Transcendence and Self-Transcendence

INDIANA SERIES IN THE PHILOSOPHY OF RELIGION
MEROLD WESTPHAL, GENERAL EDITOR

Transcendence and Self-Transcendence: On God and the Soul

Merold Westphal

INDIANA UNIVERSITY PRESS
BLOOMINGTON AND INDIANAPOLIS

This book is a publication of

Indiana University Press
601 North Morton Street
Bloomington, IN 47404-3797 USA

http://iupress.indiana.edu

Telephone orders   800-842-6796
Fax orders   812-855-7931
Orders by e-mail   iuporder@indiana.edu

MANUFACTURED IN THE UNITED STATES OF AMERICA

Library of Congress Cataloging-in-Publication Data

Westphal, Merold.
Transcendence and self-transcendence : on God and the soul / Merold Westphal.
p. cm. — (Indiana series in the philosophy of religion)
Includes bibliographical references
and index.
ISBN 0-253-34413-1 (alk. paper) — ISBN 0-253-21687-7 (pbk. : alk. paper)
1. Religion—Philosophy. 2. Transcendence (Philosophy)
I. Title. II. Series.
BL51.W3735 2004
212—dc22

                                                                    2003025352

1 2 3 4 5 09 08 07 06 05 04

Contents

ACKNOWLEDGMENTS

I would like to thank Fordham University and the Pew Evangelical Schol-ars Program for their generous support, providing me with time to work on this project. I also offer my thanks to Harvard Divinity School for giving me the opportunity to give this book as a course while it was in preparation, and to the students in that class for the help they gave me in clarifying what I was trying to say. Finally, I am pleased to express gratitude to the Society of Christian Philosophers for giving me the opportunity to present an overview of my argument in the form of a keynote address to a conference at Bethel College and for the further clarification that afforded.

ABBREVIATIONS

The following abbreviations will be used in text and notes.

Aquinas

CDA   *A Commentary on Aristotle's De Anima.* Trans. Robert Pasnau. New
      Haven, Conn.: Yale University Press, 1999.
CMA   *Commentary on the Metaphysics of Aristotle.* Trans. John P. Rowan.
      2 vols. Chicago: Henry Regnery Co., 1961.
DEE   *Aquinas on Being and Essence (De Ente et Essentia).* Trans. Joseph
      Bobik. Notre Dame, Ind.: University of Notre Dame Press, 1965.
DP   *On the Power of God (Quaestiones Disputatae de Potentia Dei).*
      Trans. Dominican Fathers. 3 vols. London: Burns Oates & Wash-
      bourne, 1934.
DV   *Truth (Quaestiones Disputatae de Veritate).* 3 vols. Trans. Robert
      W. Mulligan, S.J., James V. McGlynn, S.J., and Robert W.
      Schmidt, S.J. Indianapolis, Ind.: Hackett, 1994.
ST   *Summa Theologiae,* in *Basic Writings of Saint Thomas Aquinas.*
      Ed. Anton C. Pegis. 2 vols. New York: Random House, 1945.

1.2.3 signifies article 1, question 2, reply to objection 3. In the case of ST, the
initial number signifies the part, thus 1–2 signifies the first part of the second
part.

Augustine

C   *Confessions.* Trans. R. S. Pine-Coffin. Baltimore, Md.: Penguin,
      1961.
T   *The Trinity.* Trans. Edmund Hill, O.P. Brooklyn, N.Y.: New City
      Press, 1991.
TC   *Teaching Christianity (De Doctrine Christiana).* Trans. Edmund
      Hill, O.P. Hyde Park, N.Y.: New City Press, 1996.

Barth

A   *Anselm: Fides Quaerens Intellectum.* Trans. Ian W. Robertson. New York: World Publishing Company, 1962.

BQ   "Biblical Questions, Insights, and Vistas." In WG (1920 lecture).

CD   *Church Dogmatics*
> I/1, *The Doctrine of the Word of God.* Trans. G. T. Thomson. Edinburgh: T & T Clark, 1936.
> I/2, *The Doctrine of the Word of God.* Trans. G. T. Thomson and Harold Knight. Edinburgh: T & T Clark, 1956.
> II/1, *The Doctrine of God.* Trans. G. W. Bromiley and T. F. Torrance. Edinburgh: T & T Clark, 1957.

CP   "The Christian's Place in Society." In WG (1919 lecture).

ER   *The Epistle to the Romans.* Trans. Edwyn C. Hoskyns. London: Oxford University Press, 1933, 1968.

FI   "Fate and Idea in Theology." In *The Way of Theology in Karl Barth: Essays and Comments,* ed. H. Martin Rumscheidt. Allison Park, Pa.: Pickwick Publications, 1986 (1929 lecture).

HG   *The Holy Ghost and the Christian Life.* Trans. R. Birth Hoyle. London: Frederick Muller Limited, 1938. Three 1929 lectures.

P   *Prayer.* Ed. Don E. Saliers. 2nd ed. Philadelphia, Pa.: Westminster Press, 1985.

PT   *Protestant Thought: From Rousseau to Ritschl.* Trans. Brian Cozens et al. New York: Harper & Row, 1959.

RC   "The Doctrinal Task of the Reformed Churches." In WG (1923 lecture).

RG   "The Righteousness of God." In WG (1916 lecture).

TC   *Theology and Church.* Trans. Louise Pettibone Smith. London: SCM Press, 1962.

TM   "The Word of God and the Task of Ministry." In WG (1922 lecture).

WG   *The Word of God and the Word of Man.* Trans. Douglas Horton. New York: Harper & Brothers, 1957.

Hegel

A   Addition or *Zusatz.* This signifies material taken from lecture notes to supplement Hegel's text of EL, PM, and PR.

DFS   *The Difference between Fichte's and Schelling's System of Philosophy.* Trans. H. S. Harris and Walter Cerf . Albany: SUNY Press, 1977.

EL   *The Encyclopedia Logic.* Trans. T. F. Geraets et al. Indianapolis, Ind.: Hackett, 1991. First part of the *Encyclopedia of the Philosophical Sciences.*

ETW   *Early Theological Writings.* Trans. T. M. Knox. Philadelphia: University of Pennsylvania Press, 1971.

FS   *Frühe Schriften.* Band 1 of *Werke in zwanzig Bänden.* Frankfurt: Suhrkamp, 1971.

FK   *Faith and Knowledge.* Trans. Walter Cerf and H. S. Harris. Albany: SUNY Press, 1977.

HIN   Hegel's Foreword to H. Fr. W. Hinrichs' *Die Religion im inneren Verhältnisse zur Wissenschaft* (1822). In *Beyond Epistemology: New Studies in the Philosophy of Hegel,* ed. Frederick G. Weiss. The Hague: Martinus Nijhoff, 1974.

H&S   *Hegel's Lectures on the History of Philosophy.* Trans. E. S. Haldane and Frances H. Simson. 3 vols. London: Routledge and Kegan Paul, 1963.

HL   *Hegel: The Letters.* Trans. Clark Butler and Christiane Seiler. Bloomington: Indiana University Press, 1984.

LHP   *Lectures on the History of Philosophy: The Lectures of 1825–26,* Vol. 3. Trans. R. F. Brown et al. Berkeley: University of California Press, 1990.

LP   *Lectures on the Proofs of the Existence of God.* In vol. 3 of *Hegel's Lectures on the Philosophy of Religion.* Trans. E. B. Spiers and J. Burdon Sanderson. New York: Humanities Press, 1962.

LPR   *Lectures on the Philosophy of Religion.* Trans. R. F. Brown et al. 3 vols. Berkeley: University of California Press, 1984–87.

LWH   *Lectures on the Philosophy of World History: Introduction.* Trans. H. B. Nisbet. Cambridge: Cambridge University Press, 1975.

PR   *Hegel's Philosophy of Right.* Trans. R. M. Knox. Oxford: Clarendon Press, 1945.

PM   *Hegel's Philosophy of Mind.* Trans. William Wallace and A. V. Miller. Oxford: Clarendon Press, 1971. Third part of the *Encyclopedia of the Philosophical Sciences.*

PS   *Phenomenology of Spirit.* Trans. A. V. Miller. Oxford: Clarendon Press, 1977.

SL   *Science of Logic.* Trans. A. V. Miller. London: George Allen & Unwin, 1969.

Heidegger

AWP   "The Age of the World Picture." In QT.

BT   *Being and Time.* Trans. John Macquarrie and Edward Robinson. New York: Harper & Row, 1962.

BW   *Basic Writings.* Ed. David Farrell Krell. New York: Harper & Row, 1977.

DT   *Discourse on Thinking.* Trans. John M. Anderson and E. Hans Freund. New York: Harper & Row, 1966.

EGT	*Early Greek Thinking.* Trans. David Farrell Krell and Frank A. Capuzzi. San Francisco: Harper & Row, 1984.
EP	*The End of Philosophy.* Trans. Joan Stambaugh. New York: Harper & Row, 1973.
EPTT	"The End of Philosophy and the Task of Thinking." In BW.
ER	*The Essence of Reasons.* Trans. Terrence Malick. Evanston, Ill.: Northwestern University Press, 1969.
ID	*Identity and Difference.* Trans. Joan Stambaugh. New York: Harper & Row, 1969.
IM	*Introduction to Metaphysics.* Trans. Ralph Manheim. Garden City, N.Y.: Doubleday, 1961.
LH	"Letter on Humanism." In BW.
MWP	"My Way to Phenomenology." In *Existentialism from Dostoevsky to Sartre,* ed. Walter Kaufmann. 2nd, expanded ed. New York: New American Library, 1975.
N	*Nietzsche.* Ed. David Farrell Krell. San Francisco: Harper & Row, 1991. Four volumes in two.
OM	"Overcoming Metaphysics." In EP.
PLT	*Poetry, Language, Thought.* Trans. Albert Hofstadter. New York: Harper & Row, 1971.
PR	*The Principle of Reason.* Trans. Reginald Lilly. Bloomington: Indiana University Press, 1991.
QT	*The Question Concerning Technology and Other Essays.* Trans. William Lovitt. New York: Harper & Row, 1977.
WM/1929	*What Is Metaphysics?* In Kaufmann. See MWP.
WM/1943	Untitled postscript to WM/1929 in Kaufmann. See MWP.
WM/1949	"The Way Back into the Ground of Metaphysics." Introduction to WM/1929 in Kaufmann. See MWP.
WNGD	"The Word of Nietzsche: 'God Is Dead.'" In QT.

Kierkegaard

CUP	*Concluding Unscientific Postscript.* Vol. 1. Trans. Howard V. Hong and Edna H. Hong. Princeton, N.J.: Princeton University Press, 1992.
EO II	*Either/Or: Part II.* Trans. Howard V. Hong and Edna H. Hong. Princeton, N.J.: Princeton University Press, 1987.
FT	*Fear and Trembling/Repetition.* Trans. Howard V. Hong and Edna H. Hong. Princeton, N.J.: Princeton University Press, 1983.
JP	*Soren Kierkegaard's Journals and Papers.* Trans. Howard V. Hong and Edna H. Hong. Princeton, N.J.: Princeton University Press, 1967–78. Volume number followed by entry, not page number.
PF	*Philosophical Fragments.* Trans. Howard V. Hong and Edna H. Hong. Princeton, N.J.: Princeton University Press, 1985.

SLW   *Stages on Life's Way*. Trans. Howard V. Hong and Edna H. Hong. Princeton, N.J.: Princeton University Press, 1988.

SUD   *Sickness unto Death*. Trans. Howard V. Hong and Edna H. Hong. Princeton, N.J.: Princeton University Press, 1980.

WL   *Works of Love*. Trans. Howard V. Hong and Edna H. Hong. Princeton, N.J.: Princeton University Press, 1995.

Levinas

BI   "Beyond Intentionality." In *Philosophy in France Today*, ed. Alan Montefiore. Cambridge: Cambridge University Press, 1983.

BPW   *Basic Philosophical Writings*. Ed. Adriaan T. Peperzak, Simon Critchley, and Robert Bernasconi. Bloomington: Indiana University Press, 1996.

DEH   *Discovering Existence with Husserl*. Trans. Richard A. Cohen and Michael B. Smith. Evanston, Ill.: Northwestern University Press, 1998.

DEL   "Dialogue with Emmanuel Levinas." In *Face to Face with Levinas*, ed. Richard A. Cohen. Albany: SUNY Press, 1986.

EFP   "Ethics as First Philosophy." In LR.

EN   *Entre Nous: On Thinking-of-the-Other*. Trans. Michael B. Smith and Barbara Harshav. New York: Columbia University Press, 1998.

GCM   *Of God Who Comes to Mind*. Trans. Bettina Bergo. Stanford, Calif.: Stanford University Press, 1998.

IOF   "Is Ontology Fundamental." Cited from BPW. Also in EN.

LP   "Language and Proximity." In *Collected Philosophical Papers*. Trans. Alphonso Lingis. Dordrecht: Martinus Nijhoff, 1987.

LR   *The Levinas Reader*. Ed. Seán Hand. Oxford: Basil Blackwell, 1989.

OBBE   *Otherwise Than Being; or Beyond Essence*. Trans. Alphonso Lingis. Dordrecht: Kluwer, 1991.

PN   *Proper Names*. Trans. Michael B. Smith. Stanford, Calif.: Stanford University Press, 1996.

TI   *Totality and Infinity*. Trans. Alphonso Lingis. Pittsburgh, Pa.: Duquesne University Press, 1969.

TIHP   *The Theory of Intuition in Husserl's Phenomenology*. Trans. André Orianne. Evanston, Ill.: Northwestern University Press, 1973.

WEH   "The Work of Edmund Husserl." In DEH.

Pseudo-Dionysius

Citations in the text from Dionysius will be from *Pseudo-Dionysius: The Complete Works*, trans. Colm Luibheid (New York: Paulist Press, 1987), using the following abbreviations:

DN = *The Divine Names*
MT = *The Mystical Theology*
CH = *The Celestial Hierarchy*
EH = *The Ecclesiastical Hierarchy*

The column numbers given after the slash are from the Corderius edition in J. P. Migne, *Patrolrogiae Cursus Completus, Series Graeca* III. Paris, 1857.

Spinoza

References to Spinoza will normally be from *A Spinoza Reader*, ed. and trans. Edwin Curley (Princeton, N.J.: Princeton University Press, 1994). It incorporates translations that will appear in vol. II of *The Collected Works of Spinoza* and corrections of translations that have already appeared in Vol. I (Princeton, N.J.: Princeton University Press, 1985). Citations from the *Ethics* will use the following abbreviations, keyed to any edition:

E = *Ethics* (followed by a numeral to signify which Part)
Def = Definition (followed by an identifying numeral)
A = Axiom
P = Proposition (followed by an identifying numeral)
D = Demonstration
C = Corollary
S = Scholium
Pref = Preface
App = Appendix

Thus "E1 P32C2" signifies the second corollary to proposition 32 from Part I. Where necessary, these references will be supplemented by the Gebhardt volume and page, found in Curley's margins, e.g., "II/46."

The *Tractatus theologico-politicus* (henceforth *Tractatus* or TTP) will be cited by Curley's page numbers, followed by Gebhardt's. Thus TTP 32, III/64.

Transcendence and Self-Transcendence

Introduction

For Orientation

The story is told of a theologian who thought that Methodists had no theology. But he was invited to join the faculty of a Methodist divinity school, and after he had been there a while, he acknowledged that he had been mistaken. "Methodists do have a theology," he said, "and it comes down to this: God is nice. Moreover," he added, "there is an ethical corollary: we should be nice too."

Now some of my best friends are Methodists, but not many, so I have no opinion about the degree to which this story captures the spirit of contemporary Methodists. But I have two opinions about the theology attributed to them, whether fairly or not. Negatively speaking, it is very thin soup. On such a theological diet one's soul could become malnourished quite quickly, or, more likely, turn to constant snacking on spiritual junk food from other sources. More important, in the present context, is the positive opinion. Because of the essential link between theology and ethics, or, if you prefer, metaphysics and spirituality, this theology has the proper form. God's niceness (indicative) and our niceness (imperative) are intimately intertwined conceptually. The practical implications of theory are so immediate that it would be misleading to speak of the application of theory to practice.

I have spoken of spirituality to leave open the possibility that the practice in question might involve loving God, and I have spoken of ethics to leave open the possibility that it might involve loving one's neighbor. In either case, the basic idea is that what we say about God should have a direct bearing on our own self-transformation. Descriptions of divine being and prescriptions for human becoming are flip sides of the same coin. Within this paradigm, I propose to explore the transcendence of God in strict correlation with human self-transcendence.

I write as a Christian theist engaged in a personal journey of faith seeking understanding and growth in faithfulness. My hope is that my shared reflections will help both believers and unbelievers avoid misunderstandings that theism is heir to and thus to think more clearly about the God they affirm or deny. Thus the same analysis has an apologetic intention for readers who do not believe and a pastoral intention for readers who do.

Kant has argued that in philosophy "we must not imitate mathematics by beginning with definitions." Rather, "the definition in all its precision and clarity ought, in philosophy, to come rather at the end than at the beginning of our enquiries."[1] Because I believe him to be right, I do not begin by offering definitions of divine transcendence and human self-transcendence. Rather than assuming that we know at the outset what these terms mean, my hope is that in the course of the reflections that follow we will learn new and surprising things about them.

This leaves us vulnerable, of course, to the question with which Meno once responded to Socrates' intention to inquire into virtue without already knowing what it is: "But how will you look for something when you don't in the least know what it is?"[2] In our case the question is how we will know what conversations to listen in on to learn about transcendence and self-transcendence by exploring their interrelation. Most of us would be in big trouble if asked to go out and study sphlinks and bring back a report on their breeding habits. What are we looking for? How will we know when we find one? This is where it is important to have at least a preliminary, heuristic idea of what it is we wish to examine. So let our pre-judice (in the Gadamerian sense of pre-judgment) about transcendence be that a transcendent God is one that is to be found "beyond" or "outside" the world (as well as within it); and let us preunderstand self-transcendence to be the movement that draws us away from our natural preoccupation with ourselves.[3]

---

1. Kant, *Critique of Pure Reason*, A730–31 = B758–59.
2. Plato, *Meno*, 80d.
3. In other words, the hermeneutical circle as developed by Heidegger and Gadamer replaces Platonic recollection, granting the force of Meno's question but invoking a weaker sense of the *a priori* than Plato's (or even Kant's, since this preliminary understanding is revisable).

My hope is that by exploring these two notions in relation to each other I will be able to deepen and expand two analyses I first developed in *God, Guilt, and Death*.[4] There I reflected on divine transcendence and on human self-transcendence, but I did not attempt to think them in strict correlation with each other as I am attempting here. I devoted a couple of chapters to divine transcendence by taking a cue from Rudolf Otto and reflecting on God (or, more generally, the Sacred) as Wholly Other in the mode of *mysterium tremendum et fascinans*. It is sometimes argued that if any Other is Wholly Other then it is so completely outside the range of my experience that I can stand in no cognitive relation to it whatever. But obviously I cannot experience the *mysterium* as either *tremendum* or as *fascinans*, nor can I experience the ambivalence before the Sacred that was the theme of my earlier analysis if it falls entirely outside my experience. So the question arises: If the Wholly Other is not wholly wholly other, in what sense is it wholly other? I believe that in the latter chapters of the present essay we get an answer: an other can rightly be said to be wholly other if it enters my experience on its own terms and not mine, if it *permanently exceeds* the forms and categories of my transcendental ego and *permanently surprises* my horizons of expectation. This, I believe, is what Levinas means in describing the self-revelation of the Other as "καθ᾽ αὐτό" and what Kierkegaard means by saying that in revelation the Teacher must not only give the truth but also the condition for recognizing it as such. These notions clearly have implications for self-transcendence.

A central thesis of *God, Guilt, and Death* is that a common feature of religions in their rich variety is that they offer the believing soul solutions to the problems of guilt and death. But does that mean that religion is nothing but an instrumental relation in which God is reduced to being a solution to our problems, a means to our ends?[5]

My reply was negative. Throughout their variety, religions present the divine-human relationship as both a means and as an end in itself. Useless self-transcendence is the name I gave to that crucial dimension of the religious life in which through love of God (spirituality) and neighbor (ethics) we are drawn out of our usual preoccupation with the question of what's in it for me, or for

---

4. Merold Westphal, *God, Guilt, and Death: An Existential Phenomenology of Religion* (Bloomington: Indiana University Press, 1984), ch. 7–8. See also Merold Westphal, "Religious Experience as Self-Transcendence and Self-Deception," *Faith and Philosophy* 9, no. 2 (April 1992): 168–92.

5. As developed by Marx, Nietzsche, and Freud, the hermeneutics of suspicion can be seen as the claim that religion is nothing but instrumental religion, a means to the gratification of our individual and collective egos. In *Suspicion and Faith: The Religious Uses of Modern Atheism* (Grand Rapids: Eerdmans, 1993), I argue that religion is all too often a set of techniques for getting the goodies from God, but that biblical religion and not secular modernity (Marx and Freud) and postmodernity (Nietzsche) is the original source of protest against this form (is there any other?) of idolatry. In a sense, then, the present exploration of self-transcendence is a sequel to both *God, Guilt, and Death* and *Suspicion and Faith*, though I would hesitate to call them a trilogy.

us. It is useless because it makes the God relation of intrinsic rather than instrumental value; and it is self-transcendence because it displaces us from the center in our relations with God and neighbor.

Here are a few samples of what I mean. St. Teresa of Avila writes:

> Oh, my sisters . . . how little one should care about honours, and how far one ought to be from wishing to be esteemed in the very least if the Lord makes His special abode in the soul. For if the soul is much with Him, as it is right it should be, it will very seldom think of itself; its whole thought will be concentrated upon finding ways to please Him and upon showing Him how it loves Him. This, my daughters, is the aim of prayer . . .[6]

Simone Weil writes:

> We live in a world of unreality and dreams. To give up our imaginary position as the center, to renounce it, not only intellectually but in the imaginative part of our soul, that means to awaken to what is real and eternal, to see the true light and hear the true silence. A transformation then takes place at the very roots of our sensibility . . .[7]

Evelyn Underhill writes:

> Our spiritual life is [God's] affair; because, whatever we may think to the contrary, it is really produced by His steady attraction, and our humble and self-forgetful response to it. It consists in being drawn, at His pace and in His way, to the place where He wants us to be; not the place we fancied for ourselves. . . . If our practical life is centered on our own interests, cluttered up by possessions, distracted by ambitions, passions, wants and worries, beset by a sense of our own rights and importance, or anxieties for our own future, or longings for our own success, we need not expect that our spiritual life will be a contrast to all this. . . . The old writers [speak of] Mortification and Prayer. . . . Or, to put it the other way round and in more general terms, first turning to Reality, and then getting our tangled, half-real psychic lives—so tightly coiled about ourselves and our own interests, including our spiritual interests—into harmony with the great movement of Reality.[8]

Carlo Carretto asks why God told Abraham to sacrifice Isaac, and writes:

> God wants to communicate with the depths of Abraham's being and tear him from himself and his involvement with his own problems, which are like self-centered possessions; He wants to make this creature of His "more His," this man who is destined not for the tents of earth, but for those of Heaven.[9]

---

6. St. Teresa of Avila, *Interior Castle*, trans. E. Allison Peers (Garden City, N.Y.: Doubleday, 1961), p. 228.

7. Simone Weil, *Waiting for God*, trans. Emma Craufurd (New York: Harper & Row, 1973), p. 159.

8. Evelyn Underhill, *The Spiritual Life* (New York: Harper & Row, n.d.), pp. 39, 37, 58–59.

9. Carlo Carretto, *The God Who Comes*, trans. Mary Rose Hancock (Maryknoll, N.Y.: Orbis Books, 1974), p. 22.

Thomas à Kempis writes:

> O Lord, Thou knowest what is the better way, let this or that be done, as Thou shalt please. Give what Thou wilt, and how much Thou wilt, and when Thou wilt. Deal with me as Thou knowest, and as best pleaseth Thee, and is most for Thy honour. Set me where Thou wilt, and deal with me in all things just as Thou wilt. I am in Thy hand: turn me round, and turn me back again, even as a wheel. Behold, I am Thy servant, prepared for all things; for I desire not to live unto myself, but unto Thee: and O that I could do it worthily and perfectly![10]

The anonymous author of the *Theologia Germanica* writes:

> A truly humble, illumined person does not demand that God disclose His secrets. He does not ask why God does or prevents this or that. . . . He asks only how to become reduced and surrendering and how the eternal Will might become powerful in him, unhampered by other wills, and how the eternal Will may be fully manifested by and in him.[11]

Pseudo-Dionysius writes:

> This divine yearning brings ecstasy so that the lover belongs not to self but to the beloved. . . . We should be taken wholly out of ourselves and become wholly of God, since it is better to belong to God rather than to ourselves.[12]

Passages such as these could be reproduced indefinitely, and it is in terms of such notions of self-transcendence that I plan to explore the meaning of divine transcendence. Whatever their date, texts like these express a spirituality that is premodern. Long before either modernity or postmodernity, the believing soul has understood the God relation as a call to abandon the project of being the alpha and omega of its own existence. But since the decentered self is a central theme of postmodern philosophy, there will be something surprisingly postmodern about the life of the faith that lives out this spirituality.

The premodern character of this exploration includes the attempt to evoke and recover a patristic ethos in which "dogmatic theology" and "mystical theology" were "fundamentally bound up with one another" and it was not yet possible to read Augustine's *The Trinity* "as an exercise in speculative theology rather than as an attempt to give an account of the ascent of the soul to God."[13] As we shall see, on this journey the soul moves at once away from itself and toward itself, in accord with Jesus' paradoxes about losing and finding, dying and being reborn.

---

10. Thomas à Kempis, *Of the Imitation of Christ*, Book III, ch. XV.

11. Anonymous, *The Theologia Germanica of Martin Luther*, trans. Bengt Hoffman (New York: Paulist Press, 1980), p. 137. Luther published an edition of this essay but was not its author.

12. *The Divine Names*, in *Pseudo-Dionysius: The Complete Works*, trans. Colm Luibheid (Mahwah, N.Y.: Paulist Press, 1987), pp. 82 and 106.

13. Andrew Louth, *The Origins of the Christian Mystical Tradition: From Plato to Denys* (Oxford: Oxford University Press, 1981), pp. xi–xxi. Cf. Vladimir Lossky, *The Mystical Theology of the Eastern Church* (Crestwood, N.Y.: St. Vladimir's Seminary Press, 1976), pp. 7–9.

To speak of mystical theology in this context does not imply, however, a privileged position for unitive experience in theological reflection.[14] Without denying either the reality or the importance of such experience, I am using the term 'mystical' in a broader sense in which it means something like 'direct experience,' so that for 'dogmatic theology' and 'mystical theology' one could just as easily substitute 'metaphysics' and 'spirituality.' In the former faith seeks understanding; in the latter it seeks to "taste and see that the Lord is good" (Ps. 34:8). Nor, by speaking of spirituality, am I contrasting it with religion, as in "I see myself as a spiritual person, though I am not at all religious." This usually means something like, "I want to keep a safe distance from all 'organized' religion while keeping touch with some source of deeper meaning in my life." As a Christian, I believe that the church, for all its failings, is the best place to encounter transcendence and experience self-transcendence. But my phe-nomenological analyses will signify structures that might occur, *mutatis mu-tandis*, in relation to synagogue, church, mosque, temple, or none of the above, as in what Derrida calls "religion without religion."[15] Of course, the fact that these sites *might* have a general structure in common does not mean that there are not substantive, even crucial differences among them.

At one time I thought the subtitle for this essay would be "A Postmodern Essay on God and the Soul." The jarring character of this phrase can be clarified from the following historical sketch. When Reason asks **Augustine** what he wants to know, we are not surprised at the following exchange:

> Augustine: I desire to know God and the soul.
> Reason: Nothing more?
> Augustine: Nothing whatever.[16]

By contrast, we are surprised and more than a bit skeptical when **Descartes** prefaces his *Meditations* with an assurance to the Faculty of Theology at the Sorbonne

> that the two questions respecting God and the Soul were the chief of those that ought to be demonstrated by philosophical rather than theological argument. For although it is quite enough for us faithful ones to accept by means of faith that the human soul does not perish with the body, and that

---

14. Evelyn Underhill describes mysticism in terms of both the "unitive life" and the "unitive way." See *Mysticism* (New York: New American Library, 1955).

15. For a useful guide and overview, see John D. Caputo, *The Prayers and Tears of Jacques Derrida: Religion without Religion* (Bloomington: Indiana University Press, 1997), especially the indexed passages on religion without religion and on the distinction between the messianic and the messianisms.

16. Augustine, *The Soliloquies*, in *Augustine: Earlier Writings*, trans. John H. S. Burleigh (Phila-delphia, Pa.: Westminster Press, 1953), pp. ii, 7.

God exists, it certainly does not seem possible ever to persuade infidels of any religion, indeed, we may almost say, of any moral virtue, unless, to begin with, we prove these two facts by means of natural reason.[17]

It is hard to believe that, even if Descartes sincerely believes in God and immortality,[18] he writes out of the moral and evangelistic zeal he here professes. It is far more likely that, with an eye to Galileo, he is blowing smoke in the eyes of censors he has reason to fear on account of his physics. Still, Descartes might have held to Thomistic or deistic views about proving God and immortality, even if his primary concern was to make the world safe for mechanistic physics.

In this respect, Descartes stands closer to such premodern Parisians as Aquinas than to such postmodern Parisians as, say, Derrida. For even with the quasi-religious turn in his later writings,[19] Derrida is dramatically further removed from Augustine than is Descartes. All the more so his fellow, more unambiguously secular, Parisian poststructuralist prophets of alterity. Postmodern discourse is antipodal to God-and-the-soul talk.

Or so it seems; in any case, so it is often assumed. But by blending postmodern themes such as alterity and the decentered self with a patristic, premodern ethos, I hope to show that postmodern insights are not inherently secular and that, seen from another angle, Derrida stands closer to Augustine than does Descartes. As Edith Wyschogrod has argued that postmodernism can open up new appreciation for the moral significance of saints and the distinctly premodern hagiographic literature about them,[20] so I want to argue that postmodern arguments can be helpful in bringing both philosophical and dogmatic or systematic theology back in touch with pastoral theology. Paul Ricoeur describes his relation to his philosophical predecessors as reinterpretation and reappropriation "thanks to a meaning potential left unexploited, even repressed" by traditional readings.[21] I seek to appropriate unexploited and even repressed possibilities of secular postmodernism for the renewal of theism and its essential linkage to the renewal of theists.

The postmodern dimensions of my project are twofold. On the side of the soul stand the arguments for the decentering (not the death) of the self; while on the side of God there is the critique on onto-theology. The postmodern

---

17. Descartes, *Meditations on First Philosophy*, in *The Philosophical Works of Descartes*, trans. Elizabeth S. Haldane and G. R. T. Ross (n.p.: Dover, 1955), I, 133.
18. This is the standard view. The case for doubting it is perhaps best presented in Hiram Caton, *The Origin of Subjectivity: An Essay on Descartes* (New Haven, Conn.: Yale University Press, 1973).
19. For a splendid interpretation of this "turn," see John D. Caputo, *Prayers and Tears.*
20. Edith Wyschogrod, *Saints and Postmodernism: Revisioning Moral Philosophy* (Chicago: University of Chicago Press, 1990).
21. Paul Ricoeur, *Oneself as Another*, trans. Kathleen Blamey (Chicago: University of Chicago Press, 1992), p. 298.

assumption is that a self genuinely open to alterity will no longer be the autonomous arbiter of truth and goodness of which modernity has been so enamored. Heidegger alerts us to this difference between alterity and autonomy when, at the end of his 1921 lecture course, *Augustine and Neoplatonism*, he sharply contrasts Augustinian certainty of self with the Cartesian *cogito*. Augustine understood that the evidence of the *cogito* has a deeper foundation in a factical life of which we are not masters, in his case the life of faith, and that all science has its foundation in such factical life, that is, an everyday, pretheoretical life not grounded in the certainty of clear and distinct ideas. Instead of deepening Augustine's insights, Descartes watered them down (literally, made them insipid) and led modern thought in the wrong direction. This early version of Heideggerian postmodernism wants to detour around Descartes in order to engage Augustine directly.[22]

The decentered self, as the French put it, or the self immersed in factical life, as Heidegger puts it, will not be a substance, serenely exercising its inherent powers.[23] Such a self is better construed as a task, seeking to find and to become itself (discovering to its dismay that it has always found more than it has become, that it does not consistently live up to its best insights). Unable to be, like the turtle, its own home, it will find itself *in medias res, unterwegs,* always on the road again. As in the premodern traditions here invoked, selfhood is a journey.[24]

My second postmodern motif is the critique of onto-theology. I will argue that the overcoming of onto-theology is a necessary (but not sufficient) condition for the recovery of the transcendence of God. Like the first such motif, this one is intricately intertwined with a third theme central to postmodern philosophy: alterity. The attempt to overcome onto-theology will be the attempt to rediscover the ways in which the Holy is, as Otto has argued, "wholly other."[25] As I read it, the critique of onto-theology is simply the theological dimension of postmodernism's broader concern to preserve the full alterity of whatever is other to the self.

Because of the importance of the critique of onto-theology for my project

---

22. Martin Heidegger, *Phänomenologie des religiösen Lebens, Gesamtausgabe,* Band 60 (Frankfurt: Klostermann, 1995), pp. 298–99. It would appear that there is an important regard in which Heidegger, like Derrida, is closer to Augustine than (to) Descartes (is). The double meaning of this suggestion becomes clear by omitting, one at a time, the two words in parentheses.

23. Calvin O. Schrag presents postmodernism as resisting "recurring tendencies to construct a sovereign and monarchical self, at once self-sufficient and self-assured, finding metaphysical comfort in a doctrine of an immutable and indivisible self-identity." *The Self after Postmodernity* (New Haven, Conn.: Yale University Press, 1997), p. 27.

24. It is because Kierkegaard is so powerfully premodern and postmodern in the senses here sketched that I was able to give the title *Becoming a Self* (West Lafayette, Ind.: Purdue University Press, 1996) to my commentary on his *Concluding Unscientific Postscript.*

25. Rudolf Otto, *The Idea of the Holy,* trans. John W. Harvey (New York: Oxford University Press, 1958), especially pp. 25–30.

as a whole (and especially for my discussion of Spinoza and Hegel) and because of the lack of clarity, even to the point of obfuscation, that surrounds the concept of onto-theology, I will turn in the next chapter to a more detailed analysis of it. The ongoing assumption will then be that properly to think and speak of the transcendence of God is to avoid thinking and speaking onto-theologically.

But first a brief map of the longer journey that begins with that analysis. The movement of this essay is a dialectical argument or ascending movement through three ways of construing divine transcendence, showing that each stage illuminates the otherness of God just to the degree and in the manner that it evokes self-transcendence.

Divine transcendence is usually construed as a question concerning God's relation to the world. I will call this **cosmological transcendence.** This is where the debate between pantheism and theism comes in. Pantheism makes God wholly immanent by identifying the divine with the world as a totality. This totality can be nature, as in Spinoza's *Deus sive natura*, or history, as in Hegel's *Gott oder Geist*. In neither case is the totality crudely conceived as a heap of finite things, none of which got left out. The God of pantheism is rather the integrated wholeness of all those finite things which the analytic intellect, murdering to dissect, reduces to a heap. Or, to be a bit more precise, it is the totalizing power wholly within the whole, something like an Aristotelian soul that in this case animates the whole world and gives it unity and coherence. God is thus the power that generates all finite things and gathers them into wholeness. By oneing the many, God provides identity in difference, unity in plurality.

There is a theistic version of the last two sentences; but its meaning will be different because the theist cannot affirm the sentence prior to these two. Theism differs from pantheism in two ways: (1) creation *ex nihilo* involves an asymmetrical God/world relation—there can be God without world, but there cannot be world without God, and (2) God's immanence **in** the world includes those incursions **into** the world that are properly described as God speaking to us, whether directly or indirectly, sometimes accompanied by those incursions properly called miracles.[26]

Pantheism is not entirely without a sense of divine transcendence, but, as I will try to show, it is minimal enough to warrant calling pantheism a philosophy of immanence. Theism has a significantly stronger sense of divine otherness, but I will argue that when theism is content to distinguish itself from

---

26. For a superb theistic analysis of divine speech and especially of its indirect modes, see Nicholas Wolterstorff, *Divine discourse: Philosophical reflections on the claim that God speaks* (New York: Cambridge University Press, 1995). I have discussed the relation of this project to the overcoming of onto-theology in "Theology as Talking about a God Who Talks," *Modern Theology* 13, no. 4 (October 1997), 525–36. A more detailed analysis, with Wolterstorff's response, can be found in my "On Reading God the author," *Religious Studies* 37 (2001): 271–91.

pantheism as a distinct variety of onto-theology, it defends but does not cash in on the personal nature of God to which it is committed, and just for that reason it represents a minimal transcendence correlated to a minimal self-transcendence that barely goes beyond the pantheistic equivalents. Calling the self to represent God as "outside" the world rather than wholly "inside" the world is not to call the self away from its preoccupation with itself and may do little more than encourage cognitive complacency and self-congratulation. To be fully itself, theism needs to overcome its own onto-theological tendencies.

Just as some find it convenient to identify religion with ideology, so others find it convenient to identify theism with onto-theology. It is not hard to find historical instances of theism put to both ideological and onto-theological work. But to treat the linkage as essential rather than accidental is doubly mistaken. Conceptually, theism has other possibilities, and historically, it has sometimes actualized them. In *Suspicion and Faith,* my response to the hermeneutics of suspicion in Marx, Nietzsche, and Freud was (1) to concede that religion is all too often placed in the service of personal and/or communal egoism and is, in this generic sense, ideological, (2) to insist that there are good religious reasons to resist this tendency, and (3) to plead for a religious appropriation of the critical analyses associated with the three great masters of the school of suspicion.[27] My argument here makes the same three points in relation to postmodern critiques of onto-theology.

By looking at historical moments in the debate between theism and pantheism, in particular the pantheisms of Spinoza and Hegel, I will show that cosmological issues are not the only ones at stake; even more fundamental are epistemological and ethical/religious concerns. A deeper appreciation of divine otherness can be gained at the level of **epistemological transcendence.** Here the self is called away from satisfaction with its representations, whatever their content or source. The realism/antirealism debate, like that between modernity and postmodernity, has its theological dimensions, and I will suggest that theistic antirealism may do more justice to divine transcendence than realism can do, precisely because of the former's challenge to our claims to cognitive autonomy and adequacy. The latter point is not a denial that our knowledge of God is adequate for, say, our salvation, but a question as to whether the truth about God, understood classically as the *adequatio intellectus et rei,* is available to us. Much to the horror of some of my best friends, I will argue that when it comes to the knowledge of God, Augustine and Aquinas are as antirealist as Kant (whose antirealism is explicitly theological). Like Kant, they deny that our knowledge of God, whether derived from reason or revelation, passes the adequation test in terms of which truth has

27. It is Paul Ricoeur who describes the three great modern atheists in this way, in *Freud and Philosophy: An Essay on Interpretation,* trans. Denis Savage (New Haven, Conn.: Yale University Press, 1970), p. 32.

been traditionally defined. But as with Pseudo-Dionysius himself, the insights of "negative theology" do not reduce the believer to silence but rather provide epistemic qualification on discourse that is robustly theistic and specifically Christian. In a rather different register, the theology of Karl Barth is shown to be in deep agreement with his premodern predecessors on this matter.

Finally, I will claim that it is **ethical/religious transcendence** that does most justice to the otherness of God, that the God who commands, judges, and, by grace, forgives, is the God who evokes the deepest levels of self-transcendence in human selves. This progression can be summarized by thinking of God as other to the world, as other to my/our cognitive achievements, and finally as other to my/our volitional aims and achievements. I take it to be *prima facie* evident that the movement from cosmological to epistemological to ethical/religious transcendence correlates to an ascending scale of self-transcendence. Shifting the focus from God vis-à-vis the world to God vis-à-vis myself and my communities ups the ante considerably. Then, shifting the focus from a challenge to my cognitive autonomy and adequacy to a challenge to my behavioral and even affective autonomy and adequacy signifies the call to an even deeper decentering of myself in which, as Marcel has put such a complex task so simply, "I must somehow make room for the other in myself."[28] For ethical transcendence, here explored through Levinasian texts, that Other will be the neighbor. For religious transcendence, here explored through Kierkegaardian texts, that Other will be God. To speak of ethical/religious transcendence is to assume the inseparability of these two. *This three-stage journey in which cosmological transcendence is* aufgehoben *in epistemic transcendence, which in turn is teleologically suspended in ethical/religious transcendence, signifies my answer to the central question of this book: How shall we think the transcendence of God, or, to borrow Levinasian language, how can our God talk avoid reducing the Divine Other to the human same?*[29]

While in substance this study is at once premodern and postmodern, in method it is phenomenological—but with two important qualifiers. First, it is a hermeneutical phenomenology. Its goal may well be said to be essences, structures that can be embodied in many different times and places. But rather than looking for these in some Platonic heaven, I look for them in texts that are embedded in their own times and places. In seeking to tease essential structures out of hiding under the cover of particularity, I will make no pretense of rigorous science but rather exhibit and acknowledge the particular time and

---

28. Gabriel Marcel, *Creative Fidelity*, trans. Robert Rosthal (New York: Fordham University Press, 2002), p. 88.

29. I take Hegel's *Aufhebung* and Kierkegaard's teleological suspension to be closely related ways of speaking about recontextualizing the abstract in the more fully concrete setting that is its proper home. The earlier stages are not abandoned but are required to abandon any pretense of finality or self-sufficiency.

place of my own location. My hope is not to escape the hermeneutical circle but to make it fruitful.

Second, this is an existential phenomenology. Like any phenomenology, this one is about possibilities. It does not seek to establish the facts of the case but rather to explore possible modes of experience or being-in-the-world. But as such, these are existential and not merely phenomenological possibilities. They do not merely signify experiences I might have, but places I might dwell and ways that I might be. At issue is the meaning of my life.

PART I.
ONTO-THEOLOGY AND THE NEED TO TRANSCEND COSMOLOGICAL TRANSCENDENCE

one
Heidegger

How Not to Speak about God

One of the deepest concerns of postmodern philosophy is to preserve alterity, to keep the subject, whether personal or corporate, from reducing its object, whether it be God, or neighbor, or social world, or natural world, from its own representations and purposes. Heidegger's critique of onto-theology expresses this concern in relation to God. But if we are to examine the claim that overcoming onto-theology is necessary for the recovery of divine transcendence and of the corresponding human self-transcendence, we need to be as clear as possible what the term 'onto-theology' means. Frequently it is used as a generic term of abuse, much like 'fascist' among sixties leftists or 'liberal' among eighties and nineties conservatives. This becomes even more irresponsible when the term is treated like 'yellow,' a term which cannot be defined, but need not be since its meaning is obvious. For it then becomes possible to dismiss various texts or points of view without argument or careful examination simply by labeling them. All too often any discourse about God (unless, perhaps, it is pagan and polytheistic) is dismissed as beneath discussion simply by calling it onto-theological.

This is more like the worst of politics than the best of philosophy. But the critique of onto-theology need not degenerate into self-congratulatory verbal abuse. It can become a useful hermeneutical tool if it is willing to answer the question: What precisely is onto-theology? And it can become a useful critical tool if it is willing to answer the question: What precisely is wrong with it? Why should we try to avoid it, or go beyond it? My appreciation of this strand of postmodernism presupposes clear answers to these two questions.

Fortunately, it is unnecessary to look any farther than Heidegger, who introduced 'onto-theology' into our vocabulary in the first place.[1] He offers answers to both questions, giving at once precision and limitation to his critique. Because on his account onto-theology involves the sacrifice of divine alterity and *a fortiori* of the correspondence of divine transcendence and human self-transcendence, it is of great importance for my project, and I will devote the present chapter to Heidegger's account of what onto-theology is and how he finds it problematic. This will lay the foundation for my interpretation of Spinoza and Hegel as onto-theologians in the next two chapters, where I will try to show that onto-theological interpretations of the divine either enact a fatal separation of speculation from spirituality or, what may not be so very different, reduce spirituality to speculation. This will lead us from the debate with theism over cosmological transcendence to the further issues of epistemic and ethical/religious transcendence.

The original point of reference for Heidegger is Aristotle. The science Aristotle calls wisdom or first philosophy, but which we know as metaphysics, deals "with the first causes and the principles of things."[2] But Aristotle gives two accounts of what this means. According to one, 'first' signifies all-inclusive scope. Thus the science which

> investigates being as being . . . is not the same as any of the so-called special sciences; for none of these others deals generally with being as being. They cut off a part of being and investigate the attributes of this part. Now we are seeking the first principles and the highest causes, clearly there must be some thing to which these belong in virtue of its own nature. If then our predecessors who sought the elements of existing things were seeking these same principles, it is necessary that the elements must be elements of being not by accident but just because it *is* being. Therefore it is of being as being that we also must grasp the first causes.[3]

In this passage 'highest' functions logically to signify what is most generic, the all-encompassing.

But Aristotle also speaks in quite a different manner about what makes first philosophy first. There are three theoretical sciences: natural science or physics, mathematics, and "a science prior to both." For while physics deals with

---

1. Kant used the term, but in a much narrower sense, restricting it in effect to the ontological argument. See *Critique of Pure Reason*, A 632 = B 660.
2. Aristotle, *Metaphysics*, 981b27.
3. Aristotle, *Metaphysics*, 1003a24ff.

movable objects, and mathematics at least sometimes deals with objects inseparable from matter, "the first science deals with things which are both separable and immovable." It will be called theology because "it is obvious that if
the divine is present anywhere, it is present in things of this kind," that is,
outside of space (separable) and time (immovable). And it will be called first
philosophy because "the theoretical sciences are superior to the other sciences, and this to the other theoretical sciences." But now comes the question

> whether first philosophy is universal [dealing with the highest genus in the
> logical, all-inclusive sense], or deals with one genus, i.e. some one kind of
> being. . . . We answer that if there is no substance other than those which are
> formed by nature, natural science will be the first science; but if there is an
> immovable substance, the science of this must be prior and must be first
> philosophy, and *universal in this way, because it is first*. And it will belong to
> this to consider being *qua* being . . .[4]

Here what makes first philosophy first is a unique object that is first or prior.[5]
This is the Highest Being, not in terms of the logical priority of the all-inclusive
genus, but in terms of the cosmological primacy of the most perfect being, in
Aristotle's case God as the Unmoved Mover. To say that theology is universal
because it is first is to say that all beings essentially, and thus being *qua* being,
must be understood in the light of the Supreme Being.

In the 1949 Introduction to *What Is Metaphysics?* (1929), onto-theology is
simply Heidegger's name for this dual approach to metaphysics beginning
with Aristotle. Metaphysics represents things "in a twofold manner: in the first
place, the totality of beings as such with an eye to their most universal traits . . .
but at the same time also the totality of beings as such in the sense of the
highest and therefore divine being." In the former mode it is ontology; in the
latter, theology. This is the "onto-theological nature of philosophy proper"
(WM/1949 275). At one time Heidegger had sensed a "tension between ontology and speculative theology" (MWP 235). He has now come to see them as
inextricably intertwined.

In a subsequent essay, "The Onto-theo-logical Constitution of Metaphysics" (1957), Heidegger gives the same account.

> Western metaphysics, however, since its beginning with the Greeks has
> eminently been both ontology and theology. . . . For this reason my inaugu-
> ral lecture *What Is Metaphysics?* (1929) defines metaphysics as the question
> about beings as such *and* as a whole. The wholeness of this whole is the
> unity of all beings that unifies as the generative ground. To those who can
> read, this means: metaphysics is onto-theo-logy. (ID 54)[6]

---

4. Aristotle, *Metaphysics*, 1026a13ff. Emphasis added.
5. Since Aristotle leaves open the possibility of there being many unmoved movers, strict accuracy
would require speaking of the highest being or beings. Like most of the tradition, Heidegger
ignores this subtlety, and, except for this note, I do as well.
6. In the context of pp. 54–70.

> Metaphysics thinks of the being of beings both in the ground-giving unity of what is most general, what is indifferently valid everywhere, and also in the unity of the all that accounts for the ground, that is, of the All-Highest. . . . Ontology, however, and theology are "Logies" inasmuch as they provide the ground of beings as such and account for them within the whole. . . . Thus they are more precisely called onto-logic and theo-logic. More rigorously and clearly thought out, metaphysics is: onto-theo-logic. (ID 58–59; cf. 61, 69)

These 1957 formulations differ from those of 1949 by occurring in the context of a lecture course on Hegel's *Science of Logic.* Here it is Hegel rather than Aristotle who is the prime instance of onto-theological thinking. This is doubly significant. First, it becomes clear that when Heidegger speaks of the onto-theological constitution of metaphysics, he has in mind a tradition that includes Aristotle and Hegel among its high points. (In 1949 he had identified it as reaching from Anaxagoras to Nietzsche [WM/1949 268].) Second, when Absolute Spirit or the Idea replaces the Unmoved Mover as the All-Highest, it is clear that onto-theology is a structural concept and that a variety of beings can play the role of the Supreme Being in relation to which all beings must be understood. Thus, to anticipate our next chapter, for Spinoza the one substance he designates as God or Nature is the All-Highest, and everything that is not this substance must be understood in relation to it as either its attributes or its modes.[7]

Onto-theology is thus a bit like Baskin-Robbins or Heinz. It comes in thirty-one flavors or fifty-seven varieties or who knows how many different versions. In discussing Nietzsche on the death of God, Heidegger lists the following as God surrogates in secular modernity: conscience, reason, historical progress, the earthly happiness of the greatest number, and even business enterprise. No "flight from the world into the suprasensory" is necessary to find that particular being whose task will be to give unity and intelligibility to the whole (WNGD 64).

But all forms of onto-theology have a common purpose. Each puts its God, whether it be the Unmoved Mover, or Nature, or Spirit, or the Market to work as the keystone of a metaphysical theory designed to render the whole of reality intelligible to philosophical reflection. Thus, for example, those writers who identify freedom with free enterprise and make this the immanent telos of human history are onto-theologians in an era of the death of God.[8]

---

7. The *sive* (or) in Spinoza's *Deus sive Natura* signifies apposition, a distinction of names rather than of entities. It is not the or of "football or soccer" when an American athlete is asked which sport he plays in the fall. It is rather the or of "football or soccer" when the three tenors identify their favorite sport and suddenly remember that they are in the United States where what they call football is called soccer. Similarly, Spinoza means that one being has two alternative names, God and Nature.

8. Onto-theology can be ahistorical, as in Aristotle and Spinoza, or, under the impact of biblical messianism, historically oriented. Thus Christian, Hegelian, Marxist, evolutionist, positivist, and

The concept of onto-theology will become even more precise as we explore Heidegger's critique, his answer to our second question: What is wrong with onto-theology? I will examine three such criticisms; they can be briefly summarized as follows:

1. Onto-theology is calculative thinking.
2. Onto-theology is representational thinking.
3. Onto-theology is bad theology.

The first two of these are so closely linked that while we might distinguish them we cannot ultimately separate them. We can best approach them by tracking the history of *What Is Metaphysics?* from the original essay of 1929 to the Postscript of 1943 to the Introduction of 1949, which bears the title "The Way Back into the Ground of Metaphysics" and introduces the concept of onto-theology. In spite of important differences, they share a common concern to break free from what we might call, in a heuristic and preliminary way, a rationalist demand for total intelligibility.

The movement from 1929 to 1949 will take us to both sides of the "turn" that separates *Being and Time* and the writings associated with it from the writings of the "later" Heidegger. On both sides of this divide the "ontological difference" between being and beings is of major importance to Heidegger,[9] and one might encapsulate Heidegger's critique of onto-theology by saying it represents the forgetfulness, or oblivion, or withdrawal of being in favor of a preoccupation with beings. The theologizing of ontology is a move from beings to a being, but not a move beyond all beings, including the Supreme Being, to the being of these beings. Already in *Being and Time* Heidegger insists that "the being of beings 'is' not itself a being. If we are to understand the problem of being, our first philosophical step consists in not . . . 'telling a story'—that is to say, in not defining beings as beings by tracing them back in their origin to some other being, as if being had the character of some possible being" (BT 26).

Heidegger's true believers find this way of putting it helpful. I do not. It is

---

classically liberal onto-theologies tell big stories with happy endings. At this point Heidegger's postmodernism as the overcoming of onto-theology meets Lyotard's postmodernism as "incredulity toward metanarratives." See Lyotard, *The Postmodern Condition: A Report on Knowledge,* trans. Geoff Bennington and Brian Massumi (Minneapolis: University of Minnesota Press, 1984), p. xxiv. Elsewhere I have argued that the Christian *meganarrative* is essentially different from modernity's metanarratives. See *Overcoming Onto-Theology* (New York: Fordham University Press, 2001), Introduction.

9. Heidegger regularly uses nominalized forms of the infinitive *sein* and the related participle *seiend.* English translations vary. For *das Sein* I shall use 'being', a gerund form meant to preserve its verbal sense. To avoid the temptation of equating being with God there will be no upper case b. To preserve the etymological link between *sein* and *seiend* I shall use 'a being' for *ein Seiendes* and 'beings' for *das Seiende,* a singular form Heidegger uses to refer to the realm of beings in general and as a whole. Cf. the notes on pp. 1 and 4 of BT.

far from clear what we are to understand by being in distinction from beings, and *a fortiori* far from clear that we should care. However, Heidegger keeps trying (for decades) to tell us what he means by being and why it matters. In the process he develops a number of themes I do find philosophically important, quite independent of the question whether they are happily summarized in terms of the "ontological difference" (about which I remain skeptical). So, while it will not be possible to avoid allusions to "the difference," I will try to present Heidegger's critique of onto-theology in terms of the other themes he introduces while trying to think being.

All three stages of *What Is Metaphysics?* are concerned to distinguish a mode of thinking that is inadequate to the highest task of thought from a truly authentic mode of thinking.[10] In 1929 the contrast is between science and metaphysics. Science is "a freely chosen attitude [world-relationship] on the part of our human existence," such that "it and it alone explicitly allows the object itself the first and last word. In this objectivity of questioning, definition and proof there is a certain *limited* submission to beings so that they may reveal themselves" (WM/1929 243; emphasis added). It is the specifics of this quest for objectivity that Heidegger will in due course describe both as representational thinking and as calculative thinking.

In its concern to represent objects correctly, science, along with its allies, sound common sense and logic, is concerned exclusively with "beings—and beyond that, nothing. . . . Science wishes to know nothing of Nothing." Metaphysics, in contrast to science, asks, "But what about this 'nothing'?" (WM/ 1929 244). Heidegger suggests that in such moods as boredom, joy, and dread we become aware of the background out of which beings emerge as the foreground of our experience. This background is not itself a being, and as nothing it is the nothing which metaphysics tries to think. Such thinking arises out of the experience of the sheer contingency of things, an experience that reveals the totality of beings "in all its till now undisclosed strangeness as the pure 'Other'" (WM/1929 251; cf. 256). Metaphysics is transcendence, not the transcendence of God, to be sure, but the human movement beyond beings to the nothing that essentially belongs to them.[11] But this takes us beyond the securities of common sense, science, and the logic they share.

By the time we get to 1943, Heidegger sees the task of thinking not as

---

10. Heidegger doesn't speak here either of authenticity or adequacy, and it is not clear how best to express his purpose. To speak of thinking that is adequate to the nature of thought is not to suggest that it lives up to the ancient ideal of *adequatio intellectus et rei*. Quite to the contrary, it involves giving up on the "adequacy" of this ideal to tell us what the task of thinking is. In this regard Heidegger remains a Kantian even when he becomes critical of the transcendental subjectivism of *Being and Time*.

11. *The Essence of Reasons*, like *What Is Metaphysics?* was written in 1928, the year after *Being and Time* was published. Heidegger links the two in such a way as to make it clear that thinking nothing and thinking being are essentially the same. "Nothingness is the Not of beings and thus is being experienced from the point of view of beings" (ER 3).

metaphysics but as the overcoming of metaphysics (WM/1943 257).[12] This is not because he has abandoned the effort to think the ground (*Grund*) of beings as an abyss (*Abgrund*). "Late Heidegger" represents, if anything, an intensification of that effort. But he now uses 'metaphysics' not to stand for his own project but for the Western philosophical tradition insofar as it stands cheek by jowl with science as the objectivizing preoccupation with beings.

Between 1936 and 1943 most of what Heidegger would publish in 1961 as *Nietzsche* had been written. So it comes as no surprise that he now describes modern science as calculative thinking. "As a method of objectivising beings by calculation it is the condition, imposed by the will to will [Heidegger's phrase for Nietzsche's will to power], through which the will to will secures its own sovereignty." The truth of science "is merely the truth about beings. Metaphysics is the history of *this* truth" (WM/1943 258; emphasis added).[13]

If we think of Aristotle and Descartes we will be reminded of the tight link between science and metaphysics to which Heidegger here refers. The history of metaphysics is the history of the regional ontologies, the most basic paradigms, if you like, within which the sciences, natural and social, have operated. In the modern period, the role of mathematics and the link to technologies of various sorts warrant the name calculative thinking for the partnership between metaphysics and the sciences. But the seeds for this development were sown in ancient Greece.

While playing a grounding role for the sciences, metaphysics lacks clarity about its own "unfathomable ground" (*ungegründete Grund = Abgrund*; WM/1943 258, 260). As a result, calculative thinking "has no notion that in calculation everything calculable is already a whole before it starts working out its sums and products, and whole whose unity naturally belongs to the incalculable which, with its mystery, ever eludes the clutches of calculation" (WM/1943 262). If, then, we were to follow "the way back into the ground of metaphysics," we would discover "the onto-theological constitution of metaphysics," its tendency to answer the question of being in terms of a Highest Being, seeking desperately to ignore that which escapes the grasp of our concepts, the "speechlessness" of "dread in the sense of the terror into which the abyss of Nothing plunges us" (WM/1943 264). In other words, we would discover that metaphysics is more the partner than the alternative to science as the calculative representation of beings. The task of God is to make science possible, and metaphysics will treat any God who shirks this responsibility as an illegal immigrant in the brave new world of modernity.

---

12. It is tempting to speak of the task of philosophy or philosophical thinking, but Heidegger will eventually equate overcoming metaphysics with the end of philosophy. See "The End of Philosophy and the Task of Thinking" (1966) along with the earlier essays collected as *The End of Philosophy*.

13. On the link between knowledge and the will to power, see Nietzsche, "The Will to Power as Knowledge," in *The Will to Power*, ed. Walter Kaufmann (New York: Random House, 1968), pp. 261–331 and Heidegger, *The Will to Power as Knowledge and as Metaphysics*, Vol. III of N.

In 1949 the task is still that of overcoming metaphysics, which Heidegger insists is not its abolition but its transformation (WM/1949 267). But the theme of nothingness and the abyss has been largely replaced by the themes of the light of being and the truth of being as the ground of metaphysics, that which is beyond the ken of metaphysics and whose thinking will be the overcoming of metaphysics. The emphasis has shifted from the sheer contingency, strangeness, and mystery of beings to their unconcealedness or revealedness, from the black hole out of which beings emerge to their emergence into the light of day.[14]

In this context, to think beings instead of being (= the light of being = the truth of being) is to think what is revealed, what comes to presence, rather than to think the mystery of the unconcealment, the coming to presence. Metaphysics does the former, as we have already seen above, in the dual manner of onto-theology. It "has this twofold character because it is what it is: the representation of beings as beings . . . it always represents beings (ὄν) only with an eye to what of being has already manifested itself as beings (ἡ ὄν)" (WM/1949 276). Metaphysics is less the science of being *qua* being than the science of beings *qua* beings. As such it is ontology, but when it "sets out on the way back into the ground of metaphysics," the path of overcoming metaphysics, "with its first step it immediately leaves the realm of all ontology." By calling itself "fundamental ontology," *Being and Time* misunderstood its deepest impetus. "Coming from the ancient custom of representing beings as such, [it] became entangled in these customary conceptions." Against this background, reflection on the question "What is metaphysics?" serves "to prepare the transition from representational thinking to recollective thinking [*das andenkendende Denken*]" (WM/1949 276–77).

Implicit in this self-critique is the suggestion that transcendental philosophy is inherently metaphysical by virtue of assigning to the transcendental subject, Dasein in the case of *Being and Time*, the onto-theological role of God, the being whose task it is to be the unifying ground of the intelligibility of the whole.[15] Like theologies of creation, transcendental philosophy ends up "'telling a story' . . . tracing [beings] back in their origin to some other being" (BT 26; cf. LH 211, 216), this time the transcendental subject, or, ironically in the case of *Being and Time* itself, to Dasein.

But what is more immediately of interest here is the introduction of

---

14. Important background for this shift of focus is found in the "Letter on Humanism" (1947), in BW, and in "Aletheia (Heraclitus, Fragment B 16)" (1943), in EGT. In ID, pp. 51 and 71, Heidegger will speak of the *Wesen* and *Herkunft* of metaphysics, rather than its *Grund* as that which is beyond its ken.

15. Cf. the opening chapters of Robert Tucker, *Philosophy and Myth in Karl Marx* (2nd ed.; Cambridge: Cambridge University Press, 1972) for a more explicit interpretation of German idealism along these lines; and for an interpretation of Descartes as an onto-theologian of the subject, see Jean-Luc Marion, "Descartes and onto-theology," in *Post Secular Philosophy: Between Philosophy and Theology*, ed. Phillip Blond (New York: Routledge, 1998), pp. 67–106.

the notion of representational thinking alongside the notion of calculative thinking as descriptive of metaphysics in its onto-theological constitution. If we would understand Heidegger's critique we must try to get clearer about these two ideas. There are times when he runs them together, speaking of "representational-calculative thinking" (EPTT 377; cf. OM 100).[16] But while there is significant overlap, the two notions are not finally synonymous.

* * *

What Heidegger calls calculative thinking (and the Frankfurt school calls instrumental reason) is thought in the service of technology. On his view modern science has its roots in metaphysics and its fruits in technology; or, to modify a Cartesian image only slightly, for Western modernity philosophy is like a tree whose roots are metaphysics, whose trunk is the sciences modeled on mathematical physics, and whose branches are the technologies that emerge from these sciences.[17] Although the sciences are an intermediary, modern technology is so closely linked to metaphysics that the former can be called the completion (*Vollendung*) of the latter (WNGD 56; ID 51–52; LH 220; EPTT 375–76; OM 86; QT 21–23; WM/1943 258).

Heidegger often refers to the phenomena of modern technology: atomic power, urbanization, large corporations and a consumerist economy, computers, cybernetics, information sciences, and the power of the media (LH 199; EPTT 375–76; OM 87; DT 48). But when he distinguishes technology from the essence of technology, he transforms Montesquieu's and Tocqueville's question about the spirit of the laws into a question about the spirit of modern technology. He sees technology more as a culture than as a collection of machines (OM 93). It is less a way of doing things than a way of seeing things, a mode of revealing (QT 12–13). One can be engaged in calculative thinking even if one "neither works with numbers nor uses an adding machine or computer" (DT 46).

The essence or spirit of modern technology is an attitude, both in the older, neutral sense, and in the more recent sense in which having an attitude signifies an aggressive posture toward those around one. The technological attitude sees everything at my (or our) disposal (WNGD 77, 84, 100) or command (QT 16). The world is transformed into a stable, standing reserve of whatever I (or we) need (QT 17; WNGD 73). Since energy is high on the list of such needs, nature comes to be seen as a giant gas station (DT 50). Ironically, in the process human beings become human resources, which is to say they become a standing reserve of labor power, or buying power, or voting

---

16. Thus *Discourse on Thinking* combines a "Memorial Address" devoted to calculative thinking with a "Conversation on a Country Path about Thinking" focused on representational thinking.

17. Descartes' famous metaphor is found in the letter to Picot that serves as the preface to *The Principles of Philosophy*. See Descartes, *The Philosophical Works of Descartes*, trans. Elizabeth S. Haldane and G. R. T. Ross (n.p.: Dover, 1955), I, 211.

power, or whatever needs to be manipulated to my (or our) ends (QT 18; OM 104).

The spirit of modern technology sets upon the world in a challenging mode that Heidegger finds "unreasonable" and even "monstrous" (QT 14–16). In our "swaggering comportment" (DT 81), we set ourselves up as lords of the earth, not in any benign sense but as the "tyrant of being" (QT 27; LH 210; cf. 221). Here we encounter a harsh hostility toward modernity, but Heidegger is not a philosophical Luddite.[18] We should not blindly attack technology as a work of the devil. Our attitude should be both Yes and No—Yes because calculative thinking is justified in its own way, and No because it constantly threatens to become the only thinking, to become the sole criterion by which we operate (DT 46, 53–56; EPTT 379; OM 100). It is "the rising up of modern humanity into the *unconditional* dominion of subjectivity" that is unreasonable, and it is "subjectivity's *unconditional* self-assertion" in its collective as well as in its individual forms that is monstrous (WNGD 68; LH 221, emphasis added; cf. WNGD 95, 101, and OM 85).

One of the ways in which this self-will is unconditional is the "aimlessness" with which it "denies every goal . . ." (OM 101). It is like the child that takes a toy from another child only to discard it immediately. Why? Simply because it can. The "goal" was not to enjoy the toy by playing with it but simply to establish the sovereignty of the bully's will. This is why Heidegger speaks of the will to will where Nietzsche speaks of the will to power. "Pure will wills itself. . . . Pure will is the sole content for itself as form" (OM 101). In the technological attitude we say, in effect, "I want whatever I want whenever and however I want it." This means that technology is constrained by no standards other than those internal to its own practices (QT 26) and that value becomes the name for whatever we happen to want and think we can get (WNGD 71).[19]

Heidegger calls this an "insurrection." Does this mean that in describing modernity's will to power "Nietzsche puts man in the place of God"? In one sense, no, because God is creator and technological humanity leaves that role unfilled. But in another sense, yes, because humankind now stands as the only subject. Actually this Supreme Being is not very divine, for while the God who died was in loving relation with other subjects, the revolutionary subject is one before whom all else is object (WNGD 99–100). It is the end before which all else, including, ironically itself, is means (cf. OM 99).

In this context, overcoming metaphysics means refusing to grant such a monopoly to the spirit of technology, refusing to let it be the tail that wags every dog. Over against its blitzkrieg, another kind of thinking must establish

---

18. For the dark side of Heidegger's antimodernism, see Michael E. Zimmerman, *Heidegger's Confrontation with Modernity: Technology, Politics, Art* (Bloomington: Indiana University Press, 1990).

19. On this point of technology's immunity to criteria outside of itself, Heidegger's analysis strongly resembles that of Jacques Ellul in *The Technological Society*, trans. John Wilkinson (New York: Random House, 1964).

itself as an underground resistance movement. This is a thinking that "lets itself be claimed by being" (LH 194; cf. 199, 204, 209, 236). Human dignity consists in "being called by being" (LH 221). The thought that "listens to being" and lets itself be presided over by being (LH 196) knows that we are for the sake of being, that it and not we is essential (WNGD 97; LH 213).

It is passages like this that convince some that 'being' is Heidegger's post-modern pen name for God. But Heidegger denies this and supports his denial by pointing to his consistent refusal to equate being with any being, even the Highest Being. But if we are skeptical about Heidegger's being talk, as I am, we can read 'being' as a cipher for whatever speaks to me, calls me, claims us, reminding both me and us that we are not the subject for which everything else is object, nor the end for which everything else is means. Since both God and neighbor play that role in the religious contexts of concern in this study, we can read Heidegger's being talk as a merely formal indication that can be filled in, contrary to his intentions, with such beings as God and neighbor.

Alongside this biblical language of listening for the voice that calls and claims, Heidegger speaks in a Buddhist tone of voice about a thinking that is "non-willing" and wills "willingly to renounce willing" (DT 59). He also speaks in a Taoist tone of voice about the "passivity" of releasement (*Gelassenheit*), a "higher acting" that "is yet no activity" (DT 61).[20] In these ways, as well as in his turn to poetry and the visual arts, Heidegger seeks an alternative to the revolutionary insurrection that is modernity.

But our concern is not with Heidegger's account of the saving power; it is rather with his diagnosis of the danger.[21] And that diagnosis, at this point, is that onto-theology is dangerous because it is calculative thinking. But a fairly obvious objection might well be raised. "Have we not lost track of onto-theology altogether? What does the brave new world where calculative thinking presides over cyberspace, mega-mergers, and public opinion polls have to do with gods of metaphysics in its onto-theological mode? Doesn't the Easter greeting and response of modernity go something like this?

> The Lord is dead!
> He is dead indeed!"

---

20. On Heidegger's relation to Eastern thought, see *Heidegger and Asian Thought*, ed. Graham Parkes (Honolulu: University of Hawaii Press, 1987); Reinhard May, *Heidegger's Hidden Sources: East-Asian Influences on His Work*, trans. Graham Parkes (New York: Routledge, 1996); and Michael Zimmerman, "Heidegger, Buddhism, and deep ecology" in *The Cambridge Companion to Heidegger*, ed. Charles B. Guignon (New York: Cambridge University Press, 1993). Note 1 on pp. 264–65 gives further references.

21. At QT 28, 34, and 42, and at PLT 118, Heidegger quotes Hölderlin

> But where danger is, grows
> The saving power also.

The essays collected in PLT provide a good orientation to Heidegger's aesthetic alternative to calculative thinking.

When Heidegger calls technology "the metaphysics of the atomic age" (ID 52), does he not mean that technology has replaced metaphysics, that while the great minds of other eras were philosophers and theologians, the great minds of today are engineers and entrepreneurs?

"No," Heidegger will reply. "Windows 98 may be the *summa* of this *fin de siècle*, but the calculative thinking at the heart of modern technology is still metaphysics and, as such, is still onto-theologically constituted." Heidegger might well defend this thesis in a two-semester lecture course on the history of modern philosophy entitled *Von Nietzsche bis Descartes*.

The first semester will be devoted to the following argument. Originally metaphysics was Platonism or some footnote thereto. The supersensible world was original and primary, the sensible world derivative and secondary. Nietzsche and Marx enact the great reversal by arguing that the supersensible world is but an epiphenomenon of the sensible world, neither inevitable nor admirable. This is the meaning of their atheism. But this overturning of metaphysics is less its overcoming than its completion. For the supersensible God is replaced by a very sensible humanity, not as creator to be sure, but as The Subject, the Supreme Being in relation to which all else derives its meaning. For Marx this very material Subject is human production and reproduction, while for Nietzsche this very earthly Subject is the will to power. But in both cases it is universal because it is highest. It is the being that gathers all beings into intelligible unity.[22] Again we are reminded that secularism is no barrier to onto-theology (see WNGD 75; OM 86, 92; EPTT 375).

The second semester of Heidegger's course will deal with the turn to the subject in Descartes and Kant. The argument will be very similar because Heidegger sees Descartes and Kant as also making human subjectivity the originating, centering ground of meaning.[23] This replacement of divine by human subjectivity is a timid version of the wholly shameless move made by Marx and Nietzsche,[24] but it is essentially the same. The Subject has been

---

22. For Marx, the modernist, this intelligibility is quite unified. For Nietzsche, the postmodernist, it is anything but; it is disseminated and diversified, pluralized and perspectivized, and so forth. This is because of what we might call the fickleness of the will to power, the "aimlessness" with which, as we have seen, it "denies every goal" (OM 101). Does Nietzsche think that truth may be a woman partly because he thinks *la donna è mobile*? (See the preface to the second edition of *The Gay Science*, Section 4.)

23. The reference to origin and center here is meant to link Heidegger's analysis to Derrida's in "Structure, Sign, and Play in the Discourse of the Human Sciences," *Writing and Difference*, trans. Alan Bass (Chicago: University of Chicago Press, 1978). See also the reference to Marion in note 15 above.

24. Marx expresses his kinship with Feuerbach in terms of "the doctrine that man is the highest being for man . . ." "Towards a Critique of Hegel's *Philosophy of Right*: Introduction," in *Karl Marx: Selected Writings*, ed. David McLellan (New York: Oxford University Press, 1977), p. 69. And Nietzsche has Zarathustra say, "*if* there were gods, how could I endure not to be a god! *Hence* there are no gods . . . what could one create if gods existed?" *Thus Spoke Zarathustra*, Second Part, "Upon the Blessed Isles." Or again, "Rather no god, rather make destiny on one's own, rather be a fool, rather be a god oneself!" Fourth Part, "Retired." See note 15 above.

transcendentalized so as to neutralize the empirical evidence against its divinity (whereas Marx and Nietzsche will assign the onto-theological task to a fully empirical ego, individual or collective, stripped of all transcendental pretense). Still, the *ego cogito* is "what is present without question, what is indubitable and always standing within knowledge, what is truly certain, what stands firm in advance of everything, namely as that which places everything in relation to *itself*" (OM 87; for Kant see 88 and cf. LH 211).[25]

This is a pretty good answer to the objection that the analysis of calculative thinking has not so much shown us what is wrong with onto-theologically constituted metaphysics but has lost touch with the latter altogether. But we do not have to sit through the entire two semesters to realize that this reply will seem to a certain kind of philosopher simply to have missed the point. The philosopher I have in mind is a Christian theist who, among other things perhaps, does philosophical theology. She is quite likely an analytic philosopher, but in any case works in a realist framework that is uncontaminated by the antirealist thrust of Kantian transcendentalism and, *a fortiori*, of Nietzschean perspectivism. She has given up on the foundationalist project and does not genuflect before the Cartesian *ego cogito*. In other words, our philosopher is by choice a non-participant in both the Nietzschean/Marxian death of God and the Cartesian/Kantian transcendental turn. Accordingly, the historical figures with whom she is in most frequent dialogue are almost always pre-Kantian and frequently pre-Cartesian as well. Even if she is a Protestant, she takes the medieval philosophers more seriously than do many Catholic philosophers whose contemporary orientation is continental.

This philosopher will reformulate the earlier objection as follows. "When I questioned the link you draw between onto-theology and calculative thinking, it was not to deny what you have just sketched, namely that there is something formally onto-theological about modern technology. It was conversely to deny that there is something technological about the original 'Platonic' forms of what you call onto-theology. It does not seem to me that 'calculative thinking' is a very good description of the metaphysics of Plato, Aristotle, Plotinus, Augustine, and Aquinas,[26] or of the work that I and those with whom I am in conversation do. As theists, we affirm God, not the death of God and the unconditional self-assertion of human will to power. Trying to get clear, for example, about relation between divine foreknowledge and human freedom, so far from being tightly linked to the world of multinational corpora-

---

25. This reading of Descartes and Kant ignores the role God plays in the thought of each as a limit to human subjectivity. But most of modern and postmodern philosophy has ignored or eliminated these aspects of their thought as well. It can be argued that Heidegger's Nietzschean interpretation gives us the *wirkungsgeschichtliches Denken* of these two.

26. I shall argue in subsequent chapters that Augustine and Aquinas are not onto-theologians and that whatever onto-theological tendencies may be found in their work are kept in check by explicit counter-themes.

tions and the information superhighway, is refreshingly free from the instrumental rationalities of our increasingly irrational world. It leaves open the possibility that there is something deeper than the bottom line."

So far as the phenomena of modern technology are concerned, Heidegger will grant the point immediately. But the question concerns the essence or spirit of calculative thinking and whether it is prefigured in those philosophical theologies we might describe as pre-Nietzschean, pre-Kantian, and even pre-Cartesian.[27] Heidegger will think that we interrupted his second semester too quickly, allowing him to show the anticipations of the Marxian/Nietzschean reversal in early modern philosophy, but not listening to the ways in which the Cartesian/Kantian turn to the subject has premodern roots going back to Plato and Aristotle. Although there is no sharp line to be drawn between Heidegger's account of calculative thinking (*rechnendes Denken*) and representational thinking (*vorstellendes Denken*), it is the latter concept that now comes to the fore in Heidegger's diagnosis of the onto-theological constitution of metaphysics. It is the representational dimension of calculative thinking that links modern technology to classical metaphysics. The image of roots, trunk, and branches can be translated into a story of kinship. But it is not only a diachronic story of about how science grows out of metaphysics and then technology out of science; it is also, and for Heidegger more importantly, a synchronic story of the deep family resemblance among the three elements. Kinship is about affinity as well as lineage.

* * *

Modern technology is a way of seeing the world, namely as a conglomerate of human and natural resources at the disposal of human will to power. But on Heidegger's analysis, having the world at our disposal practically presupposes having it at our disposal theoretically, and it is the theoretical mastery of the world in science **and metaphysics** that Heidegger calls representational thinking. "The uprising of man into subjectivity transforms beings into objects. But that which is objective is that which is brought to a stand through representing. The doing away with that which *is* in itself, i.e., the killing of God, is accomplished in the making secure of the constant reserve by means of which man makes secure for himself material, bodily, psychic, and *spiritual resources* [emphasis added], and this for the sake of his own security, which wills dominion over beings" (WNGD 107). In other words, the world of objects is a world of spiritual resources at the disposal of representational thinking.[28]

---

27. One could say "post" as easily as "pre" here, for the point is substantive rather than chronological and the present scene includes astonishingly rich and vital developments in the kind of philosophical theology practiced by our objector.

28. Does this suggestion go against Heidegger's claim that "[w]hatever stands by in the sense of standing-reserve no longer stands over against as object" (QT 17; cf. 23, 26–27)? No. The distinc-

Heidegger often speaks of having the world at our disposal precisely when it is a case of represented objects at the disposal of knowledge. Thus we read of the "constant reserve" that is "at the disposal of the will" in a context not about the technological applications of science but about **truth** as a value of the will to power (WNGD 83–85; cf. DT 58). Here and in a closely related passage, objects are "at the disposal of representing" (WNGD 100). Elsewhere it is "in the realm of knowing" that beings are at our disposal or, more precisely, in the realm of representative thinking for which the world is a picture (a representation) that "the world stands at man's disposal as conquered" (AWP 130, 133).

This disposability of the world[29] sometimes signifies 'liable to subpoena,' with overtones of Kant's account of modern science as "constraining nature to give answer to questions of reason's own determining."[30] Speaking of modern science with reference to its metaphysical ground rather than its technological applications, Heidegger writes, "Knowing, as research, *calls whatever is to account* with regard to the way in which and the extent to which it lets itself be put at the disposal of representation. Research has disposal over anything that is when it can either calculate it in its future course in advance or verify a calculation about it as past. . . . Nature and history become the objects of a representing that explains" (AWP 126–27). In the "strict" formulation of the principle of reason, the *principium reddendae rationis*, this calling whatever is to account becomes the demand that reasons be given to the knowing subject to explain every fact or event and to justify every truth claim. The principle as the demand that reasons be given constitutes a "jurisdiction" (*Geltungsbereich*) that encompasses all beings, including the Highest Being, God (PR 22–30; cf. AWP 127). The judges in this court are the humans who represent objects as objects (PR 119; cf. AWP 134).

The reason representational thinking is the name of this jurisdiction is because of its underlying ontology. There is nothing except representing subjects and represented objects (LH 211; WNGD 100; DT 77–79; PR 55, 101) Or, to put it even more succinctly, to be is to be represented (AWP 127–30; PR 23, 27).[31]

There are at least two reasons why we should not read this latter formula as equivalent to *esse est percipi*. First, in order to count as a being it is not

---

tion drawn in the passage just cited between having things practically and theoretically at one's disposal is compatible with the recognition that both are ways of having things at one's disposal.

29. There's a wonderful ambiguity here. Disposability can signify 'at someone's disposal' but also 'discardable', as a disposable diaper. The two meanings are interconnected without being synonymous.

30. Kant, *Critique of Pure Reason*, B xiii.

31. Heidegger has surely not forgotten the subject when he speaks this way. But it is not clear whether he is simply presupposing the subject as correlative to the object, as the other formulations suggest, or pointing to the irony that the subjects themselves must become represented objects, just as those for whom everything is standing reserve themselves become standing reserve (human resources). He does say that "the subject is the first object of ontological representation" (OM 88).

necessary to be a representation but to be represented (or at least representable). This is why Heidegger has no qualms about attributing the ontology in question to such realists as Descartes, Lessing, and Leibniz (PR 79, 87) as well as to Kant (PR 71–74, 77, 80), whom in any case he does not interpret as a subjective idealist or phenomenalist.

Second, representation operates under the principle of reason, so it is not just a matter of producing a picture, as it were. The truth and justification that are to arise in the commerce between subject and object can only occur if reasons are given (PR 71–74, 118–19). Thus to be represented is equivalent to being "stated in a sentence that satisfies the fundamental principle of reason as the fundamental principle of founding" (PR 23). To be is to be affirmed in a justified statement.[32]

The subject, of course, is the privileged partner in this subject/object ontology. Not wanting to take the concept of subjectivity for granted, Heidegger traces it back to the Latin *subjectum*, which is a translation of the Greek *hypokeimenon*. In terms of that which is the subject of predication, Aristotle uses this notion to help explain his concept of substance or primary being (*ousia*). Heidegger focuses on its etymological sense as substratum or that which lies under or before. The modern turn to the (human) subject (both individual and collective) occurs when Descartes identifies the *ego cogito* as subject in the sense of *hypokeimenon* (WNGD 83, 100; OM 87; AWP 128; LH 211). What does this mean?[33]

Heidegger's story goes like this: modernity begins with a bad case of epistemic anxiety. As the will to power, its values all concern its own security. In this mode its highest epistemic value is truth, but only secure truth, guaranteed truth, certain truth (WNGD 82–85; OM 88, 100). Looking for something that can be its own self-grounding certainty and the basis for all other certainty, Descartes discovers the *ego cogito*. It is not merely thinker or knower in relation to what is thought or known. It is subject, *subjectum*, *hypokeimenon*, that which is most basic. (Making this a story about Kant would be little more than a good exercise for upper division undergraduates or first-year graduate students.)[34]

We can now see why Heidegger is so hostile to the subject/object ontology that is the ethos (ethic) of modernity, describing the Cartesian/Kantian turn to the subject as the "insurrection" and "assault" (WNGD 100) of a "tyrant" (LH

---

32. At this point representational thinking is virtually identical with what in other contexts is called evidentialism. See the essays by the editors in *Faith and Rationality: Reason and Belief in God*, ed. Alvin Plantinga and Nicholas Wolterstorff (Notre Dame, Ind.: University of Notre Dame Press, 1983).

33. Etienne Balibar challenges this reading of Descartes in "Citizen Subject," in *Who Comes After the Subject?* eds. Eduardo Cadava, Peter Connor, and Jean-Luc Nancy (New York: Routledge, 1991). It is significant that his interpretation stresses the role of God in Descartes' thought. See note 25 above.

34. It is worth noting that in the Second Edition Preface of the First Critique, Kant's notion of science is that of a sure or secure (*sicher*) path.

210). It is because in this move humanity "places everything in relation to *itself*" (OM 87). As *hypokeimenon*, humanity becomes the ground that

> gathers everything onto itself. This metaphysical meaning of the concept of subject has first of all no special relationship to man and none at all to the I.
>
> However, when man becomes the primary and only real *subjectum*, that means: Man becomes that being upon which all beings are grounded as regards the manner of their being and their truth. Man becomes the relational center of beings as such . . . man contends for the position in which he can be that particular being who gives the measure and draws up the guidelines for all beings. (AWP 128, 134)

At this point the two postmodern themes from the previous chapter come together: the critique of onto-theology flows into the decentering of the subject, a challenge to the way human subjectivity "places everything in relation to *itself*," thereby appointing itself "the relational center of beings as such." If modern technology is a humanism of hubris, the turn to the subject in Descartes and Kant is no less so. The theoretical will to power expressed in the latter is kin to the practical will to power expressed in the former, both as lineage and as likeness. Both are the unconditional self-assertion of human subjectivity.[35]

We must not forget, however, that we turned to Heidegger's account of representational thinking and its origin in the Cartesian/Kantian turn to the subject not in order to see more clearly its linkage to Nietzsche and modern technology, but to see whether the critique of this modern, humanistic ontotheology has any bite in relation to the premodern philosophies that our objector admires and perpetuates. Is the latter also humanistic hubris? In one sense clearly not. As the name suggests, the role of Most Valuable Player and Chief Executive Officer is assigned by prehumanistic onto-theology to a supersensible, transhuman reality and not to "Man" (the traditional name for human subjectivity).

Or so it seems. If Heidegger is to raise doubts about this apparently obvious and decisive difference, it will have to be in terms of the common ground out of which this difference grows. Both premodern and modern ontotheologies are theoretical enterprises, oriented first and foremost to knowledge and truth rather than utility and power. If it turns out that premodern ontotheology seeks, in the name of truth and knowledge, to have its "God" at the disposal of human conceptuality, its difference from modernity may not be decisive after all. This, indeed, is Heidegger's view of the matter.

Ancient and medieval thought is not representational thinking, strictly speaking; it does not construe beings as objects for the human subject. To have something "over-against" is not the same as being a "subject" for whom there are "objects" in the strict, modern sense (PR 82, 87). The "over-against" may be *physis* in the Greek sense or *ens creatum* in the Christian sense (PR 62–64,

---

35. See note 25 above.

90–91; AWP 130). Still, in one of his strongest truth-as-having-everything-at-one's-disposal passages, Heidegger points not only to the fulfillment of the Cartesian project in Nietzsche, but its anticipation in the Aristotle from whom Descartes takes the name first philosophy for his own *Meditations* (AWP 127).

Then there is Plato. When he identifies the Good as beyond being or essence (*epikeina tes ousias*), he shows that it is not an object for a subject even in the early Heideggerian sense of falling within the horizon of Dasein's understanding.[36] But when he introduces the theme of knowledge as recollection and makes even the Good an *eidos*, he elevates human subjectivity to its Cartesian centrality without quite realizing it (ER 93–97; AWP 131).[37]

In the "Letter on Humanism," Heidegger expands on the linkage between modern and premodern metaphysics. He finds in Plato and Aristotle the beginnings of "the technical interpretation of thinking" according to which even *theoria* is viewed as a kind of *techne*. One sign of this is the emergence of logic as the overriding criterion of thought's rigor. Thought itself becomes a kind of calculus (LH 194–95).[38]

Another symptom of the technical interpretation of thinking is that "philosophy becomes a technique for explaining from highest causes," a move Heidegger immediately associates with the "dominance of subjectivity" that constitutes modernity (LH 197–98). In the

> devastation of language . . . under the dominance of the modern metaphysics of subjectivity . . . language surrenders itself to our mere willing and trafficking as an instrument of domination of beings. Beings themselves appear as actualities in the interaction of cause and effect. We encounter beings as actualities in a calculative business-like way, but also scientifically and by way of philosophy, with explanations and proofs. . . . As if it were already decided that the truth of being lets itself at all be established in causes and explanatory grounds . . . (LH 198–99)

This passage is explicitly about modernity, but a modernity that is only a series of footnotes to Plato's and Aristotle's practice of making philosophy the giving of causal explanations and proofs, especially the onto-theological expla-

---

36. Levinas will regularly invoke this theme in Plato (*Republic* 508e–509b) against the tradition he calls simply "ontology." In addition to the title of his second major book, *Otherwise than Being or Beyond Essence*, see *Totality and Infinity*, trans. Alphonso Lingis (Pittsburgh, Pa.: University of Pittsburgh Press, 1969), pp. 102–103; *Face to Face with Levinas*, ed. Richard A. Cohen (Albany: SUNY Press, 1986), p. 25; and *Emmanuel Levinas: Basic Philosophical Writings*, ed. Adriaan T. Peperzak et al. (Bloomington: Indiana University Press, 1996), pp. 101, 109, 111, 117, 122, 125, 139, 141, and 147.

37. For an account of how *physis* becomes *idea* for Plato at the same time that *logos* becomes *ratio* (see next note), see IM 98–164, especially 146–52.

38. Heidegger denies that his critique of logic (cf. WM/1929) is a form of "irrationalism" and suggests, by contrast, that to subject thinking to the "technical-theoretical exactness of concepts" that logic requires is like "trying to evaluate the nature and powers of a fish by seeing how long it can live on dry land" (LH 195). For a fuller discussion of the subject, see Thomas Fay, *Heidegger: The Critique of Logic* (The Hague: Martinus Nijhoff, 1977).

nations and proofs that involve the highest causes. The "dominance of subjectivity" first emerges not when human subjectivity is posited *de jure* (by Descartes and Kant) as that which is highest, but when it is posited *de facto* (by Plato and Aristotle) as the highest in the demand that everything render itself transparent before the logical proofs and causal explanations of onto-theologically constituted metaphysics.

The spirit that links the premodern to the modern is perhaps best expressed by Hegel in his inaugural lecture at Berlin. As he begins his lectures on the *Encyclopedia*, he pleads with his hearers to bring with them

> trust in science, faith in reason, trust and faith in yourselves. The courage of truth, faith in the power of mind is the first condition of philosophical studies; we should honor ourselves and hold ourselves worthy of the highest. We cannot think highly enough of the greatness and power of mind; the hidden essence of the universe possesses no power in itself to resist the courage of knowledge; it must open itself to us, placing its riches and depth before our eyes for our enjoyment.[39]

Heidegger refers to this passage in *The Principle of Reason* (85), the text in which he develops most fully the deep affinity between premodern metaphysics and modernity's turn to subjectivity and representational thinking. His focus is on the principle of sufficient reason or ground as formulated by Leibniz,[40] and his claim is that while Leibniz was the first to give explicit formulation to the principle, it has been the guiding light of Western metaphysics during a long "incubation" period that goes back to ancient Greece (PR 4, 53, 118, 121). We have seen above how Heidegger links Leibniz with Descartes and Kant as founding fathers of representational thinking and its underlying subject/object ontology. We now need to cash in on the "incubation" metaphor and see the deep premodern roots of Leibniz's modernity.

On the one hand, the principle of reason involves giving reasons to validate statements. "For Leibniz the principle of reason is a Principle for sentences and statements. . . . The principle of reason is the fundamental principle of the possible and necessary rendering of reasons for a true sentence" (PR 22). We saw this when we saw that for Leibniz to be is to be affirmed in a justified statement.[41] But he always makes clear that his principle involves causes in the ontological order just as much as reasons in the epistemological order (PR 21–22, 26, 97). And since nothing falls outside of its sway, the

---

39. Hegel, *Werke in zwanzig Bänden*, ed. Eva Moldenhauer and Karl Markus Michel (Frankfurt: Suhrkamp), Vol. 10 (1970), p. 404. My translation eliminates Hegel's excessive italics and renders *Geist* as 'mind'. He seems oblivious to the irony involved in his "Lutheran" view of reason as having its foundation in trust and faith. For the Heidelberg version of this talk, see ch. 3, n. 31.

40. Only in its third, "complete" form does the principle specify *sufficient* reason. For a brief summary of the three forms of the principle as Heidegger presents them, see John D. Caputo, *The Mystical Element in Heidegger's Thought* (Athens: Ohio University Press, 1978), p. 60. Caputo's chapter 2 is a nice overview of Heidegger's book.

41. See note 32 above.

principle ends up demanding completeness of explanation (PR 32–33, 120). This, in turn, leads to the fundamental onto-theological gesture, the appeal to God (some supersensible reality) as first cause, as *ultimo ratio, summa ratio,* the One that is the key to the All (PR 26, 101, 117, 125).

As *prima causa,* God is under the sway and within the jurisdiction of the principle of reason (PR 26). In fact, "God exists only insofar as the principle of reason holds" (PR 28).[42] As *ultimo/summa/prima,* God is the Supreme Being. Almost! There is only one tiny exception, only one thing higher: the Principle of Reason, which kidnaps God and puts its new servant to work answering questions of reason's own determining. God's assignment is to be the keystone but not the high priest in the temple of reason, its acme but not its architect.[43] Just as Marx and Nietzsche are more candid and less ambivalent about the ultimacy of the Human Subject than were Descartes and Kant, so the latter pair are more candid and less ambivalent than Plato and Aristotle. But a common project unites them all, in spite of real differences among them, and no one enables us to see this more clearly than Leibniz. Premodern onto-theology is the incubation period of the modern, humanistic versions.

* * *

We are now in a position to understand what Heidegger means when he says that in onto-theology "the deity can come into philosophy only insofar as philosophy, of its own accord and by its own nature, requires and determines that and how the deity enters into it" (ID 56). Philosophy makes the rules that God must play by. Like the ancient Job, it subpoenas God to put in an appearance that will satisfy the human desire/demand for explanations. Precisely because of its character as calculative-representational thinking, onto-theology is bad theology. It does not let God be God and is vulnerable above all to religious critique. Heidegger's deepest objection to onto-theologically constituted metaphysics echoes Tertullian's question, "What has Athens to do with Jerusalem?" and Pascal's contrast between the God of the philosophers and the God of Abraham, Isaac, and Jacob.

This is explicit in both of the texts where Heidegger introduces the notion of onto-theology. In "The Way Back into the Ground of Metaphysics," Heidegger writes that the onto-theological character of metaphysics belongs to "philosophy proper." It is not due to the patristic and medieval merger of Greek

---

42. So much is this the case that when Leibniz's contemporary Angelus Silesius writes, "The rose is without why: it blooms because it blooms," Leibniz saw this challenge to his principle as "virtually inclining to Godlessness" (PR 35).

43. Heidegger is aware that God is often spoken of as the author of reason. "So the principle of reason holds only insofar as God exists. But God exists only insofar as the principle of reason holds. Such thinking moves in a circle" (PR 28). Heidegger does not respect this circle, which is already apparent in Descartes, the way he respects the hermeneutical circle because he thinks the first sentence ends up as empty flattery while the second sentence is the operative principle of metaphysics.

philosophy and Christian theology but rather "provided the possibility for Christian theology to take possession of Greek philosophy—whether for better or for worse may be decided by the theologians, on the basis of their experience of what is Christian" (WM/1949 275–76).

But without waiting for the theologians to respond, he reminds them to keep in mind the Pauline question, "Has not God let the wisdom of this world become foolishness?" (I Cor. 1:20). He identifies "the wisdom of this world" with what Aristotle calls first philosophy, and asks, "Will Christian theology make up its mind one day to take seriously the word of the apostle and thus also the conception of philosophy as foolishness?" (WM/1949 276).[44]

In "The Onto-theo-logical Constitution of Metaphysics," Heidegger writes that onto-theology has become problematic "not because of any kind of atheism" but because of insight into the "essential nature of metaphysics" (ID 55). The God of philosophy is *causa prima, ultima ratio,* and *causa sui,* but

> Man can neither pray nor sacrifice to this god. Before the *causi sui,* man can neither fall to his knees in awe nor can he play music and dance before this god.
> The god-less thinking which must abandon the god of philosophy, god as *causa sui,* is thus perhaps closer to the divine God. Here this means only: god-less thinking is more open to Him than onto-theo-logic would like to admit. (ID 60, 72)

In his essay on Nietzsche and the death of God, Heidegger writes that the "heaviest blow" against God is not the claim that God is unknowable or God's existence unprovable but rather that "God, the first of beings, is degraded to the highest value. . . . For this blow comes precisely not from those . . . who do not believe in God, but from the believers and their theologians who discourse

---

44. This passage echoes the appeal to Luther's Pauline polemic against Greek philosophy in Heidegger's early philosophy of religion lectures, *Phänomenologie des religiösen Lebens*, Vol. 60 of the *Gesamtausgabe* (Frankfurt: Klostermann, 1995), pp. 97, 281–82, 306–10. Luther cites this theme from First Corinthians in his *Heidelberg Disputation* as part of his distinction between the Pauline *theologia crucis* from the scholastic *theologia gloriae*, a distinction appealed to by Heidegger at pp. 281–82. See John van Buren's essay "Martin Heidegger, Martin Luther" in *Reading Heidegger from the Start*, ed. Theodore Kisiel and John van Buren (Albany: SUNY Press, 1994) and *Career of the Reformer: I*, Vol. 31 of *Luther's Works*, ed. Harold J. Grimm (Philadelphia, Pa.: Muhlenberg Press, 1957), p. 52. Heidegger's philosophy of religion lectures are a sustained polemic against the primacy of the theoretical. They repeatedly deny that philosophy is or should try to be a science (3, 8–10, 15, 17, 27, 29, 35). It is more nearly an art (8) because experience, its proper subject matter, is not itself to be construed as knowledge, for experience stands in relation to the world in its import(ance) (*Bedeutsamkeit*) rather than to "objects" (8–16). We have here a clear anticipation of the distinction in *Being and Time* between what is ready-to-hand (*zuhanden*) and what is merely present-at-hand or objectively present (*vorhanden*) as well as the later critique of the subject/object scheme as humanistic hubris. Since the analysis of experience here is largely that of religious experience, what goes for philosophy would go for theology as well (72, 97, 102, 116). For an analysis of these lectures as an anticipation of the later critique of onto-theology, see my review essay "Heidegger's '*Theologische Jugendschriften,*'" in *Overcoming Onto-theology*.

on the being that is of all beings most in being . . . seen from out of faith, their thinking and their talking is sheer blasphemy if it meddles in the theology of faith" (WNGD 105; cf. 99).

To appreciate the equivalence of this objection to the previous ones, we need to remember two things. First, in Heidegger's Nietzsche interpretation, 'value' signifies the constant reserve, whatever is required by the will to power to preserve and enhance its life. Second, while there are surely socio-political ways of reducing God to the "highest value," in his analysis of representational-calculative thinking Heidegger has identified the ways in which God becomes an epistemological value, the highest principle of explanation and justification, the key to rendering everything intelligible to human understanding. God is part of the labor pool and can remain gainfully employed only by being epistemologically useful.

Here again, although he speaks harshly about a certain kind of theology, Heidegger insists that his critique is not antireligious but just the opposite. Sounding a lot like Kierkegaard and distinguishing Christendom from New Testament Christianity, he insists that "a confrontation with Christendom is absolutely not in any way an attack against what is Christian, any more than a critique of theology is necessarily a critique of faith" (WNGD 63–64).

Perhaps the most sustained way in which Heidegger reveals the religious roots of his critique of onto-theology is the appeal to think the holy as mystery. Representational-calculative thinking cannot do this (QT 26). But constantly intertwined with his analysis and critique of this kind of thinking is the adumbration of another kind. Whether he calls it the thinking of being, or releasement (*Gelassenheit*), or meditative thinking (*besinnliches Denken*), or recollective thinking (*andenkendes Denken*), or the step back out of metaphysics, the notion is the same: instead of the demand that everything fit within the Procrustean bed of causal explanation and logical justification, this other thinking tries to think what is necessarily unthought within such conceptual schemes. When Heidegger writes, "Only from the truth of being can the essence of the holy be thought" (LH 230; cf. 218), we should remember that whether or not we are sympathetic to the "ontological difference" that underlies the notion of "the truth of being," this latter phrase points to some mode of thinking in which the demand for full intelligibility is replaced by openness to mystery.

Already in *What Is Metaphysics?* where 'metaphysics' still is the name for the good thinking to be achieved rather than the bad thinking to be overcome (limited to its proper place), this theme emerges. To think Nothing is to discover beings in their "till now undisclosed strangeness as the pure 'Other' "—a strangeness that, beyond logic, science, and common sense, evokes "wonder" (WM/1929 251, 256).

This theme is developed in the 1943 "Postscript" to *What Is Metaphysics?* That task, now described as overcoming metaphysics, is to think the mystery that escapes calculative thinking (WM/1943 262–63). As in Rudolf Otto's notion of the Wholly Other as *mysterium tremendum et fascinans*, this mystery is both repelling and attractive.[45] Before the "terror" and "horrors" of the "abyss," one experiences "dread." But there is also "awe" before "the marvel of all marvels" (WM/1943 260–61). So, in spite of the dread, the appropriate response is "surrender," "sacrifice," and "thanking" in relation to the "grace" and "favour" one has encountered (WM/1943 262–63). Any verbal response will emerge out of a prior "speechlessness," recognizing the permanent inadequacy of human discourse to that which remains mystery. "The thinker utters Being. The poet names what is holy" (WM/1943 263–64). These are two sides of the same coin, a coin not recognized as legal tender by metaphysics. The Heidegger who writes this is half thinker and half (would-be) poet, not a theologian. But his argument is clear: out of the deepest of religious motivations, the theologian has a vested interest in keeping open the space within which mystery can be encountered.

Heidegger keeps returning to these motifs. In his discussion of meditative thinking as *Gelassenheit*, he virtually equates *"releasement toward things"* with *"openness to the mystery."* Whereas subjects represent objects within a horizon of understanding, there is a thinking that asks about what lets the horizon be and recognizes that it will escape the realm of representation (DT 55, 63–68). When "language surrenders itself to our mere willing and trafficking as an instrument of domination over beings" it loses contact with the "mystery" that is only found in or as "the nameless" (LH 199). Another way of putting this is to talk about that which gives itself only as "self-concealing" and as that which "withdraws" (PR 54–55, 61–62, 68).

The Heidegger who writes all this is long past the point when he described himself as a Christian theologian. Indeed, he insists that as philosopher or thinker he operates in a realm prior to and neutral to the question of God.[46] In

---

45. Rudolf Otto, *The Idea of the Holy*, trans. John W. Harvey (New York: Oxford University Press, 1958). Heidegger read this book almost immediately after its appearance and at one time planned a review of it (see GA 60 332–34). He may have been the one to call it to Husserl's attention. See Ted Kisiel, *The Genesis of Heidegger's Being and Time* (Berkeley: University of California Press, 1993), pp. 75, 86, 96–97.

46. Heidegger first says that philosophy must be *"a-theistic* in principle" in his Aristotle lectures of 1921–22, *Phänomenologische Interpretationen zu Aristotles: Einführung in die Phänomenologische Forshung*, Vol. 61 of the *Gesamtausgabe* (Frankfurt: Klosterman, 1985), pp. 196–97. He repeats this claim repeatedly in connection with his Marburg appointment. In 1922, "Phenomenological Interpretations with Respect to Aristotle: Indication of the Hermeneutical Situation," trans. Michael Baur in *Man and World*, 25 (1992): 367; in 1924, *The Concept of Time*, trans. William McNeill (Oxford: Blackwell, 1992), p. 1; in 1925, *History of the Concept of Time: Prolegomena*, trans. Theodore Kisiel (Bloomington: Indiana University Press, 1985), pp. 79–80; and in 1928, *The Metaphysical Foundations of Logic*, trans. Michael Heim (Bloomington: Indiana University Press, 1984), p. 140. In "Heidegger's *Theologische Jugendschriften*," I have argued, with reference to the earliest of these passages, that this is a methodological and not a substantive atheism. I think that remains true for the Marburg statements, especially when compared with another Marburg piece, "Phenomenology and Theology," trans. James G. Hart and John C.

the "Letter on Humanism" (1947), Heidegger cites the following passage from *The Essence of Reasons* (1929): "Through the ontological interpretation of Dasein as being-in-the-world no decision, whether positive or negative, is made concerning a possible being toward God. It is, however, the case that through an illumination of transcendence we first achieve an *adequate concept of Dasein*, with respect to which it can now be asked how the relationship of Dasein to God is ontologically ordered." He adds that this failure "to decide either for or against the existence of God" does not mean that philosophy is "stalled in indifference" (LH 229–30; ER 91, n.56). If he is not out to make the world safe for faith, he is at least out to make it safe for the possibility of faith. "Only from the truth of being can the essence of the holy be thought. Only from the essence of the holy is the essence of divinity to be thought. Only in the light of the essence of divinity can it be thought or said what the word 'God' is to signify" (LH 230).

Heidegger distinguishes the philosopher from the believing soul (perhaps too neatly). But he knows that the latter says

> I shall never want to define You, O God,
> for I cannot worship what I comprehend.[47]

And his critique of onto-theology ultimately comes down to the attempt to leave space in the world of modern technology for this kind of faith. It will be a transgressive space rather than a merely tolerant space, for this believer denies the ultimacy of all forms of onto-theology, metaphysical, scientific, and technological. Heidegger challenges theology to join him, overcoming its own onto-theological tendencies, thereby allowing God to be worthy of worship rather than subject to human subjectivity.

His critique of onto-theology teaches us not only to distinguish among its various species, but even more importantly to recognize their generic identity. In the premodern world there are the Greek versions of Plato and Aristotle. In the modern world there are the transcendental humanisms of Descartes and Kant and the empirical humanisms of Marx and Nietzsche.[48]

At the descriptive level, their generic identity consists in the basic onto-theological gesture, seeking the clue to the universal in terms of the Highest, making sense of the whole in terms of the Center, the Origin, the Supreme Being.[49] At this level the distinction between premodern, supersensible ver-

---

Maraldo in *The Piety of Thinking* (Bloomington: Indiana University Press, 1976) and with the passage about to be cited from LH.

47. Leslie F. Brandt, *Psalms/Now* (St. Louis, Mo.: Concordia, 1973), p. 175.

48. Heidegger follows Nietzsche in linking the Greek and Christian versions. It is by treating Nietzsche as the completion of metaphysics, an ironically Hegelian aspiration, rather than the overcoming of metaphysics, that he breaks with Nietzsche's history of philosophy. The notorious "antihumanism" of postmodernism is significantly linked to its suspicions of onto-theology.

49. See note 23 above.

sions and modern, humanistic species still looks at least as fundamental as their generic kinship.

But at the critical level Heidegger's analysis points to a second dimension of generic identity that changes the picture considerably. All forms of onto-theology turn out to be humanistic hubris. Insofar as premodern onto-theologies are governed and guided by the principle of (sufficient) reason in its incubation period, that is, insofar as they admit the "Supreme Being" into philosophical discourse subject to the demand for complete intelligibility in terms of human criteria of logical justification and causal explanation, they are theoretical expressions of the will to power, the demand that everything should be at the disposal of human purpose.

In other words, the transcendence of some supersensible world is compromised not only by outright denial as in Marx and Nietzsche, but by a certain mode of affirming it. If a supersensible "God" of some sort is posited, "beyond" and "outside" the sensible world of space and time, only to be placed immediately at the disposal of the demand for complete intelligibility to human understanding, the transcendence that is offered with one hand is taken away with the other. The divine is tolerated only insofar as it is intelligible in itself and the ground of the intelligibility of everything else—to us. This means that the question of divine transcendence is not simply a question of doctrinal content. A transcendent "what" can be neutralized by an immanent "how" when human subjectivity "places everything in relation to *itself*" (OM 87), becoming "the relational center of beings as such" (AWP 128).[50]

Does this mean that we cannot approach the question of divine transcendence by looking at the difference between pantheism, as the philosophy of divine immanence, and theism, as the philosophy of divine transcendence? No, but it does mean that we will have to attend to more than the doctrinal differences between the two. In addition to asking the cosmological question, whether they place God "inside" or "outside" the world of nature and human history, we will have to ask at least two additional questions, guided by the Heideggerian critique: To what degree does this theology allow human beings, individually and collectively, to be claimed or called by a God to whom they must listen, to whom they are answerable (as distinct from being Job or Kant, demanding answers to their own questions)?[51] and to what degree is this theology open to the divine as mystery, as that which escapes our conceptual

---

50. The distinction between the "what" and the "how" is the heart of Kierkegaard's analysis, via Johannes Climacus in *Concluding Unscientific Postscript*, of truth as subjectivity. I have given a detailed analysis in chapter 8 of *Becoming a Self: A Reading of Kierkegaard's Concluding Unscientific Postscript* (West Lafayette, Ind.: Purdue University Press, 1996). Heidegger places enormous emphasis on the religious importance of the "how" in his 1920/21 lectures, *Einleitung in die Phänomenologie der Religion*, in *Phänomenologie des religiösen Lebens* (GA 60). See ch. 2 n. 44.

51. We saw this question posed above in relation to being, rather than God, in the "Letter on Humanism."

mastery by showing itself as that which hides itself?[52] A theism that would overcome its own onto-theological possibilities will have to do more than distinguish its account of God's relation to the world from pantheism's.

Accordingly, in the next two chapters we will look at two onto-theological pantheisms, those of Spinoza and Hegel, to see the way their denials of theistic transcendence is linked to these other issues of divine revelation and mystery. The hope is that it will become clearer what theism must affirm, beyond mere cosmological transcendence, if it is not to be just an alternative onto-theology, if it is not to be a doctrine of divine transcendence that functions to reduce that transcendence to human, all too human, dimensions.

---

52. We saw this theme developed at the conclusion of the introduction.

two
Spinoza
The Onto-theological Pantheism of Nature

Spinoza is the paradigmatic pantheist. But is he not *ipso facto* an atheist? This would not mean that he has overcome metaphysics in its onto-theological sense. For if the Good and Humankind (in various modes) can substitute for God as the Highest Being, why not Nature? Still, an atheist could hardly provide us with a model of divine immanence in relation to which divine transcendence could be clarified. So we'd best begin with the question of Spinoza's atheism.

There has been no shortage of those willing to label Spinoza an atheist. At the head of the list is Pierre Bayle, whose 1697 essay dominated the eighteenth-century reception of Spinoza.[1] Others include such thinkers as Leibniz,[2] Priestley,[3] Jacobi,[4] and Coleridge.[5]

---

1. Pierre Bayle, *Historical and Critical Dictionary: Selections*, trans. Richard H. Popkin (Indianapolis, Ind.: Bobbs-Merrill, 1965). The essay begins, "Spinoza, Benedictus de, a Jew by birth, and afterwards a deserter from Judaism, and lastly an atheist, was from Amsterdam. He was a systematic atheist . . . ," p. 288. Subsequent references stress, among other things, the role of the *Tractatus theologico-politicus* in preparing the way for the *Ethics*. See pp. 293, 295, 300–301.

But closer to home and during Spinoza's lifetime, the charge of atheism was anything but rare. Spinoza gives as one of his motives in writing the *Tractatus Theologico-Politicus* (1670), "The opinion of me held by the common people, who constantly accuse me of atheism. I am driven to avert this accusation, too, as far as I can."[6] Far from averting the accusation, the *Tractatus* evoked from a certain Lambert Van Velthuysen the charge that in it Spinoza "prompts atheism by stealth . . . teaching sheer atheism with furtive and disguised arguments."[7] (To which Spinoza responds that Velthuysen would have thought differently had he known "what manner of life I pursue. . . . For atheists are usually inordinately fond of honours and riches, which I have always despised . . .")[8] And in 1674 the States of Holland condemned the *Tractatus* and "other heretical and atheistic writings."[9] Later on, Alfred Burgh will tell Spinoza of his own return to the Catholic Church and in urging him similarly to convert will urge him to "reflect on the wretched and uneasy lives of atheists" and especially on "their most unhappy and horrifying death . . ."[10]

---

2. Leibniz, *Sämtliche Schriften und Briefe* (Darmstadt: Academie Verlag, 1926), II.1, p. 535.

3. "The magistrate must define strictly what he means by the term God, for otherwise Epicureans and Spinozists might be no atheists . . ." *Essay on the First Principles of Government*, in Joseph Priestley, *Political Writings*, ed. Peter N. Miller (New York: Cambridge University Press, 1993), p. 59.

4. Jacobi's charge that Lessing was a Spinozist set off the pantheism controversy about which we will hear more later on. See *The Spinoza Conversations between Lessing and Jacobi*, trans. G. Vallée et al. (Lanham, Md.: University Press of America, 1988), p. 123. Cf. p. 81. For fuller documentation, see *Die Hauptschriften zum Pantheismusstreit zwischen Jacobi und Mendelssohn*, ed. H. Scholz (Berlin: Reuter and Reichard, 1916).

5. "Spinozism consists in the exclusion of intelligence and consciousness from Deity—therefore it is Atheism." Quoted from *Critical Annotations* by Thomas McFarland in *Coleridge and the Pantheist Tradition* (Oxford: Clarendon Press, 1969), p. 190. "And, were I not a Christian, *and that only in the sense in which I am a Christian*, I should be an atheist with Spinoza." *Letters, Conversations and Recollections of S. T. Coleridge*, ed. Thomas Allsop (London: n.p., 1936), I, pp. 88–89. But Coleridge was not of one mind on the subject. See the editor's discussion of his "Note on Spinoza" and his own comments in the "Note," *Shorter Works and Fragments*, Vol. 11 of *The Collected Works of Samuel Taylor Coleridge*, ed. H. J. Jackson and J. R. de J. Jackson (Princeton, N.J.: Princeton University Press, 1995), I, pp. 608–13; *Biographia Literaria*, Vol. 7 of *The Collected Works*, ed. James Engell and W. Jackson Bate (Princeton, N.J.: Princeton University Press, 1983), I, pp. 152–53 and p. 152, n. 3; and *The Notebooks of Samuel Taylor Coleridge*, ed. Kathleen Coburn (New York: Pantheon, 1957), I, #1379. McFarland (p. 190) takes the equation of Spinozism with atheism to be Coleridge's "considered and final philosophical position."

6. *Spinoza: The Letters*, trans. Samuel Shirley (Indianapolis, Ind.: Hackett, 1995), Letter 30, p. 186. Spinoza's letters will be cited from the Shirley edition, whose page numbers will be given. The letter numbers are widely used in various editions.

7. Letter 42, p. 236.

8. Letter 43, p. 237. In today's climate we can hardly read this as other than ironical. But in Spinoza's time the link between God and morality may have been so tight that he honestly believed no person of moral principle could rightly be thought an atheist.

9. Shirley, p. 55.

10. Letter 67, p. 311.

This was the context in which Spinoza decided not to publish his *Ethics*. He writes to Oldenburg that on the verge of publication

> a rumour became widespread that a certain book of mine about God was in the press, and in it I endeavour to show that there is no God. This rumour found credence with many. So certain theologians, who may have started this rumour, seized the opportunity to complain of me before the Prince and the Magistrates. Moreover, the stupid Cartesians, in order to remove this suspicion from themselves because they are thought to be on my side, ceased not to denounce everywhere my opinions and my writings. . . . Having gathered this from certain trustworthy men who also declared that the theologians were everywhere plotting against me, I decided to postpone the publication I had in hand until I should see how matters would turn out. . . . But the situation seems to worsen day by day, and I am not sure what to do about it.[11]

By the beginning of the nineteenth century, the climate was very different. Novalis would write, "Spinoza is a God-intoxicated man."[12] And Schleiermacher would offer reverent tribute to "the holy, rejected Spinoza . . . full of religion, full of the Holy Spirit."[13] Then Hegel would respond that Spinoza's views were more nearly acosmism than atheism.[14] And Heine would describe Spinoza as one "who was for long regarded with derision and hatred, but who in our day has been raised to the throne of intellectual supremacy," adding that nothing but "sheer unreason and malice" could label his doctrine atheism.[15]

Historically, those who called Spinoza an atheist tended to be deeply hostile toward his ideas, while those who rejected this label tended to be deeply sympathetic. It has long since become possible to sort the matter out in a more dispassionate manner, and it is important to do so. For clarity is better served if terms like 'theism,' 'atheism,' and 'pantheism' (like 'onto-theology') have a fairly clear descriptive content and are not used as vague honorifics or derogatories. 'Atheism' could be defined in terms of negative answers to either of the following quite different questions. (1) Is there anything corresponding to the theistic notion of a personal creator? and (2) Is there anything that deserves to be called God?

---

11. Letter 68, p. 321.

12. *Novalis: Werke, Tagebücher und Briefe Friedrich von Hardenbergs*, ed. Hans-Joachim Mähl and Richard Samuel (Darmstadt: Wissenschaftliche Buchgesellschaft, 1978), II, p. 812 (Fragment 346).

13. Friedrich Schleiermacher, *On Religion: Speeches to its Cultured Despisers*, trans. John Oman (New York: Harper & Brothers, 1958), p. 40. Schleiermacher would later describe Spinoza as "deeply influenced by piety, even though it were not Christian piety." While insisting that he himself was not a Spinozist, he also insisted that Spinoza could be "cried down . . . as godless [only] by the literalists." P. 104.

14. G. W. F. Hegel, *The Encyclopedia Logic*, trans. T. F. Geraets et al. (Indianapolis, Ind.: Hackett, 1991), p. 97 (*Anmerkung* to ¶50).

15. Heinrich Heine, *Religion and Philosophy in Germany*, trans. John Snodgrass (Boston: Beacon Press, 1959), pp. 69, 72.

It immediately becomes clear that there is a sense in which Spinoza is indisputably an atheist and a sense in which he is indisputably not. He says no to the first question, and if a-theism consists in the denial of theism, then he clearly is and wants to be an a-theist. But he says yes to the second question, and if atheism is the denial that anything should be called God, he clearly neither is nor wants to be an atheist. The dispute is not about Spinoza's views, which on these points are clear enough, but about which sense we should give to the term 'atheism'.

Should we define 'atheism' in relation to the first question, so that all non-theists, including pantheists, are atheists; or should we define it in relation to the second question so as to allow pantheism to be a third option, distinct from both theism and atheism? As we have already seen, the latter alternative is desirable for the present project, since it would be useful to approach the question of divine transcendence by comparing theism's transcendent God with pantheism's immanent God. Fortunately, several other considerations point in the same direction:

1) 'Atheism' has come to signify a generalized opposition or indifference to religion. Making all non-theists into atheists implies, in a manner at once tendentious and descriptively misleading, that theism has a monopoly on the religious life.[16]

2) Bennett and MacIntyre point out that in the case of Spinoza in particular, the justification for calling Nature God is that "the world comes closer than anything else" to being the bearer of the divine predicates. It is "infinite, eternal, not acted on by anything else," and so forth.[17]

3) By itself this last consideration is not sufficient. For the atheist may agree that the world is infinite, eternal, and so forth. Bennett recognizes such a deep agreement between the pantheist and the atheist that "we should not be quickly confident that there is any substantive disagreement at all. . . . If Spinoza and the atheist each pointed while saying, respectively, 'That is all God' and 'None of that is God', they would point to the very same world."[18] So Bennett points to "another reason" Spinoza has for calling Nature God, "namely his view of Nature as a fit object for reverence, awe, and humble

---

16. Theism is entitled to the normative claim that other modes of religion are idolatrous, but not to the descriptive claim that only theists are religious. For a passionate rebuttal of the charge that he has "renounced all religion," see Spinoza's Letter 43, p. 238.

17. Jonathan Bennett, *A Study of Spinoza's Ethics*, henceforth SSE (n.p.: Hackett, 1984), p. 33. Alasdair MacIntyre makes the same point in "Pantheism," in *The Encyclopedia of Philosophy*, ed. Paul Edwards (New York: Macmillan, 1967), VI, 33b. He says Spinoza believed "that *all* the key predicates by which divinity is ascribed apply to the entire system of things" (emphasis added). But this is misleading, for he lists such "metaphysical" attributes as being infinite, eternal, *causa sui*, and *causa omnium*, but not such "moral" attributes (which Spinoza would deny) as goodness, beneficence, and love, which presuppose personhood. Bennett makes the necessary distinction. "Spinoza holds that the natural world answers to many traditional descriptions of God; but not to all, and in particular not to the description 'a person'" (p. 34).

18. Bennett, SSE, pp. 32–33.

love. . . . He could thus regard Nature not only as the best subject for the metaphysical *descriptions* applied to God in the Judaeo-Christian tradition, but also as the best object of the *attitudes* which in that tradition are adopted towards God alone."[19]

It is essentially the same point that Michael Levine makes when he argues that the difference between atheism and pantheism is finally evaluative and not merely descriptive. He suggests that the pantheist experiences the infinite, eternal totality as having, in Otto's language, something numinous about it that the atheist misses.[20]

***

If Spinoza's pantheism is a-theistic without being atheistic, we need to determine more closely its view of God, with special reference to divine immanence. With help from Lessing and Herder, it was under the slogan ἐν καὶ πᾶν (One and All) that Spinoza later became a fertile source of inspiration for Goethe, the German idealists, and the German romantics.[21] Spinoza's own slogan, however, is *Deus sive natura* (God or Nature) (E4 Pref, II/206–207 and E4 P4D).

To understand the 'or' (*sive*) in Spinoza's slogan we need to distinguish three cases: (1) coffee or tea, (2) New York or America's largest city, and (3) murder or homicide. '*Sive*' signifies that so far as reference is concerned, the connected terms are interchangeable; so it would be appropriate only in cases two and three.[22] But these two cases differ in that the connected terms are synonymous in the third case, having the same reference by virtue of having the same meaning or connotation, but not in the second. Spinoza's use of '*sive*' means that for him '*Deus*' and '*natura*' designate the same reality. But it does not tell us whether we are to understand the two terms as synonymous. Just how does he construe the relation between Nature and God?

---

19. Bennett, SSE, pp. 34–35. While this helps to distinguish pantheism from atheism, it does not justify listing "theism" as one of Spinoza's deepest convictions (pp. 29–35). It is as misleading to assume that anyone who isn't an atheist is a theist as it is to assume that anyone who isn't a theist is an atheist.

20. Michael P. Levine, *Pantheism: A non-theistic concept of deity* (New York: Routledge, 1994), pp. 39–40, 45, 48, 64, 69, 83–84. One might quibble that Spinoza's account of the intellectual love of God does not mesh perfectly with Otto's account of our response to the holy; but love of any sort is an affect (if not necessarily a passion) for Spinoza, and the point of distinguishing the descriptive from the evaluative is well-taken. We should note, however, that the evaluation of the world that helps distinguish Spinoza from the atheist is not the "intrinsic value" (p. 69) of which Levine speaks.

21. For Lessing see Vallée, pp. 85–86 and the discussion of the pantheism controversy in Frederick C. Beiser, *The Fate of Reason: German Philosophy from Kant to Fichte* (Cambridge, Mass.: Harvard University Press, 1987), ch. 2. For Herder, see *God, Some Conversations*, trans. Frederick H. Burkhardt (Indianapolis, Ind.: Bobbs-Merrill, 1940).

22. The theist who wants to speak about God or nature will want a coffee-or-tea 'or'. In Latin this would be '*vel*' or '*aut*'.

While working on his *Treatise on the Emendation of the Intellect,* he writes to Oldenburg that he is "afraid that the theologians of our time may take offence" because he attributes to creation much that they attribute to God and vice versa. "I do not differentiate between God and Nature in the way all those known to me have done."[23] This is open to two readings:

1) Unlike the others, I don't distinguish God and Nature.

2) Like the others, I distinguish God and nature, but not the way they do.

It is the first reading that leads to the common view that Spinoza's one, unique substance, which may be called God, is simply the whole of Nature. This is suggested by the Lessing-Herder slogan, ἐν καὶ πᾶν. It is explicit when Heine says that for Spinoza "the world is not merely God distended, God-impregnated, it is identical with God. God, called by Spinoza the Sole Substance . . . 'is All that is' "[24] and when Yovel describes Spinoza's God as "the universe itself, insofar as it could be grasped as a single whole."[25]

It is the second reading that leads to more nuanced views. Thus MacIntyre defines Western pantheism as the view that "all that is must in some sense be God, or at least a manifestation of God."[26] In his critique of the *Tractatus Theologico-Politicus,* Van Velthuysen wonders what will happen to reward and punishment "when it is asserted that all things emanate from God by an ineluctable necessity, or rather, when he asserts that this universe in its entirety is God? For I fear that our author is not very far removed from that opinion; at any rate there is not much difference between asserting that all things necessarily emanate from God's nature and that the universe itself is God."[27]

Not much difference. But perhaps some? Enough to allow for some kind of distinction between God and the world? At this point Curley has the wonderful impudence to ask, "where, exactly does [Spinoza] say that substance is the whole of nature?"[28] The prime candidate, of course, is the *Deus sive natura* formula we are exploring. So we can remind ourselves that our question about two possible readings of "I do not differentiate between God and Nature in the way all those known to me have done" is a question about how to read that formula.

---

23. Letter 6, pp. 83–84. Spinoza is probably referring to his *Short Treatise.*

24. Heine, p. 74.

25. Yirmiyahu Yovel, *Spinoza and Other Heretics: The Marano of Reason* (Princeton, N.J.: Princeton University Press, 1989), p. 5. The qualification is meant to exclude the view that the whole of Nature is to be conceived as a large heap of finite things without any inherent unity. Thus MacIntyre defines pantheism as the view "that everything that exists constitutes a unity and that this all-inclusive unity is divine," and Levine insists, "Apart from a unifying element . . . the all-inclusive whole would not be God." MacIntyre, p. 34b and Levine, p. 34.

26. MacIntyre, p. 32b. It is not clear that this definition is equivalent to the one given by MacIntyre in the previous note.

27. Letter 42, pp. 226–27.

28. Edwin Curley, *Behind the Geometrical Method: A Reading of Spinoza's Ethics,* henceforth BGM (Princeton, N.J.: Princeton University Press, 1988), p. 36. See p. 150, n. 52 for Curley's rejection of two candidates from the *Short Treatise.*

Two letters have a direct bearing on our question. In replying to Van Velthuysen's letter, Spinoza describes as "malignant" the latter's claim that "it is the same, or not very different, to assert that all things emanate necessarily from God's nature and that the universe is God . . ."[29] In a later letter to Oldenburg, he writes,

> I entertain an opinion on God and Nature far different from that which modern Christians are wont to uphold. For I maintain that God is the immanent cause, as the phrase is, of all things, and not the transitive cause. . . . However, as to the view of certain people that the *Tractatus Theologico-Politicus* rests on the identification of God with Nature (by the latter of which they understand a kind of mass or corporeal matter) they are quite mistaken.[30]

It would seem that Spinoza is directing us toward the second interpretation of his views, "Like the others, I distinguish God and nature, but not the way they do." The letter just cited specifically denies the simple identification of God and nature and tells us two things about the way his distinction between them is distinctive: (1) it is not the standard Christian account, and (2) it is a causal account, but one with God as the immanent rather than the transitive cause of the world. In other words, creation *ex nihilo* by a personal deity is not what he has in mind.[31] What he does have in mind he spells out in the *Ethics* in terms of the relation of substance to its modes and of *natura naturans* to *natura naturata*.

There is only one substance, God. It exists necessarily and is the infinite cause of all finite things, which are its modes. Whereas substance exists in itself and is conceived through itself, modes exist in God, are conceived through God. Causally speaking, they occur necessarily through the laws of God's nature; logically speaking, they follow necessarily from God's essence. In all of these ways, substance and its modes can be distinguished. If it is objected that neither separately nor collectively do these differences amount to "a Cartesian 'real distinction'"—Spinoza will only agree.[32] His distinction between God and the world of finite things is not like the others'; it is not the distinction between a creator substance and created substances.

In the midst of developing these themes in Part I, Spinoza reformulates the distinction between substance and its modes as that between *natura naturans* (nature naturing, nature active, nature as cause) and *natura naturata* (nature natured, nature passive, nature as effect). The former he identifies with "God, insofar as he is considered a free cause." The latter consists in "all the modes of God's attributes insofar as they are considered as things which are

29. Letter 43, p. 239.
30. Letter 73, p. 322.
31. In the *Ethics* Spinoza explicitly denies that substance can be created. E1 P6C, P8S2, and P15S, and his account of the relation of substance to its modes is consistently anticreationist.
32. See Curley's reference to Garrett's correspondence at the end of n. 53, p. 150 of BGM.

in God, and can neither be nor be conceived without God" (E1 P29S). *Deus sive natura* is not the simple identification of God with the whole of nature because, strictly speaking, it means *Deus sive natura naturans*. These two terms, but not *natura naturata*, have the same reference. Are they synonymous? No, so far as ordinary usage is concerned; but in the context of Spinoza's theory, yes.

Shortly before introducing this terminology Spinoza repeats the claim that "God is the immanent, not the transitive, cause of all things" (E1 P18). Our question is now quite clear. How shall we construe the distinction between substance and its modes, or between *natura naturans* and *natura naturata* as a theory of divine immanence? One could say that Spinoza's God transcends the world as cause transcends effect. But since the relation between cause and effect is not a transitive relation between two substances, creative and created, Spinoza makes God the immanent cause of the world. All this is clear enough. But what does it mean?

I believe Curley's interpretation makes the most sense out of Spinoza's text. *Natura naturans* (God, substance) is the laws of nature; *natura naturata* (world, modes) is the world of finite things/events/facts that occur in accordance with those laws.[33] On this view Spinoza's naturalism is more basic than his substance monism. One can almost say that the latter is a corollary of the former.

This reading implies a "realist" rather than a "conceptualist" or "nominalist" view of the laws of nature in relation to natural facts. They are not merely descriptions of how things regularly happen. They are forces with a kind of causal efficacy.[34] They are powers and not just patterns. They can be distinguished from the world they "govern" as energy from matter (in the ordinary sense of stuff) or as life force from organism.[35] But they cannot be separated from that world. In this respect they are like Aristotle's forms. That is why Spinoza uses the spatial metaphor 'in' in two apparently conflicting ways to describe the relation. The world, as the totality of the modes, is in God; and God is in the world as its immanent cause.

***

Spinoza's pantheism is a thoroughgoing naturalism. The laws of nature, as discovered by the sciences, are the deepest truth about the world.[36] They are

---

33. See Curley, BGM, 36–50 and E. M. Curley, *Spinoza's Metaphysics: An Essay in Interpretation*, henceforth SM (Cambridge, Mass.: Harvard University Press, 1969), ch. 1–2.

34. Yovel, p. 158, and Levine, pp. 40–41, attribute this view to Spinoza.

35. Spinoza's God would be a kind of Aristotelian world-soul, if that didn't have teleological implications.

36. This remains the case whether one gives a materialist account of Spinoza or a dualist account. For on either account, mind is as fully the product of the mechanistic laws of nature as is body. For Spinoza as materialist, see Curley, BGM, and Stuart Hampshire, "A Kind of Materialism," in *Freedom of Mind* (New York: Oxford University Press, 1972). For Spinoza as dualist, see Alan

not the product of God's creative act; they themselves are God. It follows that there is no personal creator and that all persons are "creations" of the impersonal laws of nature. But we might understand Spinoza better if we reverse the relation between theorem and corollary and make the deification of Nature (as *natura naturans*) a consequence of the case against a personal God.

This order is suggested by Yovel, who says that for Spinoza God is (1) not "a unique and separate person existing outside the world" but rather (2) "the universe itself insofar as it could be grasped as a single whole."[37] We have seen that the second formula requires revision, but our attention is now directed toward the first as a crucial, negative premise for the second. We could distinguish the question of God's separateness from the world from the question of God's personal character, but we might be more on target if we see them as abstract and concrete forms of the same question. A personal creator will be, *ipso facto*, distinct from the world, whether or not one uses the language of substance to express the fact.[38] In any event, Levine is surely right to treat the question of God's personhood as central to the debate between theism and pantheism.[39]

Spinoza leaves no doubt about this in his own case. His positive presentation of Nature as God is deeply intertwined with a fourfold assault on the notion of a personal God.

1) In the first place he denies free will (in the sense of free choice) to God. In his deterministic universe there is no room for free will anywhere. God is free, as finite beings are not, in the sense of being under no external constraints, but this is not to be construed in terms of free will. "By God's power ordinary people understand God's free will and his right over all things which are . . . they very often compare God's power with the power of kings. But we have refuted this in 1P32C1 and C2" (E2 P3S).[40] Acting from the necessity of his nature, God is the free cause of all things, which means "that all things have been predetermined by God, not from freedom of the will *or* absolute good pleasure, but from God's absolute nature, *or* infinite power" (E1 App, II/77).[41] It is a mistake to think that there is anything in God's power that he

---

Donagan, "Spinoza's Dualism," in *The Philosophy of Baruch Spinoza*, ed. Richard Kennington (Washington, D.C.: Catholic University of America Press, 1980) and Bennett, SSE. Curley finds Bennett's dualism, but not Donagan's, compatible with his materialism. See Curley, BGM, p. 157, n. 38.

37. Yovel, p. 5.

38. Levine at first distinguishes them (p. 2), but then seems to collapse the difference when he teams up with Smart to say that theistic transcendence involves " 'the belief that God is Creator' *and so* 'outside' the cosmos" (p. 107, emphasis added).

39. Levine, pp. 2–3, 11, 19, 53, 95, 147, 313–15. He quotes Feuerbach as saying, "That which separates theism from pantheism is only the conception or the imagining of God as a personal being" (p. 20, n. 16).

40. Spinoza might also have cross-referenced E1 P33 & P33S1.

41. In keeping with his theory of value, of which more hereafter, Spinoza denies that this in any way diminishes God's perfection, since perfection is solely a matter of power (E1 App, II/83).

does not produce (E1 P17S, II/61; cf. E1 App, II/83). Appeals to the will of God are merely "the sanctuary of ignorance" (E1 App, II/81).

In the *Tractatus*, God's will and intellect are "really one and the same." This means that God's will or decrees "always involve eternal necessity *or* truth" (TTP 31, III/62–63). The universal laws of nature do not stem from the eternal decrees of God; they simply are those decrees (TTP 25, III/46). As if proleptically afraid that he might be confused with Leibniz at this point, Spinoza goes beyond this in the *Ethics* to deny that will and intellect properly belong to God.[42] Actual intellect, including will, is a mode of thinking and belongs to *natura naturata* (E1 P17S, II/62; P31; P31D; P32C2). God is a thinking being and thought is an attribute of God, not because God is or has a mind, but because finite minds are modes which express the divine nature, that is, are caused by God. To say that God is a thinking being is simply to say that nature produces finite minds (E2 P1D; cf. E2 P11C).

2) Closely related to the denial of divine free will is the denial of divine purpose. In the *Tractatus*, Spinoza says the same thing about divine guidance that he says about divine decrees. To speak about either is simply to speak about natural causation. "Therefore, whether we say that all things happen according to the laws of nature, or whether we say that they are ordered according to the decree and guidance of God, we say the same thing" (TTP 25, III/45–46).

In the *Ethics*, Spinoza says it is better to attribute free will to God than to say that God acts for the sake of the good. Those who say this "seem to place something outside God, which does not depend on God, to which God attends, as a model, in what he does, and at which he aims, as at a certain goal" (E1 P33S2, II/76). If it be objected that God's own being is the model, Spinoza will focus attention on the goal. "For if God acts for the sake of an end, he necessarily wants something which he lacks" and this is an imperfection (E1 App, II/80). The very notion of a divine purpose is a human fiction and prejudice that arises from our ignorance of the true causation of things, our consciousness of our own appetites, our interpretation of our own behavior in terms of final causes, and finally, our projection of this purposiveness onto God (E1 App, II/78–80). It is in terms of this argument that Spinoza will later introduce his famous slogan, *Deus sive natura* (E4 Pref, II/206–207).

The equation of God with nature denies purpose, and thus providence in the usual sense, to God as deliberately as it denies free choice. Kolakowski simply repeats what Spinoza insists on when he writes,

---

42. On the question whether there is all that much difference between Leibniz and Spinoza, see Robert Merrihew Adams, *Leibniz: Determinist, Theist, Idealist* (New York: Oxford University Press, 1994), pp. 123–34. He writes, "Leibniz's insistence on the role of God's will, and choice of the best, in the theological explanation of the existence of the created world would remain the chief point in his differentiation of his own version of determinism from Spinoza's. . . . It is also, I believe, the point on which Leibniz can most easily be seen as defending the *personality* of God against Spinoza" (p. 125).

If, therefore, we free ourselves from Spinoza's vocabulary, we will say this: to the world it is indifferent that we are a part of it; it does not contain itself any intent, benevolent or hostile, directed toward man, it has realized in its perfection everything which can come into existence, it has no intentions of changing anything in consideration of human suffering and it is after all simply unthinkable that it would or could do this. There is no providence in the world which could keep guard over our life, there is no protection . . . nature is not interested in our constructions.[43]

3) Against this background a third denial is inevitable. A God who acts without free will or purpose is not a God who performs miracles. Spinoza's polemic against miracles differs from Hume's in that it arises from a metaphysical affirmation rather than from epistemological doubts; and it differs from the deist objection in that it arises from the conception of a God that couldn't even conceivably do miracles. God and nature are so related that the only way to understand God's power is by means of natural causes and not by means of miracles (TTP 16, III/28; 35, III/82; 37, III/84). Belief in miracles arises from ignorance of real causes and a belief in divine providence (in the traditional, non-Spinozistic sense). Were such an event to occur, it would be contrary to the divine decrees, intellect, and nature. Rather than revealing God, it would "make us doubt his existence" (TTP 34–38, III/81–86). This is not as strange as it sounds; for it is simply the claim that a miracle would make us doubt the ultimacy of the laws of nature. Spinoza consistently excludes that possibility.

After the publication of this polemic in the *Tractatus*, Spinoza asked Oldenburg "to point out to me the passages . . . which have proved a stumbling-block to learned men." Oldenburg responds by pointing to the "ambiguous" treatment of God and Nature, "which many people consider you have confused with each other. In addition, many are of the opinion that you take away the authority and validity of miracles . . ."[44] In his reply, Spinoza denies the revelatory value of miracles and repeats the claim that belief in miracles is a superstition grounded in ignorance.[45] In the *Ethics*, Spinoza alludes only briefly to this corollary of his denial of free will and divine purpose, adding only that while many believe in miracles simply out of ignorance, some are attached to these beliefs because their authority depends on them (E1 App, II/81).

4) Spinoza's fourth and final denial makes clear that God is without affects or emotions.[46] He does not simply equate the emotions with the passions, which are rather a subset of the former. Spinoza seems to hold the view that to

---

43. Leszek Kolakowski, "The Two Eyes of Spinoza," in *Spinoza: A Collection of Critical Essays*, ed. Marjorie Grene (Garden City, N.Y.: Doubleday, 1973), p. 284.

44. Letter 68, p. 322, and Letter 71, p. 329. The third item mentioned by Oldenburg concerns the Incarnation and Atonement of Jesus Christ; it thus concerns Christianity and not theism as such.

45. Letter 73, pp. 332–33.

46. Elwes and Shirley translate *affectus* as 'emotion', while Curley sticks to 'affect'.

the degree I fully understand what is going on in my emotional life, my emotions are actions and to the degree I lack this understanding, my emotions are passions. It might look as if he simply wants to deny passions to God, since they would represent an imperfection. Indeed, he insists that it would be irrational to attribute jealousy, a passion, to God (TTP 44, III/101); and he holds more generally that those who attribute passions to God "wander from the true knowledge of God" (E1 P15S, II/57).

But it is affects as such, not just passions, that Spinoza wishes to exclude from God. It is the same sort of confusion that makes God a creator that ascribes human affects to God (E1 P7S2).[47] "God is without passions, and is not affected with any affect of joy or sadness" (E5 P17). It follows that, "Strictly speaking, God loves no one, and hates no one" (E5 P17C). It also follows that, "He who loves God cannot strive that God should love him in return" (P5 P19). Does God not love himself, then? Yes, but only insofar as our own intellectual love of God (objective genitive) "is the very love of God [subjective genitive] by which God loves himself" (P5 P35–36). Since in loving himself God loves all things in himself, it follows "that God's love of men and the [human] mind's intellectual love of God are one and the same" (E5 P36C).[48]

There is nothing new here. Thought is an attribute of God (as well as extension). But this means, as we have already seen, not that God is an actual intellect or a will; these occur only in *natura naturans*. It means simply that God is the cause of every actual intellect or will. Now the same principle is applied to the emotions. God is love, not by being a person who loves, but by being the impersonal cause of all persons who love. Royce, echoing the passage quoted above from Kolakowski, summarizes this strand in Spinoza by describing his God as "rigid," "merciless," and "divine."[49]

***

We are exploring the divine transcendence embodied in theism by looking at the understanding of divine immanence found in Spinoza's pantheism. Although there are not a lot of Spinozists to be found these days, this choice is not as quixotic as it might seem. In the first place, no writings in the Western tradition have a stronger claim to being the *locus classicus* of pantheism's thesis of divine immanence. But secondly, while most naturalisms and materialisms

---

47. The passage cited from the *Ethics* in the previous paragraph links the attribution of emotions to God with belief in creation.

48. Cf. Meister Eckhart, "The eye in which I see God is the same eye in which God sees me. My eye and God's eye are one eye and one seeing, one knowing and one loving. . . . The same knowledge in which God knows himself is the knowledge of every detached spirit and nothing else." *Meister Eckhart: Teacher and Preacher*, ed. Bernard McGinn (New York: Paulist Press, 1986), pp. 270, 261.

49. Josiah Royce, *The Spirit of Modern Philosophy* (Boston: Houghton, Mifflin & Co., 1892), p. 43.

today do not deify nature, the notion that the impersonal laws of nature are the ultimate fact of the universe is widespread, both in sophisticated theories and in vague, secular common sense. One could say that pantheism, in substance if not in name, is the secular faith of the world we live in, especially since there are more than a few who, like Spinoza, would like to retain some sense of religion without any clear break from the ultimacy of the impersonal. So our examination of Spinoza's quarrel with theism is not merely of historical interest.

We have two competing pictures or cosmological theories. The immanence theory affirms that the infinite and ultimate is impersonal. The transcendence theory affirms that the infinite and ultimate is personal. The overriding question here could well take onto-theological form. Which theory of the Highest Being gives the best explanation of the whole of being? Which account renders being most fully intelligible? Whose God best satisfies the demands of the principle of sufficient reason? In onto-theological terms, that would be the significance of the debate whether God is immanent or transcendent.

We are working, however, on the hypothesis that the question of transcendence is also a question of self-transcendence, a question about our proper posture in the world and not just about the proper explanation of the world. (Simply to put the issue this way is to break with the onto-theological project. We are not so much the answer givers as the ones put in question by our own questions.) We have seen that the significance of immanence is the ultimacy of the impersonal. If we press further and ask about the significance of this ultimacy, we will find Spinoza eager to give us two answers. On the epistemic front, the impersonal character of God undermines the notions of divine mystery and divine revelation associated with biblical theism. On the ethical front, it undermines the theistic understanding of God as a moral lawgiver. In each case, the elimination or minimizing of divine transcendence is the elimination or minimizing of a significant mode of human self-transcendence. For epistemically and ethically the human remains the highest point of reference. These consequences of Spinoza's theology are at the same time its deepest motives. His philosophy of immanence is quintessentially modern in its demand for full human autonomy.[50]

We shall return to the question of ethics; for now let us look at the question of knowledge. Pantheism is not necessarily antithetical to epistemic transcendence, the claim that the divine being is a mystery significantly beyond our human capacity to comprehend.[51] One need only think of various Eastern pantheisms in the Hindu, Buddhist, and Taoist traditions or of the Western pantheisms associated with negative theology. But Spinoza's pantheism comes wrapped in a very strong commitment to the principle of sufficient reason, both as the demand that everything be rendered intelligible through the giving

---

50. See Yovel, p. xi.
51. Levine, p. 95–96; MacIntyre, 33a.

of reasons or explanations and as the confidence that this ought implies can. Reasons would not be demanded of us if we could not give them.

Thus Bennett lists rationalism as the first of five themes in Spinoza "which lie deeper than any of his argued doctrines." This doesn't just mean the superiority of reason to sense, important as this is to Spinoza. It means "explanatory rationalism," the view that "whatever is the case can be explained . . . the refusal to admit brute facts," and "causal rationalism," the view that "a cause relates to its effect as a premiss does to a conclusion which follows from it. . . . It is not that he sees logical links as weaker than they are; rather, he sees causal ones as stronger."[52] This is central to Spinoza's claim that all truth is necessary truth.[53]

Descartes' rationalism pales by comparison. As early as his attempt to transcribe Descartes' *Principles of Philosophy* into geometric form, Spinoza has Meyer point out that when he says *"this or that surpasses human understanding"* this is

> said only on behalf of Descartes. For it must not be thought that our Author [Spinoza] offers this as his own opinion. He judges that all those things, and even many others more sublime and subtle, can not only be conceived clearly and distinctly, but also explained very satisfactorily—provided only that the human Intellect is guided in the search for truth and knowledge of things along a different path from that which Descartes opened up and made smooth. . . . Different foundations are required, if we wish our intellect to rise to that pinnacle of knowledge.[54]

It is worth noting that this comes immediately after a paragraph in which Spinoza, through Meyer, disavows the Cartesian distinction of will and intellect and the free choice Descartes attributes thereby both to God and to human subjects. Since a free choice is an event that cannot be causally explained, Spinoza finds freedom (in this sense) and total intelligibility to be mutually exclusive. He was especially disturbed that Descartes not only endowed God and human persons with free choice, but made the essence of things and the laws of nature the result of such freedom on God's part. Although they are immutable and eternal "because God so wished it and brought it to pass," they are contingent and might have been otherwise.[55] But for Spinoza, "to introduce a personal creator at this point was to give up the hope of a rational explanation of things, to betray the sciences Descartes had hoped to found."[56]

Spinoza sees an irreconcilable tension in Descartes' thinking at this point.

---

52. Bennett, SSE, pp. 29–30.

53. See chapter 3 of Curley, SM.

54. Curley, *The Collected Works of Spinoza*, I, 230 (Gebhardt, I/132).

55. From Descartes' reply to Gassendi's objection to the Fifth Meditation, *The Philosophical Works of Descartes*, trans. Elizabeth S. Haldane and G. R. T. Ross (n.p.: Dover Publications, 1955), II, 226.

56. Curley, Introduction to *A Spinoza Reader* (Princeton, N.J.: Princeton University Press, 1994), p. xxv. Elsewhere Curley writes that the most fundamental difference between Descartes and Spinoza was that "for Spinoza the world was thoroughly intelligible." SM, p. 157.

"Cartesian science requires the laws of nature to be necessary truths, as a condition of the intelligibility of nature. . . . But Cartesian theology requires the laws of nature to be contingent truths, rigorously subordinated to the will of an arbitrary creator . . ."[57] Hence the need for "a different path" from the one blazed by Descartes. Nowhere is this clearer than where Descartes, with reference to his idea of God as infinite substance, writes, "I do not comprehend the infinite . . . for it is of the nature of the infinite that my nature, which is finite and limited, should not comprehend it; and it is sufficient that I should understand this . . ."[58]

At issue is our knowledge of God and, eventually, of all things in God. How good is this knowledge? The traditional hierarchy of reason over sense becomes for Spinoza the hierarchy of reason over imagination, and he maintains a steady polemic against imagination, which he understands to be the source of error (E4 P1S). In the *Tractatus*, as we shall see, the rational, philosophical knowledge of reason is superior to the imaginative, religious knowledge of ordinary people and their prophets. In the *Ethics*, Spinoza gives his three-stage version of the divided line in which the lowest, inferior stage has imagination as its prime mark.[59] Not surprisingly, Spinoza attributes traditional ideas of God, freedom, and immortality to the imagination. But the upper two stages, discursive and intuitive reason, are free of this contamination (E2 P40S2).

In praising the higher, rational knowledge, Spinoza claims for it (1) the certainty deriving from clear and distinct ideas (TTP 11, III/16), (2) the freedom not only from imagination but also from two other contaminants, personal temperament and prevailing opinion (TTP 16–17, III/30), and (3) participation in the nature of God (TTP 10–11, III/15–16).[60] But none of this precludes the possibility that God should exceed human comprehension. Descartes could make these three claims.

We might take a quantitative approach to the difference between the two. Descartes allows that "in God there is an infinitude of things which I cannot comprehend . . . and possibly likewise an infinitude of properties of which I am ignorant . . ."[61] But Spinoza also permits a finitude to human knowledge insofar as God has an infinity of attributes (E1 Def6), of which we know only two, thought and extension. Since the two seem to be in agreement about this *terra incognita* within the divine infinity, we must set aside this quantitative sense in which God exceeds human understanding in order to locate their disagreement. For they do differ on the qualitative issue: given that there are

---

57. Curley, BGM, p. 42.
58. Third Meditation, Haldane and Ross, I, 166.
59. Insofar as he distinguishes at this first level between knowledge "from random experience" and knowledge "from signs," he almost gives us a fourfold divided line.
60. In the *Ethics* this becomes the strong claim that "the human mind is part of the infinite intellect of God" (E2 P11C, P43S).
61. Haldane and Ross, I, 166.

dimensions of reality wholly outside our ken, how thorough is our grasp of those dimensions we do apprehend? Both purport to have clear and distinct, certain knowledge of God as infinite substance (there being no other kind for Spinoza). But Descartes clearly and distinctly perceives both that there is an infinite substance and that he cannot comprehend it. It is the knowledge he has that is inadequate, not the knowledge he doesn't have.

In order to disagree once more with Descartes, Spinoza will have to go beyond the claims already made for rational, philosophical knowledge. And he does. He claims that we have an adequate knowledge of God and of finite things in God, both at the second, discursive level, and at the third, intuitive level (E2 P40S2; E2 P47, P47S).

In using this language, Spinoza evokes the scholastic definition of truth as the *adequatio rei et intellectus.* He tells us that by truth he means agreement between an idea (judgment) and its object (E1 A6). We are talking the familiar language of correspondence. In a typically rationalist fashion, Spinoza defines an adequate idea, not simply in terms of agreement, but in terms of agreement that can be established *a priori* (E2 Def4).

But what is implied by calling our *a priori* knowledge of the essence of God and finite things "adequate" (*ad + aequare,* toward the equal or to make equal)? What is equal to what? Clearly Spinoza is not a Kantian for whom "objects must conform to our knowledge" but a realist for whom "all our knowledge must conform to objects."[62] Is the *intellectus* adequate to or equal to the *rei*? Does it measure up?

The measure metaphor is helpful, for it suggests the weighing device known as a balance. Even if everything that shows up on the *intellectus* side as assertion shows up on the *rei* side as fact, we would have only partial adequacy, which we might call correctness. For our scale will not be in balance unless the converse is also the case: everything on the *rei* side as fact must show up on the *intellectus* side as assertion. This two-way reciprocity is important since Spinoza gives partiality as one mark of inadequacy (E2 P11C). But it is not the point of difference. We are dealing here with essential natures, so completeness of empirical fact is not at issue, and there is nothing in Descartes' account to suggest that there is any imbalance between the essential nature of God as infinite substance and his *assertion* of this reality, no hint that his *affirmation* is incomplete.

The divine object and the human intellect fall out of balance for Descartes at the point of *comprehension.* There is more on the side of the real, in the case of God, than our clear and distinct idea of infinite substance is able to *understand.*[63] The *cogito* expresses our understanding of what a finite thinking

---

62. Kant, *Critique of Pure Reason,* B xvi.

63. Heidegger's account of the way assertion is derivative from understanding might be helpful. For my analysis, see "Hermeneutics as Epistemology," in *Blackwell Guide to Epistemology,* ed. Ernest Sosa and John Greco (Oxford: Blackwell, 1999), pp. 415–35. I am not assuming this is the way Descartes would make the distinction.

substance is. When we contrast to this a finite extended substance, we understand what we are talking about. But when the contrast is with an infinite thinking substance, we do not. We say not more than we know (for we know that God is an infinite substance), but more than we can comprehend.

Over against the weak, Cartesian sense of adequacy in terms of propositional assertion, Spinoza places a strong sense of adequacy in terms of understanding. He does not explicitly distinguish himself from Descartes in these terms. But everything he does say seems to presuppose the stronger *adequatio*. Three factors in particular deserve attention. First, he consistently rejects any notion of God, such as divine free will, that would involve a limitation on the intelligibility of God (or the world in God) to us. The only exception is quantitative, the unknown attributes of God. But within the territory of thought and extension, God is the explanation of all finite being and, to be sure that God is no unexplained explainer, Spinoza invokes the notion of God as *causa sui* and supports it with a pantheistic version of the ontological argument. Unlike Descartes, he does not qualify any of this with so much as a hint that God is incomprehensible.

Second, he represents reason as essentially pure, as constituted by its freedom from the contaminants that constrain comprehension. We have already seen this in terms of imagination, personal temperament, and public opinion. To this list we now need to add time. Such subsequent thinkers as Kant, Heidegger, and Derrida agree with Plato that nothing cuts us off from the irenic intelligibility of the eternal like time. But they find us to be incorrigibly temporal. Like Plato, Spinoza holds that we can transcend time epistemically. He makes the bold claim that reason grasps the essences of things *sub specie aeternitatis* in both the second and third kinds of knowledge. In this sense, the mind itself is eternal (E2 P44C2 & C2D; E5 P22, 29–31). It dwells in that divine ether in which we are able, as Plato puts it, to "contemplate things by themselves with the soul by itself."[64] This is the point at which ontotheology becomes the metaphysics of presence.

Finally, there is what Spinoza says about the third kind of knowledge. Like the second kind of knowledge, reason in its intuitive mode "proceeds from an adequate idea of the formal essence of certain attributes of God to the adequate knowledge of the essence of things" (E2 P40S2). Two marks distinguish this way of knowing God and all things in God in terms of adequate ideas. First there is the intuitive aspect. If given three numbers and asked to find a fourth which is to the third as the second is to the first, I may proceed discursively, employing explicit processes of inference, possibly guided by a method. This would be the second kind of knowing, and it becomes clear that the *Ethics* is an example. But if the three numbers are 1, 2, and 3, I just see "at a glance" that the fourth number is 6 (E2 P40S2).

Second, the third kind of knowledge goes beyond "universal knowledge"

---

64. Plato, *Phaedo*, 66e.

to "singular things" (E5 P36S). This movement is not inevitable. Tolstoy's Ivan Ilych knew that all humans are mortal and could even draw the syllogistic conclusion that Caius, a human, is mortal. But it had never quite dawned on him that he was mortal.[65] It is one thing to know from the proofs in the *Ethics* that all things happen inevitably in accordance with the laws of nature. It is another thing to see my cancer, or that of a loved one, from this perspective.

Spinoza tells us that "the more we understand things in this [third] way, the more we understand God" (E5 P25D) and "the more each of us is able to achieve in this kind of knowledge, the more he is conscious of himself and of God" (E5 P31S). Moreover, it is out of this third kind of knowledge that the intellectual love of God grows (E5 P33), the love which turns out to be God's love of himself (E5 P36, P36C). As we know from *The Cloud of Unknowing*, there is a love of God that is antipodal to knowledge. But this is a love tied tightly to insight. Like our consciousness of God, it grows as our understanding of God grows. This growth is gradual. We do not instantly arrive at a point where we can immediately see all things, in their particularity, in God. But there is nothing essentially mysterious about God that places any limit on this growth in understanding.

We can see that it is for the sake of his onto-theological project that Spinoza turns his back not only on the God of his fathers, Abraham, Isaac, Jacob, but even on the God of Descartes. Their God is too transcendent and is banished so that "logos, or reason" can be "restored to the natural world . . ."[66] His replacement God is "an ultimate principle of explanation."[67] It is not surprising that "he," as Spinoza regularly says, turns out to be the laws of nature construed as necessary truths.

* * *

Spinoza's onto-theological rationalism is as hostile to divine revelation as to divine mystery. For it represents a second place where divine freedom interrupts the grid of causal explanation. Insofar as God may be known through the created order (Ps. 19:1, Rom. 1:20), theism normally contains the contingency of the laws of nature just described. Neither the fact of creation nor the nature of nature is inevitable; both are the result of divine free will.[68] But the biblical God is primarily known through revelation (or, if the knowledge of God through nature is dubbed general revelation, through special revelation). This revelation consists in contingent actions in history (the Exo-

---

65. Leo Tolstoy, "The Death of Ivan Ilych."
66. Yovel, p. 127.
67. Curley, Introduction to A *Spinoza Reader*, p. xxiv. Descartes' God is also a principle of explanation, but not as consistently as Spinoza's. In crucial respects the former remains an unexplained explainer.
68. Under the spell of the onto-theological project, theists such as Leibniz may find themselves powerfully pulled in Spinoza's direction on either or both of these points.

dus, the Atonement) and in contingent speech acts, including those which interpret the actions in history.[69] Neither divine actions nor divine speech acts can be explained in terms of the laws of nature. Rather the converse is true. "For he spoke, and it came to be" (Ps. 33:9) applies not just to nature but to its laws as well.

For the same reasons that Spinoza's theology must eliminate creation and providence, it must eliminate revelation. Human cognition is radically decentered by these theistic theorems. We have seen that while he simply denies that substances can be created, he eliminates traditional views of divine providence by offering persuasive (re)definitions instead of outright denials. God is the laws of nature and to speak of divine guidance is simply to speak of events taking place in accordance with those laws, which can also be thought of as the divine decrees. It is not surprising that Stevenson gives Spinoza as a prime example of what he means by a persuasive definition, "one which gives a new conceptual meaning to a familiar word without substantially changing its emotive meaning, and which is used with the conscious or unconscious purpose of changing, by this means, the direction of people's interests."[70]

Spinoza adopts this latter strategy for dealing with revelation. He treats as superstition and insanity the belief that God would write his decrees anywhere but in the mind of the wise (TTP 7, III/5–6). But instead of giving a reason why we should replace the prophet with the sage, he offers us a redefinition of prophecy. Prophecy or revelation, properly understood, simply is reason. It is what we know with certainty by natural knowledge or the natural light. Although the human mind is the first cause of revelation, we can say that our clear and distinct ideas are dictated to us by God's nature (TTP 10–11; III/15–16). "God can communicate himself immediately to men, for he communicates his essence to our mind without using any corporeal means" (TTP 14; III/20). In other words, our knowledge of God is *a priori*.

Nothing more than this is needed. Except for the many, who are intellectually inferior! Those usually called prophets are not the true recipients of divine revelation. They interpret divine truth to those who cannot attain certain knowledge but are capable only of faith (TTP 10–11; III/15–16). They are themselves intellectually inferior, for their gifts are gifts of imagination, which is inversely related to intellect. In the absence of clear and distinct ideas, both prophets and their audience require signs to give certainty. "In this re-

---

69. See G. Ernest Wright, *God Who Acts* (Chicago: Henry Regnery, 1952). The biblical theology movement, of which this is a classic expression, probably paid insufficient attention to divine speech acts. For a valuable corrective, see Nicholas Wolterstorff, *Divine discourse: Philosophical reflections on the claim that God speaks* (New York: Cambridge University Press, 1995).

70. Charles L. Stevenson, *Facts and Values: Studies in Ethical Analysis* (New Haven, Conn.: Yale University Press, 1963), p. 32. For Spinoza, see pp. 41–42. It is no doubt the use of persuasive definition that leads Van Velthuysen to say that Spinoza "prompts atheism by stealth . . . teaching sheer atheism with furtive and disguised arguments." See note 7 above.

spect, therefore, prophecy is inferior to natural knowledge, which requires no sign, but involves certainty of its own nature" (TTP 15–17; III/26–30).[71]

By virtue of the imperfections of prophecy, we can say two things about Scripture. First, it can be said to be divine just to the degree that it teaches the truth independently established by reason (TTP 42, III/99).[72] Second, some of what Scripture teaches is contrary to reason, such as Moses' view that God is jealous (TTP 44, III/101). As such it may be called prophecy in the inferior sense, but not in the proper sense according to which it counts as revelation.

In his defense of Spinoza's pantheism, Heine writes, "God is identical with the world. . . . In man Deity reaches self-consciousness, and this self-consciousness Deity again reveals through man."[73] Heine goes on to give a Hegelian interpretation of this in terms of the history of collective humanity. For Spinoza, the "man" in whom deity comes to self-consciousness will be the Sage rather than Spirit. But since the only actual intellects are human, it will still be the case that human knowledge is the only actual knowledge there is. There is no divine knowledge, distinct from it, on which it is dependent or to which it is inferior.

Here we have a second form of epistemic self-transcendence that Spinoza disavows. In rejecting divine mystery, Spinoza denies that there is a reality that exceeds our capacities of comprehension. In rejecting divine revelation, he denies that there is an actual intellect, distinct from all human intellects (individual or collective), on which we are cognitively dependent and to which we are cognitively inferior. To grant either mystery or revelation would be to grant that we are neither the apex nor the center of the cognitive world, but are oriented toward a reality and toward a knowing that are not at our disposal, epistemically speaking. It will be clear that there is no need for such self-transcendence in Spinoza's scheme of things. Theism's affirmation of divine transcendence becomes more than merely an onto-theological alternative to Spinoza's pantheism when it affirms both divine mystery and divine revelation, which is a special instance of miracle.

* * *

We turn, finally, from the epistemic to the ethical significance of the ultimacy of the impersonal. In a famous letter to Overbeck, Nietzsche gives his interpretation. "I have a *precursor*, and what a precursor! . . . Not only

---

71. In the previously cited Letter 73 to Oldenburg, Spinoza is convinced "that the certainty of divine revelation can be based solely on the wisdom of doctrine, and not on miracles, that is, on ignorance. . . . Here I will add only this, that the chief distinction I make between religion and superstition is that the latter is founded on ignorance, the former on wisdom" (pp. 332–33). In other words, the religion of Augustine and Aquinas, who refuse to make autonomous reason the independent criterion of biblical revelation, is superstition.

72. See previous note.

73. Heine, pp. 77–78.

is [Spinoza's] over-all tendency like mine—making knowledge the *most power-ful* affect—but in five main points of his doctrine I recognize myself . . . he denies the freedom of the will, teleology, the moral world order, the unegois-tic, and evil."[74]

It is not clear that Spinoza would have welcomed this enthusiasm during his lifetime, especially from a self-designated "immoralist." Just as he finds it necessary to reject the charge of atheism, both for political and for philosophi-cal reasons, so he is eager to repudiate the charge that he undermines morality. In the *Ethics* he regularly portrays himself as the upholder of both religion and morality (E4 P37S1; E4 P73S; P4 App, II/272; E5 P41, P41S).[75]

Spinoza is an immoralist in the same sense in which he is an atheist; his ethics, like his theology, differs dramatically from that of theism. And he is not an immoralist in the same sense in which he is not an atheist; just as he offers an alternative religion, so he offers an alternative ethics. The differences will show up in many ways. For example, he holds that pity, humility, and repen-tance are not virtues (E4 P50, P53, P54). If we try to focus on the question of self-transcendence, we will find the most fundamental difference to be over the issue of divine commands.

Kant says, "Religion is . . . the recognition of all duties as divine com-mands."[76] While most theists would want to insist that it is more than this, few if any would say that it is less. Theists will differ among themselves about how to construe the moral law as divine command. Answering a question that goes back to Plato's *Euthyphro*, the divine command tradition will say that actions are right or wrong because they are commanded or forbidden by God, while the natural law tradition will say they are commanded or forbidden because they are right or wrong.[77] But the two traditions will agree that whatever the degree to which the divine nature controls the content of the divine com-mands, our moral task is to obey the commandments addressed to us by a personal God.

The nature of moral self-transcendence in this context is clear. I am not

---

74. *The Portable Nietzsche*, ed. Walter Kaufmann (New York: Viking, 1954), p. 92.

75. Cf. Letter 43, p. 238, and Letter 75, p. 337.

76. Immanuel Kant, *Religion Within the Limits of Reason Alone*, trans. Theodore M. Greene and Hoyt H. Hudson (New York: Harper, 1960), p. 142. As Descartes invoked the will of God in relation to the laws of nature, here Kant links the moral law to the will of God. But for Spinoza the notion of a divine will is an expression of ignorance (E1 App, II/81). Curley says that Spinoza finds the idea of God as a lawgiver to be unintelligible. More to the point, perhaps, is the fact that, given his model of intelligibility, the divine will represents a loss of intelligibility to any domain into which it is introduced. See "Spinoza's Moral Philosophy," in Grene, p. 370.

77. The two traditions are not hermetically sealed off from each other. According to Adams, what makes an action wrong is that it is contrary to the commands of a *loving* God. The nature of God, as loving, places constraints of a natural law type on the commands of God; but this leaves considerable freedom for divine choice. See "A Modified Divine Command Theory of Ethical Wrongness," in Robert Merrihew Adams, *The Virtue of Faith and Other Essays in Philosophical Theology* (Oxford: Oxford University Press, 1987).

the center of the moral universe. I find myself under obligation to Another who, as the source of legitimate moral claims on me, is my moral superior. My obligation to obey is not contingent upon my desires, my agreement, or my best rational insights; it derives rather from the legitimate authority of Another. I am not the ground of either the fact of obligation or the content of obligation. Just as the theistic notions of divine mystery and divine revelation leave me without epistemic autonomy or self-sufficiency, so the theistic notion of divine commands leaves me without moral autonomy or self-sufficiency. In neither case am I the measure. Rather, I am measured by Someone Other (and found wanting).

It is worth noting that the transcendence of God here is no longer cosmological (just as it ceased to be merely cosmological in theism's affirmation of mystery and revelation). It is not that of a cause outside the world but of a person other than myself with legitimate moral claims on me. We are closer to the biblical notions of God as King or Father than to that of the First Mover.[78] To that degree we have moved away from onto-theology in the direction of the God of Abraham, Isaac, and Jacob.

Of course, Spinoza will have none of this. Just as the laws of nature are not expressions of personal will, so the moral law is not such an expression, and when, under the spell of imagination rather than reason, we think of the moral life as obedience to divine commands, we misunderstand it. The one who is led by reason "complies with no one's wishes but his own" (E4 P66S). To be responsible to the commands of another is to be a slave or a child (E4 P66S; TTP 22–28, III/41–59).[79] Adam, Moses, and the prophets treat God as moral lawgiver out of ignorance grounded in imagination; Christ talks this way only out of accommodation to the intellectual defects of his audience (TTP 31–33, III/63–65). Spinoza seeks "the free man's substitute for the law of Moses."[80]

His alternative is often described in terms of a therapeutic model. Bennett puts it this way. "The ethic is totally medical or psychotherapeutic: to improve yourself you must understand your mechanism and then intervene in it so as to reduce your propensity for feeling and thinking and acting in ways that make you ill and unhappy." Spinoza's denial of a personal God is closely linked to this view of the moral life. "There is no straight conflict between the two, but it

---

78. Theism has no essential conceptual ties that I can see to either monarchy in the state nor patriarchy in family and civil society. These concern the relation of humans to each other. But it can hardly abandon for its account of the relation between God and humans the implication of moral authority carried historically by such images as king and father. The theist who abhors monarchy as a political system need not be embarrassed to say, "The Lord is king; let the peoples tremble!" (Ps. 99:1).

79. Cf. Letter 43, p. 238.

80. Curley, Introduction to A *Spinoza Reader*, p. xxxii. This is why Yovel calls Spinoza a Marrano of reason. Marranos were Iberian Jews who outwardly converted to Christianity under threat, but inwardly tried to remain Jewish. Their slogan was "not Christ, but Moses." Spinoza's slogan was "neither Christ, nor Moses, but Reason." See *Spinoza and Other Heretics: The Marrano of Reason*, pp. 20, 36, 153.

is hard to see how someone can both deeply believe that he was created by a God who loves him and whom he should love, and think that the principle route to self-improvement is to study one's own pathology and deal with it intelligently."[81]

Actually, it is not just God whose moral claims on me are excluded in this model. My relation to any Other, divine, human, animal, or environmental, is to be determined solely by what therapeutic insight determines to be in my self-interest. Ethics is reduced to looking out for Number One.

For Spinoza evaluations such as good and evil or right and wrong are relational rather than intrinsic properties of the persons, actions, institutions, and so forth to which they are attributed. But it is not relationality as such that distinguishes therapeutic ethics from theistic ethics. For theism God is intrinsically good and the will of God inherently right. To call anything other than God good or bad, right or wrong, is to speak about its relation to God. The evaluative discourse of human ethics will be relational discourse, and it will imply self-transcendence, since the ways in which I am good or evil, my actions right or wrong, will involve my relation to an Other with legitimate claims on me. By contrast, in a world where blind natural necessity is ultimate, the Supreme Being will not be a locus of intrinsic value and the basis of derivative, relational value.

Right and wrong are relative to the state. It would be wrong to think that Nature could sin or do wrong (E4 Pref, II/206–208).

Nor can there be any wrong in the state of nature, for there right is just a matter of power.[82] By natural right (power) the big fish eat the little fish, and when the strong do what they will, making the weak bear what they must, nothing wrong occurs because no norm has been violated. With the coming into being of the state by social contract, there is an agreed upon mechanism for establishing norms of justice and injustice, right and wrong. But since these norms are maintained not by reason but by threats, "the free man's substitute for the law of Moses" cannot treat these concepts as basic (E4 P37S1 & S2, II/236–39).[83]

So we turn to good and evil. They too are relational. But what makes things good or evil is their relation to me. In this respect they are like judgments of warm or cold (E1 App, II/81); they will vary from person to person and, in a single person, from time to time (E3 P51S). Sometimes Spinoza makes this sound quite subjective, as when he writes that "we neither strive for, nor will, neither want, nor desire anything because we judge it to be good; on the

---

81. Bennett, SSE, p. 13.
82. Spinoza also equates perfection and virtue with power. See E2 App, II/83; E4 Def8; E4 P20 & P24.
83. Spinoza also speaks here of sin and merit, implying that these notions have meaning only relative to some "church." Anticipating Hegel, Spinoza denies that the ethical life of a people (*Sittlichkeit*) can be the basis for the moral life. But his reason is very different from the reasons Kierkegaard and Nietzsche will give for the same conclusion.

contrary, we judge something to be good because we strive for it, will it, want it, and desire it" (E3 P9S). Referring to this passage, he later equates good and evil with whatever satisfies or frustrates "any kind of longing" (E3 P39S). Elsewhere Spinoza gives a rather objective twist to relational good and evil. Good is "what we certainly know to be useful to us" (E4 Def1; cf. Def2). Or again, "Insofar as a thing agrees with our nature, it is necessarily good" (E4 P31).

I think there is no conflict between these subjectivist and objectivist overtones. The former express Spinoza's psychological egoism. Because we are in fact only oriented to our own satisfactions, we call whatever we desire good and whatever frustrates our desire evil. The objectivist language expresses Spinoza's ethical egoism. Things are good when they are useful to us or agree with our nature, and we know them to be good when we know them to be such.

What is important is that whether we are speaking about perceived good or actual good, good is relative to the individual. That Spinoza is an ethical egoist is clear in his treatment of *conatus*.[84] "Each thing [singular thing, mode], as far as it can by its own power, strives to persevere in its being. . . . The striving [*conatus*] by which each thing strives to persevere in its being is nothing but the actual essence of the thing" (E3 P6 & P7). When Spinoza asks what reason "prescribes," "dictates," and "demands,"[85] he answers that "it demands that everyone love himself, seek his own advantage, what is really useful to him, want what will really lead a man to greater perfection [power], and absolutely, that everyone should strive to preserve his own being as far as he can" (E4 P18S, II/222). Spinoza offers this account in opposition "to those who believe that this principle—that everyone is bound to seek his own advantage—is the foundation, not of virtue and morality, but of immorality" (E4 P18S, II/223). "The striving to preserve oneself is the first and only foundation of virtue" (E4 P22C). "Acting absolutely from virtue is nothing else in us but acting, living, and preserving our being (these three signify the same thing) by the guidance of reason, from the foundation of seeking one's own advantage" (E4 P24).

I will call good whatever seems useful to me, and it will be good if it actually is useful to me. Good for me, but not necessarily for you. The fact that something actually is useful for me does not make it good for you. 'Good' never means simply 'good' but always 'good for me.' This doesn't necessarily entail the war of all against all, for "To man, then, there is nothing more useful than man" (E4 P18S, II/223). It may be in my interest to live cooperatively and peacefully rather than competitively and violently. But it is my interest, not the apprehension of some common good, much less the recognition of another's

---

84. For linguistic and historical background, see Harry Austryn Wolfson, *The Philosophy of Spinoza* (New York: Meridian, 1958), II, 195–206.

85. These quotation marks should also be read as scare quotes. We'll understand these terms best when we remember that for Spinoza the laws of nature are the decrees of God (TTP 25, III/45–46) and that natural knowledge grounded in the natural light is what God "dictates" to us (TTP 10–11, III/15–16).

legitimate claim on me, that is the sole basis of my relation to others. Bennett is right to distinguish Spinoza's view from the subjectivism of the "ignorant person [who] will call x 'good' so long as it suits *his mood then* . . ." This would be to confuse psychological egoism with ethical egoism. But I find no warrant for the claim that "Spinoza's value-judgments on x depend upon whether x is favorable to everyone's interests in the long run. Not just mine but everyone's . . ."[86]

We can see this more clearly by raising and answering an objection. "To man, then, there is nothing more useful than man," Spinoza tells us. No doubt other human beings can be useful to us in many ways: as cannon fodder for our wars, as cheap labor for our farms and factories, as sex objects for our gratification, and so forth. But is it not the task of ethics, whether taught to us by our parents, our pastors, or our philosophers, to challenge our tendencies to use others simply as means to our ends?

Spinoza's answer is not far to find. He belongs, he will tell us, to the mainstream of Western teleological/eudaemonistic ethics which teaches that true happiness is not found in the pursuit of power, wealth, or pleasure, but in a virtue (here the intellectual love of God as natural necessity) which is not part of a zero sum game in which my gain is always at the expense of another.

This is true. What is equally true is that nothing in Spinoza's therapeutic ethics requires that I concern myself with the happiness of others, forbids me to be indifferent to the widow, the orphan, and the stranger. Their sufferings, after all, are but nodes in the network of natural necessity. These were of major concern to the Hebrew prophets and to Jesus, who also was a Jew. But Spinoza finds these prophets of the hoi polloi to be immersed in imagination and seeks to replace them with the philosophical prophets of pure reason. In the ethereal regions where they see the world *sub specie aeternitatis,* the widow, orphan, and stranger disappear from view. In the quietness of eternity, their voice is not heard. Nor does any divine voice command me to love my neighbor as I love myself (Lev. 19:18).

Just as there is intellectual conversion in Spinoza, from theism to pantheism, so there is ethical conversion, from the irrational pursuit of one's advantage, whether as the inordinate pursuit of power, wealth, and sensual pleasure or as obedience to the commands of God, to the rational pursuit of one's advantage. But this conversion does not entail self-transcendence. Vis-à-vis the inordinate pursuit of power, wealth, and sensual pleasure, it involves becoming more intelligently self-centered; and vis-à-vis obedience to God's commands, it involves getting beyond the imaginative immaturity that thinks of God that way. But however the list of virtues turns out on this analysis, they will all have the form of being intelligently and self-consciously self-centered. In this context divine immanence functions to exclude the decentering lure of a self-transcendence in the direction of the Other.

---

86. Bennett, SSE, p. 11.

Hegel

The Onto-theological Pantheism of Spirit

Like Spinoza, Hegel is a pantheist, though of an importantly different sort. He provides another site at which to explore the debate over cosmological transcendence. Because for Hegel the world is only penultimately the world of nature and ultimately the world of the human spirit and its history, the term 'cosmological' is no longer quite apt. But, since the debate between both species of pantheism and theism is over the nature of the difference between God and the world of finite beings, we can retain the term, even while mentally putting it in scare quotes. N.B. The debate is not whether there is a difference between God and the world but how it should be construed. For, as we have seen in the case of Spinoza, pantheism is not the denial of any difference between the two, since he distinguishes substance or *natura naturans* from its modes or *natura naturata*. It is rather the denial that God's reality is ontologically independent of the world, in short that there could be God without the world. We will find a similar distinction and a similar denial in Hegel.

Another obvious advantage of turning to Hegel is that he is one of Heidegger's two prime paradigms of onto-theology. Heidegger introduced this term in

1949 in relation to Aristotle's completion of his ontology with a theology of the Unmoved Mover. When he returned to this theme in 1957, it was in the context of a seminar on Hegel's *Science of Logic*. It was in the latter essay that he described onto-theology as allowing God to enter philosophical discourse only on philosophy's terms and in the service of its project, and he complained, in the spirit of Pascal and Kierkegaard, that this God was religiously otiose.[1] What he says there specifically about Hegel will best be understood after we see in what sense Hegel is a pantheist.

It is possible to date quite precisely the time when Hegel abandoned theism for good. Ironically, it was in 1795 in correspondence with his two friends from seminary days at Tübingen. Schelling and Hölderlin had become Fichte enthusiasts, as we see from letters they sent to Hegel early that year. On the basis of prepublication access to Fichte's 1794 *Wissenschaftslehre*, Schelling wrote on January 5,

> Philosophy is not yet at an end. Kant has provided the results. The premises are still missing. And who can understand the results without the premises? . . . Kant has swept *everything* away, but how is the crowd to notice? One must smash it to pieces before their very eyes, so they grasp it in their hands. The great Kantians now everywhere to be seen have got stuck on the letter . . . the old superstition of so-called natural religion as well as of positive religion has in the minds of most already once more been combined with the Kantian letter. It is fun to see how quickly they get to the moral proof. Before you can turn around the *deus ex machina* springs forth, the personal individual Being who sits in Heaven above! *Fichte* will raise philosophy to a height at which even most of the hitherto Kantians will become giddy. . . . Now I am working on an ethic *à la* Spinoza. (HL 29)

Toward the end of the month, Hegel responded. Right in the middle of his famous battle cry, "May the Kingdom of God come, and our hands not be idle! . . . Reason and Freedom remain our password, and the Invisible Church our rallying point," he writes, "There is one expression in your letter concerning the moral proof that I do not entirely understand: 'which they know how to manipulate so that out springs the individual, personal Being.' Do you really believe we fail to get so far?" (HL 32).

At about the same time and as if to anticipate Schelling's reply, Hölderlin wrote to Hegel from Jena where he had been attending Fichte's lectures, expressing his enthusiasm for both the 1794 *Wissenschaftslehre* and *On the Vocation of the Scholar*.

> [Fichte's] Absolute Self, which equals Spinoza's Substance, contains all reality; it is everything, and outside it, is nothing. There is thus no object for this Absolute Self, since otherwise all reality would not be in it. Yet a consciousness without an object is inconceivable. . . . Thus, in the Absolute

---

1. For details, see chapter 1 above.

> Self no consciousness is conceivable; as Absolute Self I have no conscious-
> ness. . . . Thus did I write down my thoughts . . . as I read Fichte's first sheets
> immediately upon reading Spinoza. Fichte confirmed me. (HL 33)[2]

Schelling's own devastating reply (to Hegel) of February 4 repeats the Spinoza
connection.

> Now for a reply to your question as to whether I believe we cannot get to a
> personal Being by means of the moral proof. I confess the question has
> surprised me. I would not have expected it from an intimate of Lessing's. Yet
> you no doubt asked it only to learn whether the question has been entirely
> decided *in my own mind.* For you the question has surely long since been
> decided. For us as well [as for Lessing] the orthodox concepts of God are no
> more. My reply is that we get even *further* than a personal Being. I have in
> the interim become a Spinozist! Do not be astonished, You will soon hear
> how. For Spinoza the world, the object by itself in opposition to the subject,
> was *everything.* For me it is the *self.* . . . There is no other supersensible
> world for us than that of the Absolute Self. *God* is nothing but the Absolute
> Self. . . . Personality arises through the unity of consciousness. Yet con-
> sciousness is not possible without an object. But for God—i.e., for the
> Absolute Self—there is no object *whatsoever;* for if there were, the Absolute
> Self would cease to be absolute. Consequently there is no personal God.
> (HL 32–33)[3]

Subsequent letters from Hegel make it clear that he was convinced by this
Fichtean philosophy of God as the Absolute Self, though he adds two qualifiers. In an April letter he notes that this will have to remain "an esoteric
philosophy" and in an August letter he suggests that the concept of substance
should not be used in connection with the Absolute Self (HL 35, 42–43).

Both of these qualifications were to prove prophetic. In the first instance,
Fichte's philosophy of God as the absolute but impersonal self did not remain
esoteric enough. In a 1798–99 brouhaha appropriately called the *Atheismusstreit,* he was accused of atheism and lost his professorship at Jena.[4] In the
second instance, the category of substance came to be central to Hegel's
emphatic denial that he himself was a pantheist.

---

2. See *Science of Knowledge (Wissenschaftslehre) with the First and Second Introductions,* trans.
Peter Heath and John Lachs (New York: Appleton-Century-Crofts, 1970), and *On the Vocation of
a Scholar* in *Fichte: Early Philosophical Writings,* trans. Daniel Breazeale (Ithaca, N.Y.: Cornell
University Press, 1988).
3. Schelling's letter summarizes his own Fichtean essays of 1795–96, *Of the I as Principle of
Philosophy* and *Philosophical Letters on Dogmatism and Criticism,* essays Hegel would soon study
sympathetically. For an English translation see *The Unconditional in Human Knowledge: Four
Early Essays,* trans. Fritz Marti (Lewisburg, Pa.: Bucknell University Press, 1980).
4. A brief sketch of the main events is found in the Editor's Introduction to Fichte, *Introductions to
the Wissenschaftslehre and Other Writings,* trans. Daniel Breazeale (Indianapolis, Ind.: Hackett,
1994). This volume contains the 1798 essay that triggered the controversy, "On the Basis of Our
Belief in a Divine Governance of the World," and a couple of short pieces related to it.

The link between Hegel's departure from a theistic conception of God as a personal being "outside" (ontologically interdependent of) the world and the question of pantheism should be obvious enough. It will not have escaped the reader's notice that in both of Schelling's letters and in Hölderlin's, Fichte's new philosophy of God as the Absolute (impersonal, unconscious) Self is linked to Spinoza. Hegel's friends saw Fichte as overcoming Kant's theism by radicalizing his concept of the transcendental ego just as Spinoza overcame Descartes' theism by radicalizing his concept of substance. Whether one takes the subject or object as the starting point, the direction of movement is the same. In short, Fichte: Kant = Spinoza: Descartes. In following his friends along this path, Hegel enters pantheistic territory. Shortly he would describe the ontological basis for the moral, religious, and political revolution he hopes for as "[a]bsolute freedom of all spirits who bear the intellectual world in themselves, and cannot seek either God or immortality outside themselves."[5]

In this same spirit he describes human conscience, in the *Phenomenology of Spirit* (1807), as "the moral genius which knows the inner voice of what it immediately knows to be a divine voice." The theist, too, can say that the voice of conscience is the voice of God, but cannot continue as Hegel continues, saying of conscience that "it is the divine creative power which in its Concept possesses the spontaneity of life. Equally, it is in its own self divine worship, for its action is the contemplation of its own divinity. This solitary divine worship is at the same time essentially the divine worship of a *community* . . ." Consequently, this human divinity is actual only in the reciprocal recognition of conscientious selves which is "*absolute* spirit. . . . The reconciling *Yea*, in which the two 'I's let go their antithetical *existence* is the *existence* of the 'I' which has expanded into a duality, and therein remains identical with itself, and in its complete externalization and opposite, possesses the certainty of itself: it is God manifested in the midst of those who know themselves in the form of pure knowledge" (PS 397, 408–409).[6]

---

5. This is from a 1796 text known as "The Earliest System-Programme of German Idealism," translated in H. S. Harris, *Hegel's Development: Toward the Sunlight 1770–1801* (Oxford: Clarendon Press, 1972), p. 511. I accept the arguments of Pöggeler and Harris that pending a smoking gun to the contrary, this manuscript, which is in Hegel's hand, should be attributed to Hegel. See Harris, pp. 249–57. For pantheistic formulations in 1799–1800 drafts of the essay known as "The Spirit of Christianity and Its Fate," see ETW 253, 259–61, 264–69, and 278. In a slightly earlier draft from the same project, Hegel speaks of a "transubstantiation" of the disciples of Jesus, "an actual indwelling of the Father in the Son and of the Son in his disciples" such that like the Son they are "a modification" rather than "substances" because "there are not two substances" (FS 304). For an overview of developments in the Jena period leading up to the *Phenomenology*, see Walter Jaeschke, *Reason in Religion: The Foundations of Hegel's Philosophy of Religion*, trans. J. Michael Stewart and Peter C. Hodgson (Berkeley: University of California Press, 1990), pp. 171–84.

6. Using 'Concept' rather than 'Notion' for '*Begriff*'. That whose life follows from its concept is, of course, the "object" of the ontological argument. Like Spinoza, Hegel is a vigorous defender of this argument in a quite un-Anselmian form. See SL 86–90, 705–708; EL ¶¶51A and 193A; for

This is why, when Hegel says in the subsequent chapter on Christianity as the highest form of religion, that the "incarnation of the divine Being . . . is the simple content of the absolute religion. . . . The divine nature is the same as the human, and it is this unity that is beheld," it is clear that he is speaking of human nature as such (PS 459–60).[7] As in his early theological writings, Jesus is not uniquely the Son of God but the one through whom the essential divinity of the human as such comes to light.[8]

It is clear that it is not primarily the world of nature, as in the case of Spinoza, but rather the world of the human spirit that Hegel wishes to associate with Deity more closely than theism permits. Still, like Schelling and Hölderlin before him, Hegel saw a pantheism of the Absolute Subject to be a fraternal if not an identical twin to Spinoza's pantheism of the Absolute Object.

So we find him saying "that thought must begin by placing itself at the standpoint of Spinozism; to be a follower of Spinoza is the essential commencement of all philosophy" and "You are either a Spinozist or not a philosopher at all" (H&S 3:257, 283).[9] Or again, "The general point to notice here is that thinking, or the spirit, has to place itself at the standpoint of Spinozism. This idea of Spinoza's must be acknowledged to be true and well-grounded" (LHP 154).

If conceptual clarity were Hegel's only concern in discussing his relation with Spinoza, he might well have made use of the distinctions introduced in our last chapter. "If by pantheist you mean someone who says that God is the heap of all finite things from which none of the latter has been omitted, then neither Spinoza nor I nor anyone else is a pantheist. But if you mean the view that all finite things flow from an infinite source from which they are *reciprocally inseparable* (no world without God *and* no God without the world), then Spinoza and I are pantheists (though I differ from him in thinking that we must go beyond the category of substance in articulating the ultimate oneness of all things). And, if by atheist you mean someone who denies the theistic belief in a personal creator and redeemer whose reality is not necessarily linked to that of the world, then we are a-theists. But if you mean the view that nothing deserves to be called God, then we are not."

Sometimes Hegel takes this approach. For example, in his 1825–26 lectures on the history of philosophy, he acknowledges that there is a sense in which Spinoza is an atheist. "Spinozism is said to be atheism. This is correct in

---

the frequent references in LPR, see the indices to all three volumes under "ontological argument" and "proofs."

7. Cf. ETW 176, from an 1800 draft of "The Positivity of the Christian Religion."

8. For the early theological writings, see the passages cited in notes 5 and 7 above. For chapter 7 of the *Phenomenology*, see my *History and Truth in Hegel's Phenomenology*, 3rd ed. (Bloomington: Indiana University Press, 1998), ch. 7.

9. Haldane and Simpson translate the Michelet edition of 1840, which is based on the complete manuscript of the Jena lectures, 1805–1806, but also on materials, including student lecture notes, from various of the other eight times Hegel gave these lectures, in Heidelberg and Berlin.

one respect, since Spinoza does not distinguish God from the world or from nature. He says that God is all actuality, but all actuality insofar as the idea of God explicates itself in particular fashion, for instance, in the existence of the human spirit. So it can be said that this is atheism, and that is said insofar as Spinoza does not distinguish God from the finite, from the world, from nature" (LHP 162). It might be more accurate to say that Spinoza makes God and the world distinguishable but inseparable, but the point is clear enough. There is a quite definite sense in which Spinozism is a-theism.

However, in his 1827 lectures on the philosophy of religion and other writings of that time, Hegel feels the need to emphasize all but exclusively the other side of the story. The reason would appear to be more political than philosophical. The charge that Spinoza was an atheist, fresh in Hegel's time from the *Pantheismusstreit*, triggered in 1785 by Jacobi,[10] goes back to Spinoza's own lifetime. It played a role in his writing the *Tractatus Theologico-Politicus* and in the decision not to publish the *Ethics* during his lifetime. An even fresher memory was the *Atheismusstreit*, in which Fichte had lost his chair when his idealistic pantheism had been identified as atheism. So when the pietist theologian F. A. G. Tholuck identified the Hegelian philosophy as another version of Spinozism/pantheism/atheism,[11] Hegel had good reason to fear it might happen again and to find it prudent not to be too explicit about the quite clear sense in which he was and had been since his seminary days, an a-theist. In the 1827 lectures he launches a fourfold counter-offensive.

After a few introductory considerations, Hegel begins with a section entitled "The Concept of God" and immediately turns to the question of pantheism. "God is the absolute substance. If we cling to this declaration in its abstract form, then it is certainly Spinozism or pantheism." But "we proceed further . . . we do not stop at that point." Following the movement of the Logic from less adequate to more adequate categories, which is to be understood as a movement from abstract to concrete thinking, we (Hegelians) go on to think of God as "*subjectivity*," as "*spirit, absolute spirit*, eternally simple spirit, being essentially present to itself" (LPR 1:370–71).[12]

---

10. For details about this controversy in which Jacobi directly identified Spinozism with atheism and claimed that Lessing had confessed on his deathbed to being a Spinozist, see Frederick C. Beiser, *The Fate of Reason: German Philosophy from Kant to Fichte* (Cambridge, Mass.: Harvard University Press, 1987), ch. 2–4. Beiser notes the following irony (pp. 44–45): "Nearly all the major figures of the classical *Goethezeit*—Goethe, Novalis, Hölderlin, Herder, F. Schlegel, Hegel, Schleiermacher, and Schelling—became Spinoza enthusiasts in the wake of the controversy . . . pantheism became, as Heine later put it, 'the unofficial religion of Germany.'"

11. On Tholuck, see LPR 1:7–8. On the relation between Tholuck's charge and the 1827 lectures, see Philip M. Merklinger, *Philosophy, Theology, and Hegel's Berlin Philosophy of Religion* (Albany: SUNY Press, 1993), ch. 5.

12. Cf. PM ¶573, where, after describing a variety of systems that are customarily called pantheistic, including Spinoza's, Hegel says, "The fault of all these modes of thought and systems is that they *stop short* of defining substance as subject and as spirit." Emphasis added, using 'spirit' rather than 'mind' for '*Geist*'. Cf. EL, remark to ¶50 and SL 537.

For Hegel, then, "God remains absolute substance . . . the absolute womb or the infinite fountainhead out of which everything emerges, into which everything returns, and in which it is eternally maintained. This basic determination is therefore the definition of God as substance." Philosophies that stop at this point can be called "*pantheism*" or "*identity-philosophy*" or "more accurately . . . 'the representation of substantiality,' because in [them] God is defined above all *only* [emphasis added] as substance." But for Hegel this is only "the point of departure" for going on to define the absolute subject as spirit. "Those who say that speculative philosophy amounts to pantheism usually know nothing of this distinction; as always, they overlook what matters most" (LPR 1:373–75). In other words, Spinoza and Schelling are pantheists, but I am not.[13]

Hegel proceeds to specify three senses of pantheism which do not even apply to Spinoza, from whom he has already carefully distinguished himself. In the first place, when philosophy is accused of pantheism this might be taken to mean "that everything, the whole, the universe, this complex of everything existing, these infinitely many individual things—that all this is God . . . 'everything' meaning here this infinite multiplicity of individual things—not the universality that has being in and for itself but the individual things in their empirical existence, as they exist immediately but not in their universality." Pantheism would be the view "that everything, all individual things collectively, in their individuality and contingency, are God—for example that paper or this table is God." Hegel doubts that anyone has held such a view, but he emphatically denies that either "Oriental pantheism or genuine Spinozism" does. For them, rather, God is not the infinite pile of all finite things but rather the universal, essential substantial power through which they are united into a single whole (LPR 1:375–76).[14]

Hegel next attacks the conception of pantheism that equates it with atheism. This equation stems, he argues, from forgetting that from a religious point of view "only the substance or the One has the value of genuine actuality—individual things, in this very contrast with the One, have disappeared and no actuality is ascribed to them." Accordingly, Spinozism should be described as "*acosmism*" rather than as "*atheism*" since "in Spinozism this world or this 'all'

---

13. Cf. LPR 1:344, n. 163 (from 1824). The reference to identity philosophy is to Schelling's 1801 *Darstellung meines Systems der Philosophie*, in which he assimilated, but not for the first time, Fichte with Spinoza and sought to integrate them in a higher identity. On Hegel's early response, see DFS, including Harris' helpful Introduction. His decisive break with the identity philosophy is usually found in the Preface to PS, with its complaint about a "monochromatic formalism" of the "night in which, as the saying goes, all cows are black." In the very next paragraph, Hegel writes, "In my view . . . everything turns on grasping and expressing the True, not only as *Substance*, but equally as *Subject*" (PS 9–10).

14. In ¶573 of PM, Hegel says that "if the world were taken as it is, as everything, as the endless lot of empirical existence, then it would hardly have been even held possible to suppose a pantheism which asserted of such stuff that it is God."

simply *is not.*" Only through forgetting that "it is precisely the aggregate of finitudes (the world) that has disappeared [in Spinozism]" can it be claimed that God has disappeared, that Spinozism is atheism (LPR, 1:376–77).[15] It is as if Hegel has been reading Yeats' poem "A Meditation in Time of War."

> For one throb of the artery,
> While on that old grey stone I sat
> Under the old wind-blown tree,
> I knew that One is animate,
> Mankind inanimate phantasy.[16]

Here again, Hegel will distance himself from Spinoza, who "does not give the principle of difference (or finitude) its due. . . . Substance, as it is apprehended immediately by Spinoza without preceding dialectical mediation—being the universal might of negation—is only the dark, shapeless abyss, so to speak, in which all determinate content is swallowed up as radically null and void, and which produces nothing out of itself that has a positive subsistence of its own" (EL ¶151A). This same complaint appears when Hegel says that for Spinoza, the finite, in relation to the absolute, "*is* only as *vanishing* not as *becoming*" (SL 538). But this critique is combined with a fundamental defense: Spinoza's pantheistic acosmism is not atheism (and, in any case, I am not Spinoza).

Finally, there is the objection that Spinoza's pantheism asserts "that good is one with evil, that there is no distinction between good and evil, and therefore all religion is annulled. . . . It is said that in Spinozism the distinction of good and evil has no intrinsic validity, that morality is annulled, and so it is a matter of indifference whether one is good or evil" (LPR 1:378).[17] We saw in the previous chapter that it was just such a Spinoza in whom Nietzsche found such a welcome precursor, the Spinoza who "denies the freedom of the will, teleology, the moral world order, the unegoistic, and evil."[18] And we saw that there was good reason for Nietzsche to read Spinoza as a precursor.

In Hegel's context, such a reading could only be a politically explosive accusation rather than a cause for celebration, but in any case, he is eager to refute it. As usual, he argues that it grows from misinterpreting Spinoza, failing to see that he distinguishes God (substance) from the world (its modes). The basic truth is this: "in God there is no evil." But while the distinction between good and evil is not to be found in God, it "makes its entrance together with the distinction of God from the world, in particular from human beings. With

---

15. The acosmism defense of Spinoza also appears in EL, remark to ¶50 and in H&S 3:281–82. On the origin of the acosmic interpretation of Spinoza in earlier thinkers, see LPR 1:377, n. 27.

16. *Selected Poems and Two Plays of William Butler Yeats*, ed. M. L. Rosenthal (New York: Macmillan, 1962), p. 94.

17. This objection is also discussed in the Preface to the 1827 edition of the *Encyclopedia*, EL 8–10.

18. See ch. 2 n. 74.

regard to the distinction of God and humanity, the basic determination in Spinozism is that human beings must have God alone as their goal. . . . This is the most sublime morality." Where we place ourselves "in opposition to God . . . we are evil," and where we "posit our essential being solely in God and in our orientation toward God . . . we are good." This distinction is not found within God as absolute substance, "but for human beings there is this distinction, since distinctiveness in general enters with humane existence, and more specifically the distinction between good and evil" (LPR 1:378–79).

It is not clear that this defense of Spinoza will work. Of course, the distinctions between right and wrong and between good and evil show up in the ethics of the *Ethics*. But, as we saw, right and wrong are relative to what has been established as law by the state, and good and evil are relative to the individual, what is useful to oneself as *conatus essendi*. The objection was that such distinctions have "no intrinsic validity," and on this point Spinoza's accusers and Nietzschean celebrators would appear to be on stronger textual ground than Hegel. The reduction of morality to therapy is doubtless what the former have in mind when they see the abolition of religion and morality in Spinoza. But Hegel rather than Spinoza is our current theme, and it is clear that while distancing himself from Spinoza, he also wants to defend him against the charge of immoralism.

Hegel concludes his discussion of pantheism by returning to the distinction between substance and spirit. He speaks of the "shallow" and "superficial" objections to philosophy in terms of its designation as "an identity-system," using the language of Schelling. "It is entirely correct that substance is this identity with itself—and so is spirit." A variant reading here adds, "Identity, or unity with self is, in the end, everything." Here again he associates himself with Spinoza, but also distances himself by insisting that this identity not be thought abstractly, merely as substance, but also concretely, as spirit. "The whole of philosophy is nothing else but a study of the definition of *unity*. . . . Thus the unity of God is always unity, too, though *everything turns quite strictly upon the manner in which this unity is defined* [emphasis added]" (LPR 1:379–80). Long before any anxieties about a possible new *Pantheismusstreit*, Hegel had made it clear that this unity must be thought as spirit.

With this the 1827 lectures bring to a close the section on "The Concept of God." Looking back we discover that it has been entirely devoted to the discussion of the pantheism/atheism charge. We can summarize Hegel's fourfold argument, specifying one sense in which Spinoza can properly be called a pantheist and three in which he cannot. (1) Spinoza is a pantheist in that he affirms God to be the absolute, that is, the only substance. But I am not a pantheist in this sense because while affirming God as absolute substance, I go beyond that abstract category to the concrete category of spirit. (2) Neither Spinoza nor anything else you can think of is a pantheist in the sense of identifying God with the all-inclusive collection of finite things as such. (3) Nor is Spinoza a pantheist in a sense equivalent to atheism. Only if one mistakenly attributes the previous sense of pantheism to him can one affirm that God disappears from his system. It is rather the world that disappears in God. (4) Finally, Spinoza is not a pantheist in a sense equivalent to immoralism. Spinoza is the friend of religion and morality in that the distinction between good and evil, while not found in God, is valid for human beings in their distinctness from the divine substance as its modes.

* * *

While defending Spinoza against the charges of atheism and immoralism, Hegel regularly distances himself from Spinoza's version of God as ἐν καὶ πᾶν (One and All), both in terms of the distinction between substance (philosophy of nature) and subject (philosophy of spirit) and in terms of the more abstract issue on which, as he sees it, everything depends, namely the relation of unity or identity to difference. Already in the *Differenzschrift* of 1801 we find Hegel's prescient account of the One and the Many as it would be defined by the whole of his philosophical system: "the Absolute itself is the identity of identity and non-identity; being opposed and being one are both together in it" (DFS 156; cf. SL 74). So it is appropriate that Heidegger's discussion of Hegel as onto-theologian should come in a book entitled *Identity and Difference*.

But he is not interested in refereeing the dispute between Spinoza and Hegel over the way in which finite beings are both identical with and different from God. He is interested in the difference between Hegel as a paradigmatic onto-theologian and himself as one taking the step back out of metaphysics in its onto-theological constitution. As ontology, metaphysics seeks to understand beings as such in terms of what is most general, universal, common to all. As theology it seeks to understand beings as a whole in terms of a being "that unifies as the generative ground," the All-Highest, ultimate, and unique (ID 54, 58, 61, 69–70). These become united in onto-theology as the positing of a highest being that is the key to the meaning of the whole of being as such.

Hegel does ontology. In its concluding chapter, the *Science of Logic* specifies the matter for thinking as the absolute Idea and insists that "the absolute Idea alone is *being*" (SL 824, cited at ID 43). From the end of the journey, Hegel reminds us that from the outset we have been doing nothing but trying to think being. But Hegel also does theology. In the introductory essay, "With What Must the Science Begin?" we are reminded that for speculative thinking the true beginning can only be the result arrived at when thought has completed its dialectical movement. It is in this sense that Hegel can say that "*God has the absolutely undisputed right that the beginning be made with him*" (SL 78, cited at ID 53–54). At the beginning of the journey, Hegel reminds that from the outset we will be doing nothing but trying to think God. This is why the categories of his Logic, starting with being, can be described as "*metaphysical definitions of God*" (EL ¶85) or as "the exposition of God as he is in his eternal essence before the creation of nature and a finite mind" (SL 50; cf.

63). Speculative logic begins as ontology, becomes theology, and in recognizing these as two sides of the same coin revisits, or rather reenacts, the ontological argument in which God and being are discovered to be inseparable.[19]
Thus does the Logic give rise to the *realphilosophie* we know as the Philosophy
of Nature and the Philosophy of Spirit.

In the midst of this presentation of Hegel as onto-theologian, Heidegger
reminds us of the scope of this concept as he uses it. First, he links Hegel to
German idealism's larger project, briefly explored above in relation to Schelling, of synthesizing Spinoza and Kant (ID 47–48), locating onto-theology in
the history of speculative metaphysics. Then he reminds us that in his view
modern technology is the all too apparent heir of that tradition, "the metaphysics of the atomic age" (ID 51–52). For better or, as Heidegger sees it, for
worse, onto-theology has survived the demise of German idealism and the
many ways in which, since Hegel, philosophy has become anti-philosophy,
pursuing the overcoming of metaphysics.

But why for worse? What is so dangerous about Hegelian thinking? And
just what enables that thinking to play John the Baptist to the modern marriage
of science and technology? It is not, Heidegger hastens to tell us, a question of
atheism (ID 54–55). Nor is it a reticence to think of being as ground. Heidegger is not comfortable with the Hegelian notion that "the Being of beings
reveals itself as *the ground that gives itself ground and accounts for itself*" (ID
57, emphasis added). But he is quite willing to think of the relation between
Being and beings as that between "the grounding" and "what is grounded." In
fact, "not only does Being ground beings as their ground, but beings in their
turn ground, cause Being in their way" (ID 68–69).

The problem with Hegel's onto-theology is the way it insists on thinking
ground. It is not merely that he posits a Highest Being (the Idea, Absolute
Spirit) that is the key to the meaning of the whole of being. It is rather the
project to which this positing belongs. In other words, Hegel allows God into
his discourse "only insofar as philosophy, of its own accord and by its own
nature, requires and determines that and how the deity enters into it" (ID 56).
The project in whose service philosophy shanghais God requires "*the ground
that gives itself ground and accounts for itself*." For this reason the metaphysical
concept of God will be spelled out as "the first ground, πρώτη ἀρχή . . . the
causa prima that corresponds to the reason-giving path back to the *ultima
ratio*, the final accounting. The Being of beings is represented fundamentally,
in the sense of the ground, only as *causa sui*" (ID 60).

In portraying philosophy as setting the terms under which God will be
allowed into its discourse, there is more than a hint of hubris on its part, and
this is an important link between metaphysics and technology as the will to
power run amok. Moreover, we know that Heidegger finds this God to be

---

19. See note 6 above.

religiously vacuous. *Causa sui* is "the right name for the god of philosophy. Man can neither pray nor sacrifice to this god. Before the *causa sui*, man can neither fall to his knees in awe nor can he play music and dance before this god" (ID 72). But just what is it that makes Hegel's speculative philosophy so friendly toward modern technology and so unfriendly toward religion in Heidegger's eyes? For that is what the charge of onto-theology comes down to.

We know the simple answer to this question: neglect of the ontological difference, the failure to think the difference between Being and beings. But for those of us who do not find Heidegger's account of *the* difference all that helpful, Heidegger himself helps to formulate the issue in a manner not tied to his insistence that Being is not a being, not even the Supreme Being. What is important to Heidegger in thinking the relation between that which grounds and that which is grounded is an epistemological issue. Unconcealing (intelligibility) must remain in dialectical tension with concealment (mystery) (ID 64–67). Philosophy's project is to render the whole of reality intelligible to human thinking, and it is the hubris of this project, compounded by treating God as a means to this end, to which Heidegger objects, as we saw in chapter one.

How is Hegelian speculation an escape from this dialectic?[20] In the first place by its completeness. It professes to embody "truth in the sense of the completely developed certainty of self-knowing knowledge" (ID 49). The true beginning of the Logic is its result because it is "the rebound of thinking thinking itself out of the completion of the dialectical movement." This movement is a "self-completing fullness" (ID 53). In other words, "Hegel thinks of Being in its most empty emptiness. . . . At the same time, he thinks of Being in its fully completed fullness . . . sees the matter of thinking . . . in the movement from its emptiness to its developed fullness" (ID 56–57).[21]

Earlier reference was made to Heidegger's citation of Hegel's claim that "the absolute Idea alone is *being*." That passage continues, "imperishable *life*, *self-knowing truth*, and is *all Truth*" (SL 824, cited at ID 43). The phrase "*all Truth*" refers to the completeness motif just mentioned. The phrase "*self-knowing truth*" points to a self-consciousness motif that goes with it. Being, thought to its completed fullness, turns out to be "the absolute self-thinking of thinking. . . . For Hegel, the matter of thinking is: Being, as thinking thinking itself" (ID 43, 45). Spinoza's "standpoint of substance" is incomplete because "Being is not yet thought equally fundamentally and resolutely as thinking thinking itself." Hence the need to redo Spinoza from a Kantian standpoint (ID 47–48).

---

20. See EL ¶¶79–82 for an account of speculation as the *Aufhebung* of dialectic.

21. This passage is a good account of what is meant by the buzzword 'totalizing thinking'. The language of emptiness and fullness echoes Husserl's discussion in *Logical Investigations* of adequation in terms of fulfilled intentions. The rest or satisfaction implied by this fullness is what Jean-Luc Marion uses to distinguish idols from icons. See his *God Without Being*, trans. Thomas A. Carlson (Chicago: University of Chicago Press, 1991).

But it is important, for Hegel, not to undo Spinoza from a Kantian standpoint. For Kant makes claims to completeness based on self-consciousness for his theory of the categories of thought.[22] But the result is a theory of the finitude of human understanding whose refutation, in all its forms, Hegel identifies with philosophy (SL 45).[23] The crucial question is this: Whose self-consciousness is it whose inventory of its categoreal structure, when complete, is the confluence of logic and metaphysics (and not just a metaphysics of experience)? The latter is what Kant produces by sticking to a human subject deeply distinct from any possible creative, divine intellect. The well-known result is the thing in itself, unknowable to human thought.[24] For Hegel, this distinction has been replaced by the distinction between Understanding, human thought in its finitude, and Reason, human thought in its infinite power. In this latter mode, where Reason (*Vernunft*) prevails over Understanding (*Verstand*), Speculation over Dialectic, and Concept (*Begriff*) over Representation (*Vorstellung*), human thinking has become divine self-consciousness and its transcendental completion is *"all Truth."*

In other words, it is precisely Hegel's pantheism that enables him to pass beyond the Kantian/Heideggerian dialectic of unconcealing and concealment to what he calls speculative philosophy and Heidegger calls onto-theology, where reality is fully intelligible to human thought. In the language of the *Phenomenology*, it is because "the divine nature is the same as the human" that it is possible for philosophy to have as its goal a *"completion"* at "the point where knowledge no longer needs to go beyond itself" and to be utterly confident of its arrival "at a point at which it gets rid of its semblance of being burdened with something alien, with what is only for it, and some sort of 'other', at a point where appearance becomes identical with essence . . . when consciousness itself grasps this its own essence, it will signify the nature of absolute knowledge itself" (PS 460, 50–51, 56–57).

More vividly, Hegel quotes Meister Eckhart favorably as saying, "The eye with which God sees me is the eye with which I see him; my eye and his eye are one and the same. . . . The closeness of God and the soul admits no difference [between them]. The same knowledge in which God knows himself is the knowledge of every detached spirit and nothing else. . . . If God did not exist nor would I; if I did not exist nor would he" (LPR 1:346–48).[25]

---

22. *Critique of Pure Reason*, A xiii–xiv, xx.

23. In EL ¶¶37–60, Hegel treats the critical philosophy not as the overcoming of empiricism but as its continuation and fulfillment. This means that it is not enough for Hegel to define subjectivity or spirit in terms of presence to self (LPR 1:370). As was already the case with Fichte and Schelling, the Hegelian cogito needs to have a different ontological status from the cogito of empiricism and the critical philosophy.

24. On the essential role of the distinction between human and divine knowers in Kant's distinction between appearances and things in themselves, see my essay "In Defense of the Thing in Itself," *Kant-Studien*, 59/1 (1968): 118–41.

25. Ironically, this citation comes in a passage in which Hegel is seeking to refute the charge that

Here we see how close Hegel remains to Spinoza. Spinoza says that thought is an attribute of God. We saw in the previous chapter that for him this means that nature produces finite minds and that the only actual intellects are finite, human minds, modes of the divine substance. Thus, while we should love God (intellectually) we should not expect God to love us in return. For God's love simply is our love, not something distinct from it. As modes of the divine substance finite minds are the sole locus of thought in general and love in particular.

This is Hegel's view as well. It is the categories of the Logic that are God before the creation of the world, not an actual, personal creator. To speak of God as creator is to signify "a transition from concept to reality," and only in this positing, that is, only in creation, only when there is a world, is God actual. To think of God as an actual cause producing an actual effect is to remain tied to the Understanding, for which God remains a mystery (LPR 3:279–81).

This means, of course, that it is misleading for Hegel to complain that Spinoza's philosophy of substance falls short of the idea of God as "the absolute *Person*" (EL ¶151A), that "he lacks the principle of *personality*—a defect which has been the main cause of hostility of Spinoza's system" (SL 537). If Hegel speaks of God as "the absolute *Person*," it is not because he affirms an actual, personal creator ontologically independent of the world; it is rather because the self-actualizing Idea, like Spinoza's laws of nature, produces human persons; and Hegel is inclined to deify (and reify) humanity when, as thought, it has reached a certain standpoint, the Hegelian.

For Eckhart, God has no eyes with which to see but ours. For Spinoza, thought, as an attribute of God, is actual only in the thinking of finite human minds. For Schelling and Hölderlin, the Absolute Self is devoid of consciousness, which means that we have gone "further" than a personal God; it is called Self only because it is the ground of subjectivity (finite selves) as well as of objectivity (nature). In this tradition, Hegel presents a God who has no thought nor knowledge nor personality that is not constituted by our thought, knowledge, and personality as its locus and actuality. Writing shortly after Hegel's death, Heine described the pantheism which had been "the occult religion of Germany" since the rediscovery of Spinoza half a century earlier: "In man Deity reaches self-consciousness, and this self-consciousness Deity again reveals through man."[26]

Thus religious consciousness is God's self-consciousness, since "what God

---

speculative philosophy is pantheism. He appeals to the Catholic theology as supportive of his view, failing to mention that it was precisely for statements like this that Eckhart was condemned by the church. The first two statements are to be found in *Meister Eckhart: Teacher and Preacher*, ed. Bernard McGinn (New York: Paulist Press, 1986), pp. 270 and 261. The third is from Edmund Colledge, O.S.A., and Bernard McGinn, trans. *Meister Eckhart: The Essential Sermons*, ed. Edmund Colledge, O.S.A., and Bernard McGinn (New York: Paulist Press, 1981), p. 203.

26. Heinrich Heine, *Religion and Philosophy in Germany*, trans. John Snodgrass (Boston: Beacon Press, 1959), pp. 77–79.

creates God himself is" (LPR 1:381). But it does not know itself to be such. Thinking God to be (theistically) an actuality outside the world and a mind above our own, it is Understanding and Representation, the finitude of the many, the imagination of the hoi polloi. "Religion is for everyone. It is not philosophy, which is not for everyone" (LPR 1:180). Speculative philosophy can take the few to an infinity in which, as Reason and Concept, human consciousness is replaced by divine self-consciousness which knows itself to be such.[27] Part of what it means to call this awareness absolute or infinite is simply that the completeness of this self-consciousness leaves nothing beyond itself to be comprehended. The *dialectic* of unconcealing and concealment remains only where the standpoint of *speculative* philosophy, divine self-consciousness, has not been reached or the system of *speculative* philosophy has not been brought to completion.[28]

* * *

Like Spinoza, Hegel gives us an ontology of divine immanence which affirms the autonomous self-sufficiency of human thought and action in ways that limit human self-transcendence. God is posited as the highest being in such a way as to leave human beings at the top of the totem pole both epistemically and ethically. So we should not be surprised to find that, as with Spinoza, the notions of divine mystery and divine revelation, along with the notion of God as moral lawgiver, will either be denied altogether or be redefined beyond recognition.

In objecting that onto-theology is the speculative *Aufhebung* of the dialectic of unconcealing and concealment,[29] Heidegger is primarily concerned with the first of these, the loss of a sense of unsurpassable mystery, a theme developed at length in chapter one. Hegel is emphatic about the full intelligibility of reality to human thought, making it a central theme of his inaugural lectures both at Heidelberg and at Berlin. He concludes the former with an admonition to his hearers to trust in science and in themselves.

> The love of truth, faith in the power of mind, is the first condition in philosophy. Man, because he is mind, should and must deem himself worthy of the highest: he cannot think too highly of the greatness and the power of his mind, and with this belief, nothing will be so difficult and hard

---

27. Chapter seven of PS is perhaps the most succinct statement of this passage from theistic religious consciousness to pantheistic philosophical self-consciousness. See my analysis in chapter 7 of *History and Truth* and my essay "Hegel's Theory of Religious Knowledge" in *Hegel, Freedom, and Modernity* (Albany: SUNY Press, 1992).

28. See the satirical offer by Johannes Climacus to bow down and worship the system if only he could be assured that it was finished. Soren Kierkegaard, *Concluding Unscientific Postscript*, trans. Howard V. Hong and Edna H. Hong (Princeton, N.J.: Princeton University Press, 1992), 1:13, 106–109.

29. See note 20 above.

that it will not reveal itself [*sich eröffnete*] to him. The essence of the universe at first hidden and concealed [*verborgene und verschlossene*], has no power which can offer resistance to the search for knowledge; it has to lay itself open before the seeker—to set before his eyes and give for his enjoyment, its riches and its depths. (H&S 1:xiii)[30]

Hegel only slightly altered the wording of this challenge two years later in Berlin.[31] In both versions, Hegel refuses any limits to the availability of reality to our knowledge as enjoyment (*Genusse*). We are reminded of the passage in the *Phenomenology* in which Hegel turns to "the practical sphere" to illustrate the truth of sensible knowledge. The Eleusinian Mysteries teach the nothingness of the object in the acts of eating and drinking. "Even the animals are not shut out from this wisdom . . . for they do not just stand idly in front of sensuous things as if these possessed intrinsic being, but despairing of their reality, and completely assured of their nothingness, they fall to without ceremony and eat them up" (PS 65).

This image of knowledge as alimentary enjoyment is, in context, only about sensible knowledge. But in one of his many critiques of Kant, where he is talking about "cognition as such," he notes that Kant's transcendental ego is "the crucible and the fire through which the indifferent multiplicity is consumed and reduced to unity." Then comes his own gloss. "Now this certainly expresses correctly the nature of all consciousness. What human beings strive for in general is cognition of the world; we must strive to appropriate and conquer it. To this end the reality of the world must be crushed as it were, i.e., it must be made ideal" (EL 42 & 42A1).

Shifting from images of violence to the imagery of presence, Hegel tells us that in the Logic spirit is "purely at home with itself, and thereby free. . . . Freedom is only present where there is no other for me that is not myself." This is what enables Hegel to say, "We usually suppose that the Absolute must lie far beyond; but it is precisely what is wholly present, what we, as thinkers, always carry with us and employ, even though we have no express consciousness of it" (EL ¶24A). The categories of human thought, which are God before the creation of the world, are the Absolute "wholly present." Philosophy is the bringing of this implicit presence to full consciousness, or rather, as Hegel regularly insists, full self-consciousness, for the thought that thinks thinking knows itself and not another.

In all of these ways, Hegel testifies that he finds no ultimate mystery anywhere, no point, not even God, at which human reason reaches its limit and must point beyond itself to what it cannot fully comprehend. Philosophy is

---

30. I have altered the translation slightly, but left the translation of *Geist* as 'mind' standing as appropriate in this context. Especially against the background of the Lutheran tradition in Germany, the religious overtones of the admonition to trust (*Vertrauen*) and faith (*Glaube*), not in God but in science and in themselves, are too conspicuous to overlook.

31. The Berlin version is cited above in chapter 1 at note 39.

divine self-consciousness, "the reconciliation of God with himself." As such it is "the peace of God, which does not 'surpass all reason,' but is rather the peace that *through* reason is first known and thought and is recognized as what is true" (LPR 3:347).[32]

There is a series of passages throughout the Hegelian corpus that addresses this theme with special reference to the knowledge of God. It is especially pertinent here because the themes of divine mystery and divine revelation become inextricably intertwined as Hegel addresses both issues at once. I refer to those passages where Hegel affirms the teaching of Plato and Aristotle that the gods are not jealous or envious. There are several things to notice about these passages.[33]

1) First, Hegel gives an explicitly epistemic twist to the notion that whenever a mortal gets too big for his britches, Nemesis will take him down a peg or two by applying it to the question, so pressing since Kant, whether humans can know God. He argues that the only possible obstacle to such knowledge would be divine envy. But Plato and Aristotle were right to deny such a hindrance on the divine side. Ergo, we can know God.

2) In the strongest sense. The absence of divine envy means that in our knowledge of God there is nothing hidden, nothing secret. There is no divine mystery, except in that sense in which mystery signifies exactly the opposite of ineffability, namely that which is brought to intelligibility through speculation.[34]

3) The categorical denial of divine mystery is supported by treating hiddenness and manifestness as a simple either/or of mutual exclusiveness. This either/or excludes the Kantian/Heideggerian dialectic in which even in unconcealment God might remain concealed as exceeding our capacities of comprehension.

4) Least of all could Christians disagree with him, Hegel claims, since Christianity presents itself as the revealed religion, and this means that in it God is fully manifest and no longer mysterious.

5) In the absence of divine envy, it could only be "owing to human caprice, to an affectation of humility, or whatever you like to call it, that the finitude of knowledge, the human reason is put in contrast to the divine knowledge and the divine reason" (LP 195). Kant, along with such predecessors as Augustine and Aquinas, are reduced to caprice and affectation.

6) The appropriate contrast, rather, is that between Understanding, for which God's nature remains a secret, and Reason, for which it is manifest.[35]

---

32. The interior quotation is from Phil. 4:7. Whereas English translations usually render the Pauline νοῦς as 'understanding', Luther's translation, to which Hegel alludes, has *Vernunft*.

33. See PM ¶564; EL addition to ¶140; LP 193–95; H&S 2:72–73, 134–35; LPR 1:381–82; and HIN 243.

34. See LPR 1:382, n. 44, and 3:280.

35. Cf. the passage cited above from LPR 3:280–81 in which God remains secret and mysterious

7) These points have their ontological foundation in Hegel's pantheism. Creation is "God's self-manifesting, self-revealing" (LPR 1:381), and thus the worlds of nature and spirit are "a revelation of God" (EL ¶140A). But, just to be sure we do not take this theistically, Hegel reminds us that "what God creates God himself is" (LPR 1:381) and that what the worlds of nature and spirit reveal is their own "divine essence" (EL ¶140A).

8) The epistemic corollary is the self-consciousness motif we have already encountered. While "nature never gets to the point of being consciousness of its divine essence, it is the express task of finite spirit to achieve this" (EL ¶140A), and it remains finite just so long as it does not complete this task. Accordingly, "God is God only so far as he knows himself: his self-knowledge is, further, a self-consciousness in man and man's knowledge *of* God, which proceeds to man's self knowledge *in* God" (PM ¶564). In other words, "it is not the so-called human reason with its limits which knows God, but the Spirit of God in Man, it is, to use the speculative expression previously employed, the self-consciousness of God which knows itself in the knowledge of Man" (LP 195).

9) Finally, Hegel joins Spinoza in a gnostic interpretation of our religious responsibility. The possibility of knowing God becomes not only the command to know God but ultimately "Man's highest duty" (LP 194). Without the knowledge of God we would be but "sounding brass and a tinkling cymbal!" (HIN 243). These words are from the King James Version of 1 Cor. 13:1, translating perfectly Hegel's use of the very words Luther uses to translate the same passage. It is St. Paul's description of those who lack love. The irony of Hegel's citation of these words to describe those who lack knowledge is astonishing, since in the very next verse Paul contrasts love with knowledge. "And if I . . . understand all mysteries and all knowledge . . . but do not have love, I am nothing" (NRSV). The Pauline contrast is replaced in Hegel by Spinoza's identification in which the highest form of rational insight is the intellectual love of God. Hegel reinforces this gnosticism when he tells us that philosophy is the worship of God (LPR 1:84, 153).[36] Equally important is his description of philosophy as "a continual cultus" (LPR 1:446), since 'cultus' is his word for the practical side of religion, the correlate of its creeds and theologies.

In all of the above it is clear how closely the issues of mystery and revelation are intertwined. God may be mysterious for Understanding, but not for

---

only to the Understanding, but not to Speculation. A similar contrast between the Understanding's limited and distorted grasp of freedom and love and a truly rational, speculative comprehension is central to Hegel's political thinking. See, for instance, PR ¶¶ 5–7, 158, 182–83, and 189, with remarks and additions.

36. The translation of *Gottesdienst* as 'service of God' is misleading, since it is the ordinary word used on church bulletin boards for the Sunday morning worship service. The best treatment of Hegel's relation to the gnostic traditions is Cyril O'Regan, *The Heterodox Hegel* (Albany: SUNY Press, 1994).

Reason; for other religions, but not for Christianity, since it is the revealed religion. Revelation, like Reason, eliminates mystery. At this point, Jaeschke issues a terminological warning in relation to the *Phenomenology*. The section on Christianity as the absolute religion is entitled *"die offenbare Religion,"* not *"die geoffenbarte Religion."* Jaeschke suggests we distinguish the two as 'revelatory' and 'revealed'. "[Christianity] is 'revelatory,' not because it is revealed, but because the object of consciousness 'essentially and directly has the shape of self-consciousness.' "[37]

The point of this distinction is clear enough. The verb *offenbaren* and its derivatives naturally suggest, if they do not strictly require, the act of a personal agent, whereas the adjective *offenbar* does not. The wart on the end of my nose is *offenbar*, plainly seen for what it is, without the need for any acts of disclosure on my part; in fact, it is all too *offenbar* in spite of my best efforts to conceal it. When Jaeschke says "not because it is revealed," he presumably is reminding us that Hegel is not affirming the concept of revealed religion in the traditional sense according to which by a gracious personal act, God enables us to know and to understand what we could not have discovered with our own unaided powers of thought.[38] Revelation in this sense is a special category of miracle, a direct act by a personal God that is not part of the natural order of things.

Jaeschke is surely right to remind us that this is not what Hegel has in mind. But Hegel would be astonished by this attempt at a terminological distinction. In the very passage Jaeschke cites, Hegel writes, "Consequently, in [the Christian] religion, the divine Being is *revealed* [*geoffenbart*]. Its being revealed [*Offenbarsein*] obviously [*offenbar*] consists in this, that what it is, is known. But it is known precisely in its being known as Spirit, as a Being that is essentially a *selfconscious Being*" (PS 459).

Similarly, in the God-is-not-envious passages, Hegel uses *offenbar* and *geoffenbart* interchangeably, along with *Manifestieren, Sichmanifestieren, Sichoffenbaren,* and *sich mitteilen*. In one passage he says it is "God's nature to reveal himself, to be manifest [*sich zu offenbaren, offenbar zu sein*]. Those who say that God is not revelatory [*offenbar*] do not speak from the [standpoint of the] Christian religion at any rate, for the Christian religion is called the revealed [*geoffenbarte*] religion" (LPR 1:381–82).

---

37. Jaeschke, *Reason in Religion*, p. 204.
38. This sense is often called "special" revelation to distinguish it from "general" revelation, on which natural theology rests, the manifestation of God that *is* available to properly functioning human reason. Special revelation has traditionally included not only the "mighty acts of God" in history, such as the covenants with Abraham and David, the Exodus, the Exile, the Incarnation, and the Atonement, but also the indirect speech acts through prophets and apostles, which eventually became canonized as the biblical texts, through which those events are rightly interpreted. On the notion of indirect divine speech acts, see Nicholas Wolterstorff, *Divine Discourse: Philosophical reflections on the claim that God speaks* (Cambridge: Cambridge University Press, 1995).

Hegel is not in the least bashful about using the traditional language of Christianity as a revealed religion, just as he uses traditional language about creation, trinity, incarnation, and so forth. In each case he seeks to give a persuasive redefinition in terms of his own system of thought. In this case revealed [*geoffenbart*] reduces to manifest [*offenbar*]; Christianity is the revealed religion because in it God becomes fully intelligible and no longer mysterious, but only, of course, when Christianity has been properly decoded by speculative philosophy. Just as Spinoza replaces prophecy in the popular and traditional sense with the true prophecy which is the rational insight of the Sage, so Hegel replaces revelation in the popular and traditional sense with the rational insight of the speculative system. Just as the elimination of mystery removes from the scene an ontological Other beyond the powers of our comprehension, so the redefinition of revelation forbids the appearance of an epistemic Other, an actual intellect to which we are inferior and on which we are dependent. Autonomy prevails over alterity.

Jaeschke says this himself with full clarity. In his view, the Jena writings "show that Christianity is on each occasion of interest to Hegel to the extent that he can interpret its doctrines in the context of his philosophy. The Christian religion does not, however, afford a basis for understanding either the terms in which the fundamental principles are formulated or the way in which they are developed in the system." It is true that Hegel's philosophy accepts the Christian idea of the incarnation, "but only insofar as it can rethink the content in its own terms in the course of obtaining methodically secure knowledge."[39] This, of course, is the essence of onto-theology: God can enter philosophy's discourse only on the latter's terms and in the service of its project.

* * *

We saw in the previous chapter that Spinoza's philosophy of divine immanence had ethical as well as epistemic implications. When we ask about Hegel and the ethical, we remember that Kierkegaard's Climacus complained not only that the system wasn't yet quite finished, but also that it had no ethics. Moreover, he raises this issue with a reference to "pantheistic systems [that] have frequently been cited and attacked by saying that they cancel freedom and the distinction between good and evil."[40] It would seem that Climacus is neither convinced by Hegel's defense of Spinoza on this point nor persuaded that Hegel is without problems of his own. If there are problems, they would indeed be Hegel's own, for unlike Spinoza, he doesn't relativize good and evil to the *conatus essendi* of the individual. Hegel's ethic is much more a social ethic than a therapeutic individualism.

Kierkegaard understands that fully, but this is not the place to explore his

---

39. Jaeschke, *Reason in Religion*, pp. 287, 332.
40. Kierkegaard, *Concluding Unscientific Postscript*, 1:119–22.

critique.[41] We are trying to focus on Hegel through the double lens of Spinoza and Heidegger, to see how his pantheism might be construed as paradigmatic onto-theology. As with Spinoza, there is for Hegel no personal God, no actual moral lawgiver to whom we have obligations. Moreover, Hegel does not think that our highest duty is "to do justice to love kindness, and to walk humbly with [our] God" (Micah 6:8) or to "love the Lord [our] God with all [our] heart . . . [and our] neighbor as [our self]" (Matt. 22:34–40).[42] As we have already seen, he thinks it is to know God in the form of Reason (not Understanding) and Concept (not Representation)(LP 194). But as with Spinoza, good and evil do not simply disappear. Rather we might say they are teleologically suspended in speculative philosophy.

We see this in Hegel's reading of the fall.[43] It is not about transgression but about cognition. Innocence is understood as a pre-human immediacy, as the natural life of humankind which has not yet risen above the animal level. Thus innocence is evil and ought not to be. As in the gnostic versions where the serpent is the hero, God's command not to take of the tree of the knowledge of good and evil is a command to remain in innocence, not to embark on the journey toward philosophical cognition as something divine, as the *imago dei*. Innocence is evil and ought to be transcended because it signifies the need for truth, the failure yet to have achieved humanity's ownmost destiny as knowers. Creation and the fall are equivalent insofar as both involve the positing of finite spirit as separate from God. In the context of a pantheistic theology, human fallenness is the intermediate stage in which finite spirit has risen above animal innocence but has not yet achieved the reconciliation which comes with the self-consciousness of its own divine infinity. For Hegel evil is not about murder and rape, genocide and ethnic cleansing, child abuse and spouse abuse, religious and racial bigotry, cheating on your spouse and cheating on your income tax, perjury or ordinary lying, and so forth. It is what all of us are, whether atheists or theists, so long as we have not yet recognized our own inherent deity. Our redemption consists in becoming Hegelians.

One needn't be Kierkegaard to say at this point: "the system has no ethics." It begins to look like a therapeutic ethic in which, as with Spinoza, moral virtue is supplanted by intellectual virtue. But what about right and wrong? What about the earlier claim that Hegel's ethic is a social ethic? In other words, what about *Sittlichkeit*?

Over against the individualism of Abstract Right and Conscience, Hegel

---

41. I have done so elsewhere. See "Abraham and Hegel" in *Kierkegaard's Critique of Reason and Society* (University Park, Pa.: The State University of Pennsylvania Press, 1991) and *Becoming A Self: A Reading of Kierkegaard's 'Concluding Unscientific Postscript'* (West Lafayette, Ind.: Purdue University Press, 1996), especially ch. 7.

42. Both commandments are quotations from the Jewish Torah, Deut. 6:5 and Lev. 19.18, given in answer to a question about the greatest commandment and presented as the foundation of "all the law and the prophets."

43. See EL ¶24A3 and LPR 3:272–307.

presents *Sittlichkeit* or Ethical Life as an ethic of "my station and its duties."[44] The rights of liberal individualism, in particular the rights of property and of conscience, are not abolished by Hegel, but rather dethroned. They are no longer taken to be absolute but are relativized in two ways. First, rights are correlated with duties (PR ¶¶142–56). The entitlement mentality which dominates so much of our political discourse, both on the left and on the right, is wholly foreign to Hegel. Second, both rights and duties are embedded in the social institutions from which they are derived and by which they are authorized: family, civil society, and the state. As with Spinoza, for whom right and wrong were relative to the laws of the state, for Hegel my rights and duties are a function of my social order. Laws do not derive from rights, as liberalism would have it, but rights derive from laws and customs.

This means, of course, that Hegel's ethic is a worldly ethic. With the Reformation he refuses to privilege monastic chastity, poverty, and obedience over marriage, enjoying the fruits of one's labor, and citizenship. These latter are the freedoms of Family, Civil Society, and the State.[45] But Hegel is no Luther or Calvin, for the ethics of *Sittlichkeit* is also embedded in his pantheistic ontology. Just as God has no eyes to see with but ours, no thoughts in which to become self-conscious but ours, no love but ours, so God has no laws but ours. The laws and customs of my people are the highest norms for my conduct (when it is conduct and not cognition that is at issue) because there is no higher law. There is no divine law to which we, collectively, are responsible.

There are, to be sure, two things higher than the State as the laws and customs of a particular people, but neither involves ethical self-transcendence. Absolute Spirit is higher than Objective Spirit, which means that Art, Religion, and Philosophy represent higher levels of human self-realization than our life of rights and duties within the State. But Philosophy is the truth of Art and Religion, which means, to repeat, that our highest task is speculative insight into our essential deity. I am called to something higher than "my station and its duties," but it is not to a higher morality than the *Sittlichkeit* history has thrown me into.

But even if we stay within the limits of Objective Spirit, there is something higher than the State, namely World History. *Die Weltgeschichte ist das Weltgericht* (PR ¶¶340–41; PM ¶548).[46] Hegel insists that its "right," as the highest "right," is absolute (PR ¶¶30, 33, 340; LWH 92). But does it make any sense to speak here of right? History surely signifies a power that overthrows states and

44. The phrase is used by F. H. Bradley to describe his own very Hegelian ethics in *Ethical Studies*, 2nd. ed. (London: Oxford University Press, 1927). Following Bradley, Knox translates *Pflichten der Verhältnisse* as "duties of [one's] station" in PR ¶150. Hegel's account is found in PM and, in greater detail, in PR. For the introduction of *Sittlichkeit* in PS, where it is more closely linked to Hegel's epistemic concerns, see my *History and Truth*, ch. 5.
45. For a detailed analysis, see my "Hegel and the Reformation" in *Hegel, Freedom, and Modernity*.
46. The phrase is from Schiller's poem "Resignation."

the ethical order they embody. But does history thereby derive or exhibit any moral authority?

Hegel hastens to assure us that "world history is not the verdict of mere might, i.e. the abstract and non-rational inevitability of a blind destiny" (PR ¶342). There is a teleology in history, and philosophy knows "that reason governs the world, and that world history is therefore a rational process" (LWH 27). Philosophy teaches us that "the concrete good is indeed all-powerful, and that this absolute power translates itself into reality. The true good, the universal and divine reason, also has the power to fulfill its own purpose. . . . For goodness, not just as a general idea but also as an effective force, is what we call God . . . no force can surpass the power of goodness or of God or prevent God's purposes from being realised. . . . world history is nothing more than the plan of providence" (LWH 66–67).

But, in the first place, we know that we must demythologize this talk of God and providence, for there is no personal planner or overseer of history. The only actual minds are our own. Secondly, even if we grant to Hegel an impersonal teleology to history, a purposiveness without a purpose, it is far from clear that the "goodness" it unfolds has anything to do with morality. Allan Wood sees this clearly.

> . . . we might think of the [historical] transition from one ethical order to another as an *ethical* advance, the result of a growth in ethical knowledge. But it would be a fallacy to infer that we *must* think of it in that way. . . . Spirit's freedom is the ground of the ethical, but not everything founded on spirit's freedom is ethical, and some things founded on spirit's freedom may be higher than the ethical. A new and higher order embodies ethical knowledge, and superior knowledge of spirit's freedom, but it does not follow that it embodies superior *ethical* knowledge . . . in fact, exactly the opposite follows. . . . [The higher right of world history] is asserted at precisely those points where the state or the ethical order is seen to be limited and inadequate in its rationality. Thus the right of world history is a right that supercedes the ethical. It is, if you like, a right that is beyond the ethical, beyond good and evil.[47]

In other words, the teleology of history "aims" to bring Absolute Spirit to its perfection, the self-consciousness of God in human thought. But this has no perceivable link to any perfection of Objective Spirit. Wood places Spirit's freedom at the center of his analysis. We have seen that for Hegel, "Freedom is only present where there is no other for me that is not myself" (EL ¶24A2). This is the teleology of history. It is achieved through the pantheistic self-consciousness in which Hegel's ontology and epistemology merge. But it has little if anything to do with more just laws or more loving customs.

Even if it did, the judgment of the Court of World History in which our

---

47. Allen W. Wood, *Hegel's Ethical Thought* (New York: Cambridge University Press, 1990), p. 223.

Sittlichkeit is "judged" and "found wanting," that is, overthrown, is not a verdict to which we are privy until after the fact. It is not a higher law or norm of any kind to which we collectively are responsible. Although world history's icebergs may sink us, we are, so long as we are afloat, the king of the universe. In ethics as in epistemology, autonomy prevails over alterity.

***

With this we return to Heidegger's critique of Hegel's philosophy as onto-theology. On his view onto-theology culminates in modern science and technology. Now we can answer the question asked above: How is Hegel's speculative pantheism a friend to modernity's will to power, its John the Baptist, if you will? In his essay, "The Word of Nietzsche: 'God Is Dead'," Heidegger portrays modern technology as an "insurrection," an "assault," as "the struggle for unlimited exploitation of the earth as the sphere of raw materials and for the realistic utilization of 'human material,' in the service of the unconditional empowering of the will to power in its essence" (QT 100–101). He sees Nietzsche's announcement of the death of God as clearing the way for the absolute self-assertion of the human will to power; moreover, he sees Nietzsche as playing this role, not as the overcomer of metaphysics but as its fulfillment. We can make sense of this claim if we hear Heidegger saying, in effect, "Modern technology is the will to power devoid of moral constraint. The death of God announced by Nietzsche is its precondition and presupposition. Nietzsche, in turn, is simply unpacking the implications of Hegelian speculation, which, appearances to the contrary notwithstanding, has won so decisively that 'only a god can save us now.' "[48]

If Heidegger sees Hegel as a John the Baptist for modern technology, he himself would be a John the Baptist for this god. His call to repentance is a call to abandon onto-theological presumption for the dialectic of unconcealing and concealment, to allow mystery to be the horizon within which intelligibility, no longer absolute, occurs.

Perhaps he has Nietzsche in mind—the Nietzsche who sets Dionysius over against the Socrates "whose supreme law reads roughly as follows, 'To be beautiful everything must be intelligible' . . ."[49] This opposition translates into that between the artist and the theoretical man. "Whenever the truth is uncovered, the artist will always cling with rapt gaze to what still remains covering even after such uncovering; but the theoretical man enjoys and finds satisfaction in the discarded covering and finds the highest object of his pleasure in the process of an ever happy uncovering that succeeds through his own efforts . . . there is, to be sure, a profound *illusion* that first saw the light of the

---

48. The closing words are the most famous line from the famous 1966 interview of Heidegger by *Der Spiegel*, used as the title of the English translation in *Graduate Faculty Philosophy Journal* 6, no. 1 (winter 1977), p. 18.
49. *The Birth of Tragedy*, Section 12.

world in the person of Socrates: the unshakable faith that thought, using the threat of logic, can penetrate the deepest abysses of being . . ."[50] If Heidegger attributes the birth of onto-theology to Anaxagoras and Aristotle, Nietzsche gives that palm to Socrates.

In the same spirit, he will later distance himself from the Egyptian youths who sneak into the temple of Isis by night

> and want by all means to unveil, uncover, and put into a bright light whatever is kept concealed for good reasons. No, this bad taste, this will to truth, to "truth at any price," this youthful madness in the love of truth, have lost their charm for us. . . . *We no longer believe that truth remains truth when the veils are withdrawn.* . . . Today we consider it a matter of decency not to wish to see everything naked. . . . Perhaps truth is a woman who has reasons for not letting us see her reasons?[51]

The obvious affinity between Heidegger and Nietzsche on this point leads to the question: Is the dialectic of unconcealing and concealment somehow linked to the atheism (methodological in the case of Heidegger)[52] of these philosophies? Or could this dialectic be religiously motivated as well? More specifically, could the classical theisms of Augustine and Aquinas, so far from being onto-theological in nature, develop their own versions of this dialectic precisely in the service of a greater divine transcendence than is to be found in Spinoza and Hegel? It is to these questions that the next chapters turn.

---

50. *The Birth of Tragedy*, Section 15. Nietzsche does not propose replacing science with art, but seeing it as a *supplement* to art (Section 14) and even to nature (Section 24) which arises at the "limits" of science (Sections 15, 17–18). Cf. Derrida's discussion of the "dangerous supplement" in *Of Grammatology*, trans. Gayatri Chakravorty Spivak (Baltimore: Johns Hopkins University Press, 1976), Part II, ch. 2. For Nietzsche's slightly earlier reflections on these issues see "The Philosopher: Reflections on the Struggle between Art and Knowledge," in *Philosophy and Truth: Selections from Nietzsche's Notebooks of the Early 1870's*, trans. Daniel Breazeale (Atlantic Highlands, N.J.: Humanities Press, 1990).
51. *The Gay Science*, Second Edition Preface.
52. See ch. 1 n. 46 above.

PART II.
EPISTEMIC TRANSCENDENCE: THE DIVINE MYSTERY

four

Augustine and Pseudo-Dionysius

Negative Theology as a Break with the Onto-theological Project

We are exploring the claim that onto-theology is bad theology because it compromises the transcendence of God, that overcoming onto-theology and renewing our sense of the otherness of God are two sides of the same coin. Whether we speak in the formal mode of 'God' or in the material mode of God, the onto-theological task of the name or the named one is to render the whole of reality intelligible for human understanding. As archetypal examples of onto-theology, the nature pantheism of Spinoza and the spirit pantheism of Hegel make the double claim that 'God' is (in the proper philosophical system, though not in ordinary religious use) a clear and distinct idea, adequate to the reality it intends, and that in relation to this idea the whole of reality becomes fully intelligible to human thought. This epistemic immanence within some human conceptual apparatus is grounded in God's ontological immanence within the world of nature or history. As possessors of a system of thought which is adequate to grasp or to mirror the divine reality, we have both God and the world at our cognitive disposal.

It should be noted that the ontological claim that this immanent God is the *arche* or the *telos* or the *ultima ratio*, the center in terms of which the whole of being is unified, taken by itself, fails to meet the onto-theological demand. For even if one knew that there is a Highest Being which is the First Principle of all reality, this would not render the whole intelligible unless both that Highest Being itself and its relation to the rest of reality were themselves fully intelligible. Only the ontological claim combined with the epistemological claim will get the job done, and in Spinoza and Hegel, as we have seen, the two claims are indeed jointly propounded.

This means that to interrupt the onto-theological project, it is not necessary to deny that there is a Highest Being which is the First Principle of all reality. It is only necessary to hold (consistently, and not just on ceremonial occasions) that God is ineffable, incomprehensible, unknowable, that our conceptual systems are inadequate to the divine reality, too weak to grasp it and too dull to mirror it. Theism is committed to a God who, as creator, is ontologically transcendent, but not to a God who is epistemically immanent. When it interprets "that than which a greater cannot be conceived" also to mean "that which is greater than we can conceive," it resists the onto-theological aspirations of Plato[1] and Aristotle, Spinoza and Hegel; and, if it does this consistently and not just on ceremonial occasions, it undermines its own onto-theological tendencies, that is, recognizes them as temptations to be resisted.

It is thus no accident that when Rudolf Otto wants to reflect on the divine as "wholly other," he introduces this phrase as a gloss on the "*mysterium*" in "*mysterium tremendum et fascinans*," or that he argues that while the superiority of Christian theism lies in the rational concepts it uses to articulate the divine attributes, by themselves these leave us with "a wrong and one-sided interpretation of religion. . . . For so far are these 'rational' attributes from exhausting the idea of deity, that they in fact imply a non-rational or supra-rational Subject of which they are the predicates . . . we have to predicate them of a subject which they qualify, but which in its deeper essence is not, nor indeed can be, comprehended in them." Thus "orthodoxy has been the mother of rationalism" (read onto-theology) when it has "found in the construction of dogma and doctrine no way to do justice to the non-rational aspect of its subject," when by this failure it has given to the idea of God "a one-sidedly intellectualistic and rationalistic interpretation."[2] Or, in other words, when it has abandoned or sought to suppress the dialectic of unconcealment and concealment.

Augustine, for one, does not succumb to this temptation. This will come as a surprise to those who assume that classical theism is automatically and paradigmatically onto-theological. It would be foolish to suggest that with all

---

1. I use 'Plato' to signify the onto-theological tendencies in the Platonic corpus and 'Socrates' to signify the intratextual resistance to these tendencies.
2. Rudolf Otto, *The Idea of the Holy*, trans. John W. Harvey (New York: Oxford University Press, 1958), pp. 25, 1–3.

the Platonism Augustine has imbibed his thought is entirely free of onto-theological tendencies, especially in connection with the metaphorics of light and vision. But he is not uncritically Platonic, as we see when we find him contrasting the "confession" of humble Christian believers who are willing to be dependent on Christ and the Scriptures from the "presumption" of Platonists who think they can do just fine without either (C VII, 20).

But it should be clear that the issue here is not in the first instance about the need to go beyond reason and so-called natural theology to a theology based on special revelation. For the question is not whether the source of theology's concepts is reason or revelation but whether in either case they are up to the task of eliminating the *mysterium,* thereby rendering God and the world wholly intelligible to us. And Augustine's theory of language looks to be headed in this direction. It has an onto-theological look about it and would seem to be a paradigm of what Derrida calls the metaphysics of presence, his term for the onto-theological project of eliminating hiddenness by flushing everything out into the light at once.

Just as *Confessions* I, 8 is a foil for Wittgenstein's theory of language in the opening paragraphs of *Philosophical Investigations,* so the theory of language Augustine presents in *De Trinitate* reads like a textbook instance of what Derrida wishes to deny, the priority of meaning and knowledge to language.[3] For Augustine, the inner word or word of the heart belongs to no natural language, but is derived from the direct presence of sense or intellect to its appropriate object. The secondary, outer word, which does belong to some human language, is arbitrarily assigned to the inner word simply for the purpose of communication.[4] And, just to assure us he has read his Derrida carefully, Augustine insists on the secondary character of writing. The written word is a sign of the outer, spoken word (which remains such when we silently think it); only this latter is a sign "of the things we are thinking of" (C XV, 19).[5]

---

3. See especially XIII, 4; XIV, 10 and 13; and XV, 19–20, 22, and 40. Aquinas has a similar theory of language. See *Summa Theologiae,* 1,13,1 and *De Veritate,* 4.1. But as we shall see in the next chapter, instead of a metaphysics of presence we get a dialectic of presence and absence.

4. The link with Wittgenstein's critique of the notion of a private language should be clear. While critiquing Augustine's theory of ostensive definition as a "primitive idea of the way language functions" (I, 2) and a "general notion of the meaning of a word [which] surrounds the working of language with a haze which makes clear vision impossible" (I, 5), Wittgenstein sees him speaking "as if the child could already *think,* only not yet speak. And 'think' would here mean something like 'talk to itself'" (I, 32). For further discussion see John Turk Saunders and Donald F. Henze, *The Private Language Debate* (New York: Random House, 1976).

5. Of course the spoken word signifies the "things" we are thinking of only by means of the inner word. When Derrida speaks of the relation between signifier (phoneme or grapheme) and signified, the latter is sometimes a meaning, an Husserlian ideality, an Augustinian inner word, and sometimes an objective reality, a thing, a fact, an event. Perhaps the ease with which these are interchanged stems from the assumption of a direct realism in the theories under discussion. The inner word is not the object of consciousness from which it infers the outer thing, fact, or event. Rather it is the form through which or as which it perceives "the things we are thinking of." In

There is undeniably a metaphysics of presence at work here for ordinary language. But as we shall see, Augustine does not build an onto-theology on this foundation. Rather, for theological reasons he affirms hiddenness over sheer presence in our knowledge of God and even qualifies the presence of creatures to our consciousness in a rather Kantian way so that our knowledge of them too, "compared with [God's] is ignorance" (C XI, 4).[6] Ignorance, we might note, is not a standard metaphor for full intelligibility.

Let us begin with the central point, our knowledge of God. Augustine speaks unambiguously at the very beginning of one of his most widely influential works, *De Doctrina Christiana*. "God, Father, Son and Holy Spirit, is the ultimate thing to be enjoyed; but he is inexpressible." This Trinity is

> one supreme thing, and one which is shared in common by all who enjoy it; if, that is to say, it is a thing, and not the cause of all things; if indeed it is a cause. It is not easy, after all, to find any name that will really fit such transcendent majesty. . . . Have I said anything, solemnly uttered anything that is worthy of God? On the contrary, all I feel I have done is to wish to say something; but if I have said anything, it is not what I wished to say. How do I know this? I know it because God is inexpressible. . . . And from this it follows that God is not to be called inexpressible, because when even this is said about him, something is being expressed. And we are involved in heaven knows what kind of battle of words. (TC I, 5–6)[7]

Augustine's sense of the incomprehensibility of God is most dramatically expressed in a question that reverberates throughout the *Confessions:* "What, then, is the God I worship?" (C I, 4). His answer is most interesting. "You, my God, are supreme, utmost in goodness, mightiest and all-powerful, most merciful and most just. You are the most hidden from us and yet the most present amongst us, the most beautiful and yet the most strong, ever enduring and yet we cannot comprehend you. . . . For even those who are most gifted with speech cannot find words to describe you."

There are three things to notice here. First, the original "what" question is a properly philosophical question about essence. But Augustine knows he is not inquiring about the unconscious laws of nature or the impersonal Idea but

---

Aristotelian/Thomistic language, the very same form of a thing has a dual existence, as an abstracted, intramental reality and as an embodied, extramental reality.

6. I have argued elsewhere that Kant's entire distinction between appearances and things in themselves depends on and expresses the difference between divine and human knowledge. See "In Defense of the Thing in Itself," *Kant-Studien* 59, no. 1 (1968), pp. 118–41. Augustine, it would seem, is an antirealist.

7. In a gloss on Augustine's "if indeed it is a cause," Edmund Hill adds, "In the ordinary, human sense of cause, or of thing. He is simply adverting to the total inadequacy of all human language when applied to the divine mystery, or at least of all language that is not purely and simply scriptural. But if pressed, he would have agreed that the scriptural terms he goes on to deploy are not adequate either, though they cannot be improved upon" (TC p. 126, n. 5). Cf. T I, 3, where Augustine describes the future goal of the soul's purification as the ability "to see that ineffable thing in an ineffable manner."

about "You, my God," the Highest Being, to be sure, but at the same time the personal God with whom he is and long has been in conversation. The essence about which he inquires is the essence of an interlocutor.[8] Second, Augustine seems to know a great deal about God and gives a long list of traditional attributes, as if to answer his own question. But finally, he insists that in the very act of thus naming God, God remains hidden, incomprehensible, indescribable.

This question lies at the center of Book X, where it is repeated twice. In chapter 6 Augustine asks, "But what do I love when I love my God?" After giving a few negative answers and some metaphors based on them, he puts his question to the earth, the sea, the living things, the winds, the air, the sky, the sun, the moon, and the stars. "Clear and loud they answered, 'God is he who made us.'" In short, God is here identified not through divine attributes but as Creator. But this answer, which Augustine has affirmed throughout his text, does not put his question out of business. So he begins the very next chapter with the question, "What then, do I love when I love God?"—to which he adds, in the style of Hebrew parallelism, a second version of the same question, "Who is He that is above the summit of my soul?"

This time the question sets him off on his journey through memory, during which it becomes increasingly clear that the task of Book X is to wrestle with the question rather than to remove it from the agenda by giving a definitive answer. Accordingly, the book ends with a quotation from Psalm 22, ". . . and they shall praise the Lord who seek Him." Even for an Augustine who has found enough of God to become a bishop and theologian, the life of faith is still a life of seeking. On this path of wondering who God is, both praise and prayer (of which the *Confessions* is a sustained instance) are possible. Onto-theological satisfaction is neither possible nor necessary.

It is not necessary precisely because a life of prayer and praise are possible without it. Even in the absence of comprehension, Augustine can love his God. "So Something can be loved which is unknown, provided it is believed" (T VIII, 6). And why is it not possible to escape the dialectic of unconcealing and concealment? Augustine gives two reasons, one temporary, the other quite possibly permanent. He states the former this way: "This much I know . . . *at present I am looking at a confused reflection in a mirror*, not yet *face to face*, and therefore, as long as I am away from you, during my pilgrimage, I am more aware of myself than you." This condition will obtain "until I see you face to face and *my dusk is noonday*" (C X, 5; cf. T VIII, 6; XV, 22).

---

8. With the metaphorics of vision and light, Augustine easily sounds like an onto-theological metaphysics of presence. But in the *Confessions* vision is *aufgehoben* by the divine voice, a theme I have developed in "Divine Excess: The God Who Comes After," in *The Religious*, ed. John D. Caputo (Oxford: Blackwell, 2002), pp. 258–76. Cf. Jean-Luc Marion, "L'Interloqué," in *Who Comes After the Subject*, ed. Eduardo Cadava, Peter Connor, and Jean-Luc Nancy (New York: Routledge, 1991).

The second reason is that corresponding to the permanent ontological disparity between Creator and creatures is an epistemic disparity, and it is not clear how this could be overcome even when, in the life to come, we see God "face to face." After earth and the heavens once again declare, "We exist . . . because we were made," Augustine reflects

> It was you, then, O Lord, who made them, you who are beautiful, for they too are beautiful; you who are good, for they too are good; you who ARE, for they too are. But they are not beautiful and good as you are beautiful and good, nor do they have their being as you, their Creator, have your being. In comparison with you they have neither beauty nor goodness nor being at all. This we know, and thanks be to you for this knowledge. *But our knowledge, compared with yours, is ignorance.* (C XI, 4, emphasis added)

Since God is Creator, it is true "of all his creatures . . . that he does not know them because they are, but that they are because he knows them . . . he created because he knew, he did not know because he had created. . . . Our knowledge therefore is vastly dissimilar to this knowledge" (T XV, 22). Created things depend on divine knowledge, while human knowledge depends on created things, and, of course, on the uncreated God. It would appear that Augustine is a Kantian, for it is precisely this distinction between human, receptive knowledge and divine, creative knowledge that generates the distinction between appearances (the world as humanly known) and the thing in itself (the world as divinely known).[9] Since we are vastly dissimilar to God in being, "our knowledge, compared with yours, is ignorance." Not only is God ultimately ineffable, because *all* our knowledge is ignorance in relation to the knowing which is truly adequate to its objects by being their infinite origin, the world, too, escapes our conceptual nets. It is indeed possible, pace Hegel, to think too highly of our intellectual powers. The intelligibility in which we make our cultural homes is second-class, penultimate at best, or, to be more blunt, not even of the right kind to be ultimate. It is an island of *terra firma* surrounded by a sea of mystery.

If Augustine is right about the incomprehensibility of God, then his question, "What, then, do I love when I love God?" defines the theologian's task (and every believing soul is a theologian, one who speaks of God) in a special way. It is to keep asking that question, to keep answering it as well as one is able, and to recognize in each answer, which can indeed motivate praise and prayer, an inadequacy sufficient to motivate asking the question anew. But our task at the moment is more nearly meta-theological. If Augustine is right to challenge onto-theological demands in terms of an ineffable otherness of God, the theological task is to express The Inexpressible, while the meta-theological question becomes how best to understand the simultaneous possibility and impossibility of God talk.

---

9. See note 6 above.

The tradition of negative theology presents an obvious first candidate, and the remainder of this chapter will be devoted to it. Subsequent chapters will explore other ways of articulating God's epistemic transcendence. Negative theology affirms the divine incomprehensibility by denying the adequacy of our images and concepts of God. This is an attempt to overcome onto-theology or, to put it more positively, to explore the possibilities of a post-metaphysical theology. This latter term is less than perfect; but it has these three advantages. First, Heidegger speaks of the onto-theological constitution of metaphysics, so that his critique of onto-theology is intimately linked with, if not synonymous with, his project of overcoming metaphysics.[10] Second, Derridean deconstruction is closely linked to these motifs in Heidegger and has generated important discussions of the relation between deconstruction and negative theology.[11] Since deconstruction is often and appropriately described as a critique of the metaphysics of presence, the term 'postmetaphysical' engages the Derridean as well as the Heideggerian critique of onto-theology.

Finally, in contrast with 'non-metaphysical', 'postmetaphysical' does not commit us to the view that we can escape metaphysics. 'Post' signifies 'after' to be sure, but just as 'postwar Europe' and 'postmodern philosophy' do not signify a Europe or a philosophy that have simply left the war and modernity behind, respectively, and are no longer deeply entangled with their lineages, so postmetaphysical theology is precisely not to be understood as purified of all metaphysical residues and temptations.

Derrida does not think that Heidegger's "step back" from metaphysics can ever be a step "out of" metaphysics. Just as we are never simply present to any meaning or fact, so we are never simply beyond metaphysics, having left it safely and completely behind. To deconstruct the metaphysics of presence is not to abolish it or to escape it but to wound it, limit it, interrupt it, embarrass it. I use the term 'postmetaphysical' to express my agreement with Derrida on

---

10. See OM in relation to ID and WM/1949.

11. I have developed the linkage between the critique of onto-theology and the critique of the metaphysics of presence in "Kierkegaard's Climacus—A Kind of Postmodernist," in *International Kierkegaard Commentary: Concluding Unscientific Postscript*, ed. Robert L. Perkins (Macon, Ga.: Mercer University Press, 1997). The primary discussions by Derrida of deconstruction and negative theology are: "Différance" in *Margins of Philosophy*, trans. Alan Bass (Chicago: University of Chicago Press, 1982); "How to Avoid Speaking: Denials" in *Derrida and Negative Theology*, ed. Harold Coward and Toby Foshay (Albany: SUNY Press, 1992); and "Sauf le nom" in *On the Name*, ed. Thomas Dutoit (Stanford, Calif.: Stanford University Press, 1995). The dates of the original French publications are, respectively, 1968, 1987, and 1993. Helpful discussion is to be found in John D. Caputo, *The Prayers and Tears of Jacques Derrida: Religion without Religion* (Bloomington: Indiana University Press, 1997); in Kevin Hart, *The Trespass of the Sign* (New York: Cambridge University Press, 1989); and in the essays that accompany Derrida's in the Coward and Foshay volume. It is precisely in discussing the relation of Derrida to negative theology that Caputo notes Derrida's appropriation of Augustine's question, "What do I love when I love my God?"—on which, he suggests, "Derrida's life and work is an extended commentary." *Prayers and Tears*, p. xxii. Cf. pp. 12–13, 25, 37, 61.

this point. As we have seen, Augustine describes God in undeniably metaphysical ways while, at the same time, denying their ultimate adequacy.

We can turn first to an objection which, if sound, would immediately eliminate the apophatic strategy for overcoming onto-theology within a theistic framework. It is the claim that within the cloud of unknowing, anything goes. To worship an unknown God is to open the door to any and every representation of deity and thus to the worship of what is not God, to idolatry. For nature abhors a vacuum, or, as Jesus taught, if an unclean spirit returns to a person in whom it once lived and finds its old home "empty" and "swept," it will go and find seven friends and move back in, "and the last state of that person is worse than the first" (Matt. 12:43–45). To make matters worse, an unknown God is an invitation to antinomianism, to an anything goes policy at the practical level that would make religion the enemy of morality.[12] This objection is closely related to the assumption that deconstruction is a nihilistic abolition of all values, especially the True and the Good.

But it is doubly mistaken. First, if negative theology is a certain kind of skepticism, it is not agnosticism in any usual sense. It operates on the assumption that God is real, indeed, as superessential, more real than the most exalted creature. Moreover, it makes the paradoxical claim that it knows enough about God to know that God is unknowable, that no image of the human senses or concept of the human intellect (whether its origin is reason or revelation) is adequate to the divine reality. The Highest is higher than our comprehension can take us. Even at this abstract level, the cloud of unknowing is not a vacuum. Indeed, as we shall see in due course, it can be objected that it is all too full of the divine presence.

Second, the objection fails to notice that the primary home of negative theology, in the Christian forms that primarily concern us here, has been orthodoxy.[13] Pseudo-Dionysius begins *The Mystical Theology* with a prayer to the Trinity (MT 135/997A) and surrounds this treatise with three others, *The Divine Names*, *The Celestial Hierarchy*, and *The Ecclesiastical Hierarchy*, given over to interpretation of the Bible and Christian liturgy.[14] He opens the first of these by telling Timothy that it is precisely because of the epistemic transcendence of God that "we must not dare to resort to words or conceptions concerning that hidden divinity which transcends being, apart from what the

---

12. I have addressed the form this objection takes in Hegel and Feuerbach in "Faith as the Overcoming of Ontological Xenophobia," in *The Otherness of God*, ed. Orrin F. Summerell (Charlottesville: University Press of Virginia, 1998).

13. There are, of course, important moments of negative theology in Judaism, Islam, Hinduism, Buddhism, and Taoism. I focus on Christian versions because my primary interest is in the renewal of theism in a Christian context.

14. In *The Divine Names*, Dionysius reminds his pupil Timothy that "we should really begin with an invocation of the Trinity" and follows this up with a short discourse on the utter importance of prayer for the theologian (DN 68/680B-D). He begins both *The Celestial Hierarchy* and *The Ecclesiastical Hierarchy* with appeals to Jesus and to Scripture (CH 145/121A and EH 195/372A).

sacred scriptures have divinely revealed" (DN 49/585B, 588A). In addition to the doctrine of the Trinity, he regularly invokes that of the Incarnation (DN 61–66/640D-649B).

The writings of Dionysius may have a monophysite origin, for the first known reference to them, in the early sixth century, was in defense of the monophysitic view that, contrary to Chalcedon, Christ had only one and not two natures. There are also links between Dionysius and the Nestorian, Donatist, Monergist views that the mainstream church condemned as heresies. But early on, glosses on his work by John of Scythopolis and Maximus the Confessor gave a thoroughly orthodox reading of his corpus, and it was in this form that it first became central to the Greek, Eastern church and later to the Latin, Western church.[15]

In the East, apophaticism (some of it predating Dionysius) is at the heart of the writings of the Cappadocian fathers, St. Basil, St. Gregory of Nyssa, and St. Gregory Nazianzus, as well as of the hesychast traditions associated with St. Symeon the New Theologian and St. Gregory Palamas.[16] And in the West, Dionysius was an important source in the twelfth century for the Victorines and in the thirteenth for Robert Grosseteste, Albert the Great, Aquinas, and Bonaventure.[17]

It might be objected that just as Dionysius was claimed by orthodox and heretics alike, so later on he was as much the heritage of John Scotus Eriugena and Meister Eckhart, whose views were condemned as compromising the divine transcendence, as of Aquinas and Bonaventure. Further, there are Jewish and Islamic forms of apophaticism that would begin with prayer, but not to the Trinity, and Hindu and Buddhist forms for which meditation, but not prayer, would be appropriate. All of which shows that anything goes in the temple of negative theology, which was the original objection.

Whether one's sympathies are with orthodoxy or with one or another of the heretical traditions, it must be acknowledged that apophaticism has not been able to decide the issue between them; nor the issue between Christians, Jews, and Muslims regarding the Trinity; nor the differences among the six

---

15. See Jaroslav Pelikan, Introduction to *Pseudo-Dionysius: The Complete Works*, pp. 1213–24; Paul Rorem, "The Uplifting Spirituality of Pseudo-Dionysius," *Christian Spirituality: Origins to the Twelfth Century*, ed. Bernard McGinn et al. (New York: Crossroad, 1988), pp. 145–46.

16. See Vladimir Lossky, *The Mystical Theology of the Eastern Church* (Crestwood, N.Y.: St. Vladimir's Seminary Press, 1976), pp. 33–37. Introducing an important later work from this tradition, H. A. Hodges writes, "The practice of spiritual disciplines is always dangerous when it is not governed by a sound rule of faith . . . the most fervent devotion will go wrong if it is not kept under the control of a sound rule of faith." Lorenzo Scupoli, Nicodemus of the Holy Mountain, and Theophan the Recluse, *Unseen Warfare*, trans. E. Kadloubovsky and G. E. H. Palmer (Crestwood, N.Y.: St. Valdimir's Seminary Press, 1987), pp. 27 and 34.

17. Jean Leclercq, Introduction to *Pseudo-Dionysius: The Complete Works*, pp. 28–29. Historically, at least, negative theology has not been the path at whose end "atheism and mysticism can shake hands." Franz Rosenzweig, *The Star of Redemption*, trans. William W. Hallo (Boston: Beacon Press, 1972), p. 23.

schools of orthodox Hinduism (perhaps analogous to the distinction between Orthodox, Roman Catholic, and Protestant within Christian orthodoxy as defined by the ecumenical creeds); nor the differences between the Therevada and Mahayana traditions in Buddhism. But what method, what scripture, what practice (e.g., prayer, meditation), what tradition neutral to the combatants in any given case, has ever been able to resolve these differences and reduce plurality to unity? The fact that negative theology cannot satisfy the triumphalist longing for a single truth established beyond dispute does not mean that it is an invitation to intellectual anarchy any more than is the Hebrew Bible, which has not been able to put to an end the conflict of interpretations, Jewish and Christian, it has engendered. Those who raise the "anything goes" objection fail to notice that they are themselves engaged in disputes over matters of interpretation and of substance that have not been resolved and show no signs of resolution. But they do not draw an "anything goes" conclusion from this fact.

The following advice is typical. "Should [any thought that arises during the ascent into the cloud of unknowing] ask, 'What is this God?' answer that it is the God who made you and redeemed you, and who has, through his grace, called you to his love. 'And', tell him, 'you do not even know the first thing about him.' "[18] The "I don't know the first thing about God" response signifies the ascent into what Dionysius calls "the truly mysterious darkness of unknowing" (MT 137/1001A). The "God is the one who made me and redeemed me and called me by grace to a life of love" response is the base camp from which the ascent is made and to which, in this life, the believer returns. Different climbers will have different base camps, to be sure. But each will have one, made up of texts, traditions of interpretation, practices, communities, and so forth, and that base camp will be utterly indispensable to the ascent. Debates over which base camp is to be preferred will continue, but they will be carried on with precisely those logical and rhetorical tools which are believed in advance to be useless for the ascent itself. Negative theology is not a method for resolving theological disputes. It is a meta-theory about the epistemic status of whatever names or attributes we predicate of God.

The practical side of the anything goes objection can be met more briefly. We only have to notice that the typical home of negative theology is the religious community, not only in its doctrinal position, but in the practical disciplines that make up the purification that precedes illumination and union or perfection.[19] These include the cultivation of the virtues, prayer and meditation, reading and study, ascetic practices such as fasting, monastic vows, and participation in the liturgical life of the community. While this world is not

---

18. *The Cloud of Unknowing*, ch. 7. This advice is very Augustinian.
19. This triad has its origin with Dionysius. See CH 154–55/165B–168A; 163–68/208A–240D; EH 235–39/504A–509A; 248–49/536D–537C. Cf. Evelyn Underhill, *Mysticism* (New York: New American Library, 1955), Part Two, ch. III, IV, and X.

necessarily legalistic, it is surely at a far remove from antinomian license, from the slogan, "God is unknowable; everything is permitted."

A second objection arises out of what might appear to be quintessentially onto-theological gestures in negative theology itself. Dionysius places the whole of being in relation to the Highest Being. Thus, he regularly refers to God as the Cause of all there is. But God is no mere origin. "The Good returns all things to itself and gathers together whatever may be scattered, for it is the divine Source and unifier of the sum total of things. . . . In it 'all things hold together' [Col. 1:17] and are maintained and preserved as if in some almighty receptacle. All things are returned to it as their own goal. All things desire it" (DN 75/700A–B; cf. 102/825B). God is called omnipotent because "He founds [the world]. He makes it secure. He holds it together. He binds the whole universe totally to himself. He generates everything from out of himself as from some omnipotent root and he returns all things back to himself as though to some omnipotent storehouse" (DN 119/936D; cf. 79/708A; CH 145/121A). Clearly no being can be properly understood apart from its relation to the Highest Being.

Is this not onto-theology? No, it is not. For onto-theology is not merely the ontological claim that there is a Highest Being who gives unity to the whole of being; it is above all the epistemological claim that with reference to this Highest Being we can render the whole of being fully intelligible to human understanding. And, to understate the obvious, this latter claim is conspicuously absent from Dionysius.

Do we find anything here analogous to the calculative-representational thinking that is Heidegger's target? Only negatively in the repeated claim that none of our images and none of our concepts is adequate to the divine reality. The Highest Being is not at the disposal of even such a lofty concept as 'being', for our intellect, like our senses, falls short of the glory of God. In the Dionysian gloss on Plato's *epikeina tes ousias*, God is beyond being not because God is unreal, but because 'being' is a category strictly correlated to human knowing.[20] Dionysius is an idealist who affirms the identity of (human) thought and being, but instead of drawing the Hegelian conclusion that God as the Highest Being is fully intelligible to speculative theology, he draws the Kantian conclusion that our descriptions of God have phenomenal but not noumenal validity. 'Being' is an all too human category.

But perhaps there is an appeal to presence here that would run afoul of Derrida's critique? We must proceed carefully. Given a theistic rather than

---

20. For the repeated equivalence of being with thought or knowing, see DN 49/588A; 50/589B; 53/592C–593A; 63/645A; MT 135/997B; 138/1025B; and Letter One, p. 263. When arguing, against Dionysius, that being is prior to goodness, Aquinas agrees with the former about the correlation of being and human knowing. "Now the first thing conceived by the intellect is being, because everything is knowable only inasmuch as it is actually. Hence, being is the proper object of the intellect, and is thus the first intelligible, as sound is the first audible." *Summa Theologiae,* I.5.2.

neoplatonic interpretation, Dionysius is rightly seen as making the "totalizing" claim that being is gathered into a whole since all of being is fully present to God. But while Derrida can "quite rightly pass for an atheist," deconstruction is not a philosophical justification for atheism.[21] While some Derrideans act as if it were, where is the argument? What resources do his quasi-transcendental semantics, his quasi-Kantian analysis of how meaning works for us, have for making such a strong claim about what there is?[22] One has to know a great deal to know that there are no pink pumpkins in the universe, or no God to whom the whole of being is present.

Deconstruction is rather the claim that neither at the level of meaning or of fact/event do we have the whole of being, or God as the Highest Being, or any other being, however lowly, simply and fully present to our cognition. Neither in the mode of immediacy nor totality can we achieve a full and simple presence beyond the dialectic of presence and absence in which anything (partially) present is a trace that points beyond itself to what is not present. **Metaphysics,** and this cannot be emphasized too strongly about the pejorative use of the term, turns out to be precisely the **epistemological claim** that "presence absolutely precedes representation." Thus the sensible/ intelligible hierarchy is metaphysical when the latter, privileged member is interpreted as "present to consciousness."[23]

---

21. The quotation is from Jacques Derrida, *Circumfession: Fifty-nine Periods and Periphrases,* in Geoffrey Bennington and Jacques Derrida, *Jacques Derrida* (Chicago: University of Chicago Press, 1993), p. 155. John Caputo and Kevin Hart both insist, rightly and repeatedly, that deconstruction has no necessary links to atheism and/or death of God theology. See *Prayers and Tears,* pp. 4–5, 13, 18, 67; and *Trespass,* pp. x, 26–27, 29–30, 37, 39, 43–47, 64, 74, 94.

22. Interpretations of Derrida as a radical Kantian are to be found in Rodolphe Gasché, *The Tain of the Mirror: Derrida and the Philosophy of Reflection* (Cambridge, Mass.: Harvard University Press, 1986); Irene Harvey, *Derrida and the Economy of Différance* (Bloomington: Indiana University Press, 1986); and Christopher Norris, *Derrida* (Cambridge, Mass.: Harvard University Press, 1987). For a dissenting view, see Richard Rorty, "Is Derrida a transcendental philosopher?" in *Essays on Heidegger and Others* (Cambridge: Cambridge University Press, 1991). John Caputo's response to Rorty is "On Not Circumventing the Quasi-Transcendental: The Case of Rorty and Derrida," in *Working Through Derrida,* ed. Gary B. Madison (Evanston, Ill.: Northwestern University Press, 1993). Gasché introduces the term 'quasitranscendentals' to talk about conditions of possibility that are at the same time conditions of impossibility (pp. 316–17). One might say they are what you get when you cross a Kantian category with a Kantian idea.

23. These definitions of the "metaphysical" are Hart's reading of Derrida. See *Trespass,* p. 11. Derrida speaks of traces instead of signs to remind his readers that on his analysis, that which is not presently present was not previously present either, as if the sign were the memory of a past presence. It is a quasitranscendental law of " 'experience' in general" that "there is no experience consisting of *pure* presence . . ." "Signature Event Context" in *Limited Inc,* trans. Samuel Weber and Jeffrey Mehlman (Evanston, Ill.: Northwestern University Press, 1988), p. 10. This is why "[t]here never was any 'perception' " (the scare quotes signifying the empiricist attempt to find *pure* presence in sense experience). *Speech and Phenomena and Other Essays on Husserl's Theory of Signs,* trans. David Allison (Evanston, Ill.: Northwestern University Press, 1973), p. 103. For the relation of Derrida to Levinas on the issue of the trace, see Robert Bernasconi, "The Trace of

In other words, if there is a site where the whole of being is fully intelligible by being fully present to some mind, we are not that mind and we cannot occupy that site. When Kierkegaard's Climacus says that reality is a system for God but not for any human observer,[24] Derrida can claim to have strengthened the latter, negative claim. But with regard to the assertion that reality is a system for God, deconstruction as such (and as distinct from Derrida himself) can only remain undecided. Of the theological interpretation for which "God would be the truth of all negativity," Derrida says, "This reading will always be possible. Who could prohibit it? In the name of what?" But deconstruction means that "what is thus permitted is never necessary as such . . ."[25]

The epistemic/semiotic account of the "metaphysics" of presence, combined with the clear awareness that deconstruction is not able and does not try to settle the question of the reality of God, means we should not go along with Hart when he says that presence is "both an ontological and an epistemological category" and draws the conclusion that vis-à-vis deconstruction "a good deal of the traditional doctrinal content attached to 'God' is put under critical pressure." For example, "Christian theology, with its doctrinal emphasis upon purity of origins—*creatio ex nihilo*, Mary's immaculate conception and Jesus's virginal conception—stands as a paradigm of the metaphysics of presence."[26]

But what resources does a deconstructive semantics have to settle disputes over how Jesus or Mary or the world came to be? We lapse into metaphysics, in Derrida's sense of the term, not when we affirm these doctrines, but when we make them metaphors for our own language, texts, interpretations, and so forth, attributing pure and unmediated origination to the latter. The doctrine of the immaculate conception, for example, becomes metaphysics when we claim that it was itself immaculately conceived, the miraculous offspring of a pure reason unconditioned by our life in the cave. The expansion of presence to an ontological category is undermined by Hart's own recognition "that Derrida seeks to situate epistemology with respect to *différance* . . . [and] that he makes no claims about anything other than the *status* of our knowledge and

---

Levinas in Derrida," in *Derrida and Différance*, ed. David Wood and Robert Bernasconi (Evanston, Ill.: Northwestern University Press, 1988).

24. Søren Kierkegaard, *Concluding Unscientific Postscript to Philosophical Fragments*, trans. Howard V. Hong and Edna H. Hong (Princeton, N.J.: Princeton University Press, 1992), I, 118. On the epistemic nature of metaphysics as onto-theology, see Catherine Pickstock, who claims that "an ontology separated from theology is reducible to an epistemology." *After Writing* (Oxford: Blackwell, 1998), p. 62. Cf. pp. 63–64, 70, 127. In context she clearly means by theology a discourse which, unlike onto-theology, preserves the epistemic transcendence of God. As with Kierkegaard, Socrates is paradigmatic of genuine theology on this point.

25. "How to Avoid Speaking?" pp. 76–77. This possibility, this permission, means that those who insist on reading deconstruction as nihilism "could indeed, if they wished, recognize in it the last testimony—not to say the martyrdom—of faith in the present *fin de siècle*." The link between deconstruction and faith (undecidability and decision) is a recurring theme in *Prayers and Tears*.

26. Hart, *Trespass*, pp. 23, 39, and 36.

truth claims. *Différance* may block the way to a totalized ontology, but it is not concerned with questions of what there is in the universe and what conditions its coming into presence."[27]

But these considerations, important as they are, do not put the negative-theology-as-appeal-to-pure-presence objection to rest. To see why not, we need to distinguish two modes in which negative theology relates to positive theology. One relation is successive-diachronic, the other simultaneous-dialectical. It is the former that concerns us at present. It emphasizes the *via negativa* precisely as *via*, as the practices that constitute a journey of ascent. The first stage is from sense to intellect. With the help of negation, the symbols of scripture and liturgy are stripped of the sensible literalness and interpreted in conceptual terms. The second stage moves beyond both sense and intellect to what is better than either, union with God beyond knowing (DN 53/592C–593A; 109/872A–B; MT 136–37/1000C–1001A).[28]

In both of these stages negation stands in relation to the affirmations, first of sense and then of intellect, whose adequacy to their intended reality it persistently denies. But in the second stage it goes beyond "serving to correct positive theology" to a stand-alone role which can be argued "to be correct in itself."[29] The second 'correct' needs to be in scare quotes to signify something like this: correctness as correspondence or *adequatio* is not available to us, but the proper goal, which correctness talk misconstrues, is available to us when we leave the sphere of correctness behind and move on to something higher and better. It is this movement that *The Cloud of Unknowing* describes as the "naked intention directed to God."[30] Our intention is naked when it has been stripped not only of the desire for some benefit other than God's own self, but also of the images and concepts in which it is normally clothed. In this second stripping, negation goes beyond reminding us of the poverty of our noematic treasures to remaking the noetic posture that is willing to give them up.

The goal here is not better representations, but union, a union regularly described as unknowing, as darkness, and as silence. But the light does not quite disappear in this darkness. Beyond sense and intellect we are in touch with the "intangible and invisible darkness of that Light which is unapproachable" (DN 107/869A). In union, the mind, having turned away from all things and even from itself, "is made one with the dazzling rays" (DN 109/872A–B). The goal of mystical theology is "the brilliant darkness of a hidden silence" (MT 135/997A–B). This is why Dionysius can say that God is "known through knowing and through unknowing" (DN 108–109/872A). It is why *The Cloud of Unknowing* can say that it is "only to our intellect that [God] is incompre-

27. Hart, *Trespass*, p. 94. Cf. p. 165.
28. For a nice account of this double movement, see Rorem, "The Uplifting Spirituality," pp. 133–40.
29. Hart, *Trespass*, pp. 199–201.
30. *The Cloud of Unknowing*, ch. 7 and 24.

hensible; not to our love . . . to the intellect, God who made [the powers of knowing and loving] is forever unknowable, but to the second, to love, he is completely knowable . . ."[31] It is very much in keeping with this language that a monk of the Eastern church interprets the "mystical theology" of Dionysius as "a theory of contemplation" and sees union as "a supernatural and unspeakable intuition, as distinct from 'apodeictic' or demonstrative theology."[32] And it is surely a gloss on the notion of knowing by unknowing that Gregory Palamas says that those who experience union pass beyond sense and intellect and are "admitted to the true vision because they have ceased to see, and endowed with supernatural senses by their submission to unknowing . . . they have indeed seen, yet their organ of vision was, properly speaking, neither the senses nor the intellect."[33]

The language of contemplation, intuition, and vision tells us that we are still dealing with cognition, even if we are beyond the operation of human cognitive powers. The union that takes place in the cloud of unknowing is a kind of knowing. If Lossky describes this as bringing "a presence and a fullness which are without measure,"[34] he merely echoes Dionysius, who writes of the mysteries of God's Word,

> Amid the wholly unsensed and unseen
>> they completely fill our sightless minds
>> with treasures beyond all beauty. (MT 135/997B)

If deconstruction works "against the pleasure the present takes in itself, in order to prevent it from closing in on itself,"[35] it can easily be distinguished from negative theology. For according to one story the latter tells about itself, the diachronic story we are presently exploring, the apophatic goal would seem to be the pleasure of a present, outside of time, to be sure, closed in upon itself. Caputo can describe this as "a higher modalization of onto-theo-logy, an ontotheology *eminentiore modo*, a variation on the philosophy of presence which takes the form of a theology of super- or hyperpresence, delivering a surge of presence of which the metaphysics of presence can only dream."[36] In

---

31. *The Cloud of Unknowing*, ch. 4.

32. *Orthodox Spirituality*, by a monk of the Eastern church (2nd. ed.; Crestwood, N.Y.: St. Vladimir's Seminary Press, 1978), pp. 19 and 10. Cf. Hodges' Introduction to *Unseen Warfare*, ". . . this ignorance of creatures is at the same time a luminous knowledge of God, a formless contemplation of Him Who is without form or mode." Beyond sense and intellect there is "only an imageless intuitive apprehension of the soul itself and of God" (pp. 19 and 23).

33. Gregory Palamas, *The Triads*, trans. Nicholas Gendle (New York: Paulist Press, 1983), p. 35. He describes Paul, during his experience of ecstatic union, as all eye in the midst of light. See p. 38.

34. Lossky, *Mystical Theology*, p. 43. Cf. Derrida's complaint about the "complicity of theoretical objectivity and mystical communion" that both he and Levinas resist. "Violence and Metaphysics," *Writing and Difference*, trans. Alan Bass (Chicago: University of Chicago Press, 1978), p. 87.

35. Caputo, *Prayers and Tears*, p. xx.

36. Caputo, *Prayers and Tears*, pp. 7–8. Cf. p. 11: "As a hyperousiology, negative theology drops anchor, hits bottom, lodges itself securely in pure presence and the transcendental signified, every

other words, as Derrida puts it, there is "a certain complicity" between rationalism and mysticism.[37]

On this story negative theology is the map for a detour. The direct road to full presence, followed by onto-theology in its rational mode, is blocked. The *Mystical Theology* points out another *via* that will get us to the same goal, although in wonderfully Hegelian fashion the path and the goal are so intimately intertwined that we discover that the goal isn't quite the same when we take the Apophatic Avenue to get there. We are still immersed in light, but it is so bright as to be blinding to our finite faculties of sense and intellect. Still, negative theology ends up making a claim to presence diametrically opposed to deconstruction. So the negative-theology-as-appeal-to-pure-presence objection is still with us.

But there are three important things to notice about this pot of golden presence at the end of the rainbow *negativa*. First, for the same reasons that deconstruction is not inherently atheistic, it must remain agnostic about the possibility of such experience. It can point out how radically different it is from ordinary experience and language (though it will hardly outdo the theological sources on this point), and it can steadfastly undermine the attempts of empiricists and rationalists to sneak pure presence into their accounts of our sensible and intellectual powers. But it has no resources for denying that such a mode of "experience" is possible, either temporarily in this life or permanently in some life to come. We would have to be rewired, so to speak, radically remade; but once again deconstruction is not likely to stress this point more strongly than the diachronic Dionysians.

Second, the radical remaking of the self that is necessary to union means that God is not so much at the soul's disposal as just the opposite. Divine transcendence evokes human self-transcendence rather than human mastery. We can see this in several ways, each of which pulls our reading of union away from the hyperpresence model (for which, to be sure, there is plenty of textual support).

To begin with, the way of negation "stands the soul outside everything which is correlative with its own finite nature" (DN 130/981B). This means that union is not something achieved by the exercise of its own powers, including above all, the power of the intellect. It is to be found only beyond any act or capacity of the mind. It is a gift of grace which the soul receives in a passive and

---

bit as much as any positive onto-theo-logy, and in a certain sense more so. . . . Far from providing a deconstruction of the metaphysics of presence, negative theology crowns the representations of metaphysics with the jewel of pure presence, and effects in a still higher way . . . the triumph of presence over representation." It would seem that Caputo now agrees with Hart's critique of his own earlier attempt, in *Heidegger and Aquinas: An Essay on Overcoming Metaphysics* (New York: Fordham University Press, 1982), to read mysticism as a "step back" out of metaphysics. See Hart, *Trespass*, pp. 68–69, 102.

37. Jacques Derrida, *Of Grammatology*, trans. Gayatri Chakravorty Spivak (Baltimore, Md.: Johns Hopkins University Press, 1976), p. 80. See note 30 above.

dependent mode.[38] Even if we are talking here about total presence, so far is it from signifying mastery or having God at one's (cognitive) disposal that it rather signifies being overwhelmed and out of control.

But it is not necessary to interpret union in terms of total presence. This is clear from the interpretation by Gregory of Nyssa of Moses' ascent into the dark cloud of unknowing. His request to see God face to face is denied precisely in order that his desire for God not be quenched in satisfaction, that journey not be terminated by arrival.[39]

Perhaps the fullest development of this motif in Gregory of Nyssa is found in Gregory Palamas. Union involves a "supernatural vision of God" to be sure, for "God is not only beyond knowledge, but also beyond unknowing." However, this vision is "not seeing the divine essence, but seeing God by a revelation appropriate and analogous to Him . . . the divine manifestations . . . remain unknowable by reason of their transcendence . . . being, as it were, for us yet beyond us . . ."[40] St. Benedict, according to Palamas,

> saw the whole universe contained in a single ray of this intelligible sun—even though he himself did not see this light as it is in itself, in its full extent, but only to that extent that he was capable of receiving it. By this contemplation and by this supra-intelligible union with this light, he did not learn what it is by nature, but he learnt that it really exists, is supernatural and superessential, different from all things; that its being is absolute and unique, and that it mysteriously comprehends all in itself . . . when the vision comes to him, the recipient knows well that it *is* that light, even though he sees but dimly . . . always he is being borne on to further progress. . . . He understands then that his vision is infinite because it *is* a vision of the Infinite, and because he does not see the limit of that brilliance; but all the more, he sees how feeble is his capacity to receive the light. . . . God, while remaining entirely in Himself, dwells entirely in us by His superessential power; and communicates to us not His nature, but His proper glory and splendour.[41]

Here we get an interesting twist on the complicity between mysticism and rationalism. For what these two Gregorys give us is an extension to mystical vision of the limitations previously ascribed to the intellect (and, of course, to the senses). The discrepancy between the infinite reality of the Creator and the

---

38. *The Cloud of Unknowing*, ch. 4 and 34. Cf. DN 53/592C–D. Gregory Palamas says that the vision of the incomprehensible God occurs incomprehensibly, since it is by gift of divine grace beyond all activity of the intellect. He also identifies the giver of this gift as the Spirit. See *The Triads*, pp. 34–38.

39. Gregory of Nyssa, *The Life of Moses*, trans. Abraham J. Malherbe and Everett Ferguson (New York: Paulist Press, 1978), pp. 114–16/II, 231–33, 235, 238–39. Cf. the discussion of Jean Daniélou in *From Glory to Glory*, trans. Herbert Musurillo, S.J. (Crestwood, N.Y.: St. Vladimir's Seminary Press, 1995), pp. 26–33.

40. Palamas, *The Triads*, p. 32.

41. Palamas, *The Triads*, pp. 38–39.

finite reality of the creatures means that while the knowing by unknowing that takes place in union is higher than conceptual knowledge, just as conceptual knowledge is higher than perceptual, the third and highest level, like the lower two, remains finite and does not experience total presence. *The Cloud of Unknowing* agrees. For while it holds forth the hope of "a real knowledge and experience of God as he is" in the cloud, this will not be of God "as he is in himself, of course, for that is impossible to any save God."[42]

Moreover, this is not true only of temporary mystical ecstasy in this life. Appealing explicitly to Gregory of Nyssa, Palamas claims that no eye can see the divine Beauty "even if it gaze forever."[43] "The super-essential nature of God is not a subject for speech or thought or even contemplation, for it is far removed from all that exists and more than unknowable . . . incomprehensible and ineffable to all for ever."[44] Summarizing this theme in Gregory of Nyssa and Palamas, John Meyendorff writes, "Even in the Age to Come, there can be no end to the good things that God has to reveal; so the soul is always *in via*, always moving on."[45]

Of this yearning that is never satisfied, this desire that is never quenched, Dionysius says that it "brings ecstasy so that the lover belongs not to self but to the beloved" (DN 82/712A; cf. 106/868A). This is true in the cognitive or hypercognitive realm to which we have so far restricted ourselves. On at least one interpretation of union, God remains, in and through all manifestation, beyond our reach, our possession, our mastery, our control. God never becomes our cognitive property; and whatever sight or insight we do have at the highest levels possible for us, we have not through the exercise of our own powers but as a free gift of grace.

But there is another sense in which union or ecstasy is the experience of not belonging to oneself. We are often told that the goal of mystical longing is beyond *theoria*, that love and communion rather than contemplation or speculation are what it is all about.[46] No doubt Hart is right when he says, "There can be no strict division between 'knowing' and 'loving' with regards to mystical experience."[47] But that is at least in part because, as the endless commentaries on the Song of Solomon remind us, 'knowing' always has its "biblical" sense and is never reducible to its cognitive dimensions. Union, then, involves

---

42. *The Cloud of Unknowing*, ch. 14. Pseudo-Dionysius also holds that only God can know God. Speaking of "the inexpressible God, this One, this Source of all unity, this supra-existent Being . . . [that] is gathered up by no discourse, by no intuition, by no name," he writes, "Cause of all existence, and therefore itself transcending existence, it alone could give an authoritative account of what it really is" (DN 50/588B).

43. Palamas, *The Triads*, p. 34.

44. Quoted from Palamas by Lossky in *Mystical Theology*, p. 37.

45. Palamas, *The Triads*, p. 123, n. 45.

46. See, for example, Andrew Louth, *The Origins of the Christian Mystical Tradition: From Plato to Denys* (Oxford: Oxford University Press, 1981) pp. 82 and 85, and Lossky, *Mystical Theology*, p. 42.

47. Hart, *Trespass*, p. 103.

not only a mode of "cognition" higher than the perceptual and conceptual powers of the mind, but also such transformations of our "affections" and "will" as are properly designated as love, agape, charity.

Dionysius tells us that the goal of the journey is "to be made godlike" (CH 147/124A). But God is not God simply by staring at God. For Dionysius God is above all goodness construed as giving, generosity, grace. This motif is perhaps best developed in *The Cloud of Unknowing*. To love God is not just to long to see God face to face. It is to desire "that the will of him whom [one] loves be fulfilled" since "spiritual oneness" means "harmony of will."[48] This means that while the "naked intent" for God alone is stripped of any mercenary motive, any desire for a benefit from God other than God's own self, it is not stripped of concern for the neighbor. "For charity is nothing else than loving God for himself, above all created things, and loving men in God just as we love ourselves." Because of this refusal to separate love of God from love of neighbor, "the perfect contemplative holds no man as such in special regard. . . . For all men alike are his brothers, and none strangers. He considers all men his friends, and none his foes. To such an extent that even those who hurt and injure him he reckons to be real and special friends, and he is moved to wish for them as much good as he would wish for his very dearest friend." In this way one becomes "charitable through contemplation, that ever afterwards when he comes down from the heights . . . his will will be as readily directed to his foes as to his friends, to strangers as to relatives."[49]

Whether mystical union is to be understood cognitively in terms of pure presence or a new experience of the inseparability of presence and absence, the divine presence has a peculiarly repelling effect. The *mysterium* is *tremendum* as well as *fascinans*. It is as if one knows in advance that any audience granted by the Great King will be cut short by the command to go back out and care for the widows, the strangers, and the orphans. Or, to add a chapter to the Song of Solomon, the raptures of intimacy between the lovers will be temporary. Soon enough there will be kids to take care of.

So perhaps it was premature to distinguish deconstruction from negative theology on the grounds that the former works "against the pleasure the present takes in itself, in order to prevent it from closing in on itself."[50] In the texts

---

48. *The Cloud of Unknowing*, ch. 24, 47, and 67. Cf. *Orthodox Spirituality*, p. 23. "Will—not intellect or feeling—is the chief human instrument of union with God. There can be no intimate union with God if our own will is not surrendered and conformed to the divine will. . . ."

49. *The Cloud of Unknowing*, ch. 24–25. Since the cultivation of the virtues is part of the purification that precedes illumination and union, it is trivially true that the contemplative must practice charity. In these texts, beyond that, charity becomes an essential ingredient and consequence of union. Cf. *Orthodox Spirituality*, p. 15, where the *apatheia* of the Desert Fathers is "something quite different from a kind of anaesthesia of the feelings. . . . It is, in reality, the state of a soul in which love towards God and men is so ruling and burning as to leave no room for human (self-centered) passions."

50. See note 35 above.

of diachronic apophaticism, union is presence to be sure. But any tendency for this presence to close in on itself is challenged, deconstructed, if you like, in the texts themselves. Both in terms of the contemplative life and the active life of the contemplative, there is always more to "see" and always more to do. The argument is not grammatological or (quasi)transcendental. In the one case it is onto-epistemic, insisting that the gap between Creator and creature resists epistemic closure in pure presence. In the other case it is ethical, insisting that the bond between self and neighbor (which, as we have seen, includes the enemy) resists rupture even in the name of loving what is higher than both self and neighbor.

We have been exploring the argument that diachronic negative theology runs afoul of deconstruction's critique of the metaphysics of presence, that in it mysticism betrays its complicity with rationalism, differing not in the depth of its commitment to pure presence but only in the *via* it takes to get there. The first (brief) response was that deconstruction is not in a position to deny the possibility of what the mystic claims, any more than Kant, for example, can deny the possibility of modes of "experience" radically different from the one he describes. Perhaps, outside the textuality of life as we know it, something like pure presence is possible. The second (longer) response was to notice several ways in which Christian apophaticism has significantly qualified the claims to presence implicit in the idea of union with God.

The third response will be the final one, for it will take us back to dialectical negative theology. But before taking leave of negation as the path to union, we might well notice that its account of divine transcendence includes several dimensions of human self-transcendence.

1. At least on one reading, our knowledge is never adequate to the divine reality it intends, either in this life or in the life to come. Truth (mastery, possession) in the fullest sense is always beyond us.

2. The highest that we can attain is not within the powers of our intellect or will. We are deeply dependent.

3. God is not at our disposal. It is rather the other way around, and the more so the further we have progressed toward union or perfection. We do not so much belong to ourselves as to Another.

4. It turns out that the Other to whom we belong is human as well as divine. The Other is plural as well as One, ugly as well as Beautiful, mean as well as Merciful, needy as well as Numinous, greedy as well as Good, and so forth.

We might describe the self that journeys on the *via negativa* as a radically decentered self. Any inclination, which it comes to see as a temptation, to place itself at the center of things is resisted. It is not the Source, nor can it come to stand at the Origin. It is not the Goal, nor can we occupy the Omega Point. Its truth is not a sufficient guide, nor its power a sufficient ability to get it where it most deeply wants to get. And when it gets there, it is sent back where it is not eager to go, to a world of strangers and even enemies requiring charity.

We come, finally, to a third consideration. We need to recall that in its diachronic mode, negative theology is a journey, a *via* whose motive is love and whose goal is not knowledge but union. As Hart puts it, in this mode it has moved beyond "the discourse which reflects upon positive theology by deny- ing that its language and concepts are adequate to God" and has become "a religious programme of practices by which the soul progressively denies all that is not God in order to become one with God . . ."[51]

We have seen that union is sometimes described as if it were pure and total presence, while at other times it is seen as the continuation at a higher level of the inseparability of presence and absence, unconcealment and concealment, that characterizes our perceptual and conceptual knowledge. But there is no ambivalence on one point: union means silence. The movement beyond the correlation of being and knowing is a movement beyond words and speech (DN 53/592D). The goal is "the brilliant darkness of a hidden silence" (MT 135/997B). There is "no speaking" of the supreme Cause because it is "beyond assertion *and denial*" (MT 141/1048A–B).[52] On the upward flight, "as we plunge into that darkness which is beyond intellect, we shall find ourselves not simply running short of words but actually speechless and unknowing . . . my argument now rises from what is below up to the transcendent, and the more it climbs the more language falters, and when it has passed up and beyond the ascent, it will turn silent completely, since it will finally be at one with him who is indescribable" (MT 139/1033B–C).

It comes as no surprise that the mystical journey ends in silence. But this means that negative theology in its diachronic mode is not a good answer to the question we are asking because it is not an answer to that question at all. Our immediate question is how best to express the divine transcendence of our cognitive capacities. And to this question, "with silence" is a legitimate answer. But we posed this question as part of another question: How do we do theol- ogy? We are looking for ways to do theology that would not lapse into onto- theology. But to do theology is to engage in God talk. To look for a theology that might, in the Heideggerian and Derridean senses of the term, be a post- metaphysical discourse with God as its subject matter is to presuppose that we are going to be talking and to ask how best to do so.

Negatively speaking, we want to learn how not to speak about God. But this phrase is ambiguous. It can mean learning not to speak about God at all. But it can also mean learning to speak this way rather than that way. And it is this second meaning that is presupposed by our larger project. But to this question it is only negative theology in its dialectical mode, in its simultaneity

---

51. Hart, *Trespass*, pp. 175–77. On p. 29 Hart suggests that Derrida's critique is not directed against every use of God talk but against claims to its adequacy.

52. Cf. MT 136/1000B. "Now we should not conclude that the negations are simply the opposites of the affirmations, but rather that the cause of all is considerably prior to this, beyond privations, beyond every denial, beyond every assertion."

with positive theology, that is an answer. We encountered this simultaneity when Augustine affirmed the ultimate goodness, power, mercy, and justice of God, only to insist immediately that God remains hidden, incomprehensible, and indescribable. And we encountered it in the advice of *The Cloud of Unknowing* to say that God is the One "who made you and redeemed you, and who has, through his grace, called you to his love," then immediately to add that "you do not even know the first thing about him." We need to turn our attention to negative theology as "the discourse which reflects upon positive theology by denying that its language and concepts are adequate to God."[53] Its basic answer to our question is that we speak most appropriately about God when we fully realize and acknowledge the inadequacy of whatever we say. But that is not the whole story. And since that story will take us from the *via negativa* of Dionysius to the *via analogiae* of Aquinas, one of the former's most enthusiastic readers, it belongs to our next chapter.

---

53. See note 51 above.

five
Pseudo-Dionysius and Aquinas

How to Speak Nevertheless about God—
The Analogy of Being

Deconstruction has been described as a "generalized apophatics."[1] It reminds us how not to speak about anything at all, namely not to speak as if meaning were prior to language, as if the presence of the signified were prior to the use of the signifier,[2] making it a transcendental signified available to us outside the chain of references (differences) which language is.[3] Because negative theology is a reflection on the transcendence of God rather than on

---

1. John D. Caputo, *The Prayers and Tears of Jacques Derrida: Religion without Religion* (Bloomington: Indiana University Press, 1997), pp. 28, 32, 41, 46, 55.

2. See the discussion of Augustine's philosophy of language in ch. 4.

3. Since fully determinate meaning is always deferred in language by references not yet explicitly present to consciousness, linguistically embedded meaning is, in Heidegger's language, always a combination of unconcealment and concealment. If language games are forms of life and, as Heidegger insists, meaning is also a function of our practices, the tacit dimension, the dialectic of presence and absence is extended even further. See Hubert L. Dreyfus, "Holism and Hermeneutics," *Review of Metaphysics*, XXXIV, 1 (September 1980) and my discussion in "Hermeneutics as Epistemology," in *Overcoming Onto-theology* (New York: Fordham University Press, 2001).

the (quasi)transcendental conditions for language as such, it is a particularized apophatics. It tells us how not to speak of God, namely not to speak of God as if any images derived from our perceptual powers or any concepts derived from our intellectual powers, including the divinely authorized images and concepts of biblical revelation, were adequate to the divine reality. God is never at the disposal of our cognitive equipment.

We have seen that learning how not to speak about God can mean learning how to become silent. In the previous chapter we have focused on this dimension of Pseudo-Dionysius' thought according to which negative theology reveals the inadequacy of all human language about God in order to loosen our grip on that language (or its grip on us). Thus freed, we are prepared for the gift of loving union in the silent darkness of the cloud of unknowing. *After* we have seen the inadequacy of all cognitive acts in relation to God, we leave them *behind* and move on *beyond* them to something *higher* and *better*. This is the **successive-diachronic** mode of negative theology.

But the life of Moses is not lived at the top of Mt. Sinai, and except for rare moments of mystical ecstasy, the life of faith is lived at lower altitudes. There is an important dimension of negative theology that addresses itself to the life of faith in the cave, as it were, of language, images, and concepts. Here the task of negative theology is not to abandon the language of positive theology and lead us to silence, but to teach us how most properly to speak of God. Learning how not to speak of God means learning how to speak appropriately of God. In this **simultaneous-dialectical** mode, negative theology and positive theology are hopelessly inseparable. Dionysius "seeks to hold together affirmation and negation, similarity and dissimilarity as a dialectical way of understanding the many symbols of his tradition. A 'dissimilar similarity,' as he puts it, is *simultaneously* a similarity to be affirmed and a dissimilarity to be negated . . . affirmation and negation can never be separated entirely."[4] This dialectic involves seeing at one and the same time that "positive affirmations are *always unfitting* to the hiddenness of the inexpressible" and that "forms, even those drawn from the lowliest matter, can be used, *not unfittingly*, with regard to heavenly beings. Matter, after all, owes its subsistence to absolute beauty and keeps, throughout its earthly ranks, *some echo of intelligible beauty*" (CH 150/141A & 151–52/144B, emphasis added).

Hart relates negative theology in this dialectical mode to deconstruction and develops the thesis that while deconstruction is not negative theology, negative theology is a deconstruction of positive theology.[5] Similarly, Caputo argues that deconstruction's role in relation to negative theology is "to resituate

---

4. Paul Rorem, "The Uplifting Spirituality of Pseudo-Dionysius," *Christian Spirituality: Origins to the Twelfth Century*, ed. Bernard McGinn et al. (New York: Crossroad, 1988), pp. 136–37. The quoted phrase is from CH 148/137D.

5. Kevin Hart, *The Trespass of the Sign* (New York: Cambridge University Press, 1989), pp. 193, xi, 186, 198.

[it] *within faith*" as distinct from sight, even the "sight" of mystical darkness. It "recommits theology to the grammatological flux from which negative theology [in its diachronic mode] would take its leave" in search of "silent union."[6] But this is not a violent appropriation by deconstruction nor an obsequious attempt on the part of negative theology to pacify its critics. No doubt Dionysius, like the apostle Paul who allegedly introduced him to the Christian faith, thinks it is better to see God face to face than in a mirror dimly (1 Cor. 13:12). But given that the life of faith is lived all but entirely at the lower altitudes where we breathe the oxygen of language rather than the ether of silent union, he takes it to be a central task of theology to teach us how to speak of God.

Dionysius (and, by extension, deconstruction) has no special advice on what to say about God. The images and concepts of positive theology he discusses come from the biblical and liturgical traditions of his Christian community. He treats them as given, presupposing both divine revelation and its formulation in the *regula fidei*. His focus is not on the "what" but on the "how."[7] He says, in effect, that so far as negative theology is concerned, all the scriptural and traditional affirmations about God are appropriate *as long as we never lose sight of the way in which they are inappropriate,* namely their inadequacy. Language, even biblical language, can never mirror, master, grasp, or encompass the divine reality. The proper "how" for God talk is epistemic humility—not the Cartesian humility that admits that we do not always get it right and that even when we do we do so gradually and piecemeal, but the Kantian humility that acknowledges that, *strictly speaking,* we never get it right. Our discourse may be appropriate, but it is never adequate to the reality it intends.

As we shall see, this is not the whole story. But this first gesture of negative theology in its dialectical mode makes a decisive break with onto-theology. Like the latter, and unlike its diachronic cousin, dialectical apophaticism locates itself in those noisy regions where God talk abounds. It seeks neither to abolish nor to abate such discourse, only to abash it. But the humility it seeks to foster can only be viewed as humiliation by onto-theology, which reveals itself to be a form of pride. (Augustine would say "presumption.") For it is the nature of pride not to be able to distinguish humility from humiliation.

Let us for a moment play the role of the would-be but humiliated onto-theologian and ask this question: If we must continually confess not only what we believe but also that all of our beliefs, no matter how firmly held, always fall short of their intended reality, what is the point of our discourse? If our theological affirmations are always under erasure, if they will not enable us to bring the whole of reality to intelligible unity, if they do not arise from those mo-

---

6. Caputo, *Prayers and Tears*, pp. 6, 11.
7. In this regard there is an interesting link between Dionysius and Kierkegaard's Johannes Climacus, whose famous discussion of truth as subjectivity revolves around the distinction between the "what" and the "how." See ch. 1. n. 50.

ments of pure presence that will leave us with at least some fixed and final truths, beyond doubt and beyond further interpretation, what is our God talk good for, after all?

Dionysius welcomes the question. In his dialectical mode negation teaches epistemic humility, which in itself is a virtue. But beyond this, his answer to the question just posed points to the proper use of improper predication, a use in which the distinction between love and knowledge takes on meaning. No doubt what was said about self-transcendence in relation to the diachronic mode also applies here. Our God talk teaches us that we belong to Another and not to ourselves; this means that our love for the Beloved is not merely an erotic longing to see. What keeps that longing from lapsing into pious voyeurism are the tasks of bringing our will into conformity with the divine will and of manifesting this obedience by loving our neighbors, who are not always very loveable.

But Dionysius will emphasize another aspect of what it means to belong to Another. In a word, praise. What is our God talk good for if it doesn't provide full intelligibility and pure presence? It enables us to praise. Because "we offer worship to that which lies hidden beyond thought and beyond being," our "wise silence" is accompanied by "songs of praise" (DN 50–51/589B). Although it is secondary to the name 'Good', the name 'Being' is "rightly applied by theology to him who truly is. But I must point out that the purpose of what I have to say is not to reveal that being in its transcendence, for this is something beyond words, something unknown and wholly unrevealed. . . . What I wish to do is to sing a hymn of praise for the being-making procession of the absolute divine Source of being into the total domain of being" (DN 96/816B). What looks at first glance to be an onto-theological gesture, bringing the whole of being into relation with the Highest Being, is just the opposite. God does not come onto the scene, with our permission, to grant the full understanding human reason wishes to claim for itself. Reminding us that this is precisely what we cannot have, God enters to call us out of our preoccupation with ourselves to give the gift of praise to Another.

The theme of praise reverberates throughout the Dionysian corpus, and it has not gone unnoticed. Derrida distinguishes deconstruction from negative theology, not only because the latter begins with prayer, but also because that prayer is accompanied by encomium.[8] Louth writes, "The first thing to notice about these various theologies [of Dionysius] is that in them we learn how we can *celebrate* (*hymnein*). These theologies are not about how we can predicate qualities of God, but about how we can praise him. For [Dionysius] theology is not concerned primarily with intellectual, academic matters . . . rather it is concerned with the creature's response of praise and worship to the Love of

---

8. Derrida, "How to Avoid Speaking: Denials" in *Derrida and Negative Theology*, ed. Harold Coward and Toby Foshay (Albany: SUNY Press, 1992), pp. 81, 108, 111.

God."[9] Most succinctly, Marion says that "predication must yield to praise" when we realize that "among the divine names, none exhausts God or offers the grasp or hold of a comprehension of him."[10]

This is an important confirmation of the suggestion that negative theology, here in its dialectical mode, makes a decisive break with onto-theology. In his critique of the latter, as we have seen, Heidegger complains, "Before the *causi sui,* man can neither fall to his knees in awe nor can he play music and dance before this god" (ID 72).[11] Dionysius comes close to describing God as *causa sui.* God is regularly described as the "Cause of all existence . . . transcending all existence" (DN 50/588B). As the "absolute divine Source of being" (DN 96/816B), God is clearly a Source that has no source, an uncaused Cause. Yet in the recognition of the cognitive impotence of these descriptions, this theology bursts into songs of praise (if not dance). For, at least in its dialectical mode, praise is its primary purpose. The problem, it would seem, is not so much with the notion of *causi sui* as such, but with putting it to speculative rather than worshipful uses. When we are content to let God's being remain a "mystery" rather than a "theorem,"[12] onto-theology is replaced by doxology.[13]

If epistemic humility is a negative form of self-transcendence, praise is here its positive, flip side. On the one hand we have "I am not adequate." On the other, "God is great." How traumatic doxological self-transcendence is to the self that wishes to be the center is clear from Marcel's account of admiration, which for present purposes is interchangeable with praise or adoration. Not unimportantly, we find ourselves in the midst of an essay entitled "Belonging and Disposability," which explores what it means to belong to another and to be at another's disposal. Marcel writes,

> It is clear that the function of admirations to tear us away from ourselves and from the thoughts we have of ourselves . . . [it] can only occur in a being who is not a closed or hermetic system into which nothing new can pene-

9. Andrew Louth, *The Origins of the Christian Mystical Tradition: From Plato to Denys* (Oxford: Oxford University Press, 1981), p. 166.

10. Jean-Luc Marion, *God Without Being,* trans. Thomas A. Carlson (Chicago: University of Chicago Press, 1991), p. 106. Similarly, Catherine Pickstock argues for "the mainly *doxological* character of language. That is to say, language exists primarily, and in the end only has meaning as, the praise of the divine." *After Writing* (Oxford: Blackwell, 1998), xiii. Cf. pp. 37–49. She is not discussing negative theology directly, but she sees the claim to univocal language in Duns Scotus as fatal to a liturgical, praise-oriented understanding of language. See pp. 62–64 and 121–40. For the primacy of praise over absolute knowledge, see Jean-Yves Lacoste, "Liturgy and Kenosis," from *Expérience et Absolu,* in *The Postmodern God,* ed. Graham Ward (Oxford: Blackwell, 1997).

11. See discussion in chapter 1 above.

12. *Orthodox Spirituality,* by a monk of the Eastern Church (2nd. ed.; Crestwood, N.Y.: St. Vladimir's Seminary Press, 1978), p. 31.

13. For a contemporary attempt to do theology as doxology, see Geoffrey Wainwright, *Doxology: The Praise of God in Worship, Doctrine, and Life* (New York: Oxford University Press, 1980).

trate. . . . We should . . . study first the *refusal* to admire, then the *inability* to admire, in order to determine how both imply a basic indisposability.

Not long ago a dramatist affirmed during an interview that admiration was for him a humiliating state, which he resisted with all his force. . . . An analysis similar to the one Scheler has given of resentment should disclose that there is a burning preoccupation with self at the bottom of this suspicion, a "but what about me, what becomes of me in that case?" . . .

To affirm: admiration is a humiliating state, is the same as to treat the subject as a power existing for itself and taking itself as a center. To proclaim on the other hand, that it is an exalted state is to start from the inverse notion that the proper function of the subject is to emerge from itself and realize itself primarily in the gift of oneself . . .[14]

We can almost hear Dionysius saying, "My sentiments exactly!" The language of scripture and liturgy, and, for that matter, of philosophical theology, may be desperately inadequate to mirror or encompass the divine reality. But it is not inadequate for every purpose. In Dionysius' eyes, it is more than sufficient to provide both the incentive and the vocabulary for praise.

> *Venite adoramus.*
> *Gloria in excelsis Deo . . .*
> *Laudamus te. Benedicimus te.*
> *Adoramus te. Glorificamus te.*
> *Gratias agimus tibi propter magnam gloriam tuam.*[15]

To learn to say such words as these is surely the task of a lifetime (and perhaps of eternity as well). Such self-transcendence is not quickly accomplished. "But what about me?" is never too far beneath the surface, which means that progress is likely to be slow and relapse easy. It is the view of Dionysius, and of a significant tradition within both Eastern and Western Christianity that follows him, (1) that the kind of knowledge required by onto-theology and the metaphysics of presence is not necessary for the journey on which we learn to praise, and (2) that both the pursuit of such knowledge and the claim to have

---

14. Gabriel Marcel, *Creative Fidelity*, trans. Robert Rosthal (New York: Fordham University Press, 2002), pp. 47–49.

15. The first line, "O come let us adore him," is the refrain from the Christmas carol, "O Come All Ye Faithful." The remaining lines are from the Gloria of the Latin Mass. "Glory to God in the highest. . . . We praise you. We bless you. We adore you. We glorify you. We give you thanks for your great glory." Whereas Marion often suggests that praise replaces predication, I have argued that it always presupposes predication, without which it would be meaningless. See "Continental Philosophy of Religion," forthcoming in the *Oxford Handbook for Philosophy of Religion*, ed. William J. Wainwright. What Jean-Louis Chrétien says about prayer is equally true of praise. Noting Aristotle's claim that prayer is neither true nor false, he writes, "A demand, a supplication, a lament are not, in effect, open to truth in the same manner as a predicative proposition. But prayer always has norms that determine its rectitude, and these norms put truth into play, including the truth of the *logos apophantikos*. . . . The mere linguistic form of the demanding prayer is not enough to put out of play the question of truth." "The Wounded Word: The Phenomenology of Prayer," in Dominique Janicaud et al., *Phenomenology and the "Theological Turn": The French Debate* (New York: Fordham University Press, 2000), pp. 154–55.

achieved it, so far from being helps, are hindrances on that journey. In this way, one of the most deeply Platonic of all Christian thinkers echoes the question of Tertullian: What has Athens to do with Jerusalem?

***

We don't associate that question with Aquinas. As with Augustine, it is often assumed that as a classical theist who affirms the reality of a Highest Being who is the key to the meaning of all being, he is an onto-theologian. But, as with Augustine, he is not. Far from requiring God to be the means of rendering the whole of reality intelligible to human thought, he insists, as does Augustine, that God remains mysterious. Thus, "It is because human intelligence is not equal to the divine essence that this same divine essence surpasses our intelligence and is unknown to us: wherefore *man reaches the highest point of his knowledge about God when he knows that he knows him not*, inasmuch as he knows that that which is God transcends whatsoever he conceives of him" (DP 7.5.14, emphasis added).

In a related passage, Aquinas seems to be taking aim specifically at the totalizing[16] character of onto-theological thought.

> Creatures fail to represent their creator adequately. Consequently, through them we cannot arrive at a perfect knowledge of God. Another reason for our imperfect knowledge is the weakness (*imbecillitatem*) of our intellect. . . . It is for this reason that we are forbidden to scrutinize God's attributes overzealously in the sense of aiming at the completion [*ad finem*] of such an inquiry. . . . If we were to act thus, we would not believe anything about God unless our intellect could grasp it. We are not, however, kept from humbly investigating God's attributes, remembering that we are too weak to arrive at a perfect comprehension of Him. Consequently, Hilary writes as follows: "Even if a man who reverently seeks the infinite ways of God never reaches the end of his search, his search will always profit him." (DV 5.2.11).[17]

---

16. This postmodern buzzword is often used without any clear meaning. I use it to signify thought that claims to be ultimate rather than penultimate both "spatially," since it has a place for everything and has put everything in its place, and temporally, since it envisages no substantive future amendment.

17. Aquinas' notion of overzealous scrutiny has a surprising affinity with Nietzsche's complaint about the "*barbarizing* effects of science" because of its "unselective," "unmeasured," "indiscriminate," and "unlimited" knowledge drive. See *Philosophy and Truth: Selections from Nietzsche's Notebooks of the Early 1870's*, trans. Daniel Breazeale (Atlantic Highlands, N.J.: Humanities Press, 1990), pp. 5–9. A year after these notebook entries, Nietzsche will protest the "hypertrophy" of the logical nature in Socrates, who requires that everything be intelligible. See *The Birth of Tragedy*, Sections 12–13. He sets Lessing, who "dared to announce that he cared more for the search after truth than for truth itself" over against the "profound *illusion*" of Socrates' "unshakable faith that thought, using the threat of logic, can penetrate the deepest abysses of being . . ." See Section 15. Taking Socratic ignorance and irony into account, Kierkegaard associates Socrates

There is a dialectic of unconcealment and concealment in Aquinas, precisely because he is a practitioner of simultaneous-dialectical negative theology. Like Augustine before him and *The Cloud of Unknowing* after him, at the same time he affirms this or that about God he denies the epistemic adequacy of the predication to its subject. In spite of his Aristotelian epistemology, he has deep roots in the Christian neoplatonism and is an admirer and student of Pseudo-Dionysius. It is of no small import in the present context that his commentary on Dionysius is not on *The Mystical Theology*, which presents a successive-diachronic apophaticism, but on *The Divine Names*, in which Dionysius develops his simultaneous-dialectical negative theology. Aquinas belongs to a tradition for which "God must be deemed unknowable . . . to assure the required transcendence, while [at the same time] allowing us to have some notion of what it is we are referring to in addressing 'the Holy One,' 'our Father,' or 'Allah Akbar' " and for which articulating this dialectical tension is the proper task of philosophical theology.[18]

It is well known that Aquinas articulates this tension in his doctrine of analogy. But before we turn to his account of divine names, his epistemology of God talk, we need to look at his understanding of creation, and this for two reasons. First, as Josef Pieper writes, "there is a fundamental idea by which almost all the basic concepts of [Aquinas'] vision of the world are determined: the idea of creation, or more precisely, the notion that nothing exists which is not *creatura*, except the Creator Himself; and in addition, that this createdness determines entirely and all-pervasively the inner structure of the creature." This notion shapes "the interior structure of *nearly all* the basic concepts in St. Thomas' philosophy of Being."[19] The doctrine of analogy is no exception to this general rule.

But we have an equally pressing reason for looking at the ontology of creation before turning to the epistemology of analogy. We have begun our exploration of divine transcendence at the usual place, the debate between pantheism and theism over "cosmological" transcendence. We have looked at two pantheistic systems, have found them to be paradigmatically onto-theological, and have explored the implications of such theories for human self-transcendence. Turning to classical theism, I have argued that Augustine's insistence on the incomprehensibility of God makes a clear break with the onto-theological project as described by Heidegger (and Derrida), that this involves an epistemic self-transcendence for us that is not to be found in

---

with Lessing when he praises this same move by the latter, adding, "Only he has style who is never finished." *Concluding Unscientific Postscript*, Part II, Section I, Chapter II.

18. David B. Burrell, C.S.C., *Knowing the Unknowable God: Ibn-Sina, Maimonides, Aquinas* (Notre Dame, Ind.: University of Notre Dame Press, 1986), p. 2.

19. Josef Pieper, *The Silence of St. Thomas: Three Essays*, trans. John Murray, S.J., and Daniel O'Connor (Chicago: Henry Regnery, 1965), pp. 47–48.

Spinoza and Hegel, and that the dialectical apophaticism of Dionysius' *The Divine Names* articulates this epistemic self-transcendence for a tradition that precedes him in thinkers like the Cappadocians and Augustine and follows him in thinkers like Aquinas. But I have postponed until now consideration of the creationist ontology that separates classical theism from all forms of pantheism. That could easily enough have been done with Augustine, but because Aquinas is so much more systematic in his presentation and because the basic shape of his account of God's relation to the world is generically theistic and not specifically Thomistic, I will present his account of creation (1) as the way theism distinguishes itself from pantheism and (2) as the presupposition of theistic thought on epistemic and ethical matters.

David Burrell calls our attention to Aquinas' special concern, in affirming creation, to distinguish it from the emanationist thinking to be found among such Islamic philosophers as Alfarabi and Avicenna (Ibn-Sina).[20] Of course he doesn't speak of pantheism by name, but his concern is that by making the world come from God necessarily or inevitably, these philosophers compromise divine transcendence. And, although he does not speak of onto-theology, he fears the emanationist scheme has unfortunate epistemic consequences. Thus he has Avicenna in mind when he distinguishes himself from those whose philosophical theology aspires "to have delineated in [the soul] the entire order and causes of the universe" (DV 2.2), or, in other words, to be the locus of the simultaneously whole and perfect possession of unlimited intelligibility.[21]

Occasionally Aquinas will use emanationist language, showing how deeply neoplatonic he is. Thus ST 1.45.1 concerns "The Mode of Emanation of Things from the First Principle." But when he speaks of "the emanation of all being from the universal cause, which is God," he notes that "this emanation we designate by the name of *creation*," and this in an article devoted to affirming creation *ex nihilo*. The world is created neither out of the divine substance nor from a pregiven and possibly recalcitrant matter.

It is crucial to Aquinas, in distinguishing creation from what we might call pantheistic interpretations of emanation, that "the emanation of things from the first principle" occurs not of necessity but by virtue of a free act. Thus he affirms that "God wills the being of His own goodness necessarily, even as we will our own happiness necessarily," but he denies that God wills "things other

---

20. See Burrell, *Knowing* and *Freedom and Creation in Three Traditions* (Notre Dame, Ind.: University of Notre Dame Press, 1993). On Spinoza's relation to these two philosophers, see Harry Austryn Wolfson, *The Philosophy of Spinoza* (New York: Meridian Books, 1958).

21. I have paraphrased Boethius' definition of eternity from *The Consolation of Philosophy* (V, Prose 6) which Aquinas affirms of God (ST 1.10.1) in order to highlight the linkage between the onto-theological project as a form of totalizing thinking and what Derrida calls the metaphysics of presence, signifying both presence as opposed to absence and present as opposed to past and future.

than Himself" in this way. For "we do not will necessarily those things without which the end is attainable, such as a horse for a stroll . . . since *the goodness of God is perfect and can exist without other things . . .* it follows that for Him to will things other than Himself is not absolutely necessary" (ST 1.19.3; cf. 1.46.1, emphasis added).

This is the crucial differentiation of classical theism from pantheism. In neoplatonic contexts, emanation is often described in terms of the radiation of heat and light from a fire, such as the sun.[22] The fire is the cause of the heat and light and they proceed from their source necessarily in a very specific sense. It is not possible to have the fire without the heat and light. Accordingly, for Plotinus it is not possible to have the One without the many just as for Spinoza and Hegel it is not possible to have God without the world.

But that is just the implication Aquinas wants to deny. Creation did not have to occur; it is no more necessary to God than a horse is necessary for a stroll. Without ever creating a world, God could be God. That is what it means to say that God is "outside" the world, not that God is not present within the world, but that God's existence does not require the world's. There is "no necessity in the divine will for willing this or that concerning a creature. *Nor is there any necessity in it as regards the whole of creation, since the divine good-ness is perfect in itself, and would be so even though no creature existed*" (DV 23.4, emphasis added).

We will necessarily all those things that it belongs to our essence to will, and in that sense we will them naturally, by virtue of our nature. So Aquinas also affirms the contingency of creation by denying that God has a natural inclination to create. It is "not natural to God to will any of those other things that He does not will necessarily; and yet it is not unnatural or contrary to His nature, but voluntary" (ST 1.19.3.3).[23]

A compatibilist might try to introduce necessity into creation by treating reasons for voluntary acts as causes. But Aquinas insists that the divine will has no cause at all. God is, to be sure, a purposive, rational agent, which means that in creation God's willing has a this-for-the-sake-of-that, means-end struc-ture. But since in God means and end are willed together, "in Him, to will an end is not the cause of His willing the means" (ST 1.19.5).

Still another way to affirm that "whatever [God] wills to be concerning creatures He does not will from necessity," is to note that "God's action is purely liberal, because nothing accrues to Him from what He wills or does regarding any creature" (DV 23.4) Such a claim is not without its problems, but its purpose is clear: to deny that God acts erotically, out of need, and in that sense of necessity. Rather, "the goodness of God is perfect and can exist with-

---

22. See Plotinus, *Enneads*, IV.8.4 and V.1.6.
23. Where Aquinas says voluntary, Burrell says intentional. See *Knowing*, pp. 2, 15, 73, 99. The latter term is nicely ambiguous, signifying both the intentionality of consciousness as conscious-ness of . . . and the intentionality of agency, as in "he did it on purpose."

out other things, inasmuch as no perfection can accrue to Him from them" (ST 1.19.3; cf. 1.32.1.3).[24]

In his account of Aquinas' attempt to distinguish creation from necessary emanation, Burrell places great emphasis on "the distinction"[25] between God and creatures, and he locates this distinction in Aquinas' claim that God's essence and being are the same, that it is God's essence or nature to exist (ST 1.3.4; DEE 89–91). This is the divine simplicity, for God is not only not composed of form and matter, or of act and potency, but not even of essence and existence. For all creatures, by contrast, essence and existence are separate in the sense that they embody an essence that might not have become actual or instantiated.

Clearly this distinction is sufficient to distinguish God from all created beings. Burrell is right to claim that it exhibits God's uniqueness.[26] But just as clearly, it is not sufficient to distinguish theistic creation from pantheistic emanation. For, to begin with, it is with the very Avicenna from whose emanationism Aquinas seeks to distinguish his doctrine of creation that this distinction between God and creatures arises, and Burrell himself notes that it is not sufficient to guide Avicenna away from necessary emanation.[27] We can perhaps see this more clearly by recalling that for Spinoza and for Hegel it is the essence of God to exist. Each defends a version of the ontological argument that makes this clear.[28] But both deny creation in any sense Aquinas or Augustine would recognize.

It may be, as Burrell suggests, that on the emanationist scheme of Alfarabi and Avicenna, "there can be no adequate distinction between such a [neoplatonic] One and all that necessarily emanates from it."[29] But everything hangs on "adequate," for the pantheist can surely distinguish God from the world, just as we can distinguish the heat and light, which are here, from the fire, which is there. Spinoza distinguishes substance from its modes just as Hegel distinguishes the Idea from its actualization (*Verwirklichung*).

It is surely true that in the act of creation by which God gives to all creatures the existence they do not have from themselves, God is "intimately

---

24. On this point Burrell speaks of creation as a "gratuitous" act. See *Freedom*, pp. 5, 8, 12. Quoting Karl Barth, he calls it an act of "free love" (p. 20). Idit Dobbs-Weinstein writes that if the first cause operates "only as the result of the eternal necessity of (its) nature and only out of coexisting eternal entities, or if the divinity is the range of necessary natural forces, the relations between the divine and the world of change would, at best, be a relation of an ordering principle to its consequences." This would require "that the first cause be indifferent to this world." She is speaking of Aristotle, but might well have been speaking of Plotinus, Spinoza, or Hegel. See *Maimonides and St. Thomas on the Limits of Reason* (Albany: SUNY Press, 1995), p. 9.
25. Burrell is following Robert Sokolowski in using this term in this way. See *Freedom*, p. 185.
26. See Burrell, *Knowing*, pp. 64–65.
27. See Burrell, *Knowing*, pp. 19, 22, 76, 94.
28. Aquinas rejects the argument for epistemic rather than ontological reasons. If we could apprehend the divine essence (but we can't), the argument would be sound for us. See ST 1.2.1.
29. See Burrell, *Freedom*, p. 13.

present" to each.[30] But Spinoza and Hegel can say the same. God as *natura naturans* is intimately present to each finite mode that makes up *natura naturata*, and the Idea is intimately present to each part of nature and history in and through which it actualizes itself. Of course, these last two instances are far from what Augustine or Aquinas have in mind when they speak of divine providence.

The idea that God is a necessary being, that God's essence is to exist, that *esse* and *essentia* are the same in God is common property to theists and pantheists. It has to be qualified in a certain way for it to do the work Aquinas wants it to do. Beyond specifying the uniqueness of God, it needs to become part of a conceptual scheme in which, as indicated above, God and the world are not merely distinguished but asymmetrically separable, which means, simply, that while there cannot be the world without God, there can be God without the world. It is this to which Aquinas points in his insistence that creation is a free and not a necessary act.

Aquinas sometimes uses strange language when talking about this asymmetry. He says that creatures have a real relation to God, but that God is related to creatures "in our idea only" (ST 1.6.2.1; cf. 1.13.7).[31] But the example he gives from the world of creatures makes his meaning clear. Cognition, whether sensible or intellectual, has a real relation to its objects, but not vice versa. This is because knowledge is dependent on its objects but not vice versa. They belong to different orders in such a way that the relation of knowledge to its object is essential or internal to that knowledge, but what we would call the relation of the object to that knowledge is not essential or internal to that object. Where we might distinguish internal from external relations, Aquinas distinguishes real relations from relations in idea.

Similarly, he agrees with Dionysius, who says that while creatures are similar to God, God is not similar to them. "For what is made in imitation of something, if it imitates it . . . can be said to be like it. . . . The opposite, however is not true; for a man is not said to be similar to his image but vice versa" (DV 2.11.1).

If we were to focus only on the question of dependence or similarity, Spinoza and Hegel might well be able to adopt this usage, however awkward. For just as there is a uniqueness of God in their systems, so there is an asymmetrical relation between God and the world, especially in terms of dependence, and perhaps in terms of some kind of similarity.

But Aquinas' examples go beyond this in a way that clearly matches his intention. The asymmetries are existential. In the world of creatures, the object can exist without the knowing, and the man can exist without his image

---

30. See Burrell, *Knowing*, pp. 94–95.

31. In "Temporality and Finitism in Hartshorne's Theism," *The Review of Metaphysics*, XIX, 3 (March 1966), I have argued that a major objection posed by Hartshorne's "neoclassical" theism to classical theism rests on a misunderstanding of what Aquinas is saying here.

(portrait, photograph). But the reverse is not true. The crucial asymmetry is the one in which what is causally and archetypically first does not require for its actuality that which is derivative and secondary. Aquinas expresses this by saying that the two belong to different orders, one of which is ordered to the other. Thus the proper objects of sense and intellect have no real relation to sensible and intellectual cognition, but in such cognitions "a real relation exists, because they are ordered either to the knowledge or to the sensible perception of things; whereas the things looked at in themselves are *outside* this order." Similarly, since "God is *outside* the whole order of creation, and all creatures are ordered to Him, and not conversely, it is manifest that creatures are really related to God Himself; whereas in God there is no real relation to creatures, but a relation only in idea" (ST 1.13.7, emphasis added).

This is what it means to affirm God's transcendence by saying that God is "outside" the world.[32] It is to affirm the asymmetry of God and the world as an existential asymmetry. "Whatever things are so related to one another that one is a cause of the other's existence, the one which is the cause can have existence without the other, but not conversely" (DEE 72). By affirming an *asymmetry* in which God's *actuality* does not require that of the world, theism takes God and the world to be not merely distinguishable but separable. And thereby it distinguishes itself from pantheism.

In emphasizing the independent *actuality* of God, Aquinas often sounds as if it were Spinoza and Hegel and not just Alfarabi and Avicenna he has in mind. When we say that God is existence itself (*ipsum esse*) we should not think "that God is that universal existence whereby each and every thing formally exists. For the existence which God is, is such that no addition can be made to it. Whence by virtue of its purity it is *an existence distinct from every existence*" (DEE 90, emphasis added). If, following Hegel, Aquinas were to call his account of God before the creation of the world his Logic, it would already belong to his *realphilosophie*. We would not have to wait for a philosophy of nature or a philosophy of the human spirit to get the actuality of the self-realizing Idea.

Just as little as God is the existence of finite things is God their essence. Thus "God is in all things, not, indeed, as part of their essence, nor as an accident, but as an agent is present to that upon which it acts" (ST 1.8.1; cf. DP 3.7). As the essence of things God would require existence in order to be actual. And even if existence belongs to the essence of God and does not come to it from without but is self-generated, so to speak, if God were but the essence of things that existence would occur only in finite things. God's actuality would be the world of nature and of finite spirit, which is just how it turns out for Spinoza and Hegel.

---

32. N.B. We have just seen that this God who is "outside" the order of creation is "intimately present" to all creatures. We shall shortly see more fully that Aquinas spells this out in terms of knowledge and love as well as in causal terms.

Similarly, God is not the formal principle of all things (ST 1.3.8). If God were the form of finite things, in the Aristotelian sense of an inner, shaping force and not merely an outward, visible shape, it would only be in conjunction with the matter of those things that God would be actual. So it is not surprising that Aquinas simultaneously denies that God is the world-soul, as if the world were God's body.[33] For Spinoza extension is as much an attribute of God as thought, so that it would not be unnatural to speak of the world as the body of God, just as finite minds are the divine thought. Heine associates Spinoza with Schelling's Philosophy of Nature, which teaches "the eternal parallelism that exists between spirit and matter . . . what Spinoza calls thought and extension." For these pantheisms, God "is matter as well as spirit, both are equally divine, and he that insults the sanctity of matter is as impious as he that sins against the Holy Ghost."[34] For Hegel, too, nature is the first actualization of the Idea, which functions as the formal principle of things, their categoreal structure.

We have seen that for Spinoza God is thought as the unconscious power that produces thinkers and that for Hegel God is personal as the impersonal force that generates finite persons. Aquinas explicitly repudiates this kind of thinking, and in so doing emphasizes in still another way the independent actuality of God. He repudiates the view of Alain of Lille that when we call God good we mean that God is the cause of goodness in the created world. On this assumption there would be no reason not to call God slimy or red, for God is also the cause of slime and redness. Moreover, such a view goes "against the intention of those who speak of God," for they mean to attribute goodness to God substantially. And this can be done, for such a perfection, though we know it only from creatures and thus imperfectly, pre-exists in God in a higher way (*modum altiorem*). "Hence it does not follow that God is good because He causes goodness; but rather, on the contrary, He causes goodness in things because He is good" (ST 1.13.2; cf 1.13.6).[35] We shall return to the epistemology of such predication, but for now the point is clear: God is an independently actual goodness.

Aquinas extends this analysis to God's knowledge, to God's will, and to God's love, as a special form of will. Aquinas states explicitly that knowledge

---

33. Aquinas cross-references Augustine's similar denial in *The City of God*, VII.7. There Augustine attributes to Varro, his *bête noire*, the view that "God is the soul of the world, which the Greeks call the *cosmos*, and that this world itself is . . . by virtue of its soul, even though it too consists of soul and body."

34. Heinrich Heine, *Religion and Philosophy in Germany*, trans. John Snodgrass (Boston: Beacon Press, 1959), pp. 73–74. Heine proceeds to make it clear that by matter he primarily means the body and he rails against Jewish and Christian "spiritualism."

35. In the latter passage the perfections pre-exist in God *eminentius*. The divine simplicity is no barrier to God's possessing perfections other than existence. For "he has these perfections in a more excellent way than all things because in him they are one. . . . God has all these perfections in his existence itself" (DEE 91).

and will are "immanent" to God and are properly discussed before turning to "the power of God, which is taken to be the principle of the divine operation as proceeding to an exterior effect" (Prologue to ST 1.14). In other words, we are talking about God before the creation of the world. We don't attribute knowledge to God merely as the cause of our knowledge. Rather "because the nature of God is to have knowledge, He communicates knowledge to us, and not the other way about" (DV 2.1). "In God there exists the most perfect knowledge" (ST 1.14.1). The divine intellect understands the divine essence and through it all creatures that in some manner imitate it (ST 1.14.2; DV 1.7, 2.11). "The knowledge of God is the cause of things" (ST 1.14.8). Without any assistance from the world, God is an actual knower.

Since will and intellect belong together just as do sense and appetite, "[t]here is will in God, just as there is intellect" (ST 1.19.1). "God wills not only Himself, but also things other than Himself . . . as it befits the divine goodness that other things should be partakers therein" (ST 1.19.2). "God cannot will Himself not to be good" and hence wills the divine goodness of necessity. But "there is no necessity in the divine will for willing this or that concerning a creature. Nor is there any necessity in it as regards the whole of creation" (DV 23.4). Thus "creatures do not proceed from God through necessity *but through a free act of will*" (DV 23.4.6). This freedom of the will is to be identified as free choice (*liberum arbitrium*). God does not will creatures of necessity "because His goodness has no need of the things which are ordained to it, and the manifestation of that goodness can suitably take place in a number of different ways. There remains for Him, then, a judgment free to will this or that, just as there is in us. On this account it must be said that free choice is found in God" (DV 24.3; cf. ST 1.19.10).[36]

For Aquinas God, before the creation of the world, is an actual goodness, an actual knower, and an actual chooser. Finally, God is also an actual lover.[37] "We must needs assert that in God there is love . . ." Just as will is the natural accompaniment of intellect, so "love is naturally the first act of will" (ST 1.20.1). Divine love is not a passion, since it is not an act of sensitive appetite rooted in bodily changes. It is rather an act of intellective appetite (ST 1.20.1.1). When "anyone loves another, he wills good to that other. Thus he puts the other, as it were, in the place of himself, and regards the good done to

---

36. Given Aquinas' unequivocal attribution of free choice to God, it is puzzling why David Burrell is allergic to "the contemporary presumption that freedom is enshrined in choosing" and wishes to define divine freedom in terms of gratuity "so it need not involve *choice* . . . except quite secondarily." And given that Aquinas, in affirming free choice of God, specifically notes that divine goodness can be manifested in creation "in a number of different ways," it is puzzling that Burrell should be so skittish about possible worlds talk in connection with God and creation. In these moments Burrell's God sounds more Leibnizian than Thomist. See *Freedom*, pp. 8, 12, 33–35, and 43–48.

37. Finally only for the present context. After Question XX on God's love, Aquinas proceeds to Question XXI on the justice and mercy of God. This trio belongs to God's will absolutely.

him as done to himself. So far love is a binding force. . . . And in this way too the divine love is a binding force, inasmuch as God wills good to others" (ST 1.20.1.3).

Like the God of Augustine, the God of Aquinas is a personal creator. This God is not only the First Cause of the world of finite things; this God is an actual being who knows and loves all creatures (ST 1.20.2). The freedom of creation and the personal character of the Creator as knower and lover sharply demarcate theism from emanationist pantheism in all its forms. No doubt being dependent for one's existence on such a Creator radically undermines human aspirations toward autonomy, and we will shortly be examining the epistemic and ethical implications of this fact. The cosmological transcendence of the God of theism takes us beyond cosmological categories. But because God is a loving God, the relationship cannot be "merely *heteronomous*." By calling attention to the close link between covenant and creation in ancient Hebrew thought, Burrell reminds us of the biblical background to Aquinas' view that creation is not just about causality but above all about love.[38]

***

I have already argued that in Augustine we have a clear and by no means peripheral case of a classical theist who makes a decisive break with the onto-theological project by insisting that we cannot adequately describe God. The whole of being cannot be rendered fully intelligible to our understanding because the Highest Being, who is the key to the meaning of the whole of being, exceeds our powers of comprehension. It is mystery, we might say, all the way up. In this context, theology does not lose contact with the life of worship, but is tightly linked to prayer and praise (and love of neighbor, about which Heidegger expresses no concern).

Having paused long enough to notice how Aquinas most explicitly articulates the ways in which classical theism distinguishes itself from pantheistic emanationism, I now turn to his agreement with Augustine about the limits to our knowledge of God. Not agreement about the details, to be sure, for Aquinas spells them out in Aristotelian terms, but agreement in substance, for Aquinas is as emphatic as Augustine that God exceeds our conceptual grasp.

The argument is very direct. In the first place, essence is the principle of intelligibility. For "whatever can in any way be grasped by the intellect is called a nature. For a real thing is not intelligible except through its definition and essence" (DEE 9).[39] Aquinas uses a series of interchangeable terms to signify this principle of intelligibility: essence (*essentia, substantia*), definition (*defi-*

38. See Burrell, *Freedom*, pp. 17–19, 21–22, and 56–57.
39. See DV 1.12, where Aquinas parses *intelligere*, to understand, as *intus legere*, "to read what is inside a thing," adding that "the intellect alone penetrates to the interior and to the essence of a thing." Cf. DV 15.1.

nitio), quiddity (*quidditas*), what something was to be (*quod quid erat esse*, Aristotle's τὸ τί ἦν εἶναι), form (*forma*), and nature (*natura*) (DEE 5–11).

Secondly, the essences which make up our conceptual vocabulary are drawn from corporeal substances. This is the Aristotelian doctrine of knowledge via the immaterial reception of the forms into the intellect. The senses provide the phantasm from which the active intellect abstracts the essential form. This is the meaning of the Aristotelian doctrine that the knower becomes, in a way, the known.[40] For the very same form that is in the thing is also in the intellect. This identity is not numerical, of course, but qualitative. The same redness that informs the apple informs the intellect.

This is also the Thomistic doctrine that "the thing known is in the knower according to the mode of the knower" (ST 1.12.4; cf. DV 1.2). It is for this reason that in this life, while "it has its being in corporeal matter," the soul "knows naturally only what has a form in matter, or what can be known by such a form" (ST 1.12.11).

But, thirdly, "the knowledge of God by means of any created likeness is not the vision of His essence," so the answer to the question "whether anyone in this life can see the essence of God?" is a resounding no (ST 1.12.11). Aquinas never tires of reminding us that "in this life we cannot know God by means of that form which is identical with the divine essence."[41] This is true not only for the knowledge gained by natural reason but also that given by grace in the form of divine revelation. While this knowledge takes us beyond what reason alone can attain, in it we are still "united to Him as to one unknown" (ST 1.12.13.1). God simply doesn't fit into our cognitive apparatus, for "what is supremely knowable in itself may not be knowable to a particular intellect, because of the excess of the intelligible object above the intellect; as, for example, the sun, which is supremely visible, cannot be seen by the bat by reason of its excess of light" (ST 1.12.1).[42]

But truth is defined as the *adaequatio rei et intellectus* (DV 1.1; ST 1.16.1).

---

40. At ST 1.16.4 Aquinas quotes *De Anima* 431b 21 as saying that "the soul is in some manner all things." In his commentary, Aquinas explains that "one is in a way all things, inasmuch as one's soul is receptive of all forms" (CDA 3.13.790, p. 391). For a fuller treatment of Aquinas' general epistemology, see the essays by Norman Kretzmann and Scott MacDonald in *The Cambridge Companion to Aquinas*, ed. Norman Kretzmann and Eleonore Stump (New York: Cambridge University Press, 1993). For a detailed analysis of Aquinas' Aristotelian "empiricism" that has surprisingly Hegelian overtones, see Karl Rahner's commentary on ST 1.84.7, *Spirit in the World*, trans. William Dych, S.J. (New York: Continuum, 1994).

41. John F. Wippel, "Quidditative Knowledge of God," in *Metaphysical Themes in Thomas Aquinas* (Washington, D.C.: Catholic University of America Press, 1984), p. 217. Wippel gives a helpful overview from four works spread across Aquinas' authorship: the commentary on the *De Trinitate* of Boethius, *Summa Contra Gentiles*, *De Potentia Dei*, and *Summa Theologiae*. He could easily have extended the list to include *De Veritate* and other works.

42. Hence the concluding words of the hymn, "Immortal, Invisible, God Only Wise"—

all laud we would render, O help us to see
'tis only the splendor of light hideth thee.

Adaequatio is sometimes simply transliterated as adequation, but it is often translated as the conformity or equality of thing and intellect. *Ad-aequatio* is built on *aequatio*, a making equal. It is a mathematical metaphor suggesting an equation in which what is on one side is exactly the same (quantity) as what is on the other. In this case it is the form in the thing and the form in the intellect that are exactly the same in a non-quantitative sense. The notion of knowledge as a mirror image of the world is a twin concept.[43] Aquinas uses a number of terms interchangeably with *adaequatio*: *convenientia, assimilatio, correspondentia*, and *conformatio*. This is the language in which the correspondence theory of truth is affirmed.

Accordingly, truth is found primarily in judgments, and "the judgment is said to be true when it conforms (*adaequatur*) to the external reality" (DV 1.3). Thus, according to Aristotle, "truth is had when one affirms that 'to be which is, and not to be which is not'" (DV 1.1).[44] But if the concepts which make up the subject and predicate of the judgment are not adequate to the reality they intend, the judgments which employ them cannot be adequate to the reality they intend. They will fail to correspond and to conform. The form in the intellect will not be the same as the form in the external reality. Since in this life we cannot see the essence of God, this will always be true of our predications of God, which in turn will always be, *strictly speaking*, false. For "it is impossible to find any created species which is adequate to represent [the divine essence]" (DV 10.11; cf. 2.1). Consequently, "our intellect understands in one way, and things are in another" (ST 1.13.12.3).

Given the importance of the distinction between Creator and creature for Aquinas, it might seem as if he is claiming that a finite, created intellect cannot grasp the essence of God. But this would be heresy, on his view, for it would deny the possibility of our highest beatitude, the beatific vision (ST 1.12.1; DV 8.1). It is in this life that we cannot see the essence of God. That will change in the life to come. Before that the only exception is the state of rapture, a temporary foretaste of glory divine such as was granted to Moses and Paul.[45] In the latter case we must be "withdrawn completely from the activity of the senses . . . completely separated from mortal flesh" and therefore "not altogether in this life" (DV 10.11; cf. 13.1, 13.3, and ST 1.12.11).

In either case, there are two qualifications to notice. First, when a created intellect sees the essence of God it is not by its natural powers. Whether in rapture or in the life to come, it is a miracle, a supernatural infusion of light that is the work of grace and not of nature (ST 1.12.4–5 and 11; DV 8.3, 10.11, 13.1–2). Second, and more important in the present context, even when a created intellect sees the divine essence, it does not comprehend God (ST

---

43. See Richard Rorty, *Philosophy and the Mirror of Nature* (Princeton, N.J.: Princeton University Press, 1979).
44. The reference is to Aristotle, *Metaphysics* IV, 7 (1011b 27).
45. For extended discussion of rapture, see ST 2.2.175 and DV 13.

1.12.1.3). For when "the thing known exceeds its grasp, then the knowing power falls short of comprehension" (DV 8.2). To comprehend God would be to know God perfectly and infinitely (ST 1.12.7; cf. DV 8.2). But there is no one "who understands so perfectly that it is impossible to devise another who understands more perfectly, except God, who understands everything with infinite clarity" (DV 18.1).[46]

Another way to define comprehension would be with the spatial metaphor of inclusion. But being infinite, the divine being cannot be included in any finite being (ST 1.12.7.1; cf. DV 8.2). But the inability to include must not be thought quantitatively, as if we might comprehend some but not all of God. "God is called incomprehensible not because anything of Him is not seen, but because He is not seen as perfectly as He is capable of being seen" (ST 1.12.7.2; cf. DV 8.2).

* * *

In this life we have no concepts with which to think about God other than those which are inadequate to the divine being. Even in the life to come, when the blessed see the very essence of God, they will not comprehend God, but only grasp imperfectly that which exceeds their grasp. This is a very strong apophaticism, and if it were the whole story, it would represent a diachronic negative theology in which all God talk belongs to the *via negativa*, which is followed by silence. This would be the full meaning of Aquinas' claim that "we cannot know what God is, but rather what He is not" (Prologue to ST 1.3).

But from the strong claim that God cannot be comprehended by a created intellect, even when enabled by supernatural grace to see the divine essence, Aquinas refuses to draw the conclusion that God "cannot be known at all" (ST 1:12.1.3). This refusal occurs in Question XII, entitled "How God Is Known by Us," and Aquinas regularly assumes both that it is appropriate to assign some predicates of God and that in doing so we have a certain kind of knowledge, however imperfect. What we should learn from Dionysius is not "that [God] cannot be known at all, but that He transcends all knowledge; which means that He is not comprehended" (ST 1.12.1.3). Aquinas tries to do justice to both concealment and unconcealment in his simultaneous-dialectical apophaticism, drawing on *The Divine Names* rather than just *The Mystical Theology*. We can now see how for three different kinds of theological predication, the formula still holds good that we know what God is not rather than what God is. None of the three is an adequate expression of the divine essence.

Case #1—God is simple. The statement that "we cannot know what God is, but rather what He is not" comes in the Prologue to ST 1.3. It comes immediately after Question Two on the existence of God in which the famous five ways are presented, and it introduces Questions III–XI in which it is

---

46. Cf. the similar views of Gregory of Nyssa and Gregory Palamas, discussed in chapter 4 above.

"shown how God is not, by removing from Him whatever does not befit Him . . ." It is never appropriate to predicate of God any "perfection" that essentially involves some imperfection, moral or ontological. Thus we ought not to say that God is evil or finite. But it is appropriate to deny such imperfections of God. The predicates that do so are negative rather than positive. Thus divine simplicity signifies that God is not composite. Unlike all creatures except the angelic intelligences, God is not composed of form and matter. And unlike even the angels, God is not composed of potentiality and actuality, essence and existence. The predicates perfection/goodness, infinity, immortality/eternity, and unity similarly signify in this negative fashion. By denying or removing what is seen to be inappropriate to God, they tell us what God is not in a very straightforward way.

There are, however, two other modes of predication, metaphorical and analogical, that are both appropriate and affirmative. These are what makes Aquinas' negative theology dialectical.

Case #2—God is a lion. For Aquinas this is a paradigm case of metaphorical predication. "It is befitting Holy Scripture to put forward divine and spiritual truths by means of comparisons with material things . . . [since] it is natural to man to attain to intellectual truths through sensible things" (ST 1.1.9).[47] What is distinctive about metaphorical predicates is that they essentially signify some imperfection. Thus 'lion' signifies being a material being subject to corruption, and 'anger' signifies both passivity and change (ST 1.13.3.1, 1.20.1.2; DV 2.1 and 11). For this reason they apply primarily to creatures (ST 1.13.6). But while 'lion' does not apply "properly" to God, it may be predicated "through likeness . . . to those who share in something of the lion's nature, as for instance courage, or strength" (ST 1.13.9).[48] Thus 'lion' is an appropriate metaphor for God, for God is strong.

There is an obvious dialectic of positive and negative here, of unconcealment and concealment. To speak of God metaphorically as a lion is to say that God is both like and unlike (N.B. not just unlike) a lion. Thus Aquinas quotes Dionysius: "We cannot be enlightened by the divine rays except they be hidden within the covering of many sacred veils" (ST 1.1.9).[49] Enlightenment and hiddenness are inextricably united.

But questions arise. If God is "like" a lion in being strong, what about "God is strong"? Is that also metaphorical predication? And what about the claim that creatures are similar to God but not vice versa? Aquinas answers these questions in his theory of analogical predication, which he sharply distinguishes from metaphor. Thus

---

47. For a similar theme in Calvin, see Ford Lewis Battles, "God Was Accommodating Himself to Human Capacity," in *Readings in Calvin's Theology*, ed. Donald K. McKim (Grand Rapids, Mich.: Baker Book House, 1984).

48. Strictly speaking, of course, it is the lion who shares something of God's nature.

49. The quotation is from *The Celestial Hierarchy*, which belongs with *The Divine Names* rather than with *The Mystical Theology*.

Case #3—God is love. Aquinas holds that we can form affirmative propositions about God (ST 1.13.12) and that the names or predicates we use in doing so are used substantially and properly (ST 1.13.2–3). But the alternative to proper is metaphorical, so as long as we don't assume that 'literal' means 'univocal' we can translate 'proper' (*proprie*) as 'literal'. For Aquinas affirms that positive predicates that are applied to God substantively and properly are used neither univocally nor equivocally but analogously. Among such predicates we find not only 'goodness',[50] 'being', and 'life', but also the trio with which we have seen him distinguish his theism most emphatically from all forms of pantheism, namely actual 'knowledge', 'will', and 'love'. He is most emphatic that we do not speak metaphorically when we attribute love to God (ST 1.20.1.2).

To see how this works we need to see how analogical and metaphorical predication differ, given that the basic meaning is in both cases affirmative and takes us beyond any simple *via negativa*. Unlike metaphorical predicates, analogical predicates do not contain or imply any imperfection in their essential meaning (ST 1:13.4.1, 1.20.1.2). For this reason, while the former are said to apply primarily to creatures, the latter apply primarily to God. Aquinas often uses comparative terms "higher" (*altior*) and "more eminently" (*eminentior*) to signify how these perfections pre-exist in God. But in one case he runs the whole gamut from "excellently" (*excellenter*) to "more excellently" (*excellentior*) to "most excellent" (*excellentissimus*) (ST 1.13.2–3, 5; DEE, 91; and ST 1.6.2).

These predicates apply secondarily to creatures by virtue of their likeness to God. They are not similar as having the same form or belonging to the same order. So the predicates cannot be applied univocally to God and to creatures (ST 1.4.3). But the latter do participate in the divine exemplar "by way of a certain assimilation, although distantly and defectively" (ST 1.6.4). They are like God "in a measure that falls short" (ST 1.13.5)[51] because "the likeness of the creature to God is imperfect" (ST 1.13.5.2).

This ontological relation of similarity between God and creatures is an asymmetrical relation, as we have seen above. It will be noticed in the previous paragraph that it is creatures who are like God and not vice versa. Aquinas now translates this asymmetry as analogy. Earlier we saw that "a man is not said to be similar to his image but vice versa" (DV 2.11.1). Now we find that " 'animal' is predicated of a true animal and the picture of an animal not equivocally but

---

50. It is not immediately obvious why 'goodness' shows up in both the first and third category of names of God.

51. In this passage Aquinas subsumes the names of God under the analogy of proportion. The analogy of proper proportionality which was prominent in *De Veritate* has disappeared. This technical distinction does not affect the present analysis. For the specifics, see George P. Klubertanz, S.J., *St. Thomas Aquinas on Analogy* (Chicago: Loyola University Press, 1960), p. 27. Cf. John F. Wippel, "Metaphysics," in *The Cambridge Companion to Aquinas*, p. 92.

analogously" (ST 1.13.10.4). The picture does participate in its exemplar, however distantly, defectively, and imperfectly.

It is precisely on these points that Aquinas breaks with Maimonides,[52] who affirms that there is "no relation" and thus "no similarity" between God and creatures. Accordingly, "there is, in no way or sense, anything common to the attributes predicated of God and those used in reference to ourselves; they have only the same names and nothing else is common to them" (I, 56). Maimonides makes it clear that non-relationality and non-similarity are symmetrical relations. Thus the divine essence "is in no way like our essence," which means, for example, that God's knowledge is "totally different from [ours] and admitting of no analogy" (III, 20). But God is also "a Being to whom none of His creatures is similar, who has nothing in common with them" (I, 58). This is why Maimonides lumps together predications Aquinas would call analogous, such as existence, life, power, wisdom, and will with those the latter would call metaphorical, such as references to God's eye or ear. They are all "perfectly homonymous" (I, 56–57).

The only escape from this equivocity is negative predication. As the only truly proper form of predication, the *via negativa* provides us with "the highest possible knowledge of God" (I, 58; cf. 60). It is true, as the Sages say, that "[t]he Torah speaks in the language of men," but such language is dangerous, for "every time you establish by proof the negation of a thing in reference to God, you become more perfect, while with every additional positive assertion you follow your imagination and recede from the true knowledge of God" (I, 59).

By contrast, Aquinas builds a theory of analogical predication on his ontology of creation and participation.[53] In doing so he invokes the utterly crucial distinction between *res significata*, the thing signified, and *modus significandi*, the mode of signification.[54] The perfections in question in analogical predication involve no imperfection essentially and belong to God in an exemplary and eminent fashion. Thus, in terms of the *res significata*, they can be ascribed substantially and properly to God. But we only know these perfections through their creaturely embodiments. In terms of the *modus significandi*, neither our concepts nor our assertions are adequate to the divine

---

52. Moses Maimonides, *The Guide for the Perplexed,* trans. M. Friedländer, 2nd ed. (London: Routledge & Kegan Paul, 1904). See especially I, 156–60. Subsequent references in text. For references by Aquinas to Maimonides on these themes, see ST 1.13.2, 5; DV 2.1.

53. Aquinas' doctrine of analogy is indebted to Aristotle, especially *Metaphysics* IV, 2. But there are two important differences. First, Aristotle tends to collapse the difference between the analogical and the equivocal. See ST 1.13.10.1 and the discussion by Joseph Owens of the way in which analogy becomes a special case of equivocation. *The Doctrine of Being in the Aristotelian Metaphysics* (Toronto, Ont.: Pontifical Institute of Mediaeval Studies, 1951), ch. 3. Thus for Aristotle 'animal' is used equivocally of a real animal and a picture of one. *Categories,* 1a 2–3. Second, by virtue of the doctrine of creation, Aquinas' doctrine has a vertical character in contrast to the horizontal nature of Aristotle's. See Wippel, "Metaphysics," p. 89. In this respect it is closer to *The Divine Names* than to the *Metaphysics* or *Categories.*

54. Wippel shows how central this distinction is in "Quidditative Knowledge."

reality. But just as the creatures from which we derive our understanding of these perfections are similar to their Creator, however imperfectly, so the concepts are appropriately ascribed to God, however imperfectly. Or, in other words, analogously.

The creatures are unlike God, so the concepts conceal. If this were the whole story we would have a simple either/or between negation and equivocity, as Maimonides has it. *But the creatures are like God, so the concepts reveal.* If this were the whole story we would have univocity, and the transcendence of God, which is what Maimonides is primarily concerned to protect, would indeed be compromised. But since the whole story is the dialectical union of these two stories, we have analogy.

There is something wonderfully Kantian about all this. When it comes to God we do not know the "thing in itself." Our predicates "fail to express [God's] mode of being, because our intellect does not know Him in this life as He is . . . our intellect knows Him according to diverse conceptions because it cannot see Him as He is in Himself" (ST 1.13.1.2, 1.13.12). We cannot comprehend God, who alone "understands everything with infinite clarity" (DV 18.1).

This contrast between divine and human knowledge is important to Aquinas. By virtue of the divine simplicity, divine knowledge is not, like ours, something added to the divine essence (DV 2.1). Again, by virtue of the divine simplicity, divine knowledge is one while ours is many (DV 1.4–5). Most importantly, truth as adequation is found only in the divine intellect. "If truth is taken properly, then it will imply an equality (*aequalitatem*) of the divine intellect and of a thing. Since the first thing the divine intellect knows is its own essence, through which it knows all other things, truth in God principally implies an equality between the divine intellect and a thing which is its essence; and, in a secondary sense, truth likewise implies an equality of the divine intellect with created things" (DV 1.7).

But as we have seen repeatedly, leaving created things aside for the moment, such an equality is not to be found between any created intellect and the divine essence. *Strictly speaking,* that is, assuming univocal predication, everything positive we say about God is false.

But Aquinas is not a theological skeptic. So it should come as no surprise that while he finds truth primarily in the divine intellect he also finds it secondarily in the human (DV 1.4).

He holds that affirmative propositions "can be truly formed about God" (ST 1.13.12) and that "our intellect is not false in composing a judgment concerning God" (ST 1.13.12.3). We have many concepts of God in our minds and God "corresponds to each one of these as a thing corresponds (*respondet*) to an imperfect image of itself. Thus, even though we have several intellectual conceptions about one thing, they are all true. . . . To all of these, however, there corresponds something in reality" (DV 2.1).

We have, thus, a divine knowledge that is adequate to the divine being, that knows the divine essence as it truly is, as it is in itself. And we have a human knowledge that never achieves such adequacy, never knows the divine reality as it is in itself but nevertheless has a secondary, strictly speaking second-rate, "knowledge" that can be said to be objectively "true" in spite of failing the adequacy test. Kantian language almost forces itself upon us. God has noumenal knowledge of the divine essence; we have only phenomenal knowledge. We do not know the divine "thing in itself" but only the way God appears to human understanding, which is not the highest norm of either being or truth. It is important here to recall that it is precisely in terms of the distinction between divine and human knowledge that Kant draws these distinctions.[55]

It turns out that the distinction between divine, noumenal knowledge of the thing in itself, the thing as it truly is, and human, phenomenal knowledge of appearances extends for Aquinas, as it does for Kant, to our knowledge of finite realities. In an Aristotelian epistemology based on the immaterial reception of the form into the intellect, there would seem to be no barrier to adequation, to a finite intellect becoming or containing or being informed by the intelligible species that is the essence of a material substance.

But Aquinas, working in a creationist framework Aristotle does not share, continues to emphasize the secondary character of our knowledge. God's knowledge of created things is like an artisan's knowledge of an artifact. It is prior, it is causal, and it is the measure of the thing known, which, absent that knowledge, would not be. But our knowledge of created things is unlike God's in each of these respects (ST 1.14.8.3; DV 2.5, 8). We just saw another way to make this distinction. God, in knowing the divine essence, knows all created beings, which participate, however weakly, in that essence. God knows things through their exemplar, their archetype. Not knowing the divine essence, we do not know things in this way. We do not know the perfections they imperfectly embody. Once again, human "knowledge" is secondary and human "truth" second-rate.

Josef Pieper calls special attention to this surprising result. "Not only God Himself but also things have an 'eternal name' that man is unable to utter." In Aquinas' own words, "The essential grounds of things are unknown to us, *principia essentialia sunt nobis ignota.*"[56] The reason for this is equally surprising. It is because finite things are created. Pieper emphasizes the centrality of creation to Aquinas' thought, saying that it determines both the structure of finite beings and of Aquinas' basic concepts. It is not just that God's knowl-

---

55. See ch. 3, n. 24 above. I first presented the notion of Aquinas as a Kantian to the American Maritain Association. See "Onto-theo-logical Straw: Reflections on Presence and Absence," in *Postmodernism and Christian Philosophy*, ed. Roman T. Ciapalo (Mishawaka, Ind.: American Maritain Association, 1997).

56. Josef Pieper, *The Silence of St. Thomas*, trans. John Murray, S.J., and Daniel O'Connor (Chicago: Henry Regnery Co., 1965), p. 65. The citation is from Aquinas, CDA 1.1.15 (p. 11). Cf. DV 4.8.1, where, speaking of created things, Aquinas says that "we do not know essential [that is, specific] differences. . . ."

edge, by contrast with ours, is creative. "The essence of things is that they are creatively thought."[57] This means that the essence of finite things cannot be specified by a genus and species but also requires, continuing with the biological scheme, a family as well. We are not defined, strictly speaking, as rational animals but as created rational animals. Aquinas makes this explicit in his commentary on Aristotle's *Metaphysics,* where he gives as the definition of a human being "mortal rational animal" (CMA 7.5.1378, p. 525). For all created beings, having come into being contingently, can pass out of being; they are inherently mortal.

A paradox emerges from the fact that createdness belongs to the essence of finite things. This fact is what makes them intelligible to us. For by virtue of their imitative participation in the divine essence, the light of that which is most intelligible in itself is reflected, however dimly, in them.[58] At the same time, their createdness makes them incomprehensible. For Aquinas "it is part of the very nature of things that their knowability cannot be wholly exhausted by any finite intellect, *because* these things are creatures, which means that the very element which makes them capable of being known must necessarily be at the same time the reason why things are unfathomable."[59]

This is not a quantitative deficiency, as if there were some facts we could know quite definitively while others escape us. Aquinas is talking about our grasp of the essence of things. The truth of things, the intelligibility which makes them knowable to us, lies in "the relationship between things and the creative mind of God. . . . This relation . . . the relation between natural reality and the archetypal creative thought of God—*cannot, I insist, be known formally by us. . . .* We know the copy, but not the relation of the copy to the archetype. . . . Here we can notice how truth and unknowability belong together."[60]

Pieper relates this linkage of essence and creation to Sartre, but the point is at least equally Kantian. For Aquinas as for Kant, precisely because we are not located at the site of God's creative knowledge of finite things, we cannot know even them as they really are. In reference to both God and the world we use language intended to signify the essences of the objects of our knowledge; but in neither case do we ever really know what we mean. This double deficit of meaning means that in seeking to preserve the transcendence of God in terms of the great gulf fixed between Creator and creature, Aquinas breaks decisively with the onto-theological project. He posits a Highest Being who is the key to the meaning of the whole of being. But instead of putting God to

---

57. Pieper, *Silence,* pp. 45–51.
58. Pieper, *Silence,* pp. 55–56, 60.
59. Pieper, *Silence,* p. 60.
60. Pieper, *Silence,* pp. 58–59. Cf. p. 63: "We can never properly grasp this correspondence between the original pattern in God and the created copy. . . . It is quite impossible for us, as spectators, so to speak, to contemplate the emergence of things from 'the eye of God.'"

work in the service of rendering the whole of reality fully intelligible to human understanding, he makes God the ultimate obstacle to that project.

It is by affirming God as personal creator that Aquinas distinguishes his classical theism from all forms of pantheism. But this cosmological transcendence immediately becomes epistemic transcendence as well. Long before deconstruction, the Platonic soul and the Cartesian cogito are decentered so far as meaning, truth, and knowledge are concerned. The human mind is not the measure of truth, nor is our knowledge the measure of being. In his simultaneous-dialectical apophaticism, expressed in his doctrine of analogy, Aquinas affirms that the Highest Being, who is the key to the meaning of the whole of being, remains a mystery to us. In unconcealment, God remains concealed. We know and we know not.

In terms of this mystery motif, Aquinas' "system" remains decisively different from the onto-theological systems of Spinoza and Hegel. Without the epistemic transcendence signified by divine mystery, it is possible for Spinoza and Hegel to see the highest human knowledge as the highest knowledge there is. The only self-transcendence called for is from the lower to the higher levels of human knowing. But a very different mode of epistemic self-transcendence is evoked by Aquinas. For him God transcends all human knowing and remains beyond our comprehension (even in the life to come). Thus our knowing reaches out to what is beyond ourselves and cannot be captured and incorporated within our conceptualities, as if, having brought our thought into conformity with the Real, it has become the (divine) measure of the Real. In the act of positing a Highest Being who is the key to the meaning of the whole of being, Aquinas immediately undermines the philosophical project of rendering the whole of being fully intelligible to human understanding with the help of this Supreme Being. The Kantian side of Aquinas makes him a Kierkegaardian as well. For Johannes Climacus might well have included a footnote to Aquinas (or Augustine, or a host of other theists) when he wrote, "Existence itself is a system—for God, but it cannot be a system for any existing spirit."[61]

It is indeed Aquinas' view, like Pseudo-Dionysius' before him,[62] that God "is known to Himself alone" (ST 1.1.6). Any knowledge we may have of God can only be by participation in that divine self-knowledge, and since participation is never identity, but always partial and imperfect, divine mystery remains ineluctable and ineliminable.

But just at this point we encounter that other mode of epistemic self-transcendence for which onto-theology can find no place: divine revelation. For, on Aquinas' account, participation in the divine self-knowledge can be either by nature or by grace, by reason or by revelation. We have seen that the

---

61. Kierkegaard, *Concluding Unscientific Postscript*, trans. Howard V. Hong and Edna H. Hong (Princeton, N.J.: Princeton University Press, 1992), I, 118. For the same point with reference to history, see pp. 141 and 158.
62. See ch. 4 n. 42.

doctrine of analogy applies to all divine names or predicates, whether derived from reason or revelation. Revelation does not signify the disappearance of mystery. But it does signify a second mode of epistemic transcendence and a second theistic break with the onto-theological project. For human understanding not only relates itself to that which it cannot comprehend, it also relates itself to a Knower whose knowing exceeds its own knowing beyond measure so that, as we have seen Augustine say, our knowledge "compared with [God's] is ignorance" (C XI, 4). In receiving divine revelation in faith, human understanding transcends itself by recognizing its derivative nature; it also transcends itself by accepting its dependence on a knowing not its own. Divine grace is a personal gift, and in the faith that welcomes revelation, participation becomes an interpersonal relation. But then, in the light of the doctrine of creation, reason is as much a divine gift as is revelation, and the epistemic self-transcendence encountered in relation to both is not just an experience of limits but an encounter with love.

In our preoccupation with the Five Ways, we often overlook the fact that the *Summa Theologiae* does not begin with them but with an affirmation of the necessity of divine revelation and the "sacred doctrine" or revealed theology in which it is spelled out. For "[i]t was necessary for man's salvation that there should be a doctrine revealed by God, besides the philosophical discipline investigated by human reason . . . that certain truths which exceed human reason should be made known to him by divine revelation" (ST 1.1.1). It is precisely in this context that Aquinas affirms that God is only known by God. For in addition to philosophical knowledge, it treats of God "also so far as He is known to Himself alone and revealed to others" (ST 1.1.6).

At one level Aquinas has no more vigorous theological opponent than Karl Barth, perhaps the ultimate critic of natural theology and the doctrine of *analogia entis* on which it rests. But at another level there is deep and surprising agreement between the two. Barth also holds that God is only known by God, and the themes of mystery and revelation, concealment in unconcealment are the twin foci of his religious epistemology. For a final account of epistemic transcendence and self-transcendence, we turn to his thought.

Barth

How to Speak Nevertheless about God—
The Analogy of Faith

In his critique of onto-theology, Heidegger quotes 1 Corinthians 1:20, "Has not God let the wisdom of this world become foolishness?" links this wisdom to what Aristotle calls first philosophy and he calls onto-theology, and then asks, "Will Christian theology make up its mind one day to take seriously the word of the apostle and thus also the conception of philosophy as foolishness?" (WM/1949, 276). Apparently he had not kept up with his theological reading and was unaware of Karl Barth's *The Epistle to the Romans* (whose first and importantly revised second edition appeared in 1919 and 1922 respectively) and *Church Dogmatics* (which began to appear in 1932). For it would be hard to find a theologian closer to Paul's heart on this point than Barth. In fact, he goes so far as to lump science and history and philosophy and theology (!) together as sites in which the world not only "exists side by side with God," but "has taken His place, and has itself become God," resulting in the "deified world" of "Nature and Civilization, Materialism and Idealism, Capitalism and Socialism, Secularism and Ecclesiasticism, Imperialism and Democracy" (ER 52).

In each of the two towering texts just mentioned, God's transcendence in its epistemic mode is utterly pivotal. It is not for developmental reasons that I look at both the early and later Barth, for I agree with those who see more continuity than discontinuity between the two.[1] It is rather because in the first case the primary opponent is liberal Protestantism, while in the second the battle is waged at least as much against Roman Catholicism and permits us to bring Barthian thought into direct engagement with Thomistic thought. The different formulations of God's epistemic transcendence are at least as much due to different debate partners as they are to developmental changes. In both cases Barth sees himself as a kind of successor to Augustine in his defense of divine grace and freedom against the Pelagians. One might say that for Barth modernity is epistemic Pelagianism.[2]

His early protest is against the quintessential modernity of the theological tradition in which he had been trained, stemming from Schleiermacher, Ritschl, Troeltsch, and his own teacher, Wilhelm Herrmann, namely that it sought to make the human subject the ground and basis of our knowledge of God.[3] Anticipating Levinasian language, we can say that in any such theology Barth sees the reduction of the other (God) to the same (human being). Or, to put it in Feuerbachian terms, theology becomes anthropology. "God Himself is not acknowledged as God and what is called 'God' is in fact Man" (ER 44).[4] Barth insists that "one can *not* speak of God simply by speaking of man in a loud voice" (TM 196).

He finds liberal Protestantism to be guilty of these faults in two often closely intertwined ways: first by making religious experience the basis of theology, as in Schleiermacher, and second by making historical knowledge (of Jesus) the ground of our knowledge of God.[5] Our affective and cognitive capacities are taken to be the bridge by which we pass over from the human to

---

1. See Bruce L. McCormack, *Karl Barth's Critically Realistic Dialectical Theology: Its Genesis and Development 1909–1936* (New York: Oxford University Press, 1995), pp. 134, 244 (henceforth abbreviated as CRDT), and G. C. Berkouwer, *The Triumph of Grace in the Theology of Karl Barth*, trans. Harry R. Boer (Grand Rapids, Mich.: Eerdmans, 1956), p. 10.

2. In discussing these two texts I will draw on other writings that are properly associated with each.

3. See McCormack, CRDT 130, 182, 207.

4. Berkouwer writes that Barth "is convinced that the whole of modern Protestant theology stands or falls with its subjectivistic point of departure and that its anthropology, which forms the background and foundation of its entire structure, stands essentially defenseless against the criticism of Ludwig Feuerbach, because man is more central in that theology than the power and sovereign grace of God." *Triumph*, p. 167. Cf. ER 122, and for explicit references to Feuerbach, pp. 236 and 316, along with more extended discussions in "Ludwig Feuerbach," in TC and "Feuerbach" in PT.

5. A glimpse of what bothers Barth on this second score can be seen in a book on Ritschl's theology. A chapter entitled "A System Rooted in the Vitalities of History" has the following section headings: The Ground of Christian Faith and Theology, Problems of Methodology, A Historical Mode of Knowing and Verifying Truth for Theology, The Functioning of Historical Reason, and A Historical Norm for Theological Work. See Philip Hefner, *Faith and the Vitalities of History: A Theological Study Based on the Work of Albrecht Ritschl* (New York: Harper & Row, 1966).

the divine.[6] But *"at the moment when religion . . . becomes a psychologically and historically conceivable magnitude in the world, it falls away from its inner character, from its truth, to idols"* (BQ 68). Accordingly *Romans* carries on a sustained polemic against the historicism and psychologism that Barth sees in liberal theology (ER 30, 87, 98, 102–103, 150, 153, 277).[7]

He is especially hard on its historicism. Perhaps this is because religious experience in the form of Schleiermacher's feeling of "absolute dependence"[8] yields a God who, like the God of Aquinas' five ways and apart from the Feuerbachian problems already indicated, is too generic, lacking the specifically Christian content that is important to Barth as a theologian. In order to get this, it must be informed by knowledge of the historical Jesus. Thus the link between liberalism's psychologism and historicism. In any case, Barth is eager "to put the movement and action of God in history beyond the reach of historical investigation."[9] He writes,

> The plane which is known to us, [Jesus as the Christ] intersects vertically, from above [*senkrecht von oben*]. . . . In the Resurrection the new world of the Holy Spirit touches the old world of the flesh, but touches it as a tangent touches a circle, that is, without touching it. And, precisely because it does not touch it, it touches it as its frontier—as the new world. The Resurrection is therefore an occurrence in history which took place outside the gates of Jerusalem in the year A.D. 30, inasmuch as it there 'came to pass', was discovered and recognized. But inasmuch as the occurrence was conditioned by the Resurrection, in so far, that is, as it was not the 'coming to pass', or the discovery, or the recognition, which conditioned its necessity and appearance and revelation, the Resurrection is not an event in history at all. (ER 30)

This paradoxical formula, 'in history but not in history,' says nothing different from the slightly less paradoxical formula, 'in history but not of history.'[10] Barth makes it clear that when he says that the event of revelation that concerns him, "though it is the only real happening *in* is not a real happening *of* history," he means that it is better to treat it as myth, which he is by no means eager to do, than to deprive it of its timelessness "by being explained historically" (BQ 90). It is rather "the dissolution of history in history" (ER 103). In

---

6. Barth is not among those who find Schleiermacher's greatness to be that he "connected earth and heaven by a much needed bridge, upon which we may reverently cross" (TM 196). As we shall see, he considers such bridges to be towers of Babel.

7. McCormack writes, "These two targets of Barth's criticism are attacked separately but at times are coupled together. This occurs with increasing frequency during the course of the 1920s, becoming a shorthand for all that Barth opposes" (CRDT 249n33).

8. See Friedrich Schleiermacher, *The Christian Faith*, trans. H. R. Mackintosh and J. S. Stewart (Edinburgh: T & T Clark, 1928), pp. 5–18.

9. McCormack, CRDT 146.

10. See McCormack, CRDT 209, 233, and 252. Cf. ER 104, where the voice of God is described as a "fragment of the world" that is "detached from this world."

other words, the event of revelation by which we come to know God, being a miracle, is not a product of the historical process and *ipso facto* can neither be recognized nor explained by historical knowledge. The historical Jesus, that is, the Jesus accessible to historical research, is, from a theological point of view, an abstraction in which the human and temporal has been cut off and isolated from the divine and eternal. Barth stands with Chalcedon[11] in taking such abstraction to be heresy, not for the sake of traditionalism but for the sake of the transcendence of God in the act of revelation.

* * *

We can understand Barth's critique of liberal Protestant theology best if we see it as a critique of onto-theology that differs from Heidegger's in coming several decades earlier and in having a much broader scope. How much like Heidegger he sounds, when, complaining about the God, or rather the "No-God" who is "the complete affirmation of the course of the world and of men as it is," he writes, "The cry of revolt against such a god is nearer the truth than is the sophistry with which men attempt to justify him" (ER 40).[12] Or again, "We dare to deck ourselves out as [God's] companions, patrons, advisers, and commissioners. . . . And our relation to God is *unrighteous*. Secretly we are ourselves the masters of this relationship. We are not concerned with God, but with our own requirements, to which God must adjust Himself. Our arrogance demands that, in addition to everything else, some super-world should also be known and accessible to us. . . . Men have *imprisoned* and encased the *truth*— the righteousness of God; they have trimmed it to their own measure . . . and thereby transformed it into untruth" (ER 44–45).[13]

Now Barth is no positivist, and so far is he from eschewing matters that a positivist would dismiss as metaphysical that his critique of liberalism's psychologism and historicism can be read as a critique of a kind of Feuerbachian positivism, reducing the transcendent to the empirical. But he regularly has nasty things to say about metaphysics. He speaks disparagingly of metaphysics "developed along the lines of physics, as if this were the necessary way" (BQ 68). Then, as if to explain this comment, he insists that "the Biblical *idea of creation* is never expanded into a cosmogony. It is intended for a solemn marking of the distance between the cosmos and the Creator, and *precisely not for a*

---

11. According to the Council of Chalcedon in A.D. 451, the human and divine natures in Jesus Christ are "without confusion, without change, without division, without separation."

12. Cf. the passage already cited in chapter 1 from Heidegger. "The god-less thinking which must abandon the god of philosophy, god as *causa sui*, is thus perhaps closer to the divine God" (ID 72).

13. Cf. Heidegger's repeated question, "How does the deity enter into philosophy?" (ID 55–71), that is, into metaphysics as onto-theologically constituted, and the answer he gives, cited above in chapter 1, namely that "the deity can come into philosophy only insofar as philosophy, of its own accord and by its own nature, requires and determines how the deity enters into it" (ID 56).

metaphysical explanation of the world" (BQ 71, second emphasis added).[14] No doubt Barth has something similar in mind when he argues that the God of faith is "no metaphysical substance in the midst of other substances. . . . On the contrary, He is the eternal, pure Origin of all things" (ER 78). In other words, theology must not allow itself to come under the domination of the principle of sufficient reason. "The righteousness of God is that 'nevertheless' by which He associates us with Himself and declares Himself to be our God. This 'nevertheless' contradicts every human logical 'consequently', and is itself incomprehensible and without cause or occasion, because it is the 'nevertheless!' of God" (ER 93).[15] Metaphysics requires everything to conform to its *ratio*, the order of reasons and causes, and with the same arrogance of positivism says that whatever my net doesn't catch isn't a fish!

Barth's critique of onto-theology is very similar to Heidegger's, but whereas Heidegger focuses on the philosophical tradition from Anaximander to Nietzsche, and especially on Aristotle and Hegel, Barth is understandably more concerned about the threat the onto-theological stance poses to theology, in particular liberal Protestant theology. Jerusalem is as likely as Athens to catch the disease.

Two emphases of Barth's extended critique of onto-*theology* are especially noteworthy. The first is his critique of method, an antithesis between truth and method that will sound Gadamerian to some. In *Romans* there is a great emphasis on the divine No to all human attempts to cross the divide between the human and divine. So it is not surprising to hear Barth say, "No road to the eternal meaning of the created world has ever existed, save the road of negation. This is the lesson of history" (ER 87). This sounds like an affirmation of some *via negativa*. So how can McCormack say that Barth's purpose is to locate God beyond the realm of any and every conceptuality readily available to us, whether through a *via negativa* or a *via eminentiae* or a *via causalitatis*?[16] We've just seen Barth repudiate the *via causalitatis*, but we've also just seen him apparently affirm a *via negativa*, and, as we shall see, in his later doctrine of the analogy of faith there is a lot that can be expressed in the language of eminence. Barth himself gives us the answer. "The mystic's 'Way of Denial' [*via negativa*] is a blind alley, as are all 'ways'. The only way is the Way, and that Way is Christ" (ER 316).

Barth does not wish to deny negation, or eminence, or even causality. What he wants to deny is the notion of a way, a method by which *we* can establish a genuine knowledge of God. Thus, in "The Word of God and the Task of the

---

14. Cf. BQ 91, where Barth, speaking of genuine knowledge of God, writes, "Reality as we have known it . . . is neither verified nor explained by this new truth; but in the light of this truth, it is seen to be clothed upon with new reality."

15. Barth sees this "consequently" at work in two ideas which Paul vehemently rejects in Romans: "*Let us do evil that good may come*" (3:8) and "*Let us continue in sin that grace may abound*" (6:1, see ER 188–89).

16. McCormack, CRDT 248.

Ministry," he discusses three theological methods, the dogmatic, the critical, and the dialectical, affirms the third as the best, but critiques all three insofar as none is able to guarantee or ground our knowledge of God. "There is *no* way which leads to this event [of revelation, because] there is *no* faculty in man for apprehending it; for the way and the faculty are themselves new, being the revelation and faith, the knowing and being known enjoyed by the new man" (TM 197). This is why to witness to God is "not to leave him somewhere in the background, but to disregard the universal method of science and place him in the *foreground*" (TM 193). The clear implication is that method means putting God in the background and ourselves, our way, our faculty, our capacity, in the foreground. Feuerbach again. And Levinas—the reduction of the other to the same. This is why the faith which grounds itself in method is just as much unbelief as the faith that grounds itself in some system (ER 57).

This brings us to the second emphasis in Barth's critique of onto-*theology*. If we ask whence this hostility to method, we need but to recall a passage cited above. "We are not concerned with God, but with our own requirements, to which God must adjust Himself. Our arrogance demands that, in addition to everything else, some super-world should also be known and accessible to us" (ER 44). This arrogant demand is in the service of our desire to possess, if not God, at least our access to God, our relation to God, our knowledge of God, though this distinction is, in Barth's eyes, one without a difference. Hence we find a sustained polemic against every piety of possession (BQ 67–68, 74, 87; ER 67, 75, 81, 87, 100, 158). Theological method, it turns out, is but one of the many ways in which "Man has taken the divine into his possession; he has brought it under his management," in which religion "acts in her lofty ecclesiastical estate as if she were in possession of a gold mine" (BQ 67–68). In Marxian language, our knowledge of God can never be a commodity, nor God a fetish.

***

These last criticisms are directed at religion, not simply at theology, and here we get a further broadening of Barth's critique of onto-theology. It is not just that theology as well as philosophy can adopt an onto-theological posture; the whole of religious life can be the desire to possess, to have God at our disposal in the service of our (possibly but not necessarily pious) agenda.

Unlike Hegel, who thinks that philosophy is the highest human possibility, Barth thinks that religion holds that honor. It is "in religion that human capacity appears most pure, most strong, most penetrating, most adaptable." This is because religion is "the ability of men to receive and to retain an impress of God's revelation" (ER 183). Religion is "the last step in human progress" (ER 254). In its "purest and noblest and most tenacious achievements mankind reaches, and indeed must reach, its highest pinnacle of human possibility" (ER 185).

"But," Barth continues, "even so religion remains a human achievement" (ER 185). As such it is not merely "limited" (ER 229) but "belongs mentally and morally to the old world, and stands in the shadow of sin and death" (ER 184). Religion is "the loftiest summit in the land of sin" (ER 242).

Barth is a Reformed theologian and is here taking with utmost seriousness the doctrine of Total Depravity. This never meant merely that everyone is a sinner. Scripture itself says that directly and there is no need for theology simply to quote. Nor did it ever mean that everyone (or anyone) is as wicked as it is possible to be. It was a statement about the scope of sin, namely that no part of the human person escapes being corrupted by our fallenness. Our intellect and our emotions as well as our wills have become distorted through disobedience. Barth is simply applying this concept to human activities rather than to human faculties. Thus, in an early essay, he speaks of the ways in which in response to the call of conscience that points us to the righteousness of God, we try to take charge and make that righteousness "our very own affair." He lists three ways in which we try to make God's righteousness a human possibility: morality, politics, and religion (RG 14–21). Or again, in terms of desires, Barth says "the yearnings of religion are of the same order as our sexual and intellectual and other desires" (ER 213).[17] Neither the desire for physical pleasure, nor the desire for knowledge, nor the desire for fellowship with God is in itself evil. But all these desires have become corrupted by sin.

Accordingly, Barth's descriptions of religion are not flattering. It is the tower of Babel (ER 61 and throughout RG), arrogance (ER 37, 47, 136), a smokescreen (ER 230), an illusion (ER 136, 236), and a drug (ER 236). These last two descriptions suggest Freud and Marx, and it looks as if Ricoeur should add Barth to the names of Marx, Nietzsche, and Freud, as the great masters of the hermeneutics of suspicion.[18] Barth writes, "In the moment when we dare to say we believe, we remain always under suspicion" (ER 150).[19]

Echoing Kierkegaard's attack upon Christendom, Barth writes, "Religion is not the sure ground upon which human culture safely rests; it is the place where civilization and its partner, barbarism, are rendered fundamentally

---

17. Cf. 235 and CP 286, "The step from the *experience* of the Lord to the experience of *Baal* is a short one. The religious and the sexual are close akin."

18. Paul Ricoeur, *Freud and Philosophy: An Essay on Interpretation*, trans. Denis Savage (New Haven, Conn.: Yale University Press, 1970), p. 32.

19. While granting the legitimacy of suspicion's critique, he challenges its unbelief. It may be that "God treats [religion] as arrogance and men as illusion. But we must beware of running to the opposite misunderstanding. If religion is nebulous and lacking in security, so also is everything which is exalted to oppose religion. Anti-religious negation has no advantage over the affirmations of religion. To destroy temples is not better than to build them. . . . So long as religious as well as anti-religious activities fail to draw attention to that which lies beyond them, and so long as they attempt their own justification, either as faith, hope and charity, or as the enthusiastic and dionysiac gestures of the Anti-Christ, they are assuredly mere illusion. Everything which seeks to justify itself, whether by affirmation or by negation, is under the sentence of judgment" (ER 136).

questionable" (ER 258). In other words, in its negativity religion can have a positive function. In its prophetic form, which Barth takes to be the highest point in the history of religions, religion sets every human endeavor over against the divine requirement and finds it wanting. "In religion men know themselves to be conditioned invisibly by—sin" (ER 243–44). But in the presence of the sin it recognizes, religion as human activity is powerless.

> No religion is capable of altering the fact that the behaviour of men is a behaviour apart from God. All that religion can do is to expose the complete godlessness of human behaviour. . . . Religion neither overcomes human worldliness nor transfigures; not even the religion of Primitive Christianity or of Isaiah or of the Reformers cant rid itself of this limitation. . . . Woe be to us, if from the summits of religion there pours forth nothing but— religion! Religion casts us into the deepest of all prisons: it cannot liberate us. (ER 276)

By pointing to a problem it cannot solve, religion properly points beyond itself. Only when she "continually does away with herself" does religion have a right to exist. In her onto-theological posture, in which God enters human experience on human terms and she "acts in her lofty ecclesiastical estate as if she were in possession of a gold mine" (BQ 67), religion is just one of the forms human sinfulness takes. When religion does not point beyond itself, it is "like some great pyramid, as an immense sepulchre within which the truth lies mummified in wood and stone" (ER 129).[20]

Here as in the later *Church Dogmatics*, the contrast is not between this religion and that religion but between all religion as a human activity and revelation as a divine activity.[21] In spite of the Christocentric character of his doctrine of revelation, already well-established in *Romans*, Barth is emphatic about including Christianity in his critique of religion. All religions, even "ignorant and superstitious worship of the most terrible kind" carry an impress of revelation and are witness to the Unknown God (ER 95). This doesn't mean that all religions are equal. There are differences among them, and we have already seen the high place he gives to the religion of the Hebrew prophets. Speaking of religion, Barth writes, "May we not conclude that we should be

---

20. The notion that religion properly does not merely point beyond herself but "continually does away with herself" evokes Derridean deconstruction. For an analysis of the relation between Derrida and the Barth of *Romans*, see Walter Lowe, *Theology and Difference* (Bloomington: Indiana University Press, 1993). In *Barth, Derrida and the Language of Theology* (New York: Cambridge University Press, 1995), Graham Ward brings Derrida into conversation with the early but primarily the later Barth. For a defense of this kind of juxtaposition, see Garrett Green, "The Hermeneutics of Difference: Barth and Derrida on Words and the Word," in *Postmodern Philosophy and Christian Thought*, ed. Merold Westphal (Bloomington: Indiana University Press, 1999). The fundamental agreement between Barth and Derrida, in spite of deep differences, lies in the thought that meaning and (*a fortiori*) truth are not fixed, final, and stable *possessions* of human understanding.
21. See CD I/2, §17, "The Revelation of God as the Abolition of Religion."

right in setting every human upon one single ladder, although perhaps upon different rungs of that ladder? Are they not, at best, parables of an achievement which lies on a wholly different plane? Yes, no doubt; but nevertheless, must we not also say that the Lord permits to some human achievements a maturity which is lacking in others . . . ?" (ER 265). Some religions are better than others, but in the final analysis they are but different rungs on the same ladder of human activity, and the ladder does not reach to heaven. When it pretends to it becomes the tower of Babel.

The passage in Amos that ends with the familiar words, "But let justice roll down like waters, and righteousness like an ever-flowing stream" begins with a scathing denunciation, "I hate, I despise your festivals, and I take no delight in your solemn assemblies . . ." (5:21–24). These words are spoken by the prophet not to the pagan Canaanites, but to the covenant people of Yahweh. In a sermon as early as 1913, Barth makes it clear that in contemporary Switzerland this word of judgment is addressed to Christians and to their Christianity.[22] He makes the same point in a lecture given between the first two editions of *Romans*. "The polemic of the Bible, unlike that of the religions, is directed not against the godless world but against the *religious* world, whether it worships under the auspices of Baal or of Jehovah" (BQ 70). In a lecture simultaneous with the second edition of *Romans*, he affirms "the fact that man as man is not only in *need* but beyond all hope of saving himself; that the whole of so-called religion, and not least the Christian religion, shares in this need" (TM 195–96).

Finally, in *Romans* he writes, "The Gospel neither requires men to engage in the conflict of religions or the conflict of philosophies. . . . In announcing the limitation of the known world by another that is unknown, the Gospel does not enter into competition with the many attempts to disclose within the known world some more or less unknown and higher form of existence and to make it accessible to men." This, presumably is what both religion and philosophy in their onto-theological mode do. The Gospel, however, "is not a truth among other truths," religious and philosophical. "Rather, it sets a question-mark against all truths" (ER 35). To make sure we don't miss the point, Barth writes, "This inevitability of judgment affects all religions in so far as their reality is merely the reality of temporal and concrete things. It affects religion, even when it is upright and sincere and genuine, even the religion of Abraham and of the Prophets, even the religion of the Epistle to the Romans—and it affects, of course, the religion of anyone who undertakes to expound the Epistle" (ER 136).

Barth's break with liberal Protestantism takes the form of a critique of onto-theology as the attempt to make human subjectivity the condition for the possibility of God's entry into human life. He extends this critique beyond philosophy to Christian theology, with special reference to liberalism's psy-

---

22. See McCormack, CRDT 98–99.

chologism and historicism, and then beyond theology to religion in general—all religion, even his own. At least since 1916, he persistently developed such an argument.

> There seem to be no surer means of rescuing us from the alarm cry of conscience and religion and Christianity. Religion gives us the chance, beside and above the vexations of business, politics, and private and social life, to celebrate solemn hours of devotion—to take flight to Christianity as to an eternally green island in the gray sea of the everyday. There comes over us a wonderful sense of safety and security from the unrighteousness whose might we everywhere feel. It is a wonderful illusion, if we can comfort ourselves with it, that in our Europe—in the midst of capitalism, prostitution, the housing problem, alcoholism, tax evasion, and militarism—the church's preaching, the church's morality, and the "religious life" go their uninterrupted way. And we are Christians! Our nation is a Christian nation! A wonderful illusion, but an illusion, a self-deception! . . . Is not our religious righteousness a product of our pride and our despair, a tower of Babel, at which the devil laughs more loudly than at all the others? (RG 19–20)

McCormack sees the decisive break with the liberalism in which he had been trained in a question Barth posed to his friend Thurneysen the previous year: "Is it self-evident that 'we' 'represent' the Kingdom of God?"[23]

* * *

Barth's theology is properly called dialectical, not because it employs a dialectical method, but because its subject matter is dialectical.[24] And it remains dialectical rather than speculative[25] insofar as the tension between time and eternity, or, to speak more concretely, between the human and the divine is not resolved in any conceptual transparency. What has here been called,

---

23. McCormack, CRDT 124. Cf. CP 276–77, ". . . the seed is the word and the field is the world, but just what is the word? Which of us has it?" and BQ 85, "Let us not contrast ourselves too quickly with those to whom the cross is a stumbling block and a foolishness, for as a matter of fact we all belong with them. . . . For the sake of the suffering of the millions, for the sake of the blood shed for many that cries against us all, for the sake of the fear of God, let us not be so sure! Such sureness is only a synonym for smugness."

24. Graham Ward writes that for Barth "dialectic is, then, the relation of self or same with other. It is not simply a style of writing (though this relationship will manifest in a style that installs its own self-questioning by paradox and oxymoron). It is not simply a theological method (though the dialectical relationship must be examined in a dialectical manner and this *manner* must be a way of investigation, a *methodos* for treating the subject). The dialectic is a condition of Christian existence, a condition of distance-in-relationship to God. . . . Dialectic was a consequence for Barth of a theological reasoning in which the other of dialogue remained other, and the transcendent address of this other became the condition for thinking and speaking from the human and subjective side." *Barth*, p. 96.

25. See how Hegel makes dialectic only penultimate in *The Encyclopedia Logic*, trans. T. F. Geraets et al. (Indianapolis, Ind.: Hackett, 1991), §§ 79–82.

somewhat anachronistically, to be sure, his critique of "onto-theology"[26] signifies the divine No to everything human insofar as it would make itself the
condition for the possibility of our relation to God. It is the function of this No
to clear the way for the divine Yes, which is the only genuine condition for that
possibility. Berkouwer's *The Triumph of Grace in the Theology of Karl Barth*,
primarily concerns his later theology. But that triumph is already the central
motif in the period of *Romans.*

We have seen Barth extend the divine No to the whole of human culture,
including religion in all its dimensions. But there has been an almost gnostic
focus on epistemic matters. Writing of the period of his decisive break with
liberal theology, McCormack writes, "From now on, knowledge of God—the a
priori of all true representation of the Kingdom—would be *the* central question in Karl Barth's new theology."[27] We have seen him insist that both philosophy and theology, when they take metaphysics, or psychology, or history to be
the way to the knowledge of God, are nothing but illusion and idolatry. The
divine No reverberates through his writings loud and clear. But what about the
Yes? Barth does not read Romans as leaving us with an ironical skepticism,[28]
nor does he read Paul as pointing to a mysticism of the abyss.[29]

We should not be surprised to find that the condition for the possibility
of genuine knowledge of God will be neither human capacity nor human
achievement, but only divine grace. *Sola gratia.* Nor should we be surprised to
find that his account centers around precisely those two features that we saw to
be systematically excluded in the pantheistic onto-theologies of Spinoza and
Hegel, namely revelation and mystery.

If human capacity is not the condition for the possibility of genuine knowledge of God (or, for that matter, any other non-illusory, non-idolatrous relationship), it follows that such knowledge is impossible in human terms, and
Barth never tires of stressing this impossibility (BQ 91; TM 197; ER 59, 62,
123, 138). We cannot speak of God; "only God *himself* can speak of God" (TM
198, 214). Nor can any method we might employ make it happen that God
speaks when God is spoken of (TM 211). All of our God talk must proceed
"from God outwards" (ER 37, *von Gott aus*). In other words, our knowledge of
God will depend on the gift of revelation.

---

26. Heidegger's critique, which introduces the term in its contemporary usage, is yet to come.

27. McCormack, CRDT 125.

28. McCormack rightly rejects Stephen Webb's reading that Barth's theology is a form of skeptical
irony. See CRDT 245 n. 17 and Webb, *Re-Figuring Theology: The Rhetoric of Karl Barth* (Albany:
SUNY Press, 1991).

29. See TM 203–206, where Barth's critique of critical method in theology is that by itself it leaves
nothing but the Abyss, the Darkness, and the No. "God may be spoken of only . . . when God
himself becomes man and enters with his *fullness* into our emptiness, with his *Yes* into our No." Cf.
CP 294, "To go back to origins is not to go back to annihilation, if we go back to the Origin of
origins—to God. On the contrary, it is only in God that we can come to a positive position."

But in this context, revelation will not mean the transparency of the divine to human understanding, but a divine act of self-manifesting grace that can only be called miracle. There is no way from here to there. But there *"must still* be a way from there to here. And with this 'must' and this 'still' we confess to the miracle of the *revelation* of God" (CP 287). "He who says 'God', says 'miracle'" (ER 120). It is an "illusion that it is possible for men to hold communication with God or, at least, to enter into a covenant relationship with Him without miracle—vertical from above" (ER 50). Barth never tires of this theme, which is the corollary of the impossibility motif (BQ 91; TM 62; ER 35, 102, 115–126, 153).

The towering figure of Kant hovers in the background of the impossibility motif. Barth studied him intensely as he was about to embark on his commentary of Romans, and he was familiar with the Marburg neo-kantianism of Paul Natorp and especially Hermann Cohen, who was important for the theology of his own teacher, Wilhelm Herrmann.[30] In the Preface to the second edition of *Romans*, he lists Kant among those who influenced the changes from the first edition.[31] And his references to Kant in the text, though they come very late in the day, are favorable (ER 367, 386, 432, 468). It is as a student of Kant that he writes, "There is no object [for our knowledge] apart from our thinking of it; nor has an object any clear characteristics save when we are able to recognize them by some quick-moving previous knowledge. Therefore if God be an object in the world, we can make no statement about Him—for example, that He is capricious and tyrannical—which does not proceed from some previous superior knowledge" (ER 82). In short, the *a priori* is the condition for the possibility of experience, which, in the Kantian context, is knowledge. But, as we have been seeing, Barth insists that we have no such capacity or condition when it comes to God.

It is the comprehensive character of this "no such capacity" that is crucial here, for it does not follow immediately from the *Critique of Pure Reason* that only God can speak of God, that revelation as miracle is the only possible ground for our knowledge of God. Having denied that we have this condition or capacity in metaphysics as theoretical reason, Kant thought he could find it in practical reason and its postulates. Hegel agreed that it could not be found in the old metaphysics of the Understanding, but that it could be in the new speculative thinking of Reason. Rejecting both of these strategies, and with them any attempt to find God through theoretical or practical reason, Schleiermacher laid the foundations for liberal Protestant theology by seeking

---

30. See McCormack, CRDT 67, 75, 129–30, 136, 216. On Barth's relation to Marburg neo-kantianism, see Simon Fischer, *Revelatory Positivism* (Oxford: Oxford University Press, 1988).

31. "First and most important: the continued study of Paul himself. . . . Second, the man Overbeck. . . . Thirdly: closer acquaintance with Plato and Kant. . . . I have also paid more attention to what may be culled from the writings of Kierkegaard and Dostoevsky" (ER 3–4).

the condition in immediate intuition and feeling.[32] We have seen that later liberalism tried to graft knowledge of the historical Jesus onto this psychological foundation in order to get anything specifically Christian.[33] Barth rejects all such moves, not because he thinks they have mislocated the human capacity for knowledge of God but because he denies that there is such a capacity to be located. We can read him as belonging to the tradition that asks, After Kant's destruction of metaphysics, how is knowledge of God possible? But his answer, namely divine revelation as a miraculous gift of grace, shows that something more than Kantian skepticism, even in an extended mode, is at work. The Yes in which he affirms a genuine knowledge of God is correlated to a distinctive No in which he denies any human capacity as its ground. "Knowledge of God as an antithesis to [all] other knowledge!" (BQ 55).

If we ask what is this distinctive No that separates Barth both from idealism and from liberalism, the answer is clear: the Pauline notion, so fundamental to the Reformers, of the noetic effects of sin. Our intellects and not just our wills have been corrupted by our fallenness. As one of the great masters of suspicion, Barth finds our epistemic predicament to reside in fault rather than mere finitude. At times, however, this doesn't seem to be the case. When he says that his system, if he has one, "is limited to a recognition of what Kierkegaard called the 'infinite qualitative distinction' between time and eternity. . . . 'God is in heaven, and thou art on earth'" (ER 10), it would seem that he has created finitude in mind.[34] This seems even more explicit when he speaks of "the infinite distance between Creator and creation" (TM 205).[35] But in the latter case he goes on to speak of a dialectic of Yes and No in which the Yes points to "the creation of man in the image of God" and the No to the fact "that man as we know him is fallen man, whose misery we know better than his glory" (TM 207). And in the former case he describes revelation as the intersection of two planes: "God's creation, fallen out of its union with Him and therefore the world of the 'flesh' needing redemption" and "the world of the Father, of the Primal Creation, and of the final Redemption" (ER 29). It is not creation that needs revelation, but fallen creation.

About unfallen creation Barth has several important things to say. (1) Creation is "original grace" (CP 300). To affirm creation is already to step outside the boundaries of metaphysics, ethics, psychology, and history, for 'grace' is not a category of any of these modes of human knowledge. (2) Creation is a

---

32. See Schleiermacher, *On Religion: Speeches to Its Cultured Despisers*, trans. John Oman (New York: Harper & Brothers, 1958), Second Speech.

33. This move, or at least the need for it, is already apparent in Schleiermacher's own systematic theology, *The Christian Faith*.

34. But perhaps he remembers the argument of *Philosophical Fragments*, where Johannes Climacus links the miracle of revelation, as contrasted with recollection, with the notion of God as "absolutely different" and then argues that it is not creation but sin that renders God "absolutely different" from us. Kierkegaard, PF 9–48.

35. Cf. RC 251, where he speaks of the relation of Creator to creature as "antithesis."

"primal union with God" and a "direct relation with Him" (ER 244). Barth describes this unity as an "immediacy" to God (CP 290) and an "original synthesis" prior to the separation of thesis and antithesis of the divine Yes and No (CP 299, 312). (3) This original harmony is not a moment in history as we know it, which means for Barth, as we have seen, that it is neither explainable nor knowable as a historical phenomenon. It belongs to what Levinas would call an "irrecuperable . . . unrepresentable, immemorial, pre-historical" past[36] and what Chrétien would call the Unforgettable,[37] in either case signifying a past outside of our temporal frame of reference. The fall is "the unavoidable pre-supposition of all human history" (ER 181) and "man as we know him is fallen man" (TM 207).

(4) This past is of eschatological significance. Although lost, it is to be won again, and for this reason when theology thinks the original *and final* synthesis, it looks both backward and forward (CP 290, 299, 312; cf. ER 277). The God of revealing grace is the God "of the Primal Creation and the final Redemption" (ER 29). (5) But this past is also of present significance. Although we have never experienced it, we cannot forget it but are haunted by a reminiscence of it (BQ 55; ER 243–44).[38] This is the truth both of the idea of a divine spark in each person (CP 3310) and of the notion that we could not seek God had we not already been found (BQ 55). So we say Yes to the world and ourselves qua created and No to the world and ourselves as fallen. (6) Finally, the two are not symmetrical. "We live more deeply in the No than in the Yes. . . . True perception of life is hostile to all abstractions. It may say Yes, but only in order out of the Yes still more loudly and urgently to say No . . . the Yes becomes No" (CP 311–13). Thus we can speak of "the glory of God in creation" but only if we "pass immediately to emphasizing God's complete concealment from us in that creation" (TM 207).

In other words, in a prelapsarian condition, knowledge of God was/would have been natural and direct. The original grace of creation would have obviated any need for a subsequent grace of revelation as the miracle that overcomes the impossibility of the knowledge of God. The necessity of revelation comes from the loss of that primal immediacy. The bond has been broken and cannot be restored by our agency. We no longer have the condition or capacity for knowing God, nor is there a way or a method by which we can build a bridge from fallenness to fellowship with God. To use an Aristotelian

---

36. Emmanuel Levinas, *Otherwise Than Being or Beyond Essence*, trans. Alphonso Lingis (Boston: Kluwer, 1991), p. 38.

37. Jean-Louis Chrétien, *The Unforgettable and the Unhoped For*, trans. Jeffrey Bloechl (New York: Fordham University Press, 2002), especially ch. 3. The Unforgettable is such precisely because it cannot be remembered.

38. This reminiscence is obviously not an empirical memory, nor is it a Platonic recollection that could be the ground of genuine knowledge. It is more like what Levinas calls a trace. See Levinas, "The Trace of the Other," in *Deconstruction in Context: Literature and Philosophy*, ed. Mark C. Taylor (Chicago: University of Chicago Press, 1986), pp. 345–59.

figure, we have jumped into a hole too deep to jump out of.[39] We are like the child who has broken a toy that only a parent can fix. In Barth's view, following the Reformers, this is just as true of our epistemic as of our ethical/existential situation. Knowledge of God will depend on divine grace every bit as much as forgiveness and reconciliation. The condition for its possibility will have to be divine agency, not human capacity.

In a subtle but important nuance, Barth presents divine self-manifestation as a double agency, not God's act and our act, but God's act and God's act. He holds that revelation is not restricted to the Christ event. As we have seen, even "an ignorant and superstitious worship of the most terrible kind" can bear "an impress of revelation" and can be "a witness to the Unknown God" (ER 95). But he also holds that the definitive and decisive self-revelation of God occurs in Jesus Christ and it is in terms of that event, which took place in but not of history, that Barth spells out his account of revelation. The Bible, the whole Bible on his view, bears witness that "in Christ God was reconciling the world to himself" (2 Cor. 5:19) and in this way plays a decisive role in revelation. He holds that the scripture principle, *sola scriptura*, is utterly fundamental to the Reformed branch of Protestantism to which he belongs.

> What one may be moved to say concerning God, the world, and man because he *must* say it, having let the Scriptures speak to him—the Scriptures themselves, and not the Scriptures interpreted by any particular tradition; the whole Scriptures, and not a part of them chosen to suit a preconceived theory; the Scriptures, and not the utterances of pious men of the past or present which might be confused with them; the Scriptures, and not without the significant word of the Spirit which sustains them—what, after *those* Scriptures have spoken to him, one may be moved to say in fear and trembling concerning the things about which man of himself may say nothing, or only foolishness, *that*, if we may judge from our beginnings, is Reformed doctrine. (RC 241)

The important thing to notice here is that the appeal to the Scriptures is "not without the significant word of the Spirit which sustains them." In his Calvin lectures of 1922, Barth writes, "Calvin never spoke of the inspiration of the Bible without, at the same time, asserting a counter-principle of the most subjective character. I am thinking here of the '*tertimonium spiritus sancti internum*' the voice of the truth which causes itself to be heard not only in the Bible but also in its believing reader or hearer . . ."[40] Accordingly Barth defines

---

39. I was taught not to end a sentence with a preposition, but they never said anything about ending with two.

40. Quoted in McCormack, CRDT 307. See John Calvin, *Institutes of the Christian Religion*, trans. Ford Lewis Battles and John T. McNeill (Philadelphia, Pa.: Westminster Press, 1960), Bk. I, ch. VII, whose title reads in part, "Scripture Must Be Confirmed by the Witness of the Spirit. Thus May Its Authority Be Established as Certain." In section 5 of this chapter, Calvin writes, "For even

Reformed theology in terms of the dual principle, Scripture and Spirit. There is "no such thing as Reformed doctrine, except the timeless appeal to the open Bible and to the Spirit which from it speaks to our spirit," from which Barth draws the conclusion that there can be no creedal formulation beyond critique and reformulation (RC 229–30). For Reformed creeds, "*truth* is God—not their *thought* about God but God *himself* and God *alone*, as he speaks his own *word* in Scripture and in Spirit" (RC 235). The claim that the Bible is God's word has been called a theological axiom, but it is unlike mathematical axioms. "It expresses obedience to the *tertimonium spiritus sancti internum*, to the spirit of God in which the human spirit of the writer and the reader become one in common adoration; and the truth of the statement stands or falls with the reality of this sovereign act proceeding from God and authenticated by him" (RC 244). Just in case we haven't been paying attention, Barth says it one more time. "Reformed doctrine, in order to be itself at all, needs the free winds wherein the word of God is recognized in Scripture and Spirit" (RC 247).

The point of all this, I think, is as follows. Objectively speaking, revelation means that God puts the truth in front of us, since we have the capacity neither to do this nor to place ourselves in front of the truth. This happens in the Christ event and in the biblical witness thereto. The words of Scripture point us to the Word made flesh, the miracle in which the Invisible becomes visible, the Unknowable becomes knowable, and the Impossible becomes possible. But we have no faculty for apprehending miracle as such (ER 120). In other words, not only do we lack the capacity to find the truth, but even if it is placed right in front of us by a first divine act, we lack the capacity to recognize it as the truth apart from a second divine act of illumination, the internal testimony of the Holy Spirit. Revelation is this double miracle. Objectively, God shows us the truth we cannot discover for ourselves, and subjectively, God enables us to see that it is the truth. In the double act which overcomes our double incapacity, God give us the only genuine knowledge of God we have.

* * *

In relation to the critique of onto-theology, it would be ironical indeed if the notion of revelation as miracle meant that, with a little help from God, to be sure, the Highest Being and thereby the whole of being were to become fully transparent to human understanding. God would have entered human discourse in order to meet the human demand, or perhaps Luciferian aspiration, that we should see everything as God sees it, *sub specie aeternitatis*. Drawing on Husserlian phenomenology, Heidegger finds unconcealment and concealment to be inextricably intertwined in all human experience. In the

---

if [Scripture] wins reverence for itself by its own majesty, it seriously affects us only when it is sealed upon our hearts through the Spirit."

context of the critique of onto-theology, he finds this to be true *a fortiori* of our understanding of God (ID 64–67). In chapter 1 we have seen that the loss of mystery is, in Heidegger's view, one of the fatal flaws of onto-theology.

The irony just mentioned is not to be found in Barth's theology, for on this point he sides with Heidegger against Spinoza and Hegel. Even in revelation, God remains deeply mysterious for Barth. He does not invoke the tradition of the *via negativa* to make this point for two reasons we have already seen: first, the notion of a *via* too easily suggests that the condition for the possibility of our access to the *Sache* in question is the method we employ, and second, the *negativa* is too easily left by itself, leaving us not with faith but with abyssal skepticism, a dark night of the soul into which no light shines. But he does employ the language that others have used to express this theme. Thus with Luther he speaks of God as *deus absconditus* (ER 42). With Kierkegaard he speaks of the "infinite qualitative distinction" between time and eternity, humankind and God. And with Rudolf Otto he speaks of God as Wholly Other (*totaliter aliter*) and as the *mysterium tremendum* (BQ 74–76, 92).

In revelation the Invisible becomes visible, to be sure, but not as "a visible thing in the midst of other visible things," but rather as "visible only in its invisibility" (ER 92). We are "far from being equal to that knowledge," given to us in revelation, for the truth of God is "incomprehensible" (BQ 52, 69). This extends to the world as well as God, and "our desire to comprehend the world in its relation to God, must proceed either from the criminal arrogance of religion [as onto-theologically constituted] or from that final apprehension of truth which lies beyond birth and death—the perception, in other words, which proceeds from God outwards" (ER 37). But this latter perception only occurs in faith, and faith " 'directs itself towards the things that are invisible. Indeed, only when that which is believed on is hidden, can it provide an opportunity for faith.' . . . Faith is awe in the presence of the divine incognito; it is the love of God that is aware of the qualitative distinction between God and man and God and the world" (ER 39).[41] Subjectively speaking, in faith we know as those who don't know (ER 45, 48); objectively speaking, in faith we have "knowledge of the unknown God" (ER 48). This does not mean that in that knowledge God ceases, as Spinoza and Hegel would have it, to be unknown. It rather means that "God is known as the Unknown God" (ER 77).

Barth is not unaware of a traditional reason, perhaps *the* traditional reason in both the Eastern and Western Christian churches, for affirming the in-

---

41. The single quotes indicate a constructed quotation attributed to Luther. A similar constructed quotation is attributed to Kierkegaard, no doubt with Johannes Climacus especially in mind, on the previous page. "Now, Spirit is the denial of direct immediacy. If Christ be very God, He must be unknown, for to be known directly is the characteristic mark of an idol." Barth also writes, "In so far as our world is touched in Jesus by the other world, it ceases to be capable of direct observation as history, time, or thing." For this reason, "Jesus as the Christ, as the Messiah . . . can only be comprehended only as Paradox (Kierkegaard)" (ER 29).

comprehensibility and ineffability of God, namely that *"finitum non est capax infiniti"* (RC 231). But this maxim is not presented as the primary ground for the claim that precisely as *deus revelatus* God remains *deus absconditus*. Just as it is not human finitude that makes revelation necessary, so it is not human finitude that keeps God hidden in epiphany, concealed in unconcealment. As it turns out, it is the very nature of revelation itself, as Barth understands it, that makes the worldly medium of divine self-manifestation, whether it be a burning bush or Jesus of Nazareth, a translucent and not a transparent lens, a mirror in which we see darkly, dimly, in a riddle or enigma (ἐν αἰνίματι, 1 Cor. 13:12).[42]

Barth is not operating in the tradition of Husserlian phenomenology, but his point can best be understood with reference to others who are. In his famous analysis of The Look,[43] Sartre argues that we are aware of other persons as subjects and not objects not, as Husserl had argued,[44] by perceiving an object and somehow or other managing to construe it as a subject. It is rather when we are aware of being looked at by another that the other's subjectivity is given to us. In Husserlian language we can call this inverted or reversed intentionality, for my awareness of the other is not grounded in my intentional act (*noesis*) directed toward some intentional object (*noema*) within the horizon of my transcendental ego. The intentionality that grounds my awareness does not emanate from me but rather toward me from the other. It is as object of the other's gaze that I become aware of the other's subjectivity. This is why Levinas, whose analysis of the face as both the look and the voice that puts me in question and calls me to ethical responsibility builds on the Sartrean analysis, can tell us he is a phenomenologist interested in "an intentionality of a wholly different type,"[45] namely a type in which my awareness of myself and another has its ground in that other self. By speaking of this human other in the language of glory and revelation, Levinas introduces theological overtones into his discussion, if not exactly God. Derrida is less oblique when he iden-

---

42. The *Revised English Bible* speaks of "puzzling reflections in a mirror." The mirror Paul has in mind is probably some kind of polished metal rather than the tained glass we use as a mirror.

43. Sartre, *Being and Nothingness*, trans. Hazel E. Barnes (New York: Philosophical Library, 1956), part 3, ch. 1.

44. Husserl, *Cartesian Meditations*, trans. Dorion Cairns (The Hague: Martinus Nijhoff, 1973), fifth meditation.

45. Levinas, *Totality and Infinity*, trans. Alphonso Lingis (Pittsburgh, Pa.: Duquesne University Press, 1969), p. 23. Cf. p. 126 and p. 29, where Levinas argues that "not every transcendent intention has the noesis-noema structure." The presence of the other is a revelation inasmuch as it "constitutes a veritable inversion [of] *objectifying cognition*" (p. 67). In *Otherwise Than Being*, Levinas carries on a sustained polemic against the transcendental unity of apperception so as to point to an "experience" whose condition of possibility lies outside myself and my horizons (pp. 141, 148, 151–52, 163–64, 171. Cf. the similar polemic in "God and Philosophy"). He renders this notion more concrete by speaking of a reversed conatus (pp. 70, 75). The desire of my whole being and not merely some cognitive faculty is at issue.

tifies God, phenomenologically, as the "infinite other that sees without being seen."[46]

In the first edition of *Romans,* Barth writes that in our knowledge of God "we not only see, but *are seen,* not only understand, but *are understood;* not only comprehend, but *are grasped.*"[47] In an essay the following year he says that we are known before we know (BQ 95–96), while in the revised *Romans* he says that it is not that we know but rather that we are known (ER 61, 206). Speaking of the knowledge of our own sinfulness, which is integral to our knowledge of God, Barth first makes an explicitly Kantian gesture, denying that we are the condition for the possibility of this knowledge, and then identifies that condition as follows—"A gaze has been fixed upon us" (ER 272).

Like Levinas after him,[48] Barth gives an existential and not narrowly epistemic account of this gaze. He speaks of the way our questions have "a disconcerting way of turning about" and putting us in question (BQ 51); he speaks of a "demand" addressed to those who are "called" as those "belong no longer to themselves" (ER 31); he says it is not that we have chosen God but that God has chosen us (ER 59); and of the biblical paradigm of faith, he says, "Abraham never 'possessed God': God possessed him" (ER 123).

It may well be that, ontologically speaking, "*finitum non est capax infiniti.*" But for an epistemology (1) that takes the vision metaphor inherited in the West from Plato and reverses it so as to talk about a knowledge whose ground is being seen, (2) that goes beyond the gaze in which we are seen to the voice by which we are questioned, called, chosen, and commanded, and (3) that does this in the service of a triumph of divine grace in any genuine human knowledge of God, there is a deeper reason why God remains concealed even in divinely initiated unconcealment. God is simply not given to us in the modes in which "objects" are rendered transparent to our intentional gaze, whether that is understood in terms of Platonic recollection or in terms of any of the many footnotes thereto, such as the clear and distinct ideas of Descartes, the impressions of Hume, the transcendental unity of apperception of Kant, the speculative Idea of Hegel, or the fulfilled intentions of Husserl. In all of these modes we are the condition for the possibility of God's givenness to us, and for this reason there is at least the theoretical possibility, so unambiguously affirmed by Hegel, of replacing mystery with transparency, thereby reducing revelation to human reason. On Barth's account of revelation, it is because God alone is the possibility of our knowledge of God and is this condition as a subject who looks at us and speaks to us that God becomes

---

46. Derrida, *The Gift of Death,* trans. David Wills (Chicago: University of Chicago Press, 1995), p. 2. Cf. pp. 25, 27, 31, 40, 56, 91. In some of these passages Derrida is drawing directly on the work of Jan Patočka.

47. Cited by McCormack in CRDT 158.

48. See note 45 above.

revelatus only as *absconditus*. In this context to attempt to dissolve the divine mystery is to deface God and to silence God's voice. The God who resists every such project is one who refuses to enter human discourse on philosophy's terms (at least the terms of a major strand of Western philosophy), but who *ipso facto* gives Godself to human prayer and worship, singing and (perhaps even) dancing.

* * *

When we take our question about epistemic transcendence from the early Barth of *Romans* to the "late" or "mature" Barth of *Church Dogmatics*,[49] we find ourselves in very familiar territory. In his Foreword he complains about "the constantly increasing barbarism, tedium, and insignificance of modern Protestantism, which has gone and lost—apparently along with the Trinity and the Virgin Birth—an entire third dimension (let us say it once and for all, the dimension of mystery . . .)" (CD I/1, xi). What makes this passage especially interesting is that in the prolegomena to his systematic theology, entitled *The Doctrine of the Word of God*, it is in his defense of the doctrine of the Virgin Birth that he most succinctly resumes his theological epistemology of revelation as miracle and mystery. It comes in chapter II, §15, section 3, entitled, "The Miracle of Christmas." He begins as follows:

> God's revelation in its objective reality is the incarnation of His Word, in that He, the one true eternal God, is at the same time true Man like us. . . . [This is] not only a mystery but the prime mystery. In other words, it becomes the object of our knowledge; it finds a way of becoming the content of our experience and our thought; it gives itself to be apprehended by our contemplation and our categories.[50] But it does that beyond the range of what we regard as possible for our contemplation and perception, beyond the confines of our experience and our thought. It comes to us as a *Novum* which, when it becomes an object for us, we cannot incorporate in the series of our other objects, cannot compare with them, cannot deduce from their context, cannot regard as analogous with them. It comes to us as a datum with no point of connexion with any other previous datum.[51] It becomes the object of our knowledge by its own power and not by ours.[52]

---

49. For a detailed account of Barth's development between the second edition of *Romans* (1922) and the first half volume *Church Dogmatics* (1932), see McCormack, CRDT.

50. For example, in the formulations of Nicea and Chalcedon.

51. In other words, this "phenomenon" as epiphany shows no respect for the principle of sufficient reason. See Heidegger's critique in chapter 1 above.

52. Note that here as before the content of revelation is mysterious not because *finitum non est capax infiniti* but because we are not the condition for the possibility of this knowledge or experience. The former would be only a special case of the latter, and as we shall shortly see, it is not the operative case in the present context.

> The act of knowing it is distinctive as one which we can achieve, but which we cannot understand, in the sense that we simply do not know how we can achieve it. We can understand the possibility of it solely from the side of its object, i.e., we can regard it not as ours, but as one coming to us, imparted to us, gifted to us. In this bit of knowing we are not the masters, but the mastered. (CD I/2, 172)

But in this knowing of the event of incarnation, which is at once revelation and reconciliation, we recognize that it is "inconceivable," that we are speaking of something "really other," that our experience and thought "are delimited, determined and dominated here by something wholly outside or above us. Knowledge in this case means acknowledgment. And the utterance or expression of this knowledge is termed confession" (CD I/2, 173).[53]

Such revelation is at once grace and judgment (CD I/2, 187–88). It is grace because it is the gift of what we cannot give ourselves. It is judgment because it calls attention to this fact, namely that we do not have the capacity[54] for this knowledge. But what does judgment mean here? Does it have the logical sense of assertion or the legal sense of verdict? Clearly the latter. This judgment

> is not the difference between God as Creator and man as creature. Man as a creature—if we try for a moment to speak of man in this abstract way—might have the capacity for God. . . . But the man whom revelation reaches, and who is reconciled to God in revelation and by it, is not man in Paradise. He has not ceased to be God's creature. But he has lost his pure creatureliness, and with it the capacity for God, because as a creature in the totality of his creatureliness he became disobedient. It is with this disobedient creature that God has to do in His revelation. (CD I/2, 188)

It is as sinners that we can only receive the capacity to know God in the double miracle by which the Word becomes flesh (objectively) and we are able to recognize God in Jesus and the divine Word in the human words about him.[55]

What has all his to do with the Virgin Birth of Jesus, as attested by Matthew and Luke? Quite simply, this miracle is a sign of the double miracle by

---

53. Cf. Augustine's contrast between the "presumption" of the Platonists, who depend on recollection, with the "confession" of the believer, who acknowledges revelation. Cited above in chapter 4 from *Confessions*, VII, 20.

54. Barth uses both *Fähigkeit* and *Möglichkeit* for what the English renders as 'capacity', nicely showing that the possibility, or rather impossibility, involved is a matter of power and not formal, logical possibility.

55. These human words are in the first place the words of Holy Scripture and in the second place the preaching derived therefrom. Revelation thus has a "threefold form" that can be thought of as concentric circles. The outermost circle, preaching, derives from the second circle, the proclamation of Scripture, which in turn bears witness to the innermost circle, the event of the Word made flesh. See CD I/1, §4. Working from inner to outer, "It is just the immediate Word of God which meets us only in this twofold mediacy" (p. 136).

which both faith and its object are given to us. As such it "denotes not so much the christological reality of revelation as the mystery of that reality, the inconceivability of it, its character as a fact in which God has acted solely through God and in which God can likewise be known solely through God" (CD I/2, 177). Accordingly, this sign is anything but an explanation. Brunner would be right to reject this doctrine if it were conceived as an attempt at a biological explanation of what in fact is inexplicable mystery (CD I/2, 183–84). The connection between sign and signified "is not a causal one," nor is its function to prove or explain the sinlessness of Christ as its necessary condition (CD I/2, 189–90). It is not to be thought onto-theologically in terms of the principle of sufficient reason in either its epistemic or ontological modes, as in proof and explanation, respectively.

How, then, does the Virgin Birth function, if instead of being an explanation of anything at all it is a sign of the inconceivability of that to which it points? How is the sign appropriate to its signified? For Barth, the removal of human fatherhood is not about some supposed link between sin and sexuality but about the link between sin and male agency. With reference to a symbolic order or collective unconscious that permeates human history, at least in patriarchal contexts, Barth relates male sexuality with human sovereignty.[56] But "sovereign man as such cannot be considered as a participator in God's work. For as such he is the man of disobedience. As such, therefore, if God's grace is to meet him, he must be set aside. But this man in the state of disobedience is *a parte potiori* the male. So it is the male who must be set aside here, if a countersign is to be set up as the sign of the incarnation of God. In this sign the contradiction of grace is directed against the male because he is peculiarly significant for the world history of human genius," that is, of exceptional human capacity (CD I/2, 193–94). It is in this way that *natus ex virgine* is a sign of "the inconceivable act of creative omnipotence in which [God] imparts to human nature a capacity, a power for Himself, which it does not possess of itself and which it could not devise for itself" (CD I/1, 201).

Barth concludes, "The mystery does not rest upon the miracle." In other words, the incarnation is not mysterious because of the miracle of the Virgin Birth. "The miracle rests upon the mystery" to which it bears witness (CD I/2, 202). The incarnation is mysterious not in the realm of essences but in the realm of agencies. It is a fact which neither in its actuality nor in its knowability falls within the range of human capacity. As such it is in itself in both respects the primary miracle. The Virgin Birth is a secondary miracle that serves as a sign pointing to the primary miracle. If faith as the acknowledgment of these miracles must be, as we find in Kierkegaard's *Philosophical Fragments*, the "conquest of offense," this is because "sovereign man" would prefer to adopt

---

56. He does not mention one of the most dramatic expressions of this, the all too common linkage of military conquest with rape.

some version of the theory of recollection, according to which we already have the truth about Eternity within us and the capacity to recognize it as such as well (CD I/2, 181).

* * *

In Chapter Five of *Church Dogmatics,* entitled simply "The Knowledge of God," Barth gives us the fullest account of his mature theological epistemology. He repeatedly stresses that it is a *theological* epistemology, not just because it is about our knowledge of God but especially because it is grounded in revelation, as he understands it, and not in philosophical speculation or analysis. In his earlier writings he often referred to Plato and Kant as expressing a dialectic of time and eternity akin to that which he found in the epistle to the Romans, and in his first attempt at a systematic theology, in 1927,[57] he similarly alluded to existentialism. While he treated these philosophical references as illustrative analogs to what he was saying on the basis of biblical revelation, he came to fear that it too easily looked as if, like theologians from whom he was eager to distance himself, such as Aquinas (as we shall see) and Schleiermacher, he was trying to establish philosophical foundations for his theological system. So at the very beginning of *Church Dogmatics* he writes, "I have cut out in this second issue of the book everything that in the first issue might give the slightest appearance of giving to theology a basis, support, or even a mere justification in the way of existential philosophy" (CD I/1, ix); and he regularly reminds us that his account is not derived from some philosophical system (see CD II/1, 5–6, 183–86, 206, 221–22).

As we work our way through Chapter Five, we find ourselves in familiar territory. The theological question is not whether God is knowable but how and how far (CD II/1, 5). In answer to the first of these questions—how?—the emphatic answer is revelation as the double miracle of Word and Spirit. We have no capacity for knowledge of God, which occurs, when it does, "without and against" our power (CD II/1, 199, 213). Revelation means the divine initiative of grace as "free love" (CD II/1, 206) that can only be received in faith as obedience, and trust, and thanks and awe. God is the subject, not just the subject matter or content, of this knowing. In fact, our own subjectivity is the product of this knowing, not its producer, the constituted rather than the constitutor (CD II/1, 21, 25).[58] Neither the knowing nor the known

---

57. Barth, *Die christliche Dogmatik im Entwurf* (Zurich: TVZ, 1982).

58. Here again we encounter the motif of reverse intentionality in which the "transcendental" ego is not the ground of our knowing but is grounded in a distinctive mode of awareness. A little further on Barth will write, "God's real revelation is the possibility which man does not have to choose, but by which he must regard himself as chosen without having space and time to come to an arrangement with it within the sphere and according to the method of other possibilities" (CD II/1, 139). Cf. Levinas, who calls the presence of the neighbor a non-negotiable claim "proximity" and says that proximity is "an assignation, an extremely urgent assignation—an obligation,

falls within our horizons, is at our disposal, or is subject to our control, mastery, or possession.

In answer to the second question—how far?—Barth continues to develop the mystery motif. Even in revelation, God remains a mystery to us "because He Himself has made Himself to clear and certain to us" (CD II/1, 38). In other words, God's incomprehensibility is part of the content of revelation (and not something theology needs to learn from philosophy). In fact, "our knowledge of God begins in all seriousness with the knowledge of the hiddenness of God. . . . The first work of the worship with which we thank Him for the grace of His revelation is to know and confess Him as the hidden One" (CD II/1, 183, 197). God exceeds our cognitive grasp (1) because otherwise the one revealed would not be God, (2) because God is knowable only from God, that is, by revelation, and (3) because revelation is a knowledge mediated through parts of the created order, above all through Jesus of Nazareth, that serve as signs. These signs are the clothes or works in which God mediates self-manifestation. They are the enigmatic mirror in which we see, but only dimly or darkly (CD II/1, 52–54). When God "makes Himself visible for us through [signs], He accepts the fact that He will remain invisible as the One He is in Himself and as He knows Himself" (CD II/1, 55). To know such a sign without recognizing the inextricable mixture of unveiling and veiling in it is to know an idol (CD II/1, 55).[59]

In the midst of these familiar themes we encounter new ones, at least some new formulations and new emphases. Thus, the abstract or presummary for §27 reads as follows:

God is known only by God. We do not know Him, then, in virtue of the views and concepts[60] with which in faith we attempt to respond to His revelation. But we also do not know Him without making use of His permis-

---

anachronously prior to any commitment. This anteriority is 'older' than the a priori and is thus like an obsession or even a persecution. "This inversion of consciousness is no doubt a passivity—but it is a passivity beneath all passivity [such as Kantian receptivity which gives rise to knowledge in cooperation with the knower's conceptual spontaneity]. It cannot be defined in terms of intentionality. . . . To be sure, the intentionality of consciousness does not designate voluntary intention only. Yet it retains the initiating and incohative pattern of voluntary intention. The given enters into a thought which recognizes in it or invests it with its own project, and thus exercises mastery over it." *Otherwise Than Being*, p. 101.

59. On this point there is a deep affinity between Barth and Jean-Luc Marion, who distinguished the idol from the icon in these terms. See *God Without Being*, trans. Thomas A. Carlson (Chicago: University of Chicago Press, 1991), especially ch. 1–3 and *Idol and Distance*, trans. Thomas A. Carlson (New York: Fordham University Press, 2001).

60. The translation of *Anschauungen* and *Begriffe* as 'views' and 'concepts' hides the Kantian character of Barth's vocabulary, so I shall henceforth substitute 'intuitions' for 'views'. For Kant, intuitions (sensibility, receptivity) and concepts (understanding, spontaneity) jointly give rise to experiential knowledge. Without basing his theology on appeal to Kant, Barth describes our ordinary knowledge in Kantian terms. With Kant, but for theological reasons, Barth holds that we cannot know God by means of the cognitive equipment with which we know created beings.

sion and obeying His command to undertake this attempt. The success of this undertaking, and therefore the veracity of our human knowledge of God, consists in the fact that our viewing and conceiving is adopted and determined to participation in the truth of God by God Himself in grace (CD II/1, 179).

We have been hearing that our knowledge of God has its ground outside ourselves, that it proceeds *von Gott aus*, that God is the agent, the subject of our knowing; and we've been hearing the negative presupposition of this, namely that we lack the capacity for knowing God. Now we hear the positive presupposition, which, interestingly enough, we have already heard from Pseudo-Dionysius and Aquinas: "God is known by God and by God alone" (CD II/1, 179);[61] and we hear the corollary, namely that the knowledge of God given to us in revelation is a "participation" in God's own self-knowledge. We can know God only because "God does not wish to know Himself without Himself giving us a part in this event" (CD II/1, 204; cf. 49, 51, 57, 59). Here we encounter Barth's realism. It has two components. First, what we know is "out there." It is and it is what it is independently of whether or what we may think about it. Second, we have genuine knowledge of our "object," not of some mirage, projection, or constitution that emanates from ourselves.[62]

In his early essay on theological method, Barth praised dogmatic method, of which he was also critical, for its "taste for objectivity" (TM 201). As we have seen, Barth's early critique of liberal Protestantism included the claim that by making the human subject the ground of our knowledge of God it left itself defenseless before Feuerbach's reduction of theology to anthropology. It consists of systematically misleading expressions that seem to be about God but in fact are about ourselves. Hunsinger appropriately points out that the "objectiv-

---

61. See ch. 4 n. 42 and ch. 5 n. 62. In a footnote to the first edition of *Romans*, Barth had written that the love of God comes to us not necessarily as feeling, which may or may not be present, but "as the re-acquired knowledge of God with which God immediately knows Himself . . ." Cited by McCormack in CRDT 159n. In a 1929 evaluation of the relative strengths and weaknesses of realism and idealism, he writes that "the unity of reality and truth occurs in and only in God's Word" (FI 58). And in 1931 he writes, "Strictly speaking, it is only God himself who has a conception of God" (A 29). Thomas Merton may be thinking of Aquinas, but he is very close to Barth when he writes that God "is only known and loved by those to whom He has freely given a share of His own knowledge and love of Himself." *New Seeds of Contemplation* (New York: New Directions, 1972), p. 40.

62. I believe this usage corresponds with the sense in which McCormack calls Barth's theology realistic. It does not correspond to 'realism' as Hunsinger uses it to name a central motif in *Church Dogmatics*, since he includes in its meaning Barth's theory of analogy, which I keep conceptually distinct. 'Realism', as used here, is closer to Hunsinger's 'objectivism'. Although his preliminary definition of this motif includes only the first of the two parts mentioned above, his subsequent account includes both: "The knowledge of God as confessed by faith had been shown to be irreducible and objective, logically speaking, on the grounds that God's self-revelation in history gives faith a share in God's own self-knowledge as it is in eternity." See George Hunsinger, *How to Read Karl Barth: The Shape of His Theology* (New York: Oxford University Press, 1991), pp. 4–5, 36.

ism" of *Church Dogmatics* continues the attempt to resist such a reduction.[63] Thus we read that the revelation of God as the Word made flesh involves an "irrevocable objectivity" in which God "enters into the relationship of object to man the subject" and becomes "the object of his perception, intuition, and conception [*Wahrnehmung, Anschauen, Begreifen*]" (CD II/1, 12, 9, 3; cf. 179, 181). Although Barth insists that God is not an object like other objects and, indeed, is not only a subject but the subject of our own subjectivity,[64] he does not shy away from repeatedly saying that in revelation God becomes the object of our knowledge. This is the double miracle, objective and subjective, of revelation that we have already seen. "In His Word [God] comes as an object before man the subject. And by the Holy Spirit He makes the human subject accessible to Himself, capable of considering and conceiving Himself as object." The result is an "objective knowledge" that does not "leave out the distinction between the knower and the known" (CD II/1, 10). If this distinction were to be elided, it would make no sense to talk of God speaking to us in revelation or of us speaking to God in prayer (CD II/1, 13–14).[65]

But Barth's realism is not just about *objective* knowledge; it is also about objective *knowledge*. Faith, as the response to revelation, is not mere opinion or belief, as on Plato's divided line; it is knowledge (CD II/1, 13).[66] In contrast to skepticism or any merely negative theology, Barth regularly speaks of the "fulfillment" [*Vollzug*], "veracity" [*Wahrhaftigkeit*], and "success" [*Gelingen*] of our cognition by virtue of God's grace in revelation. In this knowledge we are not deceived because it is true or authentic [*wahrhaftig*], right or correct, valid, unassailable, trustworthy, legitimate, and genuine [*wirklich*] (CD II/1, 202–27). This knowledge is "fully true" because of its "correspondence" [*Entsprechung*] and because of the "positive relationship" and "real fellowship" [*Gemeinschaft*] between knower and known (CD II/1, 16, 224).

Has Barth forgotten everything he has said about the hiddenness of God in revelation? No, he has not, and it is time to notice the ways he qualifies these exuberantly positive claims without withdrawing them. As we do, it is worth noting that in both the affirmation and the qualification Barth speaks of our knowledge not only in terms of our intuitions and concepts, but also in terms of our words. He often links the three together (CD II/1, 213, 224, 227–28). At

---

63. Hunsinger, *How to Read*, p. 35.

64. Hunsinger refers to this as the "personalism" motif. *How to Read*, pp. 5, 40–42.

65. Barth regularly says that theology begins with prayer, perhaps thinking of Augustine and Anselm who sometimes do theology *as* prayer. One will not find this in Spinoza's or Hegel's account of our highest knowledge of God.

66. This is already true in *Romans*, though perhaps without the same emphatic emphasis. Graham Ward is mistaken to speak of "the sheer agnosticism" of *Romans*. Nor is he correct to find a theological realism in Barth only after the Anselm book of 1931. See pp. 92, 94. In a 1929 critique of Thomistic realism, Barth insists as emphatically as in *Church Dogmatics* that theology must nevertheless be realistic in the sense presently under discussion. He even calls God "the pre-eminent reality" the "*ens realissimum*" (FI 35–37).

the outset of his systematic theology, he defines dogmatics as "the scientific test to which the Christian Church puts herself regarding the language about God which is peculiar to her" (CD I/1, 1), and he reminds his readers and himself that the question of truth is a question about language (CD II/1, 195, 205). This does not mean he has fully taken the linguistic turn according to which all knowledge is linguistically embedded. Drawing on a classical distinction that goes back to Augustine and Plato, he distinguishes our thinking, to which our intuitions and concepts belong, from our speaking, to which our words belong. The former involves what we tell ourselves and thus our responsibility to ourselves, while the latter involves what we tell others and thus our responsibility to them (CD II/1, 211). This notion that language is but the means of communicating knowledge already achieved without its aid is widely disputed in contemporary philosophy. But in the present context that debate is not of great import, for in his analysis of theological knowledge, Barth ignores the distinction between thought and language and lumps our intuitions, concepts, and words together as the site where revelation happens.

Barth has not forgotten that the knowledge for which he has been making such strong claims is knowledge by participation. God is "this One first of all in Himself, and on this basis He is it secondly (not as Another, but in another way) for us" (CD II/1, 227). So Barth is a realist with quite specific "reservations" (FI 40). The objectivity he has been stressing is secondary. Primary objectivity is God's own immediate self-knowledge. Ours is a secondary objectivity, mediated "under the sign and veil of objects different from Himself" (CD II/1, 16), for "it would have to be another God who could see God directly" (CD II/1, 19). Because we cannot know God as God knows God (CD II/1, 59, 202), our knowledge is approximate, inadequate, and improper (CD II/1, 202, 205, 217, 224)—but true, at least "as true as it can be" (CD II/1, 209). The formula from the Anselm book, inadequate but true (A 29), reverberates through Chapter Five of *Church Dogmatics*.

* * *

But how shall we understand this formula, so utterly paradoxical in view of the classical definition of truth in terms of adequation (*adaequatio rei et intellectus*)? Graham Ward claims that there is an "irreducible incompleteness" in Barth's theology.

> There is no resolution of the paradox of language in chapter 5—even though that must place in doubt all that Barth has constructed for us theologically. There is no coherent account of the Word in words. In attempting to unravel the logic of divine communication, Barth is aware that the logic is beyond him and he is unable to reconstruct its economy. . . . Christology alone cannot provide a synthesis for the paradoxical foundation of Barth's theology of language. Christology as a theology of the Word, itself demands a coherent theology of language. . . . If there is to be knowledge of God at all, if

the economy of salvation is to be effected, there has to be found some ground for a theological realism.[67]

I believe a Barthian response would be fivefold: First, in order for knowledge of God to take place it is not necessary to give an account or find a ground. Faith does not require theology any more than eating requires biology. Some beliefs are properly basic and do not require evidential or explanatory support from other beliefs.[68]

Second, while faith does not require theology, theology is the attempt to give a coherent account of what the church believes and proclaims on the basis of Scripture. This methodological coherentism is one of the basic motifs of *Church Dogmatics* according to Hunsinger, who calls it, perhaps misleadingly, Barth's "rationalism."[69]

Third, the account of our language about God which theology is committed to giving does not need to be a general theory of language. Sometimes Ward talks as if what Barth's theology needs is a good philosophy of language such as Derrida can provide. But on Barth's account, theology ceases to be theology when it makes itself dependent on any philosophical theory. At other times Ward seems to recognize this, as when he writes, "So we are given, at this point, no insight into how the Word takes possession of human words and thoughts; we are merely told that it does so. There is *no account of human cognition, reasoning or imagination.* Nevertheless an account is necessary as a consequence of the shift from analyzing divine names towards a more *general theology of language.*"[70] But Barth's theology does not need even a *general theology* of language. He writes as if thought and language were distinct and separable, and he employs a Kantian analysis of ordinary, non-theological knowledge. He might well be challenged to take a more radical linguistic turn, or perhaps to give an Aristotelian/Thomistic account of ordinary knowledge. Such debates would not involve anything essential to Barth's theology, which requires only the theological claim that ordinary knowing and ordinary language as such, whatever the best philosophical theory shows their nature to be, represent no natural capacity for the knowledge of God.

Fourth, whatever "reconstruction" of the "logic of divine communica-

67. Ward, *Barth*, pp. 30–32. Ward thinks that Derrida can provide what Barth needs. In spite of the critique of Ward's analysis that follows, I think he brings the two thinkers together in ways highly illuminating both for dialectical theologians and for deconstructionists. My sympathies are with Garrett Green's defense of Ward against the critique of McCormack. See Green, "Hermeneutics," pp. 91–108.
68. There is a significant agreement here between Barth and the "Reformed epistemology" developed by Alvin Plantinga and Nicholas Wolterstorff. See their essays in the volume they edited, *Faith and Rationality: Reason and Belief in God* (Notre Dame, Ind.: University of Notre Dame Press, 1983) and Plantinga's *Warranted Christian Belief* (New York: Oxford University Press, 2000). All three reject the suggestion made in Plato's *Theaetetus* (201d), that knowledge is true belief plus an account.
69. See Hunsinger, *How to Read*, pp. 5, 49–64.
70. Ward, *Barth*, p. 21, emphasis added.

tion" theology finds itself able and obligated to give, it will involve no "resolution of the paradox of language in chapter 5" nor "a synthesis for the paradoxical foundation of Barth's theology of language." The task will be precisely to retain the paradox without resolution or synthesis. To accept such a responsibility would not just make theology dependent on philosophy but, heaven help us, on Hegelian philosophy.[71]

Finally, the doctrine of analogy as *analogia fidei* is the theologically necessary and sufficient account, coherent in relation to the other themes of this theology, of our knowledge and language about God. The "no account" charge turns out to be the expectation of an inappropriate account, one that would render this theology *incoherent*.

So we turn to Barth's theology of analogy.[72] Once Barth begins to speak the language of *participation* it is all but inevitable that he will invoke the language of *analogy* to express the notion that for all its inadequacy the God talk derived from revelation can have a "genuine and proper reference" to God.[73] The basic statement is at once straightforward and familiar to any reader of Thomas Aquinas. Having affirmed our "participation in the veracity of the revelation of God," Barth asks, "Where do we find the veracity in which we apply to God human words which as such are inadequate to describe Him?" (CD II/1, 224). Not in "simple parity [*Gleichheit*, univocity] of content and meaning when we apply the same word to the creature on the one hand and to God's revelation and God on the other." This would mean "a denial of God's hiddenness, and His revelation would no longer be understood as an unveiling in veiling." It would mean "either that God had ceased to be God and become merely a creature, or that man with his capacity had become a God." Nor should we affirm a "disparity [*Ungleichheit*, equivocity] of content and meaning," for this would mean "that we do not know God. For if we know Him, we know Him by the means given us [our intuitions, concepts, and words]; otherwise we do not know Him at all." This dilemma "does not leave us any option but to resort to this concept" of analogy, which has become "unavoidable" in spite of being "burdened by its use in natural theology" (CD II/1, 224–25).

This latter caveat portends the fundamental quarrel between Barth and Roman Catholic theology as found in Aquinas and Vatican I. With the Catholic tradition, Barth is willing to affirm both participation and analogy, but he

---

71. While Derrida's philosophy of language may illuminate Barth's theology, it is not likely to provide the "resolution" or "synthesis" spoken of here.

72. In an early essay, Barth writes that "our work in this age, though analogous to, is also disjunct from, the work of God" (CP 312). The works in question are political and no account of analogy is given. It is only later that Barth will give a *theory* of analogy in an *epistemic* context.

73. Hunsinger, *How to Read*, p. 43. Cf. Berkouwer, *Triumph*, p. 182. The use of this language is all the more inevitable in light of the fact that during the period in question, Barth comes to see Roman Catholicism as the more basic theological opponent than liberal Protestantism. See McCormack, CRDT, 376–91, and Berkouwer, *Triumph*, ch. VII.

reserves the right to ask, "What sort of a participation is it?" (CD II/1, 215) and to inquire "about the origin and constitution of [the] correspondence and agreement" built into the concept of analogy (CD II/1, 225).[74]

In relation to the doctrine of analogy found in Aquinas (see chapter 5 above), two differences arise, both significant but not equally so. Less important is the difference over the scope of analogical predication. In the last chapter we saw Aquinas affirm that analogical predication is literal because it affirms of God perfections that inhere primordially in God and only derivatively in creatures. Terms that essentially imply some "imperfection," such as materiality or passivity, can only be applied metaphorically to God. That difference disappears in Barth, who warns against being too skittish about "anthropomorphisms," since "spiritual—i.e., abstract—concepts are just as anthropomorphic as those which indicate concrete perception," since they belong to "*human* language about God" (CD II/1, 222, emphasis added).

Another way to put this is to deny that "if they are to be applied to Him, our intuitions, concepts and words have to be alienated from their proper and original sense and usage. No, He takes to Himself something that already belongs originally and properly to Him. . . . Our words are not our property, but His. And disposing of them as His property, He places them at our disposal. . . . The use to which they are put is not, then, an improper and merely pictorial one, but their proper use" (CD II/1, 228–29). Having said this, Barth proceeds to give examples of the kind of predicates he has in mind: father, son, lordship, patience, love, arm, and mouth (CD II/1, 229–30).[75]

Far more fundamental is the difference suggested by the reference to natural theology, a difference about the relation of nature and grace expressed in the contrast between Catholicism's *analogia entis* and Barth's *analogia fidei*.[76] At the outset of Aquinas' *Summa Theologiae*, he presents what he believes we can know about the existence and nature of God by human reason without appeal to scriptural revelation (ST 1.2–11). Then, after denying that we can know God by a direct apprehension of the divine essence, he inquires into the nature of proper God talk and presents his theory of analogy (ST 1.12–

---

74. Berkouwer writes that Barth's concern is "not to deny any and every kind of analogy, but rightly to understand the *nature* of the analogy that exists between God and man." *Triumph*, p. 193.

75. Speaking of such terms as 'father' and 'son', Barth writes, "These human bonds are not the original, of which the other would be the image of symbol. The original, the true fatherhood, the true filiality are in these ties which God has created between himself and us. Everything which exists among us is merely the image of this original filiality. When we call God our Father, we do not fall into symbolism; on the contrary, we are in the full reality of these two words: 'father' and 'son'" (P 46). It would appear that here Aquinas' distinction between literal but analogical predication and metaphorical predication collapses and all appropriate predication falls in the first category. It is literal in terms of the *res significata* and analogical in terms of the *modus significandi*.

76. As Barth understands the former term, though of fifteenth-century origin (see McCormack, CRDT, 385n.), it signifies what can easily be found in Aquinas. The latter term, which Barth uses to signify his distance from Catholicism, is ironically one he borrows from a Catholic theologian, Gottlieb Söhngen (see CD II/1, 81–82).

13). In this way his doctrine of analogy is linked to his natural theology. As a realist, he takes ontology to precede epistemology. So the ground both for the possibility of this knowledge and the analogical predication in which it is expressed is the ontological analogy between Creator and human creature, the similarity and difference between God's being and ours.

It should come as no surprise that Barth aims his heaviest guns against the notion that there can be a knowledge of God apart from grace as the "special help" and "miracle" of revelation received in faith (CD II/1, 84; cf. 81, 231).[77] That is why he speaks of *analogia fidei* or, on one occasion, *analogia gratiae* (CD II/1, 243). For him the correspondence posited in analogy talk is not between two beings or modes of being perceived by "nature" or "art" apart from grace (FI 29). It is rather between two acts, the gracious divine act of revelation and the human act, enabled by the same grace,[78] of faith (see McCormack, CRDT 16).

By contrast, the *analogia entis* supposes that we can build the bridge that will get us to God. Perhaps we need only "to extend our idea of lord and lordship into the infinite and absolute and we will finally arrive at God" (CD II/1, 75). Or perhaps we can "infer" God either "from the given" (FI 33) or "from general truths" (A 55),[79] forgetting that since only God knows God, "God shatters every syllogism" (A 29).

But these suppositions also suppose that we can know God without "having heard" or "having heeded . . . what is said to us about reality by the Lord of reality" (FI 29). They also treat revelation "as if it does not do the choosing but is something to be chosen" (CD II/1, 139). By ignoring the reverse intentionality that grace signifies in favor of an intentionality that signifies an inherent human capacity, they fail to apply to the justification of belief the doctrine of justification by faith, and knowledge becomes a human work rather than a divine gift (CD II/1, 239). We can hear Feuerbach grimacing in the wings as Barth asks whether such theology does "not point us to God, but to ourselves" (CD II/1, 76). In other words, is the Prime Mover of the "analogia entis really God or just an abstraction in which the unity of God is lost as creation, if it can be called that, is separated from lordship, reconciliation, and redemption? In the final analysis, isn't such an abstraction an idol?" (CD II/1, 76–84).

Two brief concluding points about Barth's *analogia fidei*. First, it seems as if the dispute is simply over the possibility of natural theology, but it isn't quite that simple. It is well known that while Aquinas begins with a natural theology, he holds that many crucial parts of Christian theology depend on revelation

---

77. Perhaps this is why Barth sees a deep affinity between Thomistic Catholicism and liberal Protestantism. See FI 41 and CD II/1, 232, 243, as well as McCormack, CRDT 418, and Berkouwer, *Triumph*, pp. 167–68.

78. Hunsinger writes that for Barth "nature has no capacity for grace apart from that miraculously granted and sustained *in actu*—in and by the act of grace itself." *How to Read*, p. 98.

79. Or with the aid of such general truths as the principle of sufficient reason in its causal form.

and are beyond the reach of unaided human reason. It seems that Barth has Aquinas, among others, in mind when he speaks of an "untenable concept of human nature . . . as though human beings themselves possessed the capacity for ascertaining what is or is not revelation, as though they had at their disposal a criterion by which they might recognize and acknowledge Christ" as distinct from his own view that we possess "no criterion by which to distinguish truth from reality [even if presented to us in an event of revelation], but that this criterion must be given to him in and with the revelation itself. . . . For not only the Word's being spoken but also our reception of it is always a matter of God's free grace" (FI 42, 48, 55). Moreover, if the capacity to receive revelation is not "something 'natural'," an "inherent human capacity . . . given with human existence as such" but rather a divine gift, this gift is not given once and for all, "something subsequently connected with human existence" as a *gratia in-haerens.* . . . For grace is the event in which God comes to us in his Word, an event over which God has sole control, and which is *strictly momentary*" (FI 39–40, emphasis added).

The critique, at least implicit here, is that even when he speaks of revelation, instead of the double miracle of Word and Spirit, Aquinas weds the Word, as a miracle of grace, not with the Spirit, but with nature as an inherent human capacity to recognize revelation. The result is an epistemological semi-pelagianism in which the "wholly other" is "no 'wholly other' at all" but "only our mirror image" (FI 55–56).

In another essay from 1929 Barth makes a similar argument. Scripture's witness to God's revelation "is no *datum,* no sum of views ready-made and existing at our disposal . . ." This is because "the hearing of the Word of God the Creator . . . is not man's work but God's: the Holy Ghost's work. Just as our spirit cannot produce the Word of God, so too, it cannot receive it . . . it is incapable unassisted, of hearing God's Word" (HG 23–25). Once again, this work of God the Spirit is not once and for all, but "it is purely and simply the office of the Holy Ghost to be *continually* opening our ears to enable us to receive the Creator's word. . . . But as the Scriptural announcement of God's revelation must be ever increasingly *becoming* the voice of the Living God to us, seeing that God is *continually* saying to us what He said by the mouth of prophets and apostles once and for all, so too the outer and inner constraints of our existence must be ever *acquiring* the character of divine indications, duties and promises through the divine speech to us" (HG 22–24, some emphasis added). The implicit critique is that by failing to link Word sufficiently to Spirit, Aquinas allows the *analogia entis* to spill over into his theory of revelation in the form of a natural or inherent capacity to recognize revelation. By contrast, Barth's view is that we have no capacity for receiving grace apart from an enabling act of grace itself.[80]

---

80. See note 78 above.

The second and final point has already been made. The gift of revelation is a divine act, but not one that gives us God or knowledge of God as a possession at our disposal. That is the point of the emphasis on the momentary character of the event of grace and the need for its continual renewal. In this sense Barth's theology privileges becoming over being.[81] This ontology of God's action as a fleeting event ever to be renewed in loving faithfulness is sometimes called Barth's "actualism."[82] From the standpoint of the onto-theological desire for cognitive autonomy, nothing could be more galling. To be dependent on an act of God's grace at the outset, as Aquinas seems to have it, is bad enough. But to know that I will never be free from this dependence if I am to know the Highest Being who is the key to the meaning of the whole of being and most especially of my own being—that is utterly intolerable.

Never? Surely this is hyperbole. What about the life to come when faith becomes sight and we see God face to face? Barth replies,

> But God as God, in Himself, will still be hidden from us even then. Even this knowing of God face to face will still be a miraculous bestowal of His grace, an incomprehensible admission of ourselves into this knowledge. . . . Even as eternal grace, freed from the whole enshrouding veil of our temporality and corruption, grace will still be the grace of God and not our nature. (CD II/1, 209)

---

81. See Green, "Hermeneutics," p. 95.
82. It is one of the six basic motifs of *Church Dogmatics* according to Hunsinger. See *How to Read*, pp. 4, 30–32 and Berkouwer, *Triumph*, pp. 184, 190, 192.

PART III.
ETHICAL AND RELIGIOUS TRANSCENDENCE: THE DIVINE IMPERATIVE

seven
Levinas
Beyond Onto-theology to Love of Neighbor

We can easily enough imagine a kind of theological "gotcha!" game in which Barth insists that he has a more radical account of sin and grace as epistemic categories than Aquinas and his *analogia entis*. To which Aquinas then replies that in spite of Barth's emphasis on the Scripture principle, he, Aquinas, is closer to biblical thinking, both with reference to Being as the first name of God in the light of Exodus 3:14 and with reference to natural theology in the light Romans 1:20. Barth will have a long and learned reply, which will provoke an equally long and learned reply from the *doctor angelicus*. Even in the ecumenical atmosphere of Vatican II, to which we have transported the two of them, it will not be easy to stop the debate.

But let us try, if not to stop the debate entirely, which is both important and legitimate, at least to sidetrack it long enough to notice the striking and surprising agreement between the two. With Pseudo-Dionysius, their common ancestor (another surprise), they affirm that only God knows God and, correspondingly, that we must say no to the onto-theological project in order to open ourselves to the genuinely theological gift. In other words, we can have saving and healing knowledge of God only as that knowledge is imparted to us by

God, who remains hidden and mysterious in this revelation. The debate over the relation of nature to this grace occurs in the context of an agreement about grace that simultaneously affirms divine epistemic transcendence and calls for human self-transcendence in abandoning the ideal of autonomy and adequation and in humbly receiving the gift in gratitude and joy. Thus Barth writes that this knowledge "does not cease to transcend us, but *we become immanent to it,* so that obedience to it is our free will. But because God remains transcendent to us even in His revelation, the subjectivity of our acknowledgment of His revelation means *our elevation above ourselves*" (CD II/1, 219, emphasis added). Both Barth and Aquinas interpret this "becoming immanent" to God's own self-knowledge in terms of participation, a term that nicely signifies both objective transcendence and subjective self-transcendence.

The time has come, however, to turn our attention from knowing to doing.[1] Over against the autonomy and adequation ideals of the Enlightenment Project in both its ancient and modern forms, epistemic transcendence has signaled the double heteronomy of revelation and mystery. But the autonomy ideal was never restricted to the cognitive realm, and it would be surprising if genuine transcendence did not entail a heteronomy of behavior as well as a heteronomy of belief. That is surely the view of Barth. He writes, "Ethics so called I regard as the doctrine of God's command and do not consider it right to treat it otherwise than as an integral part of dogmatics, or to produce a dogmatics which does not include it" (CD I/1, xiv). Once again, Aquinas would be in significant, if not total, agreement. If one gets past the anthologies' excerpts on the Five Ways, one finds both a Treatise on Law and a Treatise on Virtue in the *Summa Theologiae,* a deontological and a teleological ethics that is in each case ineluctably theological. There will still be a nature-grace scheme that will make Barth uncomfortable, but once again the agreement is more fundamental. Our highest duty is obedience to God and our highest good is loving union with God. This union is always on God's terms, not on ours, and this love has its origin in God and not in ourselves.

So we could easily proceed with either Aquinas or Barth (or Augustine, for that matter). I turn rather to Levinas. On one hand, this is quite natural since transcendence is the central theme of his thought, that by virtue of which infinity exceeds every totality and that which is otherwise than being or beyond essence. For when thought and action are governed by the categories

---

1. Let us not say from theory to practice, for the knowing we have been talking about is not in the first instance theory. Theology as a reflective, even academic, activity is always secondary and derivative from the "theology" (God talk) of the community which has not yet generated systematic and critical reflection on its God talk. Nor is 'practice' the right term for the doing in question. It could be used, but it too easily suggests either the practical in the sense of means-end instrumentality and technique or practice in the sense of the practices of a particular society and culture. The doing in question is, however, praxis in the Aristotelian sense of an activity done for its own sake and not as a means to an external end.

of totality, being, and essence,[2] the other is reduced to the same and transcendence is lost.

On the other hand, however, there is an obvious objection to this move. The transcendence with which Levinas concerns himself is that of the human other (*Autrui*), the widow, the orphan, and the stranger, the neighbor whose face I see and not the God whose face I do not. There is plenty of God talk in Levinas' writings, but apart from its secondary role, it may well be that he is an atheist. He regularly transfers such terms as absolute, infinite, revelation, height, and glory from their usual theological home to serve as descriptions of the human other, and it is far from clear that he affirms a personal God who, distinct from the world and its human inhabitants, is a creator, lawgiver, and redeemer. It often sounds as if 'God' is the name for the depth dimension in my neighbor which puts me in question with a summons to justice and even, in later writings, love.

So, it might seem, Levinas is not a leading candidate for consideration in an essay about the transcendence of *God*. I shall, however, put aside the perplexing question of the meaning of God in Levinas in order to examine his analysis of the structure of transcendence in the ethical relation to the neighbor.[3] Two reasons make this a compelling move. First, his account of the transcendence of the other is, if not entirely unique, distinctive and powerful in the way it links the transcendence of the other to the self-transcendence of the same, namely myself. Second, he tells us that his motivation is

> not some urgent need to return to ethics for the purpose of developing *ab ovo* a code in which the structures and rules for good private conduct, public policy, and peace between the nations would be set forth, however fundamental the ethical values implied in these chapters may appear to be. *The main intent here is to try to see ethics in relation to the rationality of the knowledge that is immanent in being, and that is primordial in the philosophical tradition of the West* . . . (EN xi, emphasis added)

For the philosophical tradition of the West, as Levinas understands it, it is the rationality of knowledge above all else that involves the elimination of

---

2. No strangers to the onto-theological project, it might be noted.

3. I have discussed Levinas' view of God elsewhere. See "Levinas's Teleological Suspension of the Religious," in *Ethics as First Philosophy*, ed. Adriaan T. Peperzak (New York: Routledge, 1995), pp. 151–60; "The Transparent Shadow: Kierkegaard and Levinas in Dialogue," in *Kierkegaard in Post/Modernity*, ed. Martin J. Matuštík and Merold Westphal (Bloomington: Indiana University Press, 1995), pp. 265–81; "Commanded Love and Divine Transcendence," in *The Face of the Other and the Trace of God: Essays on the Philosophy of Emmanuel Levinas*, ed. Jeffrey Bloechl (New York: Fordham University Press, 2000), pp. 200–233; "The Trauma of Transcendence as Heteronomous Intersubjectivity," in *Intersubjectivité et théologie philosophique*, ed. Marco M. Olivetti (Padova: CEDAM, 2001), pp. 87–110; and "Transcendence, Heteronomy, and the Birth of the Responsible Self," in *Calvin O. Schrag and the Task of Philosophy after Postmodernity*, ed. Martin Beck Matuštík and William L. McBride (Evanston, Ill.: Northwestern University Press, 2002), pp. 201–225.

transcendence, or, as he typically puts it in language drawn from Plato's *Sophist*, the reduction of the other to the same. This means that Levinas is interested in the recovery of epistemic transcendence *for the sake of* ethical transcendence. He sees the first as the presupposition of the latter, which, in turn, is the telos of the former. He will find it necessary to deny knowledge in order to make room for justice and love and peace. His critique of knowledge will not be like Kant's Transcendental Aesthetic and Analytic. He believes that phenomenology, especially as developed by Husserl and Heidegger, has shown well enough how the knowledge we are able to have is possible. His critique will be like Kant's Transcendental Dialectic, designed to relativize that knowledge by articulating its limits, clearly identifying that which clearly transcends our ability to grasp and comprehend and which calls us to self-transcendence.

The central target of this critique is Husserl, Levinas' teacher, whose thought he introduced into France. He sees Husserl not just as the hottest new thing on the philosophical horizon, but as "the conclusion to which one of the characteristic traditions of philosophy leads" (BI 100–101).[4] This is the tradition that defines European civilization in terms of science (WEH 47) and is thus the link between antiquity[5] and modernity, understood as Enlightenment (WEH 79). As a critique of this tradition far different from the skepticisms of nominalism and empiricism, Levinas is a "postmodern" thinker.

The titles of three essays provide a map for Levinas' critique of Husserl.[6] "Beyond Intentionality" names the central concept of Husserlian phenomenology and thereby the central target of Levinas' critique. "Ethics as First Philosophy"[7] tells us what is beyond and, for that matter, before intentionality. Traditionally one doesn't go "beyond" epistemology to get to ethics any more than one goes "beyond" ethics to get to epistemology. The two sit side by side, connected by that most democratic of conjunctions, 'and'. This "beyond" and "first" clearly suggest a challenge to this status quo. Finally, "Is Ontology Fundamental?" makes the second point negatively. Since ethics is first philosophy, ontology is not; it cannot be the primary place where wisdom is to be sought. But why ontology? Why, for example, at the outset of *Totality and Infinity* does Levinas contrast the eschatology of peace to the *ontology* of war

---

4. This more nuanced formulation expresses Levinas' view better, I think, than the more sweeping reference above to "*the* philosophical tradition of the West," as if Western philosophy spoke with only a single voice.

5. Plato and Aristotle in particular. See IOF 2.

6. What follows is Levinas' understanding of Husserl based overwhelmingly on *Logical Investigations* and *Ideas I*. It does not change substantially after two very early works, TIHP (1930) and WEH (1940). Other dimensions of thought may be found within the Husserlian corpus as a whole, as Husserl scholars will be quick to remind us, but that is not Levinas' concern. His dual task is to present the ontology of knowledge found in these "classic" Husserlian texts and to see in them an eloquent restatement of a major strand of the Western tradition. How accurate and illuminating these two moments of his thought may be is, of course, open to discussion.

7. In LR.

(TI 22; cf. 42–44)?[8] Shouldn't he have said epistemology? Isn't epistemology reflection on the nature and limits of human knowledge, and doesn't he want to supplement the phenomenological theory of the nature of knowledge with an account of its limits?[9]

Yes, but for Levinas epistemology is ontology. In the case of Husserlian phenomenology this is not because there is a concern for regional ontologies, but because, as Heidegger clearly saw and Levinas reaffirms, phenomenology is ontology as "the science of the 'meaning' of being" distinct from the sciences which study "the properties of being" (TIHP xxxii, 131).

More specifically, like any epistemological reflection it is a theory of the being of both the subject and the object of knowledge. Psychologism in epistemology presupposes and expresses a naturalist ontology which is "only a bad interpretation of the meaning of natural science" (TIHP 9). It takes physical nature to be absolute being and our experience of it to be secondary and subjective (TIHP 10). Phenomenology offers a different ontology (TIHP 12–13, 93), one that reverses the relation. Husserl's ontology "consists of attributing absolute existence to concrete conscious life . . . life in the presence of transcendent beings. . . . It will then follow that consciousness is the origin of all being" (TIHP 25).[10] It is "relative to nothing" (WEH 74; cf. TIHP 25, 28, 91). This is the heart of the freedom motif that we shall find to be so important to Levinas.

As intentionality, consciousness is "a primordial event conditioning all others" (DEH 135).[11] It is the task of the phenomenological reduction to free us from the idea (1) that the knowing subject, as absolute existence, is involved in, part of, or constituted by the world it knows (WEH 71–72; DEH 106; TIHP 146) and (2) that it deals with ready-made objects (WEH 72, 74, 79, 106). A ready-made object might be defined as one so complete in itself that its relation to human understanding is accidental and external. But for Husserl our access to beings, both the "that" and the "how" belongs to their very being

8. Where we expect a contrast between ethics and epistemology, Levinas gives us a contrast between ontology, which is tightly linked to epistemology, and metaphysics, which is tightly linked to ethics. See TI 42–48. This contrast corresponds with many others in Levinas, including totality/infinity, same/other, and transcendence/immanence.

9. A dangerous supplement indeed, for it is a direct challenge to the tradition whose completion Levinas finds Husserl to be. On the logic of the dangerous supplement, see Jacques Derrida, *Of Grammatology*, trans. Gayatri Chakravorty Spivak (Baltimore, Md.: Johns Hopkins University Press, 1976), Part II, ch. 2. In *The Philosophy of the Limit* (New York: Routledge, 1992), Drucilla Cornell links Derrida and Levinas precisely in terms of the concept of limit.

10. Following Kant's refutation of idealism, Husserl rejects the "problem of the external world."

11. To suggest that God might have a different (and possibly superior) access to things "would precisely amount to reducing intentionality to some peculiarity of conscious life, to interpreting it no longer as the initial event of transcendence that of itself makes possible the very idea of transcendence" (DEH 136). Cf. WEH 83, where for Husserl, "Thought is an absolute autonomy. . . . The monad invites God himself to be constituted as meaning for a thought responsible to itself."

(DEH 95, 97, 135; TIHP 32).[12] Being is by definition that which gives itself to human thought to be comprehended (including, of course, human thought itself).

In spite of decisively sidelining God,[13] Husserlian phenomenology is an onto-theological gesture. There is a highest being that is the key to the whole of being, and it is the task of theory to make the whole of being intelligible to human understanding in the light of this highest being.[14]

This highest being is human consciousness as intentionality. But what is intentionality? Husserl's use of this term has its prehistory in the medievals and in Brentano but is neither identical with nor reducible to either. The basic notion is that consciousness is always consciousness of. . . . It always stands in a non-causal relation to that which it is about. It is an awareness directed toward its "object." This "of" or "about" or "toward" defines consciousness as intentionality. It is thus a much broader notion than the volitional sense of intending to fix the fence or paving the road to hell with good intentions.

Levinas' understanding of Husserl on intentionality (for it is that which concerns us here) revolves around three notions: *Sinngebung,* representation, and adequation. His account of these three themes presents Husserl's phenomenology as a radical theory of freedom. Since the flip side of this freedom is immanence, as we shall see, it is a theory in which freedom prevails over responsibility as immanence prevails over transcendence.

Intentionality is *Sinngebung,* the bestowal or conferral of meaning. There can be nothing "absolutely foreign to the subject" because there can be no transcendence "that could have any other meaning than that of the intentional unity appearing within subjectivity" (DEH 69).[15] In this sense consciousness is the origin of its objects. Here is Husserl's view as Levinas understands it:

> It is necessary to dig deeper, down to the very meaning of the notion of being, and to show that the origin of all being, including that of nature, is determined by the intrinsic meaning of conscious life and not the other way around. (TIHP 18)

> We shall . . . show how [the existence of consciousness] consists in being intentional. It will then follow that consciousness is the origin of all being and that the latter is determined by the intrinsic meaning of the former. (TIHP 25 26)

---

12. Without specific reference to Husserl, Levinas opens chapters III, IV, and V of OBBE with this thought. We must think otherwise than being because to think being means "that the appearing of being belongs to its very movement of being, that its phenomenality is essential and that being cannot do without consciousness" (OBBE 131; cf. 61, 99, 134).

13. See previous note.

14. For this understanding of onto-theology as a double thesis, see the title essay in my *Overcoming Onto-theology* (New York: Fordham University Press, 2001).

15. Levinas puts the second passage in quotation marks, presumably from Husserl, but gives no reference.

Perception gives us being. It is through reflecting on the act of perception that we must seek the origin of the very notion of being. (TIHP 71)

The light of self-evidence is the sole tie with being that posits us as an origin of being . . . (WEH 61)

[Phenomenology's] vocation lies rather in grasping the meaning of objects by putting them back into the intentions in which they are constituted, and thus grasping them in their origin in the mind, in self-evidence. (WEH 71)

This last passage shows the virtual synonymity of two notions: consciousness as the origin of its objects and consciousness as constituting its objects. Thus

Husserl puts the study of every object back into the description of the meaning in which it is posited and that constitutes it. (WEH 69)

[The ego] is not constituted, but constituting. (WEH 76)

[Science] cannot renounce self-evidence, for it originally proceeds from man's concern to constitute his own existence freely. (WEH 79)

According to Husserl, Descartes' *Meditations* thus find their completion in the lucidity of the monad, in which the meaning of all reality is constituted. (WEH 83)

We must not take this talk of origin and constitution in a causal sense. Consciousness does not create the world in the sense in which God is said to do so. Nor is it *causa sui* in the sense in which God is said to be so. For Husserl, "the resistant, foreign object appears as springing forth from the mind because it is understood by it" (WEH 74). To put it a bit differently, "Being is nothing other than the correlate of our intuitive life" (TIHP 92). The pre-established harmony between thought and being is analytic, since being simply is that which gives itself to thought to be understood. There is a dimension of passivity in this. But intentional consciousness "is also the origin of what it receives. It is always active" (WEH 61). This is because *Sinngebung* is "prior to the world" (WEH 73). The world is given, to be sure, but it can only be given as what we take it to be. To be given is to be received in a certain way. "Every given, even the earth, the body, and things, are moments of the work of *Sinngebung*" (DEH 102).

As *Sinngebung*, intentionality is the activity of bestowing meaning not so much on the world, as if there were a ready-made world at hand to which meaning must somehow be added, but so that there can be a world given to us. Most of the time this seems to be a purely cognitive activity, but it has a volitional element as well. "Intentionality is thus an intention of the soul, a spontaneity, a *willing*, and the sense bestowed itself, in some way, what is *willed*: the way in which beings or their Being manifest themselves to thought in knowledge corresponds to the way in which consciousness 'wills' this manifestation through its own resolve. . . . Cognitive intention is thus a free act. The soul is 'affected', yet not passively, as it takes hold of itself again by taking responsibility for what is given in accordance with its own intention" (BI 101). In an earlier essay, Levinas anticipates this formulation when he writes, "The ego is the very freedom of consciousness, the *fiat* that it contains and of which self-evidence [the intuitive presence of the 'object' to consciousness] is but the expression" (WEH 76).

Intentionality is also representation.[16] This does not signify a mental copy of an external object but rather the very nature of the act by which consciousness renders the transcendent object (the tree by the fence, the number two, God, or whatever) present to itself (or itself present to the object). Two virtual synonyms for 'representing' are 'thematizing' and 'objectifying'. Levinas primarily relies on the second of these in explicating Husserl's view. Representation is an objectifying act. What this means in the first place is that representation is an act of consciousness, not a passivity. As such it will be intimately bound up with *Sinngebung*. *Sinngebung* and representation signify the same act under two descriptions.

In the second place, then, we must ask about the nature of objectification. It is, of course, the act by which something becomes an object of consciousness, what consciousness is directed "toward," what it is "of" or "about." But Husserl is more specific than this. An objectifying act is an identifying act.

> To Husserl, the fact of meaning is characterized by the phenomenon of identification, a process in which the object is constituted. The identity of a unity across multiplicity represents the fundamental event of all thought. For Husserl, to think is to identify. . . . The intentionality of consciousness is the fact that across the multiplicity of mental life there can be found an ideal identity, the synthesis of which the multiplicity does nothing more than bring about.
>
> The act of positing the object, the objectifying act, is a synthesis of identification. Through this synthesis all mental life participates in representation. . . . Husserl determines the very notion of representation by that of synthesis. Thus representation is not a concept opposed to action or feeling; it is prior to them. (WEH 59–60)

Levinas often complains that Husserl's theory of representation is "tainted" by an intellectualism that assumes the primacy of theoretical consciousness (e.g., TIHP 53, 61–63, 94, 128, 132–34), and in "Is Ontology Fundamental?" he praises Heidegger for overcoming this taint. He cites a passage where Husserl follows Brentano's claim that all "acts are either representations or

---

16. A detailed study of Husserl would have to distinguish between presentation, an act which takes place (more or less) fully in the present, and re-presentation, in which something past is rendered once again present. For present purposes, however, the distinction is moot because in both cases what is involved is a certain presence of the object to consciousness. The difference between various modes is secondary, and 'representation' refers equally to perception, memory, and imagination.

founded upon representations" (TIHP 57).[17] Levinas concedes "that the fact that the objects of joy, will, etc., must be represented before being pleasant, wanted, etc., does not imply . . . either for Brentano or Husserl, a denial of the intentional which is proper to these affective or volitional acts" (TIHP 57). But he worries about this "before." With Heidegger he wants to deny that we first encounter things in some value-neutral way and then, in an external and subjective manner, attach some affective or practical value to them.[18] It is not clear that there is any "before" of this sort in Husserl's view. To say that valuational intentions presuppose or are "founded upon" representations needn't mean anything more than I cannot desire an apple when I am hungry without identifying it as an apple, or at least a something edible. In any case, the concern about a taint of intellectualism is not at the heart of Levinas' worries about representation.

We get closer to the heart of that concern in the following account. "Thought, then, cannot enter into a relationship with the meaningless, with the irrational. Husserl's idealism is the affirmation that every object, the pole of a synthesis of identification, is permeable to the mind; or, conversely, that the mind can encounter nothing without comprehending it. Being can never shock the mind, because it always has a meaning for the mind. The shock itself is a way of comprehending" (WEH 68).

Nothing incomprehensible? Nothing shocking? But doesn't experience blatantly falsify these claims, along with the claim we encountered above that there is nothing foreign to the mind (DEH 69, 79)? Before we take Levinas' Husserl to be simply certifiable we must notice that Husserl's object as "a synthesis of identification"[19] is "an ideal identity, confirmed or crossed out or corrected through the evolution of subjective or intersubjective life" (DEH 137). But if my intentional expectation need not be confirmed but might need to be corrected or even crossed out, it looks as if experience can be shocking after all; in any case, the attentive reader will have noted that immediately after the denial of shock, Levinas has Husserl telling us that "[t]he shock itself is a way of comprehending." So there both is and isn't a shock. How can Levinas define representation as "a determination of the other by the same, without the same being determined by the other" (TI 170)?

To sort all this out we shall have to turn to the third dimension (for present purposes) of Husserl's theory of intentionality, his account of adequation.[20]

---

17. The citation is from Husserl, *Logical Investigations*, trans. J. N. Findlay (London: Routledge & Kegan Paul, 1970), II, 556.

18. See Heidegger, *Being and Time*, trans. John Macquarrie and Edward Robinson (New York: Harper & Row, 1962), pp. 96, 101, 121–22, 132, 141.

19. This identification occurs even "at the level of a still entirely prepredicative sensible experience." N.B. Representation as objectifying identification is not necessarily judgment, which would only be a special case. See TIHP 89 and WEH 63.

20. Levinas follows the account in *Logical Investigations*, Sixth Investigation, especially ch. 1–5.

The classical definition of truth as *adaequatio rei et intellectus* lies at the heart of common sense and of all correspondence theories of the nature of truth. In its Aristotelian-Thomistic form it refers to the immaterial reception of the form into the mind through the work of abstraction by the active intellect. For Husserl, this tradition represents too much the realism of the ready-made object. But he will take over from it the mathematical notion of an equation that is built right into the term *adaequatio*. Something is equal to or (non-numerically) identical with something. For Aristotle and Aquinas knowledge occurs when the form in the thing is exactly the same as the form in the intellect.[21]

Genuine knowledge requires complete adequation. " *'The object is actually "present" or "given," and present as just what we have intended it;* no partial intention remains explicit and still lacking fulfillment.' What happens here is therefore a genuine *adaequatio rei et intellectus*" (TIHP 74).[22] This concept of adequation is tightly linked to the prior notions of representation and *Sinngebung*. For Husserl's transcendental idealism,

> the appearance of the object, representation, is always in proportion to consciousness. It is the adequation between ego and non-ego, Same and Other. Once represented, the Other equals the Same. . . . Descartes expresses this essential equality when he affirms that by itself the ego can account for all things. . . . Consciousness will always remain the source of meaning, for in the meaning that characterizes the object, the strangeness or the heterogeneity of being takes on the measure of consciousness. . . . What exceeds the limits of consciousness is absolutely nothing for that consciousness. (DEH 127)

According to this familiar tradition,[23] if I say that the cat is on the mat and the cat is indeed on the mat, my assertion is true. There is an adequation or correspondence between my assertion (or, depending on one's philosophical commitments, either my sentence or the proposition it expresses) and the fact (or event) it picks out. But for Husserl this is partial adequation at best, or, strictly speaking, none at all, for what is on one side is not equal to what is on the other. Signifying or empty intentions aim at intuitive fulfillment and are

---

21. Thus, as we have seen, God remains incomprehensible for Aquinas precisely because the human intellect cannot grasp or contain the divine essence, even when, in the life to come, it "sees" God directly.

22. The interior quotation is from Husserl, *Logical Investigations*, II, 762. Every intention "is a self-evidence being sought," and for this reason "the presence of being marks something on the order of a fulfillment. It is a situation where being *in person* presents itself to consciousness, and confirms the thought that was intending it in an indirect way, that was 'just thinking' it without seeing it. The truth is *adaequatio rei et intellectus*" (WEH 61–63).

23. I take Tarski to be explicating this tradition in "The Semantic Conception of Truth," in *Readings in Philosophical Analysis*, ed. Herbert Feigl and Wilfrid Sellars (New York: Appleton-Century-Crofts, 1949), pp. 52–84.

meaningful before they are filled, or fulfilled, or confirmed by intuitive presence (TIHP 66–67).[24] I can *believe* that there is a refrigerator in the next room and *hope* that there is a beer inside even when I am still in this room and can see neither. For common sense my belief and my hope are confirmed when I go into the room and see the refrigerator and the beer (or, as Heidegger might prefer to put it, when I use the refrigerator to get to the beer and use the beer to satisfy my thirst).

There is a certain adequation or intuitive fulfillment of my original intentions here, for both the refrigerator and the beer are present "in person" to my sight (and touch). But neither is present *as* I intended it. So far as sight is concerned, and this is the standard example, I intend each in its totality as a three-dimensional object accessible from a virtually infinite number of perspectives, sides, or aspects, or adumbrations which Husserl calls *Abschattungen*. While looking front on I intend the sides, the back, the bottom, and the top which I do not see, along with all the possible cross-sections. But only a fraction of these are ever given to perceptual intuition at any given time.

It is characteristic of physical objects that I can never know them in the full sense because adequation is never complete. Full presence is never achieved and my beliefs are "never totally justified," nor can I have certainty about them (DEH 27; WEH 82; TIHP 23).[25] I can intend the front of a building only to discover that it is a facade for a movie set and no building at all. To acknowledge this obvious fact of ordinary experience is not to be a skeptic (TIHP 22), but rather a fallibilist. This is why my intention of a refrigerator signifies "an ideal identity, confirmed or crossed out or corrected through the evolution of subjective or intersubjective life" (DEH 137). My intention of the refrigerator may be confirmed when I go to check it out, but it may be crossed out if I discover that unknown to me someone has removed it from the room, and it may be corrected if I discover that while it is still there, it has no beer in it. Or, to put it a little differently, "disappointment" or "dissonance" occur when intuition goes contrary to expectation and leaves only partial confirmation—the room is still there, but it lacks a refrigerator or the refrigerator is still there but lacks a beer.[26]

So we can be surprised or "shocked" by experience when our expectations

---

24. It is by linking certainty, truth, and knowledge so tightly to total presence that Husserl becomes a paradigm of what Derrida means by the "metaphysics of presence." See TIHP 83 and 88 and EN 160, along with Derrida's critique in *Speech and Phenomena*, trans. David B. Allison (Evanston, Ill.: Northwestern University Press, 1973).

25. The link between knowledge and certainty characteristic of a certain philosophical rationalism that goes back at least to Plato remains unbroken for Husserl.

26. Levinas quotes from Husserl, *Logical Investigations*, II, 702, "*An intention can only be frustrated in conflict insofar as it forms part of a wider intention whose completing part is fulfilled*" (TIHP 74). This is why Husserl is a fallibilist and not a skeptic. Cognitive failure presupposes cognitive success. The facade is a physical object even if it is not a house.

are "disappointed" and have to be "crossed out" or "corrected." "The shock itself is a way of comprehending." We learn from experience and adjust our intentions accordingly. Our "knowledge" of physical objects, whether in ordinary perception or in the sciences that deal with them, does not meet the strict criteria for knowledge that has been philosophy's aspiration at least since Plato. The "truth" we gain about them is always tentative because the adequation we attain always remains anticipation and thus approximation. Such objects are transcendent, and this is the whole meaning of transcendence here, because even when they are present "in person" they always exceed what can be given in fulfilling intuition.

How, then, shall we understand the claim, "Being can never shock the mind, because it always has a meaning for the mind"? Perhaps we already have before us two clues. "*Once represented*, the Other equals the Same" (emphasis added). In the act of representation or *Sinngebung*, I take the object to be exactly what I take it to be. I posit an equality, albeit one I can never fully realize. But (1) I can always adjust my representation so that experience (to date) no longer contravenes this equality. Every "shock" is in principle eliminable. Moreover, (2) I intend objects of this kind precisely as objects of this kind, namely the kind that can (temporarily) surprise me. When they do so, they confirm my expectations about their essence, if not about their existence. For that reason, "The shock itself is a way of comprehending."

Our other clue comes in the claim that "the strangeness or the heterogeneity of being takes on the measure of consciousness. . . . What exceeds the limits of consciousness is absolutely nothing for that consciousness." This taking on is an ongoing process, subject to crossing out and correction. But every intentional act subsumes the heterogeneity of the transcendent object under the measure of consciousness, identifies it as what that act of *Sinngebung* takes it to be. These acts are revisable. We don't need a philosopher to tell us that. What exceeds the limits of this particular act of identification or meaning bestowal is not nothing for consciousness. But what exceeds the limits of all such acts "is absolutely nothing for that consciousness." The being of the object is such that there is nothing about it that *in principle* exceeds the power of consciousness to define it. It is totally accessible and has no other meaning than the reduction of its heterogeneity to the measure of consciousness, a reduction that can always be continued even if never completed.

If adequation, and thus certainty, truth, and knowledge can only be approximated but never attained in sense perception or the sciences based on it, Husserl thinks we can and must look elsewhere. Philosophy, as phenomenology, has consciousness, not the world, as its object (DEH 10). Husserl calls such intentions as are expressed as "I perceive, I remember, I imagine, I judge, I desire, I want" *Erlebnisse* and then insists that the reflection in which they are given is dramatically different from the perception of physical objects. In reflection, or what Husserl calls immanent perception, "there is no duality between what is revealed and what is only intimated. *Ein Erlebnis schattet sich nicht ab.*"[27] *Erlebnisse* are given, so to speak, all at once. For this reason full adequation occurs. "The immanent perception of reflection . . . is in full possession of its object: the anticipated and the given overlap entirely. The self-evidence of the world is thus incomplete. Only the self-evidence of conscious-ness which thus finds itself fundamentally distinct from the world, and self-evidence which consequently reveals to us a consciousness which can only be transcendental, is certain. This whole development is extremely close to the theory of Cartesian doubt" (WEH 73; cf. 74). Notice the triple claim: (1) In reflection total adequation occurs (cf. TIHP 135). (2) It is only here that it occurs (DEH 55, 82).[28] (3) The object of this knowledge, in which cer-tainty and total adequation coalesce, is not empirical consciousness, which belongs to the world, but transcendental consciousness, which is the origin of the world.

Consistently rejecting Berkeley's idealism, according to which, as Husserl understands it, the object of consciousness is a constituent part of conscious-ness,[29] and in keeping with Kant's refutation of idealism (TIHP 125, 131), Husserl affirms the transcendence of objects in the world, the paradigm of which is the physical object of sight, and he contrasts this transcendence with the immanence of reflection in which the "object" of consciousness is its own acts, given in a fully adequate intuition. At the same time he tends to override this distinction in favor of a more general immanence. According to Hus-serlian phenomenology, as Levinas understands it, knowledge is "the game of unveiling in which immanence always wins out over transcendence; for, once being is unveiled, even partially, even in mystery, it becomes immanent" (EN 56). Being as such is immanent in consciousness not by being a real part of consciousness but because it has no *raison d'être* other than to be present to intuition in human consciousness. To be is to be perceivable, to be available to adequation, whether partial or total. In this "extreme accessibility of being" to consciousness, astonishment "subsides" (BI 102). So Levinas can say,

> In truth, thought thus moves out of itself towards Being, without thereby ceasing to remain in its own proper sphere (*chez elle*). . . . Thought *satisfies* itself in Being . . . always within its own limits . . . this represented con-tent, always identical to itself and thus immanent. . . . Being is immanent in thought and thought does not transcend itself in knowledge. Whether knowledge be sensible, conceptual or even purely symbolical, the transcen-dent or the absolute, claiming, as it does, to be unaffected by any relation, can in fact bear no transcendental sense without immediately losing it: the

---

27. Levinas quotes from Husserl, *Ideas Pertaining to a Pure Phenomenology and to a Phenomeno-logical Philosophy: First Book*, trans. F. Kersten (The Hague: Martinus Nijhoff, 1983), §34, p. 68 and §42, p. 90.
28. This is not easy to reconcile with the claim that adequate self-evidence occurs in mathematics, where "the object intended is entirely covered by the object seen; the signitive intention is entirely realized" (DEH 27). But this problem is peripheral to what concerns us here.
29. This rejection is a recurring motif, especially in TIHP.

very fact of its presence to knowledge signifies the loss of transcendence and of absoluteness. In the final analysis, presence excludes all transcendence. (BI 105–106)[30]

We must never lose sight of the fact that Levinas reads Husserl as the culmination of a dominant tradition in Western philosophy. At least since Plato this tradition has understood knowledge as the subsumption of the particular under the universal. For Husserl, this universal is the horizon within which each intentional act takes place (IOF 5). Representation identifies its object by locating it within its (revisable) horizon of expectations, and "anything my net doesn't catch isn't a fish."[31] Levinas describes the catching that is cognition in strong language that is suggestive of Hegel and Heidegger as well as of Husserl. Knowing is "the overcoming of known objects." It makes them available for my "*possession*" and "*consumption*." The horizon of understanding is "the field of my freedom, power and property—in order to grasp the individual upon a familiar foundation." Comprehension is "the exercise of power . . . in which a *being* is already assimilated." Reason becomes power and domination, "a ruse of the hunter who ensnares." Understanding is "struggle and violence over things." In naming (identifying) things, comprehension is "a violence . . . without disappearing, those beings are in my power. Partial negation, which is violence, denies the independence of a being: it belongs to me." It is there for my "possession" and "enjoyment."[32]

This is why Levinas can describe thought as transcendence, yes, but as "transcendence in immanence" (BI 112). "The transcendence of the object is exactly what it is in conformity with the inner meaning of the thought that intends that object. . . . The exteriority of objects proceeds from the absolute respect given to the interiority of its constitution" (WEH 86). The "triumph of subjectivity"[33] in Husserl's phenomenology is, as Levinas sees it, the triumph of immanence over transcendence.

It is also the triumph of freedom over responsibility. Because consciousness is not constituted but in the ways we have already noticed constitutes both its world and itself, it is free (WEH 71–76, 79, 84–85; DEH 133–34). Thought is "entirely master of itself, responsible to itself, and consequently free" (WEH

---

30. For a helpful discussion of these two senses of immanence, see Jean-Luc Marion, *Being Given*, trans. Jeffrey L. Kosky (Stanford, Calif.: Stanford University Press, 2002), pp. 23–27.

31. My teacher, John Smith, loved to use this apothegm, whose origins are unknown to me, to describe positivism and related forms of reductive empiricism.

32. See IOF 7–9. Cf. the analysis of enjoyment in TI as the mode of being-in-the-world in which my satisfaction is the end to which everything else is the means. It is a fundamental mode of reducing the other to the same, the object to the subject. Also see EN 139, 219. On knowing as absorption, see DEH 121–126; as possession, TIHP 69; BI 102; as grasping, BI 103; EN 126, 139, 219.

33. This is the title of Quentin Lauer's book on Husserl as published by Fordham University Press in 1958, subsequently issued by Harper & Row in 1965 under the title *Phenomenology: Its Genesis and Prospect*.

81). In the culture of knowledge, which Hegel "glorifies as freedom . . . culture triumphs over things and men. That is the meaning of being; as in the writings of Husserl, in which, with intentionality, human consciousness gets out of itself, but remains on the scale of the *cogitatum* which it equals and which satisfies it. Culture as a thought of adequation, in which human freedom is guaranteed, its identity is confirmed, in which the subject in his identity persists without the *other* being able to challenge or unsettle him" (EN 181).

✳ ✳ ✳

Levinas is not so much interested in denying this account of knowledge[34] as in relativizing it, making it subordinate to and derivative from a relation "anterior to" and "irreducible to comprehension" (IOF 5; cf. TI 82–101). The reason is simple. He holds that if one starts with this ontology of knowledge, whether in its rationalist, empiricist, or pragmatist versions, there is no path to ethics as unconditional and infinite responsibility to and for the other. Unless ethics is first philosophy,[35] what passes as "ethics" will be fatally compromised and corrupted. His complaint is not that Husserl misdescribes certain modes of comportment with-or-in-the-world, but that he makes of the phenomenology that describes them "almost a new religion" (DEH 37). He and the tradition he culminates treat knowledge, understood in terms of presence and self-presence, as the highest vocation of the human spirit, the specifically human task (WEH 74, 79; BI 101, 107, 112).

At this point Levinas might, like Kierkegaard in *Works of Love*, invoke the divine command to love our neighbor as we love ourselves. After all, this command and the specification, so dear to Levinas, of the neighbor as the widow, the orphan, and the stranger, are to be found in his own Hebrew Bible. Moreover, his "Jewish" writings in the form of Talmudic commentary locate themselves in a particular religious tradition. But Levinas' (enormous and still growing) impact on contemporary discourse derives overwhelmingly from his "Greek" writings, which locate themselves in the Western philosophical tradition. His critique is an immanent critique, a deconstruction, if you will. It does not arise from an appeal to some religious text or tradition as normative.

Levinas sees in the Husserlian quest for rigorous science and all its historical predecessors a nostalgia for the eternal and asks if there might not be another response to that nostalgia than the quest for pure thought and absolute knowledge (DEH 134). Is there not, he asks, a mode of meaning that is "prior to my *Sinngebung*" (TI 51)?[36] Is there not a new rationality, "or perhaps we

---

34. Levinas does develop a deconstruction of Husserlian phenomenology in terms of its forgetting of the ways in which intentional acts are conditioned by the horizons in which they occur and of which they are not the origin. Sensation and history are two such horizons. But this immanent critique is secondary to the critique on behalf of ethics.

35. See "Ethics as First Philosophy" in LR.

36. Cf. TI 207, 293; GCM xi, xiii; BI 106, 111.

should say the most ancient one" (EN 72),[37] more basic than the ontology which finds the logos of the *onta*, their *raison d'être*, in their presence to the mind's eye? Is there not an alternative awareness that opens the same to the other that will "challenge or unsettle" it (EN 181)?

If the critique of what we have come to call the logocentric tradition is not a call to abandon philosophy, the critique of the phenomenological expression of that tradition is not a call to abandon phenomenology, for it is not bound to its Husserlian form (DEH 91; EN 81).[38] Levinas wants to articulate a transcendence of which Husserl neither knows nor wants to know anything. But this "beyond" is "reflected *within* the totality and history, *within* experience" (TI 23) and thereby calls for its own phenomenology. Levinas insists that "in spite of everything, what I do is phenomenology" (GCM 87).[39] This means that the possibility of another mode of meaningful thought and another rationality can be put in specifically phenomenological terms.

Since the concept of intentionality is central to Levinas' exposition and critique of Husserlian phenomenology, his quest for another phenomenology is the quest for "an intentionality of a wholly different type" (TI 23). It will be a non-objectifying intentionality (DEH 128), not a matter of representation and adequation (EN 127)[40] or of vision and aiming (GCM xii; cf. TI 174). It will bring to awareness what is prior to my activity (GCM xiii),[41] and it will be the site of "*signification without a context*" (TI 23), which is to say it will not be governed by my horizons of expectation. So why not say, as Levinas himself does on occasion (TI 109), that the ethical relation, which is "anterior to" and "irreducible to comprehension" (IOF 5), is something quite different from intentionality? For the simple reason that it occurs "*within* experience" as a consciousness or awareness of something—it will turn out to be someone—to which I can direct my attention, or better, to which I find my attention drawn. In this case, as we shall see, the intentional arrows do not emanate from me toward the object but originate in the "object" and are directed toward me. I am challenged, summoned, put in question. We can thus speak of an "inversion" (TI 67) of objectifying intentionality in which "it is the very movement of constitution that is reversed" (TI 129). *Inverse intentionality is the key to ethical transcendence.* By contrast with the intentionality of possession, it will be one of "dispossession" (GCM xiv).

---

37. Cf. EN 62, 83, 164, 228; TI 88, 204–205, 252.
38. Nor to its Heideggerian form. Levinas appreciates Heidegger's challenge to the primacy of theoretical consciousness in Husserl, but insofar as he still understands being-in-the-world as disclosure, he just presents Husserlian intentionality in a more concrete form. See IOF and TI 28, 45–47, 67.
39. Cf. Foreword and TI 28–29. Richard Cohen puts it nicely when he says that Levinas is "faithful in his own way to the phenomenological movement" (DEH xi).
40. Cf. TI 27, where adequation is trumped by non-adequation.
41. Cf. the reference above to meaning that is "prior to my *Sinngebung*."

By the same token, Levinas can speak of another phenomenological reduction, which could be called awakening, in which "the subject as intuitive reason . . . reason in the adequation of knowledge" will find itself "put into question" (EN 83–85). Why continue to speak of a reduction when everything is reversed, when the same is put into question by the other, when my acts of *Sinngebung* and identification no longer define the situation? Simply because descriptive analysis, which first moves from empirical facts to the essential structure of experience, now moves to that pole from which meaning (and thus, phenomenologically speaking, the world) originates. This is the transcendental realm in which the very transcendence of the other becomes the condition of the possibility of my experience.

It is well-known that for Levinas it is in the ethical relation that genuine transcendence shows up "*within* experience," that it is the human Other (*autrui*)[42] who puts me in question and calls me to responsibility, and that in *Totality and Infinity* and related essays, this summons emanates most especially from the face of the other. No one can view the portraits in an art gallery or art book in quite the same way after reading *Totality and Infinity*. I shall present Levinas' account of a transcendence that is "irreducible to comprehension" (IOF 7) in terms of two theses about the face of the other.

First, the face "*expresses itself*" and it does so "καθ᾽ αὐτό."[43] We can take this thesis to be a gloss on two others we have already encountered. The inverse intentionality in which transcendence is experienced involves "meaning prior to my *Sinngebung*" (TI 51; cf. 207, 293). In this appearing there is an agency prior to my agency; the other is "present as directing this very manifestation" (TI 65). In filming this scene, in playing this symphony, the other is the director whose lead I must follow. Or since, as we have seen, *Sinngebung* is the flip side of representation as identification, the face of the other identifies itself. Prior to any classifications I may bring, the other names itself.[44]

The inverse intentionality of the καθ᾽ αὐτό also brings to light the notion of "*signification without a context*" (TI 23). This points to "a knowledge without a

---

42. In his translation of *Totality and Infinity*, Alphonso Lingis translates *autrui*, signifying personal alterity, as 'Other' and the more generic *autre* as 'other'. Some translators follow him in this, while others do not, leaving it to context (in English) or better, the French text, to decide. I shall follow the latter path, but without altering Lingis' translation.

43. This Greek term is translated into Latin as *per se*, signifying in, through, or from itself. Thus καθ᾽ αὐτό simply calls attention to the strictness with which we should read 'expresses itself'. For Heidegger this is the very essence of phenomenology, which means "to let that which shows itself be seen from itself in the very way in which it shows itself from itself" (BT 58).

44. At first glance it seems strange that Levinas, who complains so bitterly about the neuter neutrality of other thinkers, should say that the face expresses "itself," making it linguistically awkward to switch suddenly to saying, perhaps, that she names herself. One advantage of his diction, however, is that it constantly poses the question of what other (*autre*) could possibly give itself in this way, to which the answer always is only the *Autrui*, the personal, human other. See IOF 6.

priori" (TI 61–62); but since the *a priori* in Husserlian context is the horizon, the καθ' αὐτό suspends the efficacy of all my horizons.[45] Where disclosure is a function of our horizons, the being disclosed is "relative to us and not καθ' αὐτό. . . . Manifestation καθ' αὐτό consists in a being telling itself to us independently of every position we would have taken in its regard, *expressing itself*. Here, contrary to all the conditions for the visibility of objects, a being is not placed in the light of another but presents itself" (TI 64–65; cf. 74).

In an interesting twist on Kant, Levinas says that "to disclose, on the basis of a subjective horizon [mine or ours], is already to miss the noumenon" and makes it clear that only the καθ' αὐτό, which depends on no "borrowed light," gives us the "thing in itself" (TI 67). In other words, when our horizons, our light, our *a priori*, are the forms into which the content presented must be fit, the "knowledge" that results is merely phenomenal. We break through to the noumenal, to the thing in itself,[46] only when by expressing itself καθ' αὐτό the other breaks through our horizons of expectation to present and to identify itself without restriction.[47] When Levinas says, "The immediate is the face to face" (TI 52),[48] he is not denying that we always bring our horizons with us as a turtle brings its shell; he is only pointing to the ability of the face to cut through and neutralize those horizons and express itself without their mediation. It is only when the other is present without the mediation of my *Sinngebung* and my horizons that the other is present in person. Here signification "is not equivalent to presenting oneself as a sign, but to expressing oneself, that is, presenting oneself in person" (TI 262; cf. 181–82).[49]

---

45. In his search for a reduction more radical than Husserl's, Marion seeks to remove the restrictions on givenness represented by the constituting ego and the horizons of its intentionality which together define the realm of possible objects of consciousness. This parallels Levinas' notion of signification (1) "prior to my *Sinngebung*" and (2) *"without a context."* See Marion, *Reduction and Givenness*, trans. Thomas A. Carlson (Evanston, Ill.: Northwestern University Press, 1998), ch. 2 and p. 204.

46. Here Husserl's famous "to the things themselves" becomes a kind of Kantian "to the things in themselves."

47. Jean-Luc Marion tells us that this is true of every phenomenon and thus of givenness as such. "The phenomenon can appear as such . . . only if it pierces through the mirror of representation. Appearing must thus remove itself from . . . the imperial rule of the a priori conditions of knowledge by requiring that what appears force its entry onto the scene . . . it breaks through the frame . . . the movement of appearing ends by bursting on the depthless surface of consciousness. . . . The given is exposed because it explodes." *Being Given: Toward a Phenomenology of Givenness*, trans. Jeffrey L. Kosky (Stanford, Calif.: Stanford University Press, 2002), p. 69. Cf. pp. 60, 117, 123, 132, 150–53, 159, 173–74. Levinas might well reply that even if every phenomenon tries to have this independence, only the face of the other succeeds.

48. Cf. OBBE 90–91 and LP 119, where Levinas writes, "The neighbor is precisely what has a meaning *immediately*, before one ascribes one to him. But what has meaning thus can only be as an other, as *he* who has a meaning before one gives meaning to him. . . . Immediacy is the obsessive proximity of the neighbor, skipping the stage of consciousness, not by default but by excess, by the 'excession' of the approach."

49. Jeffrey Kosky writes, "As expressing itself before we have disclosed it, the expression of the face

Levinas calls this immediacy revelation. Having linked the notion of disclosure to that of horizons, he writes, *"The absolute experience is not disclosure but revelation. . . . Revelation* constitutes a veritable inversion [of] *objectifying cognition"* (TI 65–67; cf. 62, 73). Although this revelation is the self-presentation of the neighbor and not, at least not in the first instance, of God, it has a structure that will be familiar from our examination of revelation in Dionysius, Aquinas, and Barth.

This is especially clear in the contrast Levinas draws between the καθ' αὐτό and the Socratic notion of recollection and the corollary notion that the "teacher" stands in a maieutic relation to the learner, that is, can never actually teach but can only be an occasion for recollecting what the learner already knows. The Socratic idea is "to receive nothing of the other but what is in me, as though from all eternity I was in possession of what comes to me from the outside—to receive nothing, or to be free." Levinas calls this the "primacy of the same" or the "self-sufficiency of the same" (TI 43–44). By contrast, for the other to express itself καθ' αὐτό means "to *receive* from the Other beyond the capacity of the I, which means exactly: to have the idea of infinity. But this also means: to be taught. . . . Teaching is not reducible to maieutics; it comes from the exterior and brings me more than I contain" (TI 51).[50] Accordingly, "The conversion of the soul to exteriority [transcendence], to the absolutely other, to Infinity, is not deducible from the very identity of the soul, for it is not commensurate with the soul" (TI 61). Teaching comes to us from a "height," a "transcendence," an "infinity of exteriority" that is the "face of the Master." But, "His alterity is manifested in a mastery that does not conquer, but teaches. Teaching is not a species of a genus called domination, a hegemony at work within a totality, but is the presence of infinity breaking the closed circle of totality" (TI 171).[51]

Although the details are different, Levinas explicitly links representation, whose Husserlian account we have already noted, to Platonic recollection. Both involve the reduction of the other to the same by incorporating it within the domain of what I can think (TI 126–27).

Revelation is dramatically different from recollection. But revelation in-

---

bears its own meaning . . . in its presentation καθ' αὐτό, in its appearance outside and prior to the context of worldly signification, it does not signal anything other than itself. . . . The face is the signifier in which *Autrui* presents himself . . . the revealer and the revealed coincide . . ." *Levinas and the Philosophy of Religion* (Bloomington: Indiana University Press, 2001), pp. 20–21.

50. Cf. TI 171, 180, 204. The other signifies infinity precisely by exceeding my capacity to contain. Norman Wirzba has given us two fine essays on teaching in Levinas. "From maieutics to metanoia: Levinas's understanding of the philosophical task," in *Man and World* 28 (1995): 129–44 and "Teaching as propaedeutic to religion: The contribution of Levinas and Kierkegaard," in *International Journal for Philosophy of Religion* 39 (April 1996): 77–94.

51. "But the relation is maintained without violence, in peace with this absolute alterity. The 'resistance' of the other does not do violence to me, does not act negatively; it has a positive structure: ethical. The first revelation of the other, presupposed in all other relations with him, does not consist in grasping him in his negative resistance and in circumventing him by ruse. I do not struggle with a faceless god, but I respond to his expression, to his revelation" (TI 197).

volves mystery. The face of the neighbor represents an alterity "irreducible to comprehension" (IOF 7). "The incomprehensible nature of the presence of the Other" (TI 195) stems in part from the fact that in revelation it presents itself καθ' αὐτό, independent of my cognitive machinery, and in part because even in revelation it "overflows comprehension" (IOF 6) and remains a mystery. Its presence is quite other than the presence of being in knowledge where "[n]othing turns up to contradict the intention of thought, nothing emerges from hiding to foil it;[52] there is no chance of an ambush, planned and set up in the darkness or in the mystery of a past or a future refractory to presence" (BI 103–104). It is possible to speak of this darkness and this mystery as that which "*withholds* itself from presence in me" (BI 113, my emphasis) or as that which *conceals* itself by failing to be identical to the form in which it presents itself (TI 192).

But more often Levinas will speak of the "overflow of the Infinite *in* the finite" (BI 113), of a "surplus" beyond what thought is able to "contain" (GCM xiii).[53] Thus we are dealing with "the unencompassable" (BI 113), with "the Uncontainable" (EN 90), with "*bedazzlement*" (EN 200),[54] and with "a *traumatism of astonishment*" (TI 73).[55]

Here once again we encounter the confluence of revelation and mystery, two themes conspicuously absent in Spinoza and Hegel, and tightly intertwined in the theologians of epistemic transcendence, namely Augustine, Dionysius, Aquinas, and Barth. How is it, we might ask, that according to Levinas' first thesis, the other as face is able to present itself καθ' αὐτό, immediately, and in person, and in this revelation withhold and conceal itself by overflowing what the recipient can contain? The answer is found in the second thesis. Just after telling us that manifestation καθ' αὐτό is revelation, Levinas tells us, "The face speaks. The manifestation of the face is already discourse. . . . This presence . . . is said" (TI 66). The face is not a facade, for it reveals itself, and "its revelation is speech" (TI 193).

Levinas' philosophy of transcendence as ethical alterity is most fundamentally a philosophy of language. Vision, the dominant metaphor of the knowledge he calls ontology as the reduction of the other to the same, is trumped by the voice.[56] In this context he will often speak of conversation,

---

52. As noted above, the fact that it may take a while to get to this place doesn't change its character for Levinas. Nothing remains in principle hidden.

53. For the overflow metaphor in TI, see 25, 28, 49, 195.

54. Bedazzlement is an important feature of the saturated phenomenon according to Marion. See "The Saturated Phenomenon" in *Phenomenology and the "Theological Turn,"* trans. Bernard G. Prusak, Jeffrey L. Kosky, and Thomas A. Carlson (New York: Fordham University Press, 255).

55. The language of trauma becomes increasingly prominent in OBBE. See my essay "The Trauma of Transcendence as Heteronomous Intersubjectivity," cited in note 3 above and Rudolf Bernet, "The Traumatized Subject," *Research in Phenomenology,* XXX (2000).

56. Absolute otherness, Levinas insists, is strictly speaking invisible. See TI 33–35 and cf. 65, 74–75.

which suggests a certain reciprocity. But language as discourse or conversation is no mere exchange of information, no negotiation, no social pastime. It embodies the asymmetry that is a trademark, and to some a stumbling block, in Levinas' account of alterity. For the voice which comes from beyond history but is heard within experience "calls [beings] forth to their full responsibility" so that they find themselves "called upon to answer at their trial" (TI 23). I cannot abandon my natural egoism, but "the very fact of being in a conversation consists in recognizing in the Other a *right* over this egoism" (TI 40).[57] Ethics simply is "this calling into question of my spontaneity by the presence of the Other" (TI 43).[58] This egoism, this spontaneity, which in *Otherwise Than Being* Levinas will identify as *conatus essendi*, he here calls the "primordial sphere, which corresponds to the same [and] turns to the absolutely other *only on call from the Other*" (TI 67, emphasis added).[59]

If there is a reciprocity in this conversation in which I am summoned, called into question, even accused, it is because discourse can be "a non-allergic relation with alterity" (TI 47). "To welcome the Other is to put in question my freedom" (TI 85). In a passage that links this welcome to the idea of revelation, Levinas writes

> To approach the Other in conversation is to welcome his expression, in which at each instant he overflows the idea a thought would carry away from it. It is therefore to *receive* from the Other beyond the capacity of the I. . . . But this also means: to be taught. The relation with the Other, or Conversation, is a non-allergic relation, an ethical relation; but inasmuch as it is welcomed this conversation is a teaching. (TI 51)

Levinas continues by insisting that this teaching is "not reducible to maieutics." Then, as if concerned lest the epistemological aspects of the situation overshadow the ethical relation which is their telos, he adds, "Finally, infinity, overflowing the idea of infinity, puts the spontaneous freedom within us into question. It commands and judges it and brings it to its truth" (TI 51).[60]

This truth is not the truth of reason. Reason, at least the reason that gives rise to ontology, the tradition so profoundly summed up in the Husserlian theory of intentionality, "speaking in the first person is not addressed to the other, conducts a monologue" (TI 72).[61] It is a monologue because it only knows the subject-object relation and reduces the other to an object. "Object"

---

57. Conspicuously absent here is any reference to my rights. That is not what the ethical relation is about.

58. Cf. TI 171–72 and 75–76, where Levinas writes, "The presence of the Other is equivalent to this calling into question of my joyous possession of the world."

59. We have already encountered the very next sentence, "*Revelation* constitutes a veritable inversion [of] *objectifying cognition.*"

60. Appropriately, it is in the very next paragraph that Levinas introduces the notion of "meaning prior to my *Sinngebung.*"

61. Here Levinas joins Gadamer, Habermas, and Rorty in raising the question of the possibility of a dialogical reason.

here does not mean "thing" in the sense of an inanimate something. Reason knows that the other is a person, but it defaces this person by making "it" a function of its own horizons and the *Sinngebung* that takes place therein. *"The other qua other is the Other*. To 'let him be' the relation of discourse is required; pure 'disclosure,' where he is proposed as a theme [read: intentional object], does not respect him enough for that. *We call justice this face to face approach, in conversation*. If truth arises in the absolute *experience* in which being gleams with its own light, then truth is produced *only* in veritable conversation or in justice" (TI 71).[62] This is why in Section I.C. of TI, entitled "Truth and Justice," Levinas can argue that "Truth Presupposes Justice" (TI 90) and that "[t]he freedom that can be ashamed of itself founds truth" (TI 83).

This reference to justice has a concrete economic meaning. Levinas regularly identifies the other whose face is in question not just as the neighbor but as the widow, the orphan, and the stranger. He emphasizes the nakedness of the face, and part of the meaning of this notion is quite literal. "The nakedness of his face extends into the nakedness of the body that is cold and that is ashamed of its nakedness. Existence καθ' αὐτό is, in the world, a destitution.... This gaze that supplicates and demands, that can supplicate only because it demands, deprived of everything ... this gaze is precisely the epiphany of the face as a face. The nakedness of the face is destitution. To recognize the Other is to recognize a hunger" (TI 75).

The proper response to this destitution is to give. Levinas emphasizes the asymmetry of the relation, but not in the sense criticized by Nietzsche in which compassion expresses the superiority of the giver. "To recognize is to give. But it is to give to the master, to the lord, to him whom one approaches as 'You' [Thou] in a dimension of height." But then Levinas returns to the economic issue. The generosity called for is the gift that is "the abolition of inalienable property" (TI 75).

We must not overlook another important point in this passage. When Levinas says that "the face speaks," he does not simply mean that utterances emerge from its mouth. Here it is the gaze itself "that supplicates and demands."[63] The gaze has, or better is, its own voice. It performs speech acts without uttering any words.[64] How is this possible? Because the gaze has the

---

62. I have added the emphasis on *only*, which underscores the sense in which all other "knowledge" is merely phenomenal and only the ethical relation puts us in touch with the thing in itself, as discussed above.

63. Cf. TI 262, where "the whole body—a hand or a curve of the shoulder—can express as the face."

64. Cf. Psalm 19:1–4:

The heavens are telling the glory of God . . .
There is no speech, nor are there words;
    their voice is not heard;
Yet their voice goes out through all the earth,
    and their words to the end of the world.

same twofold structure as the more literal speech act. First, it exhibits inverse intentionality in which the arrows of signification come toward me rather than emanating from me, and second, in being thus addressed I find myself put in the dock, my freedom questioned from the standpoint of justice.

I know of no better example of what Levinas means here than is found in a passage that Sartre quotes from Faulkner's *Light in August*. The mob of rednecks has just castrated the black man, Christmas, and he is bleeding to death.

> But the man on the floor had not moved. He just lay there, with his eyes open and empty of everything save consciousness. . . . For a long moment he looked at them with peaceful and unfathomable and unbearable eyes. Then his face, body, all, seemed to collapse, to fall in upon itself and from out the slashed garments about his hips and loins the pent black blood seemed to rush like a released breath . . . upon that black blast the man seemed to rise soaring into their memories forever and ever. They are not to lose it, in whatever peaceful valleys, beside whatever placid and reassuring streams of old age, in the mirroring face of whatever children they will contemplate old disasters and newer hopes. *It will be there, musing, quiet, steadfast, not fading and not particularly threatful, but of itself alone serene, of itself alone triumphant.*[65]

But what is this claim, or, to put it differently, what does the face say? Levinas is interested in the transcendence of the ethical relation, not in spelling out this claim into a moral code or the system of ethical norms. Accordingly he is cryptic about what the face says. But not entirely silent. I find three formulations, which I take to have, like the Christian trinity, a perichoretic relation of mutual indwelling. Each is explicated by the other two. The most familiar is "you shall not commit murder" (TI 199, 216, 303).[66] The other two are "you shall not usurp my place in the sun"[67] and "you shall not let me die alone."[68]

Although there is no personal Creator here, there is a hint of "cosmological" transcendence in these claims, since the other addresses me from beyond history (TI 23), or, as the later Levinas will put it, from an immemorial past that was never present. What is said has always already been said (OBBE 35–37). Here, if I will allow, my nostalgia for eternity can be satisfied.

For just this reason there is also epistemic transcendence in this claim (for the three are one) and the other who is its source is present only through

---

65. Sartre, *Being and Nothingness*, trans. Hazel E. Barnes (New York: Philosophical Library, 1956), p. 406 (p. 526 in the Washington Square Press paperback edition). The English is Faulkner's original, the italics Sartre's. It becomes clear that in Sartre's analysis of The Look we have a paradigm of the inverse intentionality that is so crucial to Levinas. But whereas Sartre knows only an allergic reaction to such alterity, Levinas speaks of the possibility of welcome and generosity.

66. At TI 171 Levinas speaks of "the ethical impossibility of commiting [*sic*] this murder" and at 262 of the other "as the infinite resistance to murder" and, as if referring to the Faulkner narrative, as "the hard resistance of these eyes without protection—what is softest and most uncovered."

67. See DEL 24; EN 131; EFP 82, 85.

68. See DEL 24; EN 130, 169; BI 112.

revelation and as mystery. To welcome this alterity is to suspend my own cognitive activity so as to open myself to what I do not, can not, and should not try to control, and it is to acknowledge a presence that simultaneously overwhelms and withholds itself from my cognitive capacities.

But this cognitive self-transcendence involved in opening myself to revelation and mystery is in the service of a transcendence that in its deepest reality is ethical. It is as a claim upon my freedom that I experience the other as wholly other, for this claim is not a product of my own pure practical reason, or of the general will, or of any contractual arrangement, explicit or tacit. The self-transcendence evoked by the ethical relation Levinas calls welcome and generosity.

Later he will call it substitution. I have largely limited myself in this exposition to the "early" Levinas of *Totality and Infinity,* drawing on later writings only where they seem to me not really datable as later. There are new themes in *Otherwise Than Being* and the essays that surround it. Thus in the idea of substitution and the concepts that cluster around it, he offers a more radical (I have assiduously avoided the term until now) account of the responsibility under which I find myself by the claim of the other and what is involved in the response of welcome and generosity (OBBE ch. 4). The diachronic understanding of time in the later writings, according to which there is an immemorial and irrecuperable past from which I am obligated prior to any commitments I may make, further illuminates the dialectic of presence and absence in the experience of ethical transcendence. I can never get to the one who calls me to responsibility in order to negotiate, or intimidate, or even kill.[69] And the distinction between the saying and the said only makes it clear that it is the mere fact of speaking and not the propositional content of the speech act that calls my freedom into question. These ideas enrich Levinas' analysis, but they do not give it an essentially different structure. The claim of the other may be rendered more traumatic and its essentially transempirical nature in the midst of empirical destitution emphasized more strongly, but the basic idea remains the same: ethical transcendence occurs in the mysterious self-revelation of the other who calls my freedom into question by making an unconditional claim upon me.

And what if that other were God?

---

69. See, for example, OBBE 9–10, 30–38, 86, 101, and EN 232–33.

eight

Kierkegaard

Beyond Onto-theology to Love of God

For Levinas, as we have seen, there is only the slightest hint of cosmological transcendence. The focus is entirely on epistemic and ethical transcendence, and the thesis is quite clear: transcendence is fundamentally an ethical or personal matter and epistemic transcendence is its necessary condition. Only that which exceeds comprehension retains enough alterity to put my freedom in question. Only that which is beyond intentionality by enacting an inverse intentionality in which I am no longer the *Sinngeber*, the origin of meaning, can call me to responsibility. Only the voice that escapes my vision, or perhaps turns my gaze into hearing ("the face speaks"), occupies the height that deserves the name transcendence.

It is the human other, the widow, the orphan, and the stranger, who speak to me from this height, unconstrained by my horizons, which they nevertheless interrupt and invade. God does not appear as an independent agent in this scene, which is why cosmological transcendence leaves the barest trace on the radar screen. So Levinas, whose whole thought can be said to focus on the problem of transcendence, is of no direct help in our inquiry into the nature of divine transcendence. Given the power of his account of transcendence and its crucial link to the self-transcendence of ethical responsibility, that's a pity. But perhaps we can find him helpful after all by asking how it would look if, instead of substituting the neighbor for God, as he does, we reverse his reversal and try to think God as the voice that addresses us from on high. My thesis in this chapter is that that is exactly what we find in Kierkegaard,[1] that Levinas' account of ethical transcendence provides a splendid heuristic for reading Kierkegaard's account[2] of religious transcendence because the two have the same structure.

Talk of cosmological transcendence takes place in abstract, metaphysical categories that all too easily (but not necessarily)[3] lend themselves to onto-theological thinking. Talk of ethical and religious transcendence is inescapably personal and, as such, resists onto-theological games and gestures. The mediating link is epistemic transcendence. It can be expressed in abstract, impersonal categories such as finite and infinite, capacity and incapacity, containment and excess. But the moment it goes beyond mystery to revelation, or links mystery essentially to revelation (since only God knows God and our knowledge of God depends on what God tells us), the pantheistic doctrine of mystery (as in Plotinus) is decisively left behind in an essentially interpersonal account of our knowledge of God. Revelation is an asymmetrical I-Thou relation in which the Thou has precedence over the I. This opens the door to an interpersonal religious transcendence in which the cognitive dimension with its dialectic of unconcealment and concealment is teleologically suspended in relations of obedience, trust, worship, and fellowship.

***

In *Fear and Trembling*, Johannes de Silentio presents the religious relation as faith. In other words, faith is his name for self-transcendence in the face of divine transcendence. At the very outset he sharply distinguishes faith from knowledge, at least from that knowledge thought to be the highest by the best and brightest of his culture, namely speculative philosophy, a.k.a. the system or science (FT 5–8). Were it not for the satirical disrespect he shows for the latter, it might seem that he is invoking Plato's divided line, in which *pistis*

---

1. Looking back, we can see that such address is what Spinoza and Hegel eliminate from their accounts of "revelation" and what Augustine, Pseudo-Dionysius, Aquinas, and Barth include in theirs.

2. By "Kierkegaard's account" I mean the collection of accounts he presents for our consideration, sometimes pseudonymously, sometimes in his own name. Following his wish, I shall attribute the pseudonymous works to the pseudonymous authors.

3. In theistic contexts, cosmological transcendence is understood in terms of a personal Creator, and the causal and cosmic dimensions rightly find their telos in communion and covenant, where the impersonal is *aufgehoben* in the personal and the onto-theological project pales into insignificance. The affirmation of creation is not the attempt to render the world intelligible in accord with the principle of sufficient reason but the identification of the one who is worshiped. "Our help is in the name of the Lord, who made heaven and earth" (Ps. 124:8).

(belief) and *eikasia* (imagining) as the two forms of *doxa* (opinion) constitute the lower half of the divided line in contrast with genuine knowledge (*noesis, episteme*) at the top. He even alludes to Hegel's version of this scheme, according to which philosophy consists in translating the inferior forms (*Vorstellungen*) of understanding (*Verstand*) into the superior forms (*Begriffe*) of reason (*Vernunft*) (FT 7). But he does so only to satirize the notion, which he finds at the heart of the Hegelian philosophy, that since everyone already has faith, the task is to go beyond faith to knowledge. Faith is rather the task of a lifetime. In the Preface it is likened in this respect to doubt, not the paper doubt of Descartes, but the doubt of the ancient skeptics (we might add Buddhists). In the Epilogue, which serves as the other bookend within which to tell the story of Abraham's (almost) sacrifice of Isaac (Gen. 22), Silentio repeats that faith is the task of a lifetime and this time compares it to love (FT 121–23). So, far from being at the lowest and most common level of human cognition, trying to be knowledge but never quite succeeding, faith, Silentio suspects, is one of those excellent things that is as difficult as it is rare. That's the whole point of retelling the Abraham story. If he is the paradigm of faith, who would be so bold as to claim to have achieved it or so ridiculous as to claim to have gone past it.

Silentio's goal is to rescue the discussion of faith and reason from its longstanding captivity to the model of Plato's divided line. He challenges both assumptions of that model: first, that the highest human task is knowledge as pure insight and full presence, the untrammeled gaze at truth in the full daylight outside the cave, and second, that mere belief (*pistis*)[4] is what you have to settle for when you're not good enough to raise yourself to such lofty heights. Thus Hegel, the current form of the Platonic model for Silentio, will say, "Religion is for everyone. It is not philosophy, which is not for everyone."[5]

Like Plato's belief (*pistis*) and opinion (*doxa*) and Hegel's representations (*Vorstellungen*) and understanding (*Verstand*), Silentio's faith is not knowledge in the sense to which speculative philosophy aspires (*noesis, episteme, Wissenschaft*, system), or, to say the same thing in biblical language, faith is not sight. In order (1) to rescue faith from its alleged *Aufhebung* in sight, the pure and total presence that is philosophy's pride, and (2) to retain for the "object" of faith the status of both mystery and the subject (agent and subject matter) of revelation, Silentio's version of Abraham's (almost) sacrifice of Isaac emphasizes in five ways the gulf fixed between faith and knowledge.

---

4. *Tro* in Danish and *Glaube* in German have the same ambiguity as *pistis* in Greek and can mean either everyday, garden variety belief or religious faith.

5. *Lectures on the Philosophy of Religion*, ed., Peter C. Hodgson (Berkeley: University of California Press, 1984–87), I, 180. Cf. III, 283, where Hegel says that "in religion, the content of the idea appears in forms accessible to sense experience or understanding, because religion is the truth for everyone. . . . In religion the truth has been revealed as far as its *content* is concerned; but it is another matter for this content to be present in the *form* of the concept, of thinking, of the concept in speculative form."

First, Abraham's faith is an encounter with the *mysterium tremendum*.[6] As *mysterium*, God escapes our conceptual grasp, to be sure,[7] but in a particular direction signified by the qualifier, *tremendum*. Thus Silentio emphasizes the terror and the terrifying nature of the encounter (FT 33, 72, 75, 77) along with its dreadfulness (FT 78, 114).[8] As he approached Mount Moriah, Abraham experienced "the shudder of the idea" (FT 9), and we in turn can only approach him "with a *horror religiosus*, as Israel approached Mount Sinai" (FT 61). There is nothing here of the secure serenity in which the thinker grasps the full intelligibility of being. Abraham's transcendental ego, if he has one, is shaken to its core in this experience.

Second, faith is a response to the paradox and as such is a relation irreducible to comprehension. Actually, Silentio specifies three paradoxes. The "prodigious paradox of faith" is (1) "a paradox that makes a murder into a holy and God-pleasing act" and (2) "a paradox that gives Isaac back to Abraham again, *which no thought can grasp, because faith begins precisely where thought stops*" (FT 53, emphasis added). Faith is also (3) "precisely the paradox that the single individual as the single is higher than the universal . . . that the single individual as the single individual stands in an absolute relation to the absolute . . . *a paradox impervious to thought*" (FT 55, emphasis added).[9] Silentio relates the paradox to the *tremendum* and finds himself "shattered," "repelled," and "paralyzed" because in Abraham's story "I have seen the terrifying face to face" (FT 33). He emphasizes the anxiety, the distress, and the agony evoked by the paradox (FT 63, 65). So it is not surprising that he not only confesses that he

---

6. It will be recalled that Rudolf Otto uses this term to designate the "non-rational" dimension of the holy in *The Idea of the Holy*, trans. John W. Harvey (New York: Oxford University Press, 1958), ch. 4. He spells it out in terms of the fear, the shudder, the awe, the horror, and the dread evoked by the ultimately uncanny. In presenting this idea to students, I once found myself saying, "If it isn't scary, it isn't God." In our earlier discussion of Heidegger we saw that the loss of awe was a mark of onto-theology.

7. In this respect, the *mysterium tremendum* is a special case of what Jean-Luc Marion calls the saturated phenomenon. See "The Saturated Phenomenon," in Dominique Janicaud et al., *Phenomenology and the "Theological Turn": The French Debate* (New York: Fordham University Press, 2000) and *Being Given: Toward a Phenomenology of Givenness*, trans. Jeffrey L. Kosky (Stanford, Calif.: Stanford University Press, 2002), pp. 21–24.

8. This dimension of the presentation can well be read in conjunction with Kierkegaard's *The Concept of Anxiety*, trans. Reidar Thomte (Princeton, N.J.: Princeton University Press, 1980), remembering that the original translation was entitled *The Concept of Dread*, trans. Walter Lowrie (Princeton, N.J.: Princeton University Press, 1957).

9. The two forms of this third paradox are the themes, respectively, of Problema I and II. The ethical, which is teleologically suspended or *aufgehoben* in faith, is identified with the universal. It is important to notice that Silentio understands this, not in the Platonic/Kantian sense of the apprehension of eternal truth that is universal by transcending the contingencies of history, but in the Hegelian sense of *Sittlichkeit* (see p. 55 n. 7), the laws and customs of one's people. Accordingly, Silentio presents the ethical as the nation, the state, and society (FT 57–59, 62). See "Abraham and Hegel" in my *Kierkegaard's Critique of Reason and Society* (University Park, Pa.: Penn State University Press, 1991).

does not have the faith of Abraham, but that it represents a movement he is incapable of making by himself (FT 48–51, 69). Nor can society be of any help, since the paradox includes the claim that the individual is irreducible to being but part of the social whole, merely a player in society's language games.

Third, Silentio develops the second paradox, the one about Abraham getting Isaac back, in terms of another category: the absurd. In Silentio's version, Abraham believed that he would get Isaac back *in this life,* and he believed this "by virtue of the absurd." Once again Silentio tells us that this faith is beyond him. "I cannot shut my eyes and plunge confidently into the absurd. . . . For my part, I presumably can describe the movements of faith, but I cannot make them" (FT 34, 37).[10]

But in Silentio's account of the absurd we also get something new. The absurd[11] is not absolutely or inherently absurd, but only such relative to a point of view he describes as human, all too human. Abraham "had faith by virtue of the absurd, for *human calculation* was out of the question. . . . He had faith by virtue of the absurd, for all *human calculation* ceased long ago" (FT 35–36, emphasis added). It is only relative to human calculation that faith is absurd. The norm for this calculation is "one's understanding and along with it every-thing finite, for which it is the stockbroker . . . for the understanding continues to be right in maintaining that in the finite world, which it dominates, this having [getting Isaac back] was and continues to be an impossibility. The knight of faith realizes this just as clearly; consequently, he can be saved only by the absurd, and this he grasps by faith" (FT 36, 47).

But what human understanding and its calculation leave out of the ac-count is God, and to believe by virtue of the absurd is to believe "by virtue of the fact that for God all things are possible" (FT 46) even when they are "over and beyond human powers" (FT 48). When God is factored into the equation, faith ceases to be absurd in itself, though it continues to be absurd relative to human understanding and the finitude over which it presides. What the knight of faith recognizes to be impossible is only impossible "humanly speak-ing" (FT 46), *in a human calculation from which God has been excluded.* Only for a faith that excludes this exclusion will the act of faith and its content make sense. But as long as faith has not become sight, as long as we do not see God face to face, this exclusion of the exclusion will occur in the cave and not in the pure light outside. It will not, indeed cannot, without betraying itself, satisfy the philosopher's demand for absolute knowledge and sheer presence.

Fourth, faith is a form of madness. To Silentio, "Abraham was the greatest of all, great by that power whose strength is powerlessness, great by that wisdom whose secret is foolishness, great by that hope whose form is madness, great by that love that is hatred to oneself" (FT 16–17). Once again, this madness is

---

10. In this confession we see both the possibility and the limits of the phenomenology of religion. To describe the religious life is one thing; to live it is another.

11. Or the "preposterous" (FT 20).

relative to a particular criterion of sanity. "Humanly speaking, he is mad and cannot make himself understandable to anyone. . . . Let me speak humanly about it, purely humanly! . . . Is it not madness! . . . is he not mad?" (FT 76–77). For this reason, Silentio, anticipating a move his successor Johannes Climacus will make, introduces the Socratic notion of divine madness.

> Venerable Father Abraham! . . . You who were the first to feel and to bear witness to that prodigious passion that disdains the terrifying battle with the raging elements and the forces of creation in order to contend with God, you who were the first to know that supreme passion, the holy, pure, and humble expression for the divine madness that was admired by the pagan . . . (FT 23)

In his second speech on Eros in the *Phaedrus*, Socrates disavows his earlier claim that one should turn from the lover to the non-lover "on the ground that the former is mad, and the latter sound of mind. That would be right if it were an invariable truth that madness is an evil, but in reality, the greatest blessings come by way of madness, indeed of madness that is heaven sent." He concludes this portion of his speech by asserting "the superiority of the heaven-sent madness over man-made sanity."[12] That is precisely what Silentio wishes to suggest, namely that the reason in whose name faith is judged to be absurd and insane is a "man-made sanity" which lacks the authority to be an ultimate criterion. Faith is not the failed attempt to conform to this "sight" but the deep suspicion that as human, all too human, it is full of blind spots and just at the crucial points.

Of course, the fact that Abraham has faith does not mean he has ceased to be human. Hence the terror, the dread, the anxiety, the distress, and the agony. Transcendence has sundered him deeply. As human he understands and recognizes the force of the judgment that the paradox of faith is absurd and insane; he is anything but a blithe spirit. But as open to the divine, he also understands and recognizes the limited validity of this judgment, though he goes beyond it at great personal risk and without the security of socially sanctioned guarantees. Faith is the self-transcendence that welcomes this deeply disturbing invasion of the inner sanctum of his self.[13]

Fifth, and finally, Abraham's God relation involves a private language game. This theme, in which Silentio takes the linguistic turn, helps us to understand the previous three, in particular to see how the paradox, the absurdity, and the madness of faith are not absolute but relative to a particular, contingent human point of view. In Silentio's version, Abraham does not tell his wife, Sarah, his servant Eliezer, or his son Isaac, what the trip to Mount

---

12. Plato, *Phaedrus*, 244 a–d.
13. For a more detailed analysis of this structure in both Levinas and Kierkegaard, see my essay "Transcendence, Heteronomy, and the Birth of the Responsible Self," in *Calvin O. Schrag and the Task of Philosophy after Postmodernity*, ed. Martin Beck Matuštík and William L. McBride (Evanston, Ill.: Northwestern University Press, 2002), pp. 201–225.

Moriah was all about, and in Problema III he asks whether it was "ethically defensible for Abraham to conceal his undertaking" from them (FT 82). But he has been preparing the reader for this question from the outset. Abraham's silence stems from the fact that neither Isaac, nor Sarah, nor Eliezer could understand him (FT 10, 21). Of course, this doesn't mean that they lacked the linguistic competence to comprehend the sentences he might utter; he means that it wouldn't make sense to them, that they could not imagine how the sacrifice of Isaac might be the right thing to do. As a matter of fact, Abraham can't speak because *no one* could understand him (FT 60, 67, 71, 76). He lacks the ability to appeal to the universal, in terms of which he could be understood (FT 60, 71).

This is what distinguishes Abraham as the knight of faith from the tragic hero. Silentio reminds us of three fathers who actually killed their children, Agamemnon, Jephthah, and Brutus. We have already seen that the universal is the ethical, the laws and customs of one's people. In each case there is a good reason within the *Sittlichkeit* in question, to sacrifice the individual for the good of the community, to subordinate family ties to civic duty. Because this ethos is shared by all members of the community, it is the universal to which the tragic hero can appeal and in terms of which those around him will understand him. They will weep with him and for him, but they will understand that he did the right thing.

Now it may be, as some interpreters have suggested,[14] that the story of Genesis 22 functioned to reinforce the numerous other passages in the Hebrew Bible that prohibit child sacrifice in ancient Israel. The idea is that Abraham came from a culture in which child sacrifice was a sanctioned religious act, but that God was saying to him and through him to all Israel, "No. I am different from the gods who demand child sacrifice. As a matter of fact, I forbid it." But that is not the way Silentio tells the story. Abraham already lives in a culture in which such an act would simply be murder, and unlike the situation of the tragic hero, there is no socially sanctioned higher value to trump that norm in these circumstances. As the criterion of the good the universal warrants the judgment, "This is murder," and as the criterion of the true confers upon this judgment the status of knowledge. Abraham finds himself in his God relation to be eccentric to the universal. "Humanly speaking, he is mad and cannot make himself understandable to anyone" (FT 76).[15]

Humanly speaking! The nagging qualifier is what gives interest to the question of Problema III, whether Abraham's silence is "ethically defensible." It is long since clear that it is not. Within the ethical one must justify one's actions by appeal to the universal, and the inability or refusal to do so means

---

14. See Louis Jacobs, "The Problem of the *Akedah* in Jewish Thought," in *Kierkegaard's Fear and Trembling: Critical Appraisals* (University, Ala.: University of Alabama Press, 1981).

15. As early as 1837, Kierkegaard emphasizes the importance of the distinction between "philosophy (the purely human view of the world, the *human* standpoint) and Christianity" (JP III, 3253).

that one is either a criminal or, more charitably, mad.[16] The point of the question is not to repeat this by now familiar verdict but rather to ask two questions. Q1—What must be true if the above analysis is the whole story? A1—The individual is only a part in a whole and the social totality in which one happens to find oneself is the highest norm for one's existence. In Levinas' language, no infinity interrupts this totality, and transcendence is swallowed up in immanence. Q2—What must be true if there is to be a third possibility in which the individual is *higher* than the universal, eccentric to the social totality but not by virtue of irrationality (insanity) or immorality (criminality)? A2—The ethical universal must *not* be the highest norm for human existence but must be teleologically suspended in an infinity, a transcendence that invades and relativizes this totality along with its criteria of the good and the true. This is the wager of faith.

Silentio emphasizes the linguistic nature of Abraham's loneliness. "Abraham remains silent—but he *cannot* speak" (FT 113). It is as if he has been reading his Wittgenstein and knows that the universal is a language game, a network of rules that prescribe what practices are permitted and what statements are intelligible. Anticipating twentieth century theories, he places the tragic hero in the context of a dialogical rationality. He has been reading his Gadamer and explains that Iphigenia accepts her father's resolve to sacrifice her because "they now have a mutual understanding. She can understand Agamemnon" (FT 115). Doubtless her prior horizon was limited to family values, in which it was a father's duty to protect his children. But Agamemnon has explained that their family belongs to a larger society, which has a higher claim upon them. As a fusion of horizons takes place, they come to mutual understanding. She doesn't merely understand what he is about to do; she understands that it is right.

Silentio has also been reading his Habermas and does not wish to appear partial in the debate with Gadamer. Eccentric to the prevailing language game, Abraham experiences the distress and anxiety we encountered earlier. "The tragic hero does not know this distress. In the first place, he has the consolation that every counterargument has had its due, that he has given everyone an opportunity to stand up against him: Clytemnestra, Iphigenia, Achilles, the chorus, every living person. . . . The tragic hero does not know the dreadful responsibility of loneliness" (FT 113–14).[17] It turns out that even Clytemnestra, the mother of the girl about to be sacrificed, understands Agamemnon.

But Abraham "speaks no human language . . . he speaks in a divine language, he speaks in tongues" (FT 114). What justifies his eccentricity to the prevailing language game and the temporal totality it constitutes, if anything,

---

16. "And yet 'to be mad' is the mildest expression" (FT 76).
17. On the tension between Kierkegaard and Habermas, see my "Commanded Love and Moral Autonomy: The Kierkegaard-Habermas Debate," in *Kierkegaard Studies*, Yearbook 1998, 1–22.

is a conversation with the eternal, not a private language,[18] but a private language game, a dialogue not limited by the rules that govern "humanly speaking." But these rules and the public language game they constitute define what counts as knowledge in any particular context. So faith, Silentio's name for Abraham's posture, is not knowledge in either the "modern" sense of pure, unconditioned insight or the "postmodern" sense of the beliefs that count as knowledge within a particular, human language game.[19] The Kantian formula fits Silentio quite exactly: "I have therefore found it necessary to deny *knowledge*, in order to make room for *faith*."[20]

But what is this faith for which he works so hard to make room? Surely not the mere belief/opinion on the lower half of either Plato's or Hegel's divided line. It belongs to a different domain, since, while faith is not knowledge, it is not the failed attempt at knowledge either. Accordingly, Silentio treats faith as a virtue, but not as an intellectual virtue. He regularly links it indissolubly to two moral virtues, humility and courage (FT 33–34, 48–49, 73). It is courage because of its willingness to endure the trauma and loneliness of stepping outside the security of the universal, and it is humble because it does not do so with the arrogance of the criminal ("The rules don't apply to me; I can do as I please") or of someone mad ("I can see the real truth; all these so-called sane people are quite blind"). The anguish of faith is tied to both its courage and its humility.

But this clue only reinforces the requirement that we not look for the essence of faith in the cognitive domain but in the domain of human freedom. What sort of act of freedom deserves the name of faith? The Abraham story suggests that faith is the willing vulnerability to and acceptance of divine revelation. Let us remember our Levinasian heuristic: What would it look like if we think of God as the voice of transcendence that addresses us from on high? Silentio's answer: It would look like Abraham. For Abraham God is above all a voice; with or without audible sound, God performs speech acts, and with or without physical hearing, Abraham knows himself to be addressed from on high.[21]

In the biblical story God addresses two kinds of speech acts to Abraham:

---

18. This is not the silent, interior monologue that Derrida finds in Husserlian phenomenology. See Derrida, *Speech and Phenomena and Other Essays on Husserl's Theory of Signs*, trans. David B. Allison (Evanston, Ill.: Northwestern University Press, 1973). For the "private language" debate in Wittgensteinian context, see John Turk Saunders and Donald F. Henze, *The Private Language Problem: A Philosophical Dialogue* (New York: Random House, 1967).

19. One could just as easily speak here with Marx of an ideology or with Foucault of an *episteme* or a power/knowledge discursive practice.

20. *Critique of Pure Reason*, B xxx.

21. In an interesting passage that goes, once again, beyond the biblical text, Silentio tells us that Abraham "knew it was God the Almighty who was testing him" (FT 22). Quite obviously this "knowledge" is not the "modern" or "postmodern" knowledge from which faith has been so carefully distinguished.

promise and command.[22] In Lutheran language, not strange to Kierkegaard, these are the speech acts of gospel and law. Silentio acknowledges both. "By faith Abraham received the promise that in his seed all the generations of the earth would be blessed" (FT 17). Again, "By faith Abraham emigrated from the land of his fathers and became an alien in the promised land" (FT 17). While there is reference here to the promise, the crucial speech act presupposed here is the command, "Go from your country and your kindred and your father's house to the land that I will show you" (Gen. 12:1). But, of course, Silentio is primarily interested in another command given by God to Abraham. "Take your son, your only son Isaac, whom you love, and go to the land of Moriah, and offer him there as a burnt offering on one of the mountains that I shall show you" (Gen. 22:2).

Vis-à-vis the promise, faith is trusting acceptance. Vis-à-vis the command, faith is obedience. Neither the trust nor the obedience is a merely cognitive act. To be sure, both trust and obedience presuppose belief that such and such is the case[23]—in this instance, for example, that there is a God and that it was God and not some diabolical deceiver who had issued the promise and the command—but for both trust and obedience belief-that plays a supporting role to belief-in. It is just these interpersonal elements—trust, obedience, belief-in—that are wholly lost sight of on the Platonic/Hegelian divided line and in the onto-theological project in general.

Because the God of Abraham is not merely an essence but a person who performs speech acts, revelation is not merely a manifestation of the being of God but far more fundamentally of the will of God. That will is not Abraham's will; neither the promise nor the command have their origin in him or in any human community to which he belongs. In faith Abraham abandons both the individual autonomy of belief and action to which Descartes, Locke, and Kant subscribe and the collective autonomy we find in the general will of Rousseau and the spirit of Hegel. One might say he is presciently postmodern. But the point not to be overlooked is that divine transcendence here consists not merely in an "object" that my *vision*, whether of sense or intellect, cannot capture, but above all in the alterity of a *voice* that decenters me by expressing a will not my own that is nevertheless recognized as both an unearned gift and a rightful claim which does not originate from the self and which is not presided over by the self. As the self-transcendence that welcomes this voice, faith is the willingness to be not merely reoriented but even redefined by this voice. God is not so much the Prime Mover as the Prime *Sinngeber.* The meaning of the

---

22. Nick Wolterstorff suggests that these are the two most typical speech acts in biblical religion and that what we usually call revelation does not consist primarily of God's giving us information about Godself. See *Divine Discourse: Philosophical reflections on the claim that God speaks* (New York: Cambridge University Press, 1995).

23. P. F. Strawson's account of the logic of presupposing is relevant here. See "On Referring," in *Mind*, 1950, reprinted in *Essays in Conceptual Analysis*, ed. A. G. N. Flew (London: Macmillan, 1956); and *Introduction to Logical Theory* (London: Metheun, 1952), ch. 6, pt. III.

world and even of my own existence arises not from my I nor from my We but from the Thou whose voice disrupts the certainties and the securities of both the I and the We. It is said that "faith cometh by hearing, and hearing by the word of God" (Rom. 10:17 AV). Silentio might turn this into a definition: faith is a certain hearing, a hearing that welcomes the voice of God.

* * *

Not quite eight months after *Fear and Trembling* appeared, Johannes Climacus, another Kierkegaardian pseudonym, presents us with an even smaller work, *Philosophical Fragments*. After a satirically anti-Hegelian Preface in which he contrasts his fragmentary "pamphlet" with the system, he dives immediately into a thought experiment. One fruitful way of reading the experiment is as a response to a question left unanswered in the earlier work: How did Abraham know what he was supposed to do? For Silentio assures us that Abraham "knew it was God the Almighty who was testing him; he knew it was the hardest sacrifice that could be demanded of him; but he knew also that no sacrifice is too severe when God demands it—and he drew the knife" (FT 22). There is nothing puzzling about the second of these knowings, but what about the third and especially the first? How did he come to this "knowledge" and how does it relate to the knowledge from which, as faith, it is so sharply distinguished and relative to which it is paradoxical, absurd madness? If *Fear and Trembling* gives us a negative epistemology of faith, telling us that it arises neither, as modernity would have it, in the absolute knowledge of speculative philosophy, nor, as postmodernity more modestly would have it, in some human language game or other, *Fragments* will propose a positive epistemology of faith.

Climacus does this in his thought experiment by asking what would be necessary if we were to go beyond the Socratic notion that knowledge is recollection.[24] We know that the answer will be revelation as the alternative to recollection, but Climacus is in no hurry to get there. He could say, simply, "Revelation. Abraham knew what he was supposed to do because God told him." But while that would be an answer, of sorts, to the question, "Whence this knowledge?" it would not tell us how this knowledge works and, just as importantly, just wherein it differs from the kind of knowing, especially speculative, onto-theological knowing, from which Climacus is as eager to distinguish it as was Silentio.

First he gives us the essentials of the recollection model as he understands it:

---

24. In *The Concept of Irony*, trans. Howard V. Hong and Edna H. Hong (Princeton, N.J.: Princeton University Press, 1989), Kierkegaard quite sharply distinguishes the ignorant and ironic Socrates from the speculative Plato; and Climacus, in *Concluding Unscientific Postscript*, implies a similar distinction by setting Socrates over against the speculative project. But no such distinction is operative in *Fragments*.

1) The truth is already in us. "Thus the ignorant person merely needs to be reminded in order, by himself, to call to mind what he knows. The truth is not introduced into him but was in him . . . the truth in which I rest was in me and emerged from me . . . [it is] the truth that I had from the beginning without knowing it" (PF 9, 12).

2) The teacher can never be more than a midwife, can never have more than a maieutic relation to the learner. The teacher may be the occasion for recollection, but this help is not essential. It can always be replaced by another helper or by no helper at all.[25] Thus the knower is "sufficient unto himself" (PF 10–11).

3) When it comes to the knowledge of God, "self-knowledge is God-knowledge" (PF 11). This is Climacus' epistemic reading of the Platonic claim that the soul is divine. This implies that the soul's highest knowledge is the highest knowledge there is, a thesis with which Hegel is in full agreement.[26] The claim that only God knows God becomes the claim that we, in our highest knowing, are God and that our self-knowledge is God-knowledge.

Climacus names the alternative to this scheme revelation (PF 11). Then he spells out its difference at each of these three points:

1) The truth is not already in us, or rather, we are not in the truth. "If the situation is to be different . . . then the seeker up until that moment must not have possessed the truth, not even in the form of ignorance, for in that case the moment becomes merely the moment of occasion; indeed, he must not even be the seeker . . . he has to be defined as outside the truth . . . or as untruth. He is, then, untruth" (PF 13). Why Climacus takes such a hard line here will become clearer when we get to the third point.

2) The teacher is more than a midwife and plays an essential and not merely a maieutic role. For "if the learner is to obtain the truth, the teacher must bring it to him . . ." We are not surprised; we saw that coming. But we are surprised as Climacus continues, "but not only that. Along with it, he must provide him with the condition for understanding it, for if the learner were himself the condition for understanding the truth, then he merely needs to recollect" (PF 14). The teacher gives the condition, a capacity, an ability to understand the truth which, along with the truth itself, the learner lacked.

What does it mean here to understand the truth? It might mean to comprehend something very complicated or abstruse, as in "I didn't understand Gödel's theorem until a very good teacher explained it to me." But that wasn't Abraham's problem. He had no trouble understanding what it meant to offer his son as a sacrifice. His problem was to recognize this as the truth, to see that it was the right thing to do. Of course, Climacus is thinking of Socrates and the

---

25. My geometry teacher helped me to understand the Pythagorean theorem, but presumably Pythagoras didn't need such help but figured it out for himself.

26. See my *History and Truth in Hegel's Phenomenology*, 3rd ed. (Bloomington: Indiana University Press, 1998), especially ch. 5–8.

slave boy in the *Meno*, not Abraham. But the intertextual reading is justified by the similarity of the two cases. The slave boy's problem was not to understand the idea of a square with twice the area of another square but to recognize the truth of the special case of the Pythagorean theorem presented by Socrates' diagram, namely that the square of the hypotenuse of a right triangle is equal to the sum of the squares of the other two sides. The question of the condition is simply this: When the truth is staring you in the face (somehow or other), are you able to recognize it as the truth? The slave boy was, and in this sense he was self-sufficient and the teacher dispensable. Like many others since Pythagoras, he might have discovered a proof of the Pythagorean theorem (or at least this special case of it) without help from Socrates, and it was precisely this ability that enabled him to recognize the solution as the truth when Socrates presented it to him.

Not so with Abraham. Neither his I nor his We, neither "modern" pure insight nor "postmodern" competence in his culture's language games could give rise to his frightful truth. He knew by revelation because God not only told him what he ought to do but enabled him to see that it was the right thing to do, that the command of God trumped the laws and customs of his people. Without overt reference to Abraham, Climacus gives us this structure as a general definition of revelation.

But when revelation is understood as this combination of giving the truth and giving the condition for recognizing it as the truth, recollection theory goes beyond its usual restriction to *a priori* knowledge. Much of our factual knowledge is based on the testimony of others, for example what we believe because we read it in the newspaper or heard it on the evening news.[27] It is often said that revelation is a mode of knowing based on the testimony of God. This is true as far as it goes, but for Climacus, at least, it does not go far enough. For in the ordinary case, when presented with the truth by the testimony of another, the knower has the capacity to recognize it as the truth by recognizing the trustworthiness of the witness, by comparing the testimony with that of other witnesses, by checking it out directly, and so forth. But this means that the recollection model, as presented by Climacus, is neutral with reference to the difference between *a priori* and empirical knowledge. If, when presented (somehow) with the truth, including matters of fact and not just relations of ideas,[28] I have the capacity to recognize it as such, recollection is at work, I am self-sufficient as a knower, and the teacher (witness) is in principle dispensable.

Absent any caveat to the contrary, we might understand divine revelation in just this way. Climacus' claim that the teacher must also give the condition

---

27. The important role of testimony in the structure of what we count as knowledge is stressed by Alvin Plantinga in *Warrant and Proper Function* (New York: Oxford University Press, 1993), especially in ch. 4.
28. To use a familiar empiricist way of distinguishing the empirical from the *a priori*.

is his caveat to the contrary. But in making it, so as decisively to distinguish revelation from recollection, he also enables us to see that it applies to factual knowledge, whether these are physical facts, historical facts, metaphysical facts, or moral facts.[29] If there are facts of any of these kinds that we cannot recognize as such without the gift of the condition, at that point recollection reaches its limit and revelation is the only source of knowledge. "I have therefore found it necessary to deny *knowledge*, in order to make room for *faith*,"[30] Climacus tells us, in effect, where faith is the welcoming of revelation, the willingness to be dependent on its double gift.

In revelation so construed, the teacher does not play the merely maieutic role of an occasion that is eliminable rather than essential. But such a teacher is not what we usually understand by a teacher, for "the one who not only gives the learner the truth but provides the condition is not a teacher. Ultimately, all instruction depends upon the presence of the condition; if it is lacking, then a teacher is capable of nothing, because . . . the teacher, before beginning to teach, must transform, not reform, the learner. But no human being is capable of doing this; if it is to take place, it must be done by the god himself" (PF 14–15). In other words, revelation can only come from a teacher who is also the Creator. The ontic finitude of the knower as creature is recapitulated in the noetic finitude of this epistemic heteronomy.

3) It is, of course, no surprise to find revelation linked to God as its source. But Climacus presents this as a corollary to the surprise we have been exploring, namely that the teacher must give not only the truth but also the condition. Now comes a second surprise, this one about the learner; and here it becomes unmistakably clear that the soul is not divine and that self-knowledge is not God-knowledge. How is it, Climacus asks, that the learner lacks the condition for recognizing existentially important truth? "God must have given

---

29. In speaking thus I commit myself to the belief that there are facts of all these kinds. By this I mean that there are truths of these kinds, though these may be "phenomenal" truths that do not meet the adequation test, whose truth is not recognized *a priori*, whether this latter is defined in terms of formal logic (the denial is self-contradictory), in terms of self-evidence, or in terms of being the condition for the possibility of experience. Two important recent works in religious epistemology work out such an account of revelation in relation to factual knowledge of religious import, both historical and metaphysical. See C. Stephen Evans, *The Historical Christ and the Jesus of Faith: The Incarnational Narrative as History* (New York: Oxford University Press, 1996) and Alvin Plantinga, *Warranted Christian Belief* (New York: Oxford University Press, 2000). The link to Kierkegaard is explicit only in the former case, but a reading of Climacus' thought experiment is the best introduction to Plantinga's bold project.

30. In oblique and direct references, Climacus tells us this is already going on in *Either/Or*. His "main thought," pre-empted by the appearance of *Either/Or*, "was that, because of the copiousness of knowledge, people in our day have forgotten what it means *to exist*, and what *inwardness* is . . ." The very title of *Either/Or* expresses an "indirect polemic against speculative thought, which is indifferent to existence" (CUP 249, 252; cf. 251). Existence, subjectivity, and inwardness are more or less synonymous terms for the only horizon within which ethics and religion can even occur, much less thrive.

him the condition for understanding the truth (for otherwise he previously would have been merely animal, and that teacher who gave him the condition along with the truth would make him a human being for the first time)" (PF 15). The learner must somehow have lost it. But this cannot be due to an act of God or to an accident, Climacus argues, so "it must therefore have been due to himself. . . . The untruth, then, is not merely outside the truth but is polemical against the truth. . . . But this state—to be untruth and to be that through one's own fault—what can we call it? Let us call it *sin*" (PF 15).[31] Bereft of the condition, the learner is "unfree and bound . . . the slave of sin." The teacher must therefore not merely be Creator but also "*savior*," "*deliverer*," and "*reconciler*" (PF 15, 17), and the learner must become "*a new person*" who has experienced "*conversion*," "*repentance*," and "*rebirth*" (PF 18–19). Perhaps Climacus is thinking of Paul here, who speaks of "those who by their wickedness suppress the truth" (Rom. 1:18). In any case, sin is definitely an epistemological category for him.[32] Matters epistemic are once again spilling over into the ethical domain, broadly speaking. Faith involves not only the intellect but also the will, its freedom, and even its bondage.[33] The limit of knowledge is drawn not merely by finitude but also by fault, and the faith for which Climacus makes room by denying knowledge is far more complex than mere assent or disbelief.

That this is the decisive turning point is made clear by Climacus in a section entitled "The Absolute Paradox." The "ultimate paradox of thought," he suggests, is "to want to discover something that thought itself cannot think" (PF 37), to find the limits of (human) thought. If we give the title "*the god*" to "this unknown against which the understanding in its paradoxical passion collides and which even disturbs man and his self-knowledge," this is "only a name" and we have yet to see what it means (PF 39). If this unknown god is to be a genuine frontier, it must not only be different from the knower, but

---

31. In a journal entry from 1835, when his own relation to Christianity was in a turmoil verging on despair, Kierkegaard writes that "the yawning abyss is *here* where Christianity posits man's cognition as defective on account of sin" (JP III, 3245). This entry begins, "*Philosophy and Christianity can never be united.*" It continues with an anticipation of the deconstruction of onto-theology. ". . . for if philosophy as a self-accounting for the relationship between God and the world denied itself, if it came to the conclusion that it could not explain this relationship, then philosophy at its highest perfection would involve its own total destruction, namely as evidence that it could not fulfill its own definition. Yes, seen from this standpoint, philosophy would not even serve as a transition to Christianity, for it would necessarily have to stop with this negative result . . ." Perhaps, while thinking here of Socratic ignorance, Kierkegaard is anticipating secular postmodernism.

32. For this notion in another context, see my essay "Taking St. Paul Seriously: Sin as an Epistemological Category," in *Christian Philosophy*, ed. Thomas P. Flint (Notre Dame, Ind.: University of Notre Dame Press, 1990), pp. 200–226.

33. The bondage of the will is an important Lutheran theme, going back to Augustine and eventually to Paul. Luther's polemic against Erasmus on this subject, *The Bondage of the Will*, is found in Vol. 33 of *Luther's Works*, ed. Helmut T. Lehmann (Philadelphia, Pa.: Fortress Press, 1957).

"absolutely different" (PF 44–45). Like Levinas, Climacus thinks that genuine alterity is not found in ontology but in ethics, or, in Climacus' biblical language, not in creation but in the fall. "But if the god is to be absolutely different from a human being, this can have its basis not in that which man owes to the god (for to that extent they are akin) but in that which he owes to himself or in that which he himself has committed. What, then, is the difference? Indeed, what else but sin. . . . We stated this in the foregoing by saying that the individual is untruth and is this through his own fault" (PF 46–47).[34]

For Climacus, or at least for the religious sphere as he presents it, there is epistemic transcendence. There is that which we cannot know by our own powers but only through the gift of an Other. But looked at closely, the epistemic thread leads us to the ethical, beyond the intellect to the will. The alterity to which we are allergic apart from faith is not merely the difference between an infinite mind and our finite minds; it is more fundamentally the difference between a holy will of the God who has a rightful claim on us and a sinful will, centered on itself. The self-transcendence called forth by this transcendence will begin in the consciousness of sin and the willingness to receive, not just the truth, and not just the condition, but forgiveness and reconciliation. That is why Climacus' successor, Anti-Climacus, will answer the question, What does the divine voice say? with the categorical imperative, "Thou shalt believe in the forgiveness of sins" (SUD 115).[35]

* * *

To Levinas this may not sound like ethics, and he complains bitterly that Kierkegaard is too much like a certain Augustine. In a text from the Cassiciacum period immediately after his conversion, significantly enough entitled *The Soliloquies*, Augustine imagines a conversation in which Reason asks what he wants to know, to which he replies, "I desire to know God and the Soul." To which Reason responds, "Nothing more?" To which Augustine responds, "Nothing whatever."[36] The problem for Levinas occurs precisely where Kierkegaardian texts introduce the notion of sin. He sees sin as the subject's secret, replacing and re-enacting the secret of Abraham, a secret

---

34. No doubt it is because of the centrality of the notion of sin in their account of the religious that both Climacus and Anti-Climacus develop the notion of offense as the alternative to faith. In *Philosophical Fragments* that notion is introduced immediately after this discussion of sin. Sin is also central to *The Concept of Anxiety*, written more or less simultaneously with *Fragments*.

35. Cf. "It is indeed God in heaven who through the apostle says, 'Be reconciled': it is not human beings who say to God, 'Forgive us.' No. God loved us first" (WL 336). Kierkegaard, here writing in his own name, immediately draws the ethical corollary: "the true conciliatory spirit is this: when the one who does not, note well, need forgiveness is the one who offers reconciliation."

36. *Library of Christian Classics*, Vol. VI, *Augustine: Early Writings*, trans. John H. S. Burleigh (Philadelphia, Pa.: Westminster Press, 1953), pp. 26–27. Of course, Augustine does not stay at this point. In the context of a rich account of the relation of God and the soul, he develops both a personal ethics and a politics, tasks Levinas himself does not undertake.

"that is not simply knowledge about which one refrains from speaking, but one that, identified especially with the burn of sin, remains of itself inexpressible" (PN 67).

The result, of course, is not an atomic, self-contained self, but a God relation that takes place in hidden inwardness. But Levinas sees here a "thirst for salvation . . . that consumes itself with desires." Subjectivity is "a *tensing on oneself* . . . the anxiety of A for A. The subjectivity of the subject is an identification of the Same in its care for the Same. It is egotism" (PN 67–68).

> Thus faith, the going forth from self, the only possible going forth for subjectivity, is the solitary tête-à-tête with what for Kierkegaard admits of nothing but the tête-à-tête: God. . . . The truth that suffers does not open man to other men but to God, in solitude. That existence, the interiority of which is too big for the outer world, and cannot enter it, is thus, in the eyes of many, in the violence of the modern world and its cult of Ardor and Passion. It carries within it an irresponsibility, a ferment of disintegration. . . . Thus begins the disdain for the ethical basis of being, the somehow secondary nature of all ethical phenomena that, through Nietzsche, has led us to the amoralism of the most recent philosophers. (PN 70–72)

In other words, Kierkegaard's "I have therefore found it necessary to deny *knowledge,* in order to make room for *faith*" is by no means equivalent to Levinas' "I have therefore found it necessary to deny *knowledge,* in order to make room for *responsibility.*" The two are rather sharply at odds.

This critique is, if anything, more weighty now than when Levinas made it and deserves careful consideration. To begin, we need to be clear that the ethical stage that is distinguished from the aesthetic in *Either/Or* and then teleologically suspended in the religious stage in *Fear and Trembling* is Hegelian *Sittlichkeit,* the laws and customs of one's people. So far from signifying the ethical relation as Levinas understands it, it is rather the politics he distinguishes from morality and the totality he distinguishes from infinity (see TI 21–22). Levinas understands this. He knows that the ethical stage is "a stage at which the inner life is translated in terms of legal order, carried out in society, in loyalty to institutions and principles and in communication with mankind" (PN 67). But he seems to think that unlike himself, who knows an ethics of infinity and transcendence, Kierkegaard knows only the ethics of totality and immanence and turns from mere socialization to seek salvation in a religious faith beyond ethics. He writes, "Now it is not at all certain that ethics is where [Kierkegaard] sees it. Ethics as consciousness of a responsibility toward others . . . far from losing you in generality, singularizes you, poses you as a unique individual, as I. Kierkegaard seems not to have experienced that, since he wants to transcend the ethical stage, which to him is the stage of generality" (PN 76–77).

But this is a double misreading of the Kierkegaardian corpus. First, there is the charge from Climacus that the system has no ethics (CUP 119, 121). But of course, the system does have an ethics of *Sittlichkeit,* as Climacus himself satirically acknowledges (CUP 145).[37] What it lacks is what Climacus calls subjectivity, which he distinguishes both from the gnostic, speculative point of view in which theory is the highest human task[38] and from the bourgeois language game (*Sittlichkeit*) in which social conformity is all that can be expected of one.[39] Subjectivity is the horizon, the *sine qua non* for the religious, and is presupposed by both Religiousness A and Religiousness B, to which Climacus gives extensive attention in Part Two, Section II, Chapter IV of *Postscript*.[40] But subjectivity is not coextensive with the religious. Chapter I, in which we find the complaint that the system has no ethics, has a heading that begins, "What ethics would have to judge if becoming subjective were not the highest task assigned to a human being" (CUP 129). Chapter II includes the (in)famous claim that "truth is subjectivity" (see especially CUP 203), and Climacus seems primarily concerned with matters religious. But Chapter III returns to the question of "Ethical Subjectivity" (CUP 301).

It is clear that Climacus means something different by ethics and the ethical than does Silentio. For Climacus it is demarcated on the one side from *Sittlichkeit*, since it is set as a challenge to the system, which has no ethics; and it is demarcated on the other side from the religious, although as two modes of subjectivity the two are closely enough linked to be hyphenated at times as the ethico-religious. Like Levinas, Climacus does not give us an ethics, but when he is talking about the ethical realm he is quite clearly talking about a wider range of responsibility than the God relation that takes place in hidden inwardness. In Climacus, Kierkegaard already has a conception of the ethical different from the one that gets teleologically suspended in *Fear and Trembling*.

But Climacus leaves the idea of the ethical undeveloped, and to his complaint that the system has no ethics, Levinas might be read as complaining, ironically, that his subjectivity has no ethics either. While not strictly speaking true, the complaint that Climacus has religion without ethics would at least have as much force as the counter-complaint that Levinas has ethics

---

37. An excellent treatment of Hegelian ethics is found in Allen W. Wood, *Hegel's Ethical Thought* (New York: Cambridge University Press, 1990). For a more sustained analysis of *Postscript*, see my *Becoming a Self: A Reading of Kierkegaard's Concluding Unscientific Postscript* (West Lafayette, Ind.: Purdue University Press, 1996).

38. Whether abstractly in terms of Logic or concretely in terms of World History, both of which can be adequately grasped only as totalities.

39. The speculative is the highest human task because it is the culmination of Absolute Spirit in Hegel's system, while the ethical belongs a level down at Objective Spirit. Already in *Stages on Life's Way*, Frater Tactiurnus presents an account of the ethical sphere that goes beyond conformity to social expectations. "The ethical sphere is only a transition sphere, and therefore its highest expression is repentance as a negative action . . . the ethical [is] the sphere of requirement (and this requirement is so infinite that the individual always goes bankrupt)" (SLW 476).

40. He calls these, respectively, the religion of immanence and transcendence precisely because the former is possible within the horizon of recollection while the latter presupposes revelation.

without religion, in spite of occasional, enigmatic references to God.[41] But *Postscript* is far from being the culmination of Kierkegaard's authorship,[42] and Climacus is far from being his last word on ethics.

Less than a year after publishing *Postscript*, Kierkegaard writes in his journal:

> Despite everything people ought to have learned about my maieutic carefulness, by proceeding slowly and continually letting it seem as if I knew nothing more, not the next thing—now on the occasion of my new upbuilding discourses[43] they will probably bawl out that I do not know what comes next, *that I know nothing about sociality*. The fools! Yet on the other hand I owe it to myself to confess before God that in a certain sense there is some truth in it, only not as people understand it—namely, that continually when I have first presented one aspect clearly and sharply, then the other affirms itself even more strongly.
>
> Now I have the theme of the next book. It will be called:
> Works of Love (WL 409, emphasis added)

Let us remember where we are. We have observed a structure in Levinas in which epistemic transcendence and self-transcendence are not merely derived from cognitive finitude but teleologically suspended in the service of ethical transcendence and self-transcendence. To make use of this in our investigation of divine transcendence, we have turned to Kierkegaard with the suggestion that the structure is the same except that the other is, *in the first instance*, God and not the neighbor. We have seen in Silentio and Climacus a denial of knowledge in the service of something transcognitive, namely faith. It is belief, to be sure, but wholly absorbed in the service of trust in the divine promise and obedience to the divine command. Where knowledge is a matter of vision (the seen and the unseen), transcendence is still a matter of the voice, and faith is a response to an inverse intentionality.

The objection from Levinas is that this faith is irresponsibility rather than responsibility, that in its preoccupation with its own God relation it leaves the neighbor in the lurch. Kierkegaard's reply, given with some exasperation, is simply, "Wait 'til I'm finished!"—after which he sits down to write his account of faith's responsibility for the neighbor, entitled *Works of Love*. The sad thing,

---

41. See ch. 7 n. 3 above.

42. See my account of "Religiousness C" in "Kierkegaard's Teleological Suspension of Religiousness B," *Foundations of Kierkegaard's Vision of Community: Religion, Ethics, and Politics in Kierkegaard*, ed. George B. Connell and C. Stephen Evans (Atlantic Highlands, N.J.: Humanities Press, 1992), pp. 110–29, and ch. 14 of *Becoming a Self*.

43. The reference is to *Upbuilding Discourses in Various Spirits*, Part I of which is entitled "An Occasional Discourse" but is better known as "Purity of Heart is to Will One Thing." It is an eloquent portrayal of the religion of hidden inwardness at the level of what Climacus would call Religiousness A.

so far as Levinas' response to Kierkegaard is concerned, is that he writes as if he has never even heard of this book.[44]

Writing this time in his own name, Kierkegaard proceeds in accordance with Jesus' answer to the question about the greatest commandment. " 'You shall love the Lord your God with all your heart, and with all your soul, and with all your mind.' This is the greatest and first commandment. And a second is like it: 'You shall love your neighbor as yourself' " (Matt. 22:37–39).[45] This means, contra Levinas, that the neighbor is not left out and forgotten. Nor is the second commandment second because it is of lesser importance.[46] It is second because it depends on the first. The deepest ground of my responsibility to and for my neighbor is the command of God. "Ultimately, love for God is the decisive factor; from this originates love for the neighbor . . . the Christian love commandment commands loving God above all else, and *then* loving the neighbor" (WL 57, emphasis added; cf. 140).[47] This means that God is the middle term in a triadic relation. "*Worldly wisdom is of the opinion that love is a relationship between persons; Christianity teaches that love is a relationship between: a person—God—a person, that is, that God is the middle term*" (WL 106–107).[48] Hidden inwardness is not abandoned. "Shut your door and pray to God—because God is surely the highest." But neither is it self-sufficient, for "when you open the door that you shut in order to pray to God and go out the very first person you meet is the neighbor, whom you *shall* love" (WL 51). If the first thing God says in the privacy of hiddenness is the offer of forgiveness and reconciliation, the last thing God says to the believing soul returning to the public sphere is "Don't forget to love your neighbor as yourself." So Kierkegaard cites 1 John 4:20, "If anyone says, 'I love God,' and hates his brother, he is a liar; for how can he who does not love his brother, whom he has seen, love God, whom he has not seen."

The neighbor, created in the image of God, may well be a trace of God, but not in the strict, Levinasian sense of the term. For the command to love the neighbor is not a past that was never present. It is revelation in history, originally part of the Mosaic legislation, reiterated in the teaching of Jesus, and

---

44. Neither the substance of Levinas' critique, nor the ignoring of *Works of Love* in making it, is unique to him. For a systematic and sustained response, see M. Jamie Ferreira, *Love's Grateful Striving: A Commentary on Kierkegaard's* Works of Love (New York: Oxford University Press, 2001).

45. The interior quotation marks indicate that Jesus is quoting from his own Bible, Deut. 6:5 and Lev. 19:18 respectively.

46. Jesus immediately adds, "On these *two* commandments hang all the law and the prophets" (verse 40, emphasis added). And elsewhere he teaches, "whoever breaks one of the least of these commandments, and teaches others to do the same, will be called least in the kingdom of heaven" (Matt. 5:19). Cf. James 2:10, "For whoever keeps the whole law but fails in one point has become accountable for all of it."

47. It is worth remembering that the Jesus from whom Kierkegaard takes this ordering speaks as a Jew, not as a Christian.

48. Cf. WL 58, 67, 77, 119, 121.

addressed to each one today as Word and Spirit combine to give both the truth and the capacity to recognize it as such. If it doesn't fit Levinas' account of the trace, it does fit his account of transcendence as coming from "'beyond' the totality" but also as "reflected *within* the totality and history, *within* experience" (TI 23).

For Levinas transcendence enters history and experience as the face of the human other, the neighbor. We saw in the previous chapter that the face speaks and that when it does it expresses itself καθ' αὐτό. The same structures are present when Kierkegaard makes God rather than the neighbor the First Other. Though the God who commands me to love my neighbor as I love myself is one I cannot see face to face—"you cannot see my face; for no one shall see me and live" (Ex. 33:20)—God is nevertheless the voice by which I am addressed and called into question. As when dealing with Abraham, God's speech acts are both promise and command, gospel and law. Thus Kierkegaard will write in his journals a few years after *Works of Love*

> *Christianly* the emphasis does not fall so much upon to what extent or how far a person succeeds in meeting or fulfilling the requirement, if he actually is striving, as upon his getting an impression of the requirement in all its infinitude so that he rightly learns to be humbled and to reply upon grace.
>
> To scale down the requirement in order to be able to fulfill it better . . . —to this Christianity in its deepest essence is opposed.
>
> No, infinite humiliation and grace, and then a striving born of gratitude—this is Christianity. (WL 486)[49]

In *Works of Love* the focus is on the requirement and its infinitude. The First Series of reflections are a sustained mediation on love as a duty. It has a Kantian, deontological ring to it.[50]

But there are two major differences. First, Kant insists, "*Love* is a matter of *feeling* [*Empfindung*], not of will or volition, and I cannot love because I *will* to do so, still less because I *ought* . . . hence there is no such thing as a *duty to love*."[51] Against this, Kierkegaard insists that neighbor love is a divine *command*. The second difference is that obligation does not have its origin in the autonomy of pure practical reason but in a *divine* command. Kierkegaard

---

49. Hence Jamie Ferreira's title, *Love's Grateful Striving*.

50. The Second Series is correspondingly Aristotelian, a virtue ethics focused on a single virtue, neighbor love.

51. From the Preface to the second part of Kant's *Metaphysics of Morals*, namely *The Metaphysical Principles of Virtue*. See *Kant's Critique of Practical Reason and Other Works on the Theory of Ethics*, trans. Thomas Kingsmill Abbott, 6th ed. (London: Longmans, Green and Co. Ltd, 1909), p. 312. More briefly, "love as an inclination (*Neigung*) cannot be commanded" but only "beneficence (*Wohlthun*) from duty" (*Grounding for the Metaphysics of Morals*, 399). For Kierkegaard too, it's "not about *love* but about *works* of love" (WL 3); but one of the works of love is "to be able to find [the neighbor] loveable despite and with his weaknesses and defects and imperfections." This requires one "to transform oneself *and one's taste*" (WL 158, emphasis added). This has an Aristotelian flavor, according to which ethics is about bringing both one's actions and one's affections into accord with the right and the good.

emphasizes the divine command character of his ethics[52] so vigorously that there can be no doubt about the fact that God, whose face I do not see, nevertheless speaks and in such a fashion as to claim us, not merely to inform us. "The divine authority of the Gospel . . . does not speak *about* us human beings, you and me, but speaks *to* us human beings, to you and me," so "it does not follow from this that you are to take it upon yourself to be the expert knower" (WL 14–15).

That God speaks is constantly presupposed and expressed. That in this speech God expresses Godself καθ᾽ αὐτό is thematized more explicitly, not, of course, in this language, but rather in the sustained contrast between commanded and celebrated love. There are two loves celebrated by secular culture in general and the poets in particular: erotic love and friendship. Kierkegaard regularly calls these forms of self-love. If parallelism in Hebrew poetry is saying the same thing twice or even three times in slightly different words,[53] he would have heard this trope in Elvis Presley's "I Want You, I Need You, I Love You." For in the erotic context of the song, the I Love You only repeats the I Want You and the I Need You. This example gives us a hint at why Kierkegaard sees celebrated love as self-love. He develops the point three ways.

1) Erotic love and friendship are spontaneous. They are found in my drives, inclinations, and feelings.[54] They come naturally. I need no teaching, no discipline, no urging. When, to speak of erotic love, the hormones begin to rise, I spontaneously get a crush on girls in general and "her" in particular. And long before puberty, in the absence of what is considered abnormal development, children naturally seek to have friends, even a "best friend." Nor do adults lose these tendencies. Of course, the "object" of desire may in either case not reciprocate, and I may find it difficult to find a lover or a friend. But this external difficulty in no way mitigates the spontaneous nature of the inclination. Elvis had it right. This love is in the service of my needs and wants.

2) The celebrated loves are preferential and thus exclusionary. There is an unqualified equality about commanded love (WL 44, 60, 68–74, 81) inasmuch as all, unconditionally everyone is my neighbor (WL 44, 49). This includes even the enemy, whom I am to love (WL 19, 67–68). Not so in celebrated love. In erotic love and friendship I am drawn to this one but not that one,[55] and the basis of selection is what I find attractive. Sex appeal

---

52. I have discussed this theme in "Commanded Love and Moral Autonomy: The Kierkegaard-Habermas Debate," and in "Commanded Love and Divine Transcendence," in *The Face of the Other and the Trace of God: Essays on the Philosophy of Emmanuel Levinas*, ed. Jeffrey Bloechl (New York: Fordham University Press, 2000), pp. 200–233. Just what kind of divine command theory this is calls for careful examination.

53. For example, "Bless the Lord, O my soul, and all that is within me, bless his holy name" (Ps. 103:1).

54. In contrast with commanded love. See WL 143.

55. In Mozart's opera, Don Giovanni's attempt to be an exception to this rule is at once comic and tragic.

and some non-erotic usefulness or pleasure motivates me. My spontaneity is guided by my preferences; I love what I want and need.

There doesn't seem to be much self-transcendence here, so it is not surprising that Kierkegaard calls these loves self-love. Still, there are nagging questions. Surely it isn't the case that every lover and every friend acts selfishly in those relationships where reciprocity[56] is achieved. There can be real generosity in relationships based on utility or pleasure. Moreover, Aristotle reminds us that beyond these, there are friendships of the good between those "who wish for their friends' good for their friends' sake . . ."[57] Kierkegaard knows this, and it leads him to this third point.

3) Even where individuals are not selfish in relation to each other, we have not necessarily transcended self-love, "which selfishly can unite the two in a new selfish self" (WL 56). They can form "an alliance in self-love" (WL 119) in which the primary concern is "one's own earthly advantage and that of a few others," since it is easy "to get a few people to hold together in self-love" (WL 123–24). The reference to "a few others" reminds us that the selfish we Kierkegaard has in mind, based on spontaneity and preference, need not be a twosome. It could be a family, an extended family, a tribe or clan, a class, a race, a nation. In other words, the few could in fact turn out to be many without the union ceasing to be spontaneous and preferentially exclusionary. I just naturally root for Americans in international competitions like the Olympics or the World Cup, and in doing so withhold my support from other competitors and my joy when they beat "us."

What has all this to do with God expressing and revealing Godself καθ' αὐτό in issuing the command to love the neighbor as oneself? Simply this. As we saw in the previous chapter, the immediacy of the καθ' αὐτό means that it cuts through the horizons of expectation of those addressed, neutralizing their normal, mediating role; and it means that the message that is received, whether in faith or offense, does not have its ground in the transcendental subjectivity, personal or corporate, of the receiver.[58] Transcendence takes place in a heteronomy, at once cognitive and moral, in which the other addresses, identifies, individuates, and claims the same. In the present context, the structures of celebrated love are the horizons of expectation that are invaded by the divine command quite foreign to them, and it is the spontaneity and preferences of the I and the We thus addressed that are put into question by the divine voice. Perhaps alterity of this sort is the only authentic phenomenon, if, as Heidegger

---

56. Not to be confused with symmetry, since relationships may be very lopsided.

57. *Nichomachean Ethics*, 1156b 9–10.

58. This independence of givenness from both the I and its horizons of expectation is at the heart of Jean-Luc Marion's critique of Husserl, both in *Reduction and Givenness*, trans. Thomas A. Carlson (Evanston, Ill.: Northwestern University Press, 1998), and in *Being Given*. When constrained by these *a priori* conditions, no phenomenon can show *itself* but "is staged only in a scene set by and for another besides it, actor without action, submitted to a spectator and transcendental director." *Being Given*, pp. 212–13.

says, phenomenology means "to let that which shows itself be seen from itself in the very way in which it shows itself from itself" (BT 58).[59] Perhaps other "phenomena" try to give themselves from and through themselves but never quite succeed in eluding mediation on the part of the recipient.

This reading is confirmed by the contrast, familiar from Silentio and Climacus, Kierkegaard draws between the divine command and human reason (WL 199) or a "merely human view" (WL 121) with which it comes into "collision" (WL 109, 113). It is "madness, humanly speaking" (WL 108), or at the very least "most strange"—a clear mark of "divine origin" (WL 42). According to a "worldly, a merely human but also ingeniously and poetically developed view," the goal is "to emancipate people from all bonds . . . from the bond that binds one to God and binds one in everything, in every expression of life . . . there is a more or less open intent to depose God in order to install human beings—in the rights of humanity?" Then, as if anticipating Nietzsche, Kierkegaard concludes, "If God is dismissed, the place will indeed be vacant" (WL 114–15).[60] Given the sharp contrast between "the divine conception and the merely human conception" (WL 109), it is no surprise that "to the natural man [the duty of neighbor love] is an offense" and to cultured wisdom "foolishness" (WL 58–59).

So, far from being the condition of the possibility of the neighbor love command, the merely human I and We, along with their horizons of meaning and truth, are the conditions of its impossibility. In order to make room for a faith which, like Abraham's, will be receptive to the divine command, Kierkegaard finds it necessary to deny the knowledge of human reason and worldly wisdom. Here is divine transcendence in its epistemic mode. But like the offer of forgiveness and reconciliation (gospel), the command to love my neighbor (law) is not merely or even primarily about my beliefs. It is about my actions, my attitudes, my affections, my very identity. This is the fully religious mode of divine transcendence. *God is the voice beyond my own who calls me to a life beyond my own through a promise and a command beyond any knowledge or will of my own.*

Like Levinasian ethical transcendence in which the neighbor is the First Other without God as middle term, this religious transcendence calls for a self-transforming self-transcendence.

Like Levinas, who regularly refers to encounters with the other as trauma,[61] Kierkegaard does not soft-pedal the potential for offense upon hearing the Voice. It decenters me decisively. "It is the mark of childishness to say: *Me wants, me—me*; a mark of adolescence to say: *I—and I—I*; the sign of maturity

---

59. Cf. Marion, who says of the saturated phenomenon (a more inclusive category than the voice of transcendence), but which he relates to this formula from Heidegger, "it alone appears truly as itself, of itself, and on the basis of itself . . ." *Being Given*, p. 219.

60. Read: Christendom got the Nietzsche it deserved.

61. Especially throughout OBBE. See ch. 7 n. 55 above.

and the devotion of the eternal is to will to understand that this *I* has no significance unless it becomes the *you* to whom eternity incessantly speaks and says, *You* shall, *you* shall, *you* shall" (WL 90).[62]

In decentering me, the Voice deprives me of the freedom to reduce the other to the same. It imprisons me (WL 96) by reminding me that "you belong to him" (WL 12).[63] If celebrated love is self-love, its overcoming can only be "self-renunciation" (WL 4), "self-sacrifice" (WL 113, 119), and, most frequently throughout the text, "self-denial." "Love is self-denial, rooted in the relationship to God" (WL 424).[64]

At this point some will be tempted to see only the gloomy piety in which Kierkegaard's father brought him up. But once again Levinas is a helpful guide. At this point in his own argument he insists that the traumatic challenge to my *conatus essendi*, to my freedom, is without alienation (OBBE 105, 112, 114, 118). This is because it takes me beyond the usual alternatives of freedom and slavery (OBBE 105). But how? Because I am subject to a claim that is "imposed with a good violence" (OBBE 43). By being Good, the Good "redeems the violence of its alterity" (OBBE 15; cf. 123). Or, to put it a bit differently, "no one is enslaved to the Good" (OBBE 11; cf. 138).[65] This is as close as Levinas is willing to come to saying that those who lose themselves in welcoming the other gain themselves thereby.

Kierkegaard is less reticent. If he sees the divine command as the death of the humanism of the I and the We, it is for the sake of a different, more modest, theistic humanism. It turns out that his diatribe against self-love is not directed at self-love as such but rather at its primacy. It is not to be abolished but "dethroned" (WL 44–45, 50, 58).[66] The neighbor-love command is a kind of pick with which to "open the lock of self-love" (WL 17), ironically setting free those whose pursuit of absolute freedom, whether of the I or the We, has enslaved them to themselves. But this does not mean, as in Plato's *Republic*, that we should get rid of the poets (WL 47), though we cannot expect to learn about the most truly human from them. There is a legitimate place for erotic

---

62. Kierkegaard continues, "Youthfulness wants to be the only *I* in the whole world; maturity is to understand this *you* personally, even if it were not even addressed to a single other person." This echoes two Levinasian themes: the individuating character of the voice's claim on me and the asymmetry of the ethical relation. When it is a question of my responsibility, the question of anyone else's responsibility is strictly irrelevant. This motif, in turn, echoes the Kierkegaardian reminder of Jesus' command to love the enemy.

63. Here Kierkegaard echoes the hostage motif of OBBE.

64. Cf. WL 52–56, 84, 113, 130, 191, 194–97.

65. Obviously Levinas is not equating the empirical facticity of the neighbor with the Good. However foolish or unjust, the other remains an embodiment and bearer of the Good. To this degree Levinas retains the notion of creation in the image of God.

66. At the level of *Sittlichkeit* Judge William argues that in marriage erotic love is not annihilated but dethroned, ennobled, relativized, and transfigured. See EO, II, 30–31, 61, 177, 226, 253, 271. Similarly, in speaking of the teleological suspension of the ethical (qua *Sittlichkeit*), Silentio says that it is not "invalidated" but "reduced to the relative" (FT 70–71).

love and friendship. They are good, precisely when they lose their autonomy and are subordinated to the dual command to love God and neighbor.

But when they are thus teleologically suspended in the God relation, they are transformed (WL 112). This means not only that there is a proper place for self-love, but more importantly that there is a proper self-love (WL 18). Like Luther, Kierkegaard is an Augustinian, and he accepts the latter's teaching that

> the man who knows how to love himself loves God; and the man who does not love God, even though he loves himself, which is innate in him by nature, can still be said quite reasonably to hate himself when he does what is against his own interest, and stalks himself as if he were his own enemy. . . . But when the mind loves God, and consequently as has been said remembers and understands him, it can rightly be commanded to love its neighbor as itself. For now it loves itself with a straight, not a twisted love, now that it loves God.[67]

Accordingly, for Kierkegaard the neighbor-love command contains within it another command: "*You shall love yourself in the right way*," and he comments, "To love yourself in right way and to love the neighbor correspond perfectly to one another; fundamentally they are one and the same thing." On the basis of this reading of the "as yourself" of the command, he formulates proper self-love as follows: "You shall love yourself in the same way as you love your neighbor when you love him as yourself" (WL 22–23). This means that no matter what the earthly relationship, the self-denial that overcomes self-love never means "that the one worships and the other is the one worshiped." Specifically, it precludes the codependency of "the vulnerable woman in relation to the arrogant man," and, to switch from gender to class, of the poor to the powerful in which the socially weaker parties "know of no other expression for the relation than to abase themselves and to throw themselves away" (WL 125).

With this notion of proper self-love Kierkegaard introduces a teleological humanism into his deontology that may make Levinas nervous. But in this way he keeps command and promise, law and gospel in balance. The bad news (to the false self) is that self-transcendence is self-denial. The good news (to the false self at the end of its tether) is that self-transcendence is self-discovery. Precisely as command, the voice of transcendence offers to the decentered self a triune gift—its own truest self in proper relation both to God and to neighbor.

---

67. Augustine, *The Trinity*, trans. Edmund Hill (Brooklyn, N.Y.: New City Press, 1991), XIV, 4, 18. Cf. VIII, 4, 9: "Whoever therefore loves men should love them either because they are just or in order that they might be just. This is how he ought to love himself, either because he is just or in order to be just; in this way he can love *his neighbor as himself* (Mk. 12:33) without any danger. Anyone who loves himself any other way loves himself unjustly. . . ."

Conclusion

In chapter 3, Hegel is presented as a paradigmatic example of how not to speak about God, and it is argued that in his speculative pantheism the transcendence of God is whittled away to the barest minimum. Still, my argument throughout this book has a strikingly Hegelian character. It is a matter of method rather than of substance. By this I don't mean the hermeneutical phenomenology I take from Ricoeur and Gadamer, according to which one finds the phenomena to be described not naked, as it were, but fully clothed in texts and traditions marked by historical particularity and contingency. One operates within a hermeneutic circle even if one seeks to open it wide enough to suggest the relevance of the descriptions for understanding other texts and traditions.

What I rather have in mind is the order of presentation, moving from the abstract to the concrete. For Hegel, 'abstract' does not signify the universal abstracted from concrete particularity so much as the part extracted from the concrete whole to which it properly belongs.[1] He holds that the proper pro-

---

1. This Hegelian sense of 'proper' is counter to Heidegger's sense of 'authentic' in *Being and Time* in that it suggests that X is most truly itself not all by itself but only in relation to Y, which is beyond

cedure for philosophy is to work from the abstract to concrete, to begin with what is least complete and self-sufficient, discover the larger context to which it belongs, and contextualize or recontextualize it by reinterpreting it as part of a more complex "whole." Thus, to take an example from the *Phenomenology of Spirit*, Sense Certainty needs to be reinterpreted (over against its self-presentation as self-sufficient) as belonging to Perception, which in turn needs to be reinterpreted as belonging to Understanding. Hegel calls this recontextualization *Aufhebung*. Its familiar sense of simultaneously canceling and preserving means, more concretely understood, negating the "object" of thought (which in the Logic includes the categories of thought itself) as an atomic, stand-alone entity and affirming it as part of a larger complex of which it is not the organizing principle. To be *aufgehoben* is to be put in one's place, but not as if it were the task of philosophy to set the world in order. There is already a place for everything and everything is already in its place. The task of philosophy is to see things in their proper places and thus avoid misinterpreting them.

The attentive reader will have noticed that I treat Kierkegaard's notion of teleological suspension as virtually synonymous with *Aufhebung*. It is already at work in *Either/Or*, though not by name. Judge William argues that the esthetic stage is included, though in a subordinate role, in the ethical stage. The former is not "repudiated" or "annihilated" or "destroyed" but rather "dethroned" in order that it may be "ennobled" and "transfigured" in its proper home (EO II 21, 30–31, 56–57, 61, 94, 226, 253, 271). Accordingly, "the esthetic is absolutely excluded or it is excluded as the absolute, but relatively it is continually present . . . all the esthetic returns in its relativity" (EO II 177). Similarly, in *Fear and Trembling*, where we get the teleological suspension of the ethical by name, we are reminded that "that which is suspended is not relinquished but is preserved in the higher, which is its τέλος or proper home" (FT 54).[2] Accordingly, "the ethical is reduced to the relative. From this it does not follow that the ethical should be invalidated; rather, the ethical receives a completely different expression . . ." (FT 70).

The deep affinity between *Aufhebung* and teleological suspension is qual-

---

itself. It is as a Hegelian that Derrida protests against the atomistic sense of the proper even if he neglects to reclaim the term for a relational sense of (non) identity. See, in context, *Margins of Philosophy*, trans. Alan Bass (Chicago: Chicago University Press, 1982), pp. 4, 27, 124, 333; *Of Grammatology*, trans. Gayatri Chakravorty Spivak (Baltimore, Md.: Johns Hopkins University Press, 1974), pp. 109–10; "Interpreting Signatures (Nietzsche/Heidegger): Two Questions" in *Dialogue and Deconstruction: The Gadamer-Derrida Encounter*, ed. Diane P. Michelfelder and Richard E. Palmer (Albany: SUNY Press, 1989); *Spectres of Marx*, trans. Peggy Kamuf (New York: Routledge, 1994), p. 92; and, for a brief overview, Irene Harvey, *Derrida and the Economy of Différance* (Bloomington: Indiana University Press, 1986), pp. 5–6.

2. It cannot be emphasized too much that the ethical in question is not the Platonic/Kantian ethical, pure reason's untrammeled insight into eternal truth, which neither Hegel nor Kierkegaard thinks we possess, but the Hegelian ethical, *Sittlichkeit*, the laws and customs of one's people. See my essay "Abraham and Hegel," in *Kierkegaard's Critique of Reason and Society* (Macon, Ga.: Mercer University Press, 1987).

ified by two important differences. First, relying on biological metaphors inherited from Aristotle, Hegel talks as if the movement from the atomic and abstract to the contextual and concrete is all but inevitable, as if it has a kind of developmental or historical necessity to it. The task is not to get from here to there but to recognize and understand the movement *after* it has happened. For Kierkegaard, by contrast, there is no such necessity, no DNA of the spirit, and the task is to understand the need for the movement of recontextualizing *in order to make the movement*, thereby entering a life world I might not have entered, playing a language game I might not have played. Teleological suspension is a (possible) act of freedom.

Second, Hegel is committed to philosophy as a presuppositionless science.[3] This means both (1) that one can identify the right abstract point of departure and (2) find the appropriate teleological suspensions that lead to the ultimate τέλος without presupposing that Omega point, which turns out to be the ground of the entire process and thus the Alpha point as well, at the beginning of the philosophical journey. Kierkegaard has no such pretensions and is quite willing to acknowledge the hermeneutical circle within which he operates. For him thought is faith seeking understanding,[4] and the conceptual, teleological necessities that require relativizing and recontextualizing one stage within another can only be seen as such in relation to the ultimate τέλος by which the entire process is guided.[5] Otherwise they will appear to be paradoxical, absurd, or just plain mad.

I side with Kierkegaard in qualifying the Hegelian method in these two ways. Still, the basic Hegelian structure remains, making it possible to read the text backwards. This means seeing the parts in relation to the whole in which they are eventually placed rather than in their supposed self-sufficiency. They may well be essential parts or necessary conditions, but they are only parts and they are ordered within the whole by a τέλος not automatically their own (though they can make it their own), just as on a well-functioning team the individual players are ordered by the coach's game plan and not by the autonomous aspirations of their athletic *conatus essendi*.

Such a reading of the present text would go something like this:

Ethical and Religious Transcendence The highest height of God's transcendence is that of the voice that calls to faith, where faith is understood as welcoming the voice by trusting the promises and obeying the commands it hears from on high. From on high! In other words, neither the voice, nor the promises, nor the commands are mine or ours. I would arrange things dif-

---

3. See, for example, "With What Must the Science Begin" at the beginning of the *Science of Logic*, trans. A. V. Miller (New York: Humanities Press, 1969).

4. No less for Hegel and the worshipers of the system than for himself, in spite of their huffing and puffing to the contrary.

5. N.B. For Kierkegaard there are conceptual necessities, though they are relative to an Omega point that can be accessed only by faith and not by sight.

ferently, and so would we. So there is a heteronomy without which the alterity would be compromised. Accordingly, Kierkegaard insists that faith can be reached only by passing through the possibility of offense. The voice of transcendence is a call to a double self-transcendence: (a) a transformation in which I become what I most immediately am not, one who loves God and neighbor, and (b) a relocation in which I become part of something greater than either my own *conatus essendi* or our life world—namely the Kingdom of God, a game plan in which I become myself by serving rather than by being served.[6]

Epistemic Transcendence There are two themes here, revelation and mystery, both of which can be seen to be essential to ethical and religious transcendence. This is immediately obvious in the case of revelation. If the divine voice is to be a voice from on high and not my voice or ours, the ultimate source of knowledge will have to be divine revelation and not human reason.[7]

The case with mystery is a bit more complex. Incomprehensibility is surely a form of alterity, and it calls for a self-transcendence in being open to what I cannot grasp, contain, or explain. But how does this have its τέλος in loving God and neighbor? Heidegger, Levinas, and Kierkegaard agree that the project, even the demand that every being and especially the Highest Being be fully transparent to my understanding requires me to reduce God to something dramatically less than God. For Heidegger this will be a religiously irrelevant *causa sui*; for Levinas this will be a defaced and silenced being; and for Kierkegaard this will be a speculative object rather than a gracious and demanding subject before whom life is at once a gift and a task. In each case objectivity triumphs over subjectivity, metaphysics over spirituality, knowledge over love. It isn't just that such knowledge, be it onto-theology (Heidegger), ontology (Levinas), or speculation (Kierkegaard), is not a necessary condition of the love that is the highest self-transcendence; the project or demand for such knowledge is actually a form of resistance to that self-transcendence.

It is true that the incomprehensibility of God has often been understood in terms of the transcendence of an Infinite Essence over finite minds. It is equally true that Infinite Essences do not, as such, perform speech acts. They neither love, nor evoke love, nor command love. This abstract, metaphysical language carries with it the danger of lapsing into an onto-theological discourse that ironically confesses the limit to its project without really abandoning it. If the transcendence of God as mystery is to be *aufgehoben* in the self-transcending faith that works through love (Gal. 5:6), it will have to be remembered that the ultimate mystery is that of the Thou to the I, the speaker to the

---

6. "For the Son of Man came not to be served but to serve, and to give his life a ransom for many" (Mark 10:45).

7. We have seen that Aquinas and Barth are in complete agreement on this in spite of their disagreement on what unaided human reason can accomplish.

one addressed, and not one kind of essence to another. In other words, what have traditionally been called the "moral" attributes of God need to have priority over the "metaphysical" attributes. This does not mean that the latter must be denied, for it may very well be that the infinite, eternal being of God is beyond the reach of our finite, temporal minds. But it does mean that such an insight needs to be teleologically suspended in the awareness that even more than any human speaker, the First Speaker is an interiority and a freedom that can never be fully transparent to the one who hears. Metaphysical incomprehensibility is but an aspect and anticipation of this deeper truth, its τέλος and proper home. "I shall never want to define You, O God, for I cannot worship what I comprehend."[8]

Cosmological Transcendence Similarly, if God is the Creator, maker of heaven and earth, then God is *causa prima, ultima ratio,* and *causa sui.*[9] Here again the "metaphysical" attributes need not be abolished but rather dethroned, placed in a context where they are subordinate to the "moral" attributes. The theistic way of affirming the former differs from the pantheistic way in that God's transcendence (original independence) of the world means that the creation of the world is not a necessity but a free act of self-giving love. In other words, the God of theism is personal, while the God of pantheism is impersonal. But if theistic discourse is to cash in on this difference so that it makes a difference, it will have to keep impersonal ("metaphysical") categories from becoming the tail that wags the dog. While recognizing that they point to important truth, it is crucial also to recognize that they point beyond themselves to personal ("moral") categories that are more nearly adequate to their intended referent. This means, for example, that when I speak of God as *causa sui,* I not only acknowledge, with every form of pantheism and materialistic atheism, that I am not my own origin, but more importantly that every "*causa sui* project"[10] I am tempted to undertake, every attempt to make myself (or ourselves) autonomous and self-sufficient, is an act of ingratitude toward the One from whom my (our) life is a gift and of disobedience toward the One before whom my (our) life is a task. Insight must never be separated from responsibility, metaphysics from spirituality, transcendence from self-transcendence. Where divine transcendence is preserved in its deepest sense, the affirmation of God as Creator is not merely the attribution of a certain structure to the cosmos but above all the commitment of oneself to a life of grateful striving.[11]

---

8. Leslie F. Brandt, *Psalms/Now* (St. Louis, Mo.: Concordia, 1973), p. 175.

9. See Heidegger, ID 60 as in chapter 1 above.

10. I borrow this phrase from Ernest Becker in *The Denial of Death* (New York: Free Press, 1973). It should be obvious enough that the onto-theological project is one kind of *causa sui* project.

11. I borrow these last two words from the title of Jamie Ferreira's wonderful book *Love's Grateful Striving: A Commentary on Kierkegaard's* Works of Love (New York: Oxford University Press, 2001).

INDEX

Index

Merold Westphal is Distinguished Professor of Philosophy at Fordham University.